After God

D1559374

John D. Caputo, *series editor*

PERSPECTIVES IN
CONTINENTAL
PHILOSOPHY

Edited by
JOHN PANTELEIMON MANOUSSAKIS

After God

Richard Kearney and the Religious
Turn in Continental Philosophy

FORDHAM UNIVERSITY PRESS
New York ■ 2006

Perspectives in Continental Philosophy Series, No. 49
ISSN 1089-3938

Library of Congress Cataloging-in-Publication Data

After God : Richard Kearney and the religious turn in continental philosophy / edited by John Panteleimon Manoussakis.—1st ed.
    p.   cm. — (Perspectives in continental philosophy ; no. 49)
    Includes bibliographical references and index.
    ISBN 0-8232-2531-3 (hardcover) — ISBN 0-8232-2532-1 (pbk.)
    1. Kearney, Richard. God who may be.   2. Kearney, Richard. Strangers, gods, and monsters.   3. God.   4. Philosophical theology.   5. Continental philosophy.
    I. Manoussakis, John Panteleimon.   II. Series.
BT103.K4333   2005
211—dc22

                                                                    2005018164

Printed in the United States of America
08 07 06   5 4 3 2 1
First edition

Contents

Acknowledgments

Several of the contributions published in this volume have previously appeared in the following journals: *Continental Philosophy Review*, *Faith and Philosophy*, *Metaphilosophy*, *Modern Theology*, *Philosophy and Social Criticism*, *Philosophy Today*, *Research in Phenomenology*, *Revista Portuguesa de Filosofia*, and *The Irish Theological Quarterly*. The editor would also like to thank Indiana University Press for granting their permission to reproduce here the exchange among Jacques Derrida, John D. Caputo, and Richard Kearney (originally published in *God, the Gift, and Postmodernism*).

Abbreviations

OS   Richard Kearney, *On Stories* (London: Routledge, 2001).

GMB Richard Kearney, *The God Who May Be: A Hermeneutics of Religions* (Bloomington: Indiana University Press, 2001).

SGM Richard Kearney, *Strangers, Gods, and Monsters: Interpreting Otherness* (London: Routledge, 2002).

Introduction

JOHN PANTELEIMON MANOUSSAKIS

Moses desires to see the "glory" (Ex. 33:18) or the "face" (Ex. 33:22) of God, but he is refused and receives a vision of God "only from behind," *after God*, on going by, had pressed him with his hand into the crack in the rock.

Hans Urs von Balthasar, *The Glory of God*, VI, p. 38

So here we are, like Moses, *after* God.

All the texts in this volume share, in one way or another, the adverbial ambiguity of *after*. The God they seek—the God they are after—is a God who can be seen "only from behind," that is, without being seen, in the blindness of vision, at the limits of the phenomenological horizon. This is a God who, for several of our contributors, can be known only through the dark cloud of not-knowing. A God who can be named only through the paradox of a name that refers back to itself, without name. A God *without* God, without sovereignty, power, and presence.

Who or what comes, then, after God? Such was the question that befell philosophy following the proclamation of the "death of God." In the wake of God, as the last fifty years of philosophy have shown, God comes back again, *otherwise*: Heidegger's last God, Levinas's God of Infinity, Derrida's and Caputo's *tout autre*, Marion's God without Being, Kearney's God who may be.

The stakes in this debate could not, in my view, be higher or more topical; the questioning of God has taken on a new urgency and pertinence in this time of religious and cultural conflict. This return to religion became dramatically visible in all its complexity on September 11. The event itself assumed religious dimensions in its sublimity as a *mysterium tremendum et fascinans*. It was immediately registered in terms of two religious idioms: Islamic fanaticism, which "provoked" and "justified" it, and Christian fundamentalism, which proclaimed that the West was under attack and vowed to protect it. As the name of God was invoked by politicians and common people alike, as "ground zero" became more and more a *hallowed* ground with interfaith services and memorials, gradually September 11 became less exclusively a political case, simply because such an impossible event could not be fully appropriated by political language. It called, in time, for a more philosophical discourse, as epitomized by Kearney's essay "On Terror" in his *Strangers, Gods, and Monsters*. The present volume on Kearney, I believe, elaborates and expands on such a discourse, by presenting us with a divinity at last free from the three-headed monster of metaphysics—the Omni-God of omnipotence, omniscience, and omnipresence—and the "triumphalist teleologies and ideologies of power" that it has provoked.

In the Continental tradition, religion and the question of God have always been an integral part of philosophy. Whether theistic or atheistic, intellectual movements such as phenomenology, hermeneutics, existentialism, structuralism, and poststructuralism have all engaged in various ways with questions of ultimacy, transcendence, and alterity. Two of the foremost thinkers in this dialogue are Søren Kierkegaard and Martin Heidegger. Kierkegaard emphasized faith over reason, while Heidegger gave precedence to thought over faith. Both, however, draw from a common Pauline tradition, although they interpret it differently. With the advent of phenomenology, normative questions about theistic claims—for example, the debate about the existence of God—are often bracketed (a method known as the phenomenological *epoche*) for the sake of a different and arguably more meaningful set of questions: Could God be given to consciousness as a phenomenon? What kind of phenomena are religious experiences? What sort of phenomenological method is needed in order to describe them? In recent years, this questioning of God has assumed such acute and arresting proportions as to prompt some scholars to speak of a "theological turn" in philosophy. Kearney's

work signals one of the most compelling and challenging engagements with this turn.

Following Kierkegaard and Levinas, the Continental philosophy
of religion embraces Pascal's distinction between the God of the philosophers and the God of Abraham, Isaac, and Jacob, giving precedence to the latter over the former. Such a gesture indicates a move
away from metaphysics and toward a God who surpasses the old categories of ontotheology. Contemporary French thinkers (Jacques
Derrida, Jean-Luc Marion, Jean-Luis Chrétien) have offered exemplary cases of such thinking. Marion, in particular, has greatly con-
tributed to the formation of a nonmetaphysical thinking of God.
First, by following Heidegger's critique of ontotheology, he unfet-
tered God from His ontological burden; more recently, by recovering
and reinterpreting the notion of giveness in Husserl; and finally, by
developing his own insights on a phenomenology of saturation.

In its hermeneutical trajectory, following Heidegger, Gadamer,
and Ricoeur, Continental philosophy adds a movement both of suspicion and of affirmation to this debate. Richard Kearney's *diacritical
hermeneutics* and John D. Caputo's *radical hermeneutics* are two special
instances. Besides being the chief exponent of deconstruction's implications for religion (*The Prayers and Tears of Jacques Derrida*, 1997),
Caputo's thought has been of tremendous significance in explicating
Jacques Derrida's "turn to religion," represented by a series of recent works.[1] Caputo's *Radical Hermeneutics* (1987) led him to a novel,
postmetaphysical understanding of religion "without religion" (*On
Religion*, 2001), signaling with this paradox the undecidable mystery
of God—"an infinite questionability" that is, at the same time, "endlessly questionable." Kearney's diacritical hermeneutics, on the other
hand, attempts to steer a middle path between Romantic hermeneutics (Schleiermacher), which retrieves and reappropriates God as
presence, and radical hermeneutics (Derrida, Caputo), which elevates alterity to the status of undecidable sublimity. This debate—
exemplified by this volume's concluding exchange among Kearney,
Derrida, and Caputo—has already made its mark as one of the most
challenging directions of Continental thought.

This volume attempts to represent some of the most considered responses to Richard Kearney's recent writings on the philosophy of
religion, in particular *The God Who May Be: A Hermeneutics of Religion*
(Indiana, 2001) and *Strangers, Gods, and Monsters: Interpreting Otherness* (Routledge, 2003). Since the publication of these two volumes,

over a dozen international academic societies have devoted conferences, book panels, and seminars to major aspects of Kearney's hermeneutics of religion.[2] This volume brings together seventeen essays,
seventeen different variations on the same theme: philosophy about
God *after God*—that is to say, a way of thinking God otherwise than
ontologically. Against the monotony—or, as Nietzsche has aptly put
it, the monotono-theism—of a single voice, this volume sings with a
polyphony that brings into unison different times and different
spaces. First, the thinkers included in this collection hail from different geographical coordinates: in particular, continental Europe and
North America. But they also traverse different generations: an older
one, comprising figures who have influenced Richard Kearney's
thought (Breton, Derrida, Caputo, Marion, Greisch, Janicaud, Hederman), and a younger one that includes several figures who have
been inspired by Richard Kearney's thought (Bloechl, Nichols, Ó
Murchadha, Treanor, Manoussakis). In any case, it is Kearney's recent attempts to rethink the religious that serve as the central thread
that runs throughout this collection.

Richard Kearney is still in the midday of his life (he was born in
December 1954); and his work, far from being concluded, is still in
many exciting ways in progress. This volume does not aspire to offer
a definitive statement on Kearney's philosophy of religion, but only
to put on record and make available for a larger readership the lively
debates that his writings have already generated. By doing so, this
work bears witness to two things: the relevance of Kearney's philosophical writings for the current study of religion, and the relevance
of theology and religion for the present study of philosophy as it has
been confirmed by the work of major thinkers on both sides of the
Atlantic.[3]

All of the papers presented in this volume share the common prob-
lematic of the otherness of the Other—an eminent concern in post-
Levinasian philosophy. This problematic can be expressed in the fol-
lowing dilemma: how can we think and speak of the Other *on the
Other's terms*, that is, without reducing otherness to a reflection of the
Same—while, at the same time, being able to think and speak of the
Other without falling into a sort of apophatic mysticism of the
ineffable?

Kearney's work, even when it comes to the question of the paradigmatic Other, that is, God—or, *especially* when it comes to questions of God—tries persistently to articulate a middle way (a *via*

tertia) between the two extremes of our philosophical debate: (a) the unmediated, uncritical rapport with the Other epitomized by Levinas's infinity, Derrida's *différance*, and Caputo's *khora,* and (b) certain rigid and outdated conceptions of ontotheology and metaphysics. Kearney would like to maintain the healthy criticism of a hermeneutics of suspicion without, however, letting go of a hermeneutics of suspension (that retrieves and even embraces forgotten or overlooked treasures in tradition's storehouse, such as Aristotle's *dynamis*, Gregory's *prosopon*, and Cusanus's *possest*). This position came to be known in *Strangers, Gods, and Monsters* as *diacritical hermeneutics*. The methodological equivalent of diacritical hermeneutics is the *prosopic reduction* proposed here.

It is this hermeneutical reduction of reductions—reversing the reversals and returning us to the simple eschatology of the everyday—that the essays of the present book seek to address. Almost all of the authors would agree on the necessity of a critical philosophy for providing us with the resources for discernment when it comes to distinguishing between a "good" alterity (the stranger, the widow, and the orphan) and a "bad" alterity (the monstrosity of evil). They would disagree, however, on the criteria to be chosen and the principles that would guide us in such a diacritical project.

The crucial moment in carrying out Kearney's envisioned philosophy (hermeneutical and phenomenological) comes when the road we follow reaches a fork. At that moment one needs to decide which way to go, and it is precisely in the possibility of such a decision—if, indeed, one can decide—that a number of the papers find potential disagreement. For diacritical hermeneutics seems to want to have its pie and eat it: Isn't the need for criteria canceled out by the *neutrality* of its position? And if such a neutrality is abandoned for the sake of criteria, wouldn't we eventually have to side with one or the other extreme?

The thinkers writing for this volume take two distinct and somewhat antithetical positions. There are those who question Kearney's seemingly equivocal language of the different signs and figures of God, asking how this "God who may be" does not end up to be not a God at all but rather a regulatory concept (Desmond) or a unifying idea (Nichols) around which Kearney is constructing some kind of "ethical monotheism" (Bloechl). Such criticism eventually leads to the arduous task of "defining" what or who God is supposed to be (Treanor)—a question taken up in a controversial way by Breton and O'Leary.

On the antipodes of this line of thinking, there are those who question Kearney's reluctance to cut the umbilical cord of metaphysics, asking whether his religious hermeneutics offers us an alternative *to* ontotheology or just another version of it, namely, an onto-eschatology (Olthuis). After all, as Hart and Olthuis ask, isn't the *possible* a category of metaphysics? Both Ó Murchadha and O'Leary interrogate the Judeo-Christian commitments that, in their view, inform Kearney's hermeneutical and phenomenological reading. Kearney's pledge to an understanding of God that would promote love and justice does not derive (as Janicaud argues in his essay—the last before his untimely death) from a purely phenomenological observation; and thus it seems to vitiate his claim to find God in phenomena such as *posse* or the "face" of the Other: phenomena which, if "allowed to unfold on their own terms and without theological interference, do not necessarily point to the God of Scripture" (O'Leary). As Ó Murchadha observes, "the things to come" (eschatology) are not quite the same as "the things themselves" (phenomenology).

This debate, like any debate that touches upon the fundamental questions of philosophy, cannot receive a definitive answer. It must instead be left open and ongoing. As a provisional and tentative response, however, to the arguments, questions, and objections raised by the essays collected in this volume, we have prefixed a double proposal for a phenomenological prosopic reduction that supplements the preceding three (Husserl, Heidegger, and Marion). This is an attempt to sketch out those premises according to which the conundrum of the Other's alterity, as outlined above, is rethought through an integral phenomenology that allows us to encounter the Other in the relational infinity of our everyday experience. This renewed attention to epiphanies of the ordinary universe is what Kearney calls a *microeschatology.*

Wishing to leave the much-contested question of the relationship between philosophy and religion open, we have organized the seventeen contributions presented here into two major groups: "Philosophy Facing Theology" and "Theology Facing Philosophy." We thought that such a dialogical "facing off" might best capture the relational character of *prosopon* as a being-toward-the-face-of-the-Other.

The final part of the present volume, titled "Recapitulations," provides the reader with lively debates and exchanges among leading figures on the philosophy of religion (Derrida, Marion, Caputo) and theology (Tracy, McFague, Keller) while summarizing and reviewing the main themes of thinking God *after God.*

PART I

The Return to the *Eschaton*

Epiphanies of the Everyday: Toward a Micro-Eschatology

RICHARD KEARNEY

That is God . . .
What?
A shout in the street
         James Joyce, *Ulysses*

What if we were to return to epiphanies of the everyday? What if we could come back to the end (*eschaton*) in the here and now? Back to that end after the end of time that addresses us in each instant? What if we could rediscover ourselves again face-to-face with the infinite in the infinitesimal? Touch the sacred enfolded in the seeds of ordinary things?

Such a return would invite us to experience the ultimate in the mundane. The first in the last. The most in the least. It would bring us into dialogue with those who seek the divine in the pause between two breaths. Transcendence in a thornbush. The Eucharist in a morsel of madeleine. The Kingdom in a cup of cold water. San Marco in a cobblestone. God in a street cry.[1]

In our rush to the altars of Omnipotence we often neglected theophanies of the simple and familiar. We forgot to attend to the germs of the kingdom manifest in what Gerard Manley Hopkins calls "speckled, dappled things." So doing, we tended to overlook the semaphore of the insignificant. For it is often in the most quotidian, broken, inconsequential, and minute of events that the divine signals to us—"to the Father through the features of men's faces." This insight into the sacred "thisness" of things is what Duns Scotus, the Celtic thinker, called *haecceitas*. The idea is that Creation is synonymous and synchronous with incarnation, that each moment is a new occasion for the eternal to traverse the flesh and blood of time. *Ensarkosis*, or enfleshment: the infinite embodied in every instant of existence, waiting to be activated, acknowledged, attended to. The one ablaze in the many. The timeless flaring in the transitory. The holiness of happenstance. And our calling, in the wake of such encounters, is nothing less than this: to give "beauty back to God" (Gerard Manley Hopkins). So that each of our responses serves, potentially, as an opportunity to transubstantiate flesh back into word. And by extension, word into action.

Our highest human vocation, as Hopkins puts it, is to revisit the "inscape" of the sacred in every passing particular. This activity he calls variously "aftering," "seconding," "over-and-overing," or "abiding again" by the "bidding" of the singular. This is what we might term *ana*-esthetics, heeding the semantic resonances of the Greek prefix *ana*: "up, in place or time, back, again, anew" (*Shorter Oxford English Dictionary*). We are speaking of a refiguring of first creation in second creation. Re-creation of the sacral in the carnal. Against the Grand Metaphysical Systems that construed God in terms of formal universals and abstract essences, the Scotist poet invites us back (*ana*) to the first genesis—and *at the same time* forward to the final kingdom: to that *eschaton* dwelling in each unique, material instant, no matter how lowly or profane. Here and now the sacred "selves" and "instresses" through the most transient forms of flesh. "Each mortal thing does one thing and the same: / Deals out that being indoors each one dwells; / Selves—goes itself; myself it speaks and spells, / Crying what I do is me: for that I came" ("As Kingfishers Catch Fire"). From such instantaneous and recurring incarnation no one and no thing, no single *this* or *that*, is excluded. All are invited to the table. And the table is laden. For 'This Jack, poor potsherd, patch, matchwood, immortal diamond, / Is immortal diamond."[2] Here the descent into the banal (*katabasis*) takes the form of a reascent to the precious (*anabasis*). And in the process the binary opposition between up and down dissolves.

What, then, if we could return to the *eschaton*? What if we could embrace a philosophical gesture inspired by successive radicalizations of the phenomenological method, culminating in what we might call a *fourth reduction*? Suppose we were to envisage an after-the-event return to the event. A move back to the everyday moment where philosophy first begins in wonder or pain. Would this not be the simplest of redirections? A recapture of those accidental events that escape the nets of essentialist inspection? This questioning is intended as a modest proposal fashioned in the guise of an epilogue, echo, repetition, recall (*ana-mnesis*)? Like a postscript of some "supplementary clerk" appended to the grand reductions of Husserl, Heidegger, and Marion?

Our wager is that such a fourth reduction—this last and least of returns—might eventually lead us back (*re-ducere*) to the *eschaton* curled at the heart of quotidian existence. Such a revisiting of the least of things, in order to retrieve the voice and visage of the highest in the lowest, is what we call an *eschatological reduction*. What follows is a brief sketch of what this might entail.

The phenomenological method, according to Jean-Luc Marion, has been subject to three main reductions since its inception in the early twentieth century. First came the *transcendental reduction* initiated by the founder of phenomenology, Edmund Husserl. This involved a bracketing of our "natural attitude" of habit and opinion so as to return to the "essences" of meaning. According to Husserl, the redirecting of our attention from accidental contingencies of existence to the invariant, essential structures underlying them would lead us eventually to an inner realm of transcendental consciousness—a place where we might experience an "eidetic intuition" of timeless truths.

Husserl's transcendental reduction was followed by Heidegger's *ontological reduction* (though Heidegger never used this term). This second reduction involved a further reorientation of our awareness, this time from the essences of beings to "being as being" (*Sein als Sein*). This also entailed a "turning" of our attention toward the so-called *ontological difference*, namely, the long neglected difference between being (*Sein*) and beings (*Seiendes*).

More recently, we have witnessed what Marion calls a third reduction. This we might call the *donological reduction*. It is largely identified with Jean-Luc Marion's return to the "gift" in *Being Given* and other works. As such it aims to go beyond both Husserl's epistemology and Heidegger's ontology to a tertiary intuition of what Marion calls "the saturated phenomenon." But it finds several significant prefigurations, it seems to me, in the famous "religious turn" of a third generation of phenomenologists inspired by philosophers such as Levinas, Ricoeur, and Michel Henry. Here we might also count such postmetaphysical thinkers as Derrida, Caputo, and Chrétien, not to mention Marion himself, who has made the reduction to the "givenness of the gift" a hallmark of his pioneering investigations.[3]

What we are suggesting here, then, is the possibility of a fourth reduction—one that does not aim to supplant the first three but merely to supplement them. We might call this reduction *microeschatological* insofar as it leads us through the horizons of (1) "essence," (2) "being," and (3) "gift"—*back to the everyday*: that is, back to the natural world of simple embodied life where we may confront again the other "face-to-face." Here we recover the stranger as vis-à-vis or visage, as what the Greeks called *prosopon*.[4] The other who appears to us through the accidental and the anecdotal. This fourth reduction, in short, would reverse the first three reversals (while fully acknowledging their invaluable findings) and bring us right back to the beginning: the face-to-face encounters of our ordinary universe.

While this may appear, at first blush, to be like a return to Heidegger's being-in-the-world, we recall that Heideggerian *Dasein* has no body, no sex, no unconscious, no unique answerability to the other. *Dasein* remains a universal, transcendental structure. In its most authentic expression, it is always and in each case alone before death. Inauthenticity, by contrast, is signaled by *Dasein*'s immersion in the common society of being-with-others in the mode of the "They." Our everyday social, moral, and political relations with our fellow human beings are basically, for Heidegger, a distraction from the essential questioning of Being. Everydayness poses the threat of *doxa* to the rarefied insights of the *Augenblick*, understood in terms of *Dasein*'s own self-disclosure. For, we are told, "*Dasein* exists for the sake of itself," and only secondarily for others. With the fourth reduction we are proposing to move in an alternative direction: from the ontological back to the ontical, from speculative solipsism back to the *sensus communis* of our being-for-one-another.

While our proposal may seem, at second blush, like a reiteration of the Levinasian move from ontology to ethics, it also departs from it in several crucial respects. For example, the eschatological encounter with the *prosopon* differs from Levinas's account of the face in that for us the eyes of the other *do* have color (they are embodied as particular, living, sensible flesh). We also depart from Levinas in seeking to move *back to being* from beyond being. There is something quintessentially incarnate about the *prosopon* as a way of facing an Other whose very transcendence traverses and invests its immanence here and now. Every concrete person—understood as *prosopon/persona*—is charged with the *thisness* of a specific narrative identity, of a contingent history that is both conscious and unconscious. *Prosopon* is not a mask (*prosopeion*). It is not a mere pretext for God, some faint trace of transcendence. It is the divine itself manifest in the "least of these": in the color of their eyes, in the lines of their hands and fingers, in the cracked tone of voice, in all the tiny epiphanies of flesh and blood.

So while Levinas's notion of the face leads us beyond ontology and aesthetics to a religious ethics of asymmetry between self and other, the eschatological reduction we propose here aims to (a) reconcile ethics with aesthetics and (b) bring the Good back into liaison with being. For the *prosopon* is precisely that: liaison, dialogue, chiasmus, oneself-as-another and the other-as-oneself. This epitomizes a face-to-face symmetry that Levinas and certain deconstructionists decry. For us, the being of *prosopon* is a being-good. A recipe for what we have called elsewhere an *onto-eschatology*. It signals a retrieval of God not so much beyond being as beneath being. God in and through and for being. *Deus sicut transitus ad esse*.

Moreover, the fourth reduction is characteristically "prosopic" in that it embraces the possibility of hermeneutic mediation and detour. This profoundly modifies the tendency of both the ontological and the donological reductions to ultimately sacrifice interpretation to some ineffable sublime. The fourth reduction proposes to return us to the hermeneutic resources of speech beyond the excesses of apopathic silence. And regarding religion, we would suggest that the eschatological reduction might lead us back to a God of the last and least of these (*elachistos*)—divinity encountered as incarnate *prosopon* in what may be described, with Ricoeur, as a "second naïveté" or "second faith." So that *after* God we find ourselves *returning to* God. We discover ourselves *before* God in a new way, recovering, by way of creative repetition, what was always there in the first place, but remained unseen. The fourth reduction might thus be said to move from meta-physics to ana-physics: that is, back to the most concretely enfleshed phenomenon of the *prosopon* in its infinite *capacity to be*. In other words, there is nothing at all new about the *prosopon* in itself. All that is new is our way of *seeing* and *hearing* it. But it was always already there, summoning us, from the start.

So, I repeat, the fourth reduction does not dispense with the three reductions that precede it. Rather it supplements them—to say "completes" would be pretentious—by retrieving the eschatological space that makes each reduction possible: the *eschaton* which holds and upholds "essence," "being," and "gift." It salvages what is remaindered from the three reductions. Residual seeds of possibility that have been there, unremarked, from the beginning. In other words, the eschatological reduction retrieves the *possibilizing* of essence, being, and gift, which seemed impossible before the return to the gracious gap underlying and sustaining them. Is the fourth reduction religious, then? Yes; but only if we understand here a religion *beyond* religion, *before* religion, and *after* religion. This is a form of *ana-theism*, if you will. Leaving open options of both theism and atheism. It is a repetition forward to a God of the most ordinary things of our most ordinary existence.

By extension, we might suggest that the *ana-theistic* retrieval performed by the fourth reduction is accompanied by a series of related retrievals:

1. *ana-esthetic* (retrieval of radiance after abjection);
2. *ana-dynamic* (retrieval of the possible after the impossible);
3. *ana-phatic* (retrieval of speech after silence);
4. *ana-physical* (retrieval of the natural after the supernatural);
5. *ana-ethical* (retrieval of the good after normativity);
6. *ana-choral* (retrieval of divine chora after the abyss);
7. *ana-erotic* (retrieval of desire after desirelessness).

Each of these retrievals would, of course, require extended hermeneutic explication, which is beyond the limits of this summary sketch.

For now, let me simply say this: like all philosophical enterprises, especially those of a spiritual character, this proposal of a fourth reduction is a hermeneutic wager. A matter of faith, then? Yes, but a faith sustained by as much understanding, interpretation, and wisdom as possible. A belief which never ceases to wrestle with its twin of unbelief. A hope in a light seen through the dark. Jacob's faith as he struggles with the angel in the night.

It is crucial, I believe, to emphasize this hermeneutic character of the fourth reduction. Why so? Because such acknowledgment of the *interpretive* status of our approach guarantees a pluralist reading of the *eschaton*. It keeps us humble. Whether we call it simply "God," or the "God beyond God" (with Eckhart and the mystics) — or, indeed, the not-yet-God of atheistic messianism (Bloch, Derrida) — all this is actually a matter of interpretation. A question of listening, of reading, of belief. The *eschaton* is not the prerogative of any one particular religion, monotheistic or otherwise. It is more generous than that. It is the assurance that every "I am" (and especially the divine) is inextricably linked to an "I am no one." The *ego sum* is inseparable from the *nemo*: the last and least of beings. This double movement is felicitously captured in the French word *personne*: I am someone and no one at the same time. For the *eschaton* is a creative and loving emptying (*kenosis*) which gives space to beings. It is the gap in God incarnate in the littlest of things. The infinitesimal infinite.

Perhaps this is what Plato was alluding to in the *Timaeus* when he spoke of *chora* as an empty womb that precedes and engenders all intelligible and sensible things. Or what the Upanishads were gesturing toward when they spoke of *akasa*—that infinite empty space within *both* the universe *and* the inner heart, from which all divine energy (*sakti*) flows into the world. A sacredness, at first, smaller than a seed (*bija*). And perhaps it was also what Paul had in mind when he spoke of a capacious "unknown God" who anticipates Christ—and, one might add, Krishna, the Buddha, and the other sacred figures of wisdom and compassion?

The *eschaton* may be construed, accordingly, as the least exclusive of functions. As the very opposite of Hegel's *telos* and theodicy. And if we wish to read it as One, it would be as an absolute that refuses to be reduced to any one of its manifestations. An absolute that absolves itself. As such, this irreducibility of *L'Un à l'Unique* (to borrow the formula of Stanislas Breton) is the best guarantee of interreligious pluralism.[5] Because the eschatological One cannot be named absolutely in any one way, it can be named only in multiple ways. The One in the midst of the many is not at the expense of the many. It is, rather, the path that leads to other paths. A refusal of both absolutism (one without many) and relativism (many without one). So that if Christ, for example, famously announces that it is "only" through him that one can get to the Father, we might interpret this "only" as excluding nothing but exclusiveness itself. The *eschaton* is open to everyone. It is, as it were, the germinal space that engenders numerous different religions. Thus, every attempt to define the *eschaton* is already and necessarily an interpretation. In the beginning was the Word, which is always already a multiplicity of words. From the start is hermeneutics! The first and last of methods. And the simplest. Which is why, in this free space of eschatology, we may say that Jesus and the Buddha, for example, converse without seeking to convert one another. The Scriptures and Sutras find themselves in dialogue. Theists and atheists commune.

If some of the preceding terms draw from monotheism, it is not only because this reflects my own hermeneutic wager as someone who hails from a Judeo-Christian heritage; it is also because I believe that this same tradition harbors within itself seed spaces which foster a colloquy of different voices. I am thinking here of several signal events in my own biblical narrative tradition. First, the aboriginal act of withdrawal (*zimzum*), which allows the Creator of Genesis to give space and freedom to its creatures. Second, the eschatological gap at the heart of the deity revealed in Exodus 3:15, which allows the one who "was" and "is" also to be the one who "may be"—a deity, in the guise of a common thornbush, which promises to be with its creatures forever, the God of possibility to come. Third, a Word self-emptying into the flesh of the last and least, an emptying that proceeds from incarnation right up to death on the cross and descent into the dark: kenotic acts inviting all beings to live again more fully. And, fourth, the *germen nihili* returning from the abyss of the empty tomb in the form of what Paul called the germinal or spiritual body.

Four divine descents, then, into the empty space of the ordinary—creation, exodus, incarnation, death–resurrection—each one of which solicits the return of old life in epiphanies of new life. Four revelations of the divine potentiality to plumb the depths of *khora* in order to bring forth the more from the less. An extraordinary paradox this, no? And one that is ingeniously captured, I believe, in the Patristic metaphor of the Trinity as *peri-choresis*. Three persons dancing around (*peri*) a fourth dimension, an empty space (*chora*)—that sacred milieu of mutual withdrawal, letting be, love. Three persons who would collapse into indifference and indifferentiation were it not for that free feminine spacing opening up between them: an Open that holds them at once together and apart. For *chora* has always been a she. The matrix of all things. As invoked by the anonymous artist of the mother-and-child mural in the monastery of Chora in Istanbul. *Chora Achoraton*. "Container of the Uncontainable."[6]

This is, of course, an interpretation. A "religious" interpretation, granted. A particular reading of the *eschaton* that acknowledges itself as such and does not exclude other interpretations (theistic or atheistic), but rather invites them to the chorus of philosophical exchange. For where our Western tradition speaks of *chora*, *eschaton*, and *germen nihili*, our Eastern counterparts might invoke such terms as *bija*, *guha*, or *tao*. This decisive and long-overdue conversation between the world's different wisdom traditions has hardly begun, though happily figures such as Pannikar, Abhishiktananda, Griffiths, and Thich Nhat Hanh are pointing the way. For if religion has, alas, been one of the major sources of war and hatred, it may also be a crucial ingredient of healing.

The fourth reduction, in sum, radicalizes the three phenomenological reductions to the point where they rejoin hermeneutics. And here we adhere to Paul Ricoeur's counsel that we "renounce the idea of creating a phenomenology of the religious phenomenon taken in its indivisible universality" in favor of an "interconfessional hospitality" that permits us to trace the "broad hermeneutic strands" of specific religions in dialogue with others.[7] At this critical juncture, we find intuition recovering interpretation. We see the *eschaton* selving itself in various ways, featuring itself in multiple faces, singing itself in many voices. A polyphony of call and response. A banquet of translation.

Let me offer, at this point, a few remarks on the eschatological reduction as "repetition." The fourth reduction leads us back—by leading us forward—to a sacred space at the heart of things. For too long theology and metaphysics have identified the divine with the most all-powerful of Beings. Sovereign, Self-sufficient substances. Transcendental Forms. First and Final Causes. Immutable essences. But in the process, we tended to turn our backs on the "God of little things," the holiness of this and that. Too often we forgot the fact that God is manifest in the least ones calling for a cup of cold water, asking to be fed, clothed, cared for, heard, loved. We ignored the face of the desert stranger who comes in the middle of the night and wrestles with us until we open our eyes and see face-to-face: *Prosopon*. We stopped hearing God in "a shout in the street."

The fourth reduction solicits a retrieval of the lowercase at the other side of the uppercase: after Metaphysics, after Theology, after Being, after God. So we call it a micro-eschatology. Why? To remind ourselves that we are seeking to signpost a path that brings us back to the "end" (*eschaton*) that is after the End (*telos*) and before the Beginning (*arche*). An eschatology, we repeat, that restores us to the simplicity of the face-to-face prior to all First and Final Causes. We are talking, to borrow Ricoeur's formula, about an "eschatology of the sacred" beyond both archaeology and teleology. In other words, our eschatology of the everyday defies the perverse reading of eschatology as some triumphant End of History where the divine trumps the human. It scuppers the fantasy of a Supreme Being disparaging finite creatures in some Final Settlement. Such a triumphal sense of Last Judgment travesties the enigma of the last-as-first; it betrays the logic of the "least of these." And, so doing, it remains deaf to the miracle of discernment, which may intervene in the most profane moments of our lived experience.

The fourth reduction also resists the tendency of certain sublime theologies—deconstructive or New Age—to leave us senseless before some utterly inaccessible Other. Departing from the secure syllogisms of metaphysics does not mean we have to embrace a transcendence so transcendent that it disappears off the radar screen, leaving behind not only flesh but word as well. We are not obliged to become sightless and speechless (*apo-phasis*) before the sublimity of God. No. What we seek, with the fourth reduction, is a "repetition" of speech (*ana-phasis*), a retrieval of saying beyond silence. Such saying would, in turn, be accompanied by a seeing beyond the invisible (*ana-aesthesis*) and a touching beyond the tangible (*ana-pathos*). In short, we are concerned with a way of saying, seeing, and feeling over again—of sensing otherwise, anew, for a second time. So that we may "see and touch the goodness of the Lord" in the wounds and wonders of the commonest beings. Disclose the sacramental in *le dernier des derniers*. For the *eschaton* reveals itself in the mundane as much as in the momentous, in the scarred as much as in the beautiful, in the lost as much as in the found. It elicits ways of rediscovering God in the ordinary universe which the gods—*pace* Heidegger and certain postmodern prophets of fatality—have never really abandoned.

This is why we claim that the eschatological reduction signals a return to poetics. A sort of *ana-poetics* after *aporetics*. Such a poetics, we repeat, bids us revisit the primordial sphere of everyday sayings, expressions, presuppositions, beliefs, speech acts, convictions, faiths, and commitments—namely, that realm of primary speech that the first three reductions sought, in their different ways, to bracket. Not that we want to dispense with the invaluable disclosures of *essence*, *being*, and *gift* brought about by the preceding suspensions. On the contrary, we wish rather to push these radical insights toward a recapitulation of the ordinary beyond the extraordinary. Such that one will, hopefully, never again take the given for granted nor remain deaf to the epiphany of a street cry. So that what might first appear as a presumptuous gesture—somehow to outdo such thinkers as Husserl, Heidegger, or Marion—is in fact the opposite. The fourth reduction is no more than a memo, an afterword, an epilogue after the event. It is intended, in all modesty, as a reminder posted to these great phenomenologists that there are a few small things left behind, unheard and unseen, discarded and neglected, in their seemingly exhaustive wake. In their plunge toward fundamental profundity, phenomenology often turned its sights from the treasures floating in the flotsam and jetsam of the forfeited. It overlooked the "foul rag and bone shop of the heart" (Yeats).

The return to poetics does not require the abandonment of philosophy. In fact, poetics might be said to occupy that in-between site where conceptual reflection finds its limits and poetry finds its illimitable nutrition. In this sense, the idiom of poetics promoted by the fourth reduction invites us to another kind of thinking, what we might call with Rilke an understanding of the heart, which observes a double fidelity to both philosophy and poetry. As such, it hopes to conjoin a certain rigor of mind with a special resonance of imagination. And to obviate dogmatism.

Against the Hegelian lure of a final synthesis, we insist that the four reductions be considered as a fluid interplay where each moves back and forth between the others, resisting the tendency to fix the interrelationship in some teleological hierarchy of progressive fulfillment. The cry of the fourth reduction, no less than that of the first (Husserl's), is "back to the beginning," over and over again. Indeed, our commitment to such a poetics of perpetual replay reminds us that the game of the four reductions is not confined to phenomenology per se, considered as some crowning achievement of Western metaphysics. It has been playing itself out, time after time, from the earliest instances of Western (and, no doubt, non-Western) thought. For example, Platonism might be said to mark the first reduction; Aristotelianism, the second; Neoplatonism, the third; and a certain return to the ordinary world (Augustine's questing heart, Duns Scotus's "thisness," Teresa of Avila's "pots and pans"), the fourth. The variations are multiple and recurring. There is nothing really new in what we are saying here. It has been said before, in numerous ways. The fourth reduction simply offers a poetic license to start all over. To say it again. To do it again.

As we have already indicated, the return to the *eschaton* triggers a renewed interest in the religious. But this return to the religious remains for us philosophers a hermeneutic exercise rather than a theological dogma. It is not apologetics. For the hermeneutic space opened up by the fourth reduction is necessarily a creative conflict zone of interpretations—a space where, for example, the theistic "messianisms" of monotheism can converse with the atheistic "messianicities" of postmodernism (Derrida, Bloch, Žižek, Badiou, Agamben), not to mention the wisdom interpretations of non-Western traditions. The philosophical hermeneutics we espouse acknowledges that every seeing is a *seeing-as*; every hearing, a *hearing-as*; every understanding, an *understanding-as*. True, the eschatological space disclosed by the fourth reduction is, arguably, the closest that the contemporary philosophy of phenomenological hermeneutics gets to theology. It certainly opens up the possibility of new theological interpretations. But if it may thus serve as prelude to theology, it is not yet, strictly speaking, theology. As philosophy of religion it keeps a certain methodological distance, as philosophy must. (If I were writing as a theologian, I could waive such scruples.) At best, we might say that the eschatological reduction carves out an agora where philosophy and theology may confront one another anew in "loving combat."

How, then, one might ask, does the fourth reduction relate to the "theological turn in phenomenology"? While my friend, the late Dominique Janicaud, coined this phrase with a specific polemic in mind, we would be prepared to offer a somewhat broader reading. It is not necessary, in our view, to see the encounter between phenomenology and theology as a takeover of one by the other. Rather, I would suggest that the hermeneutic space opened up by the fourth reduction allows philosophy and theology to face off against one another in a process of mutual exchange. This facing off is also a facing toward: *prosopon*. Distance in and through rapprochement. That is to say, the eschatological turn allows theology to surpass itself as theology just as it permits phenomenology to surpass itself as phenomenology. So that the theological turn in phenomenology might correspond to a phenomenological turn in theology. The fourth reduction could thus be said to emancipate both disciplines into a new reinterpretation of the rapport between Being and God. A rapport that, we recall, has preoccupied Western thinkers from its Greek and biblical origins; and that, after a temporary eclipse, is now finding voice again.

The eschatological reduction, therefore, endeavors to amplify the horizons of "theology" and "philosophy" to include neglected possibilities of experiencing divinity and sacredness, alterity and transcendence, ultimacy and depth. That is why eschatology, as I understand it, can include in its range of reference both religious phenomenologists like Marion, Henry, Levinas, and Chrétien—targeted by Jani-caud—and "postreligious" thinkers such as Bonhoeffer, Caputo, and Derrida. In sum, rather than excluding either theology or phenome-nology, micro-eschatology explores new possibilities for both by ex-ceeding their conventional limits.

Eschatological repetition calls, lastly, for another notion of *time*. Here we encounter a temporality beyond both the linear chronology of his-tory and the circular reiteration of myth (e.g., the eternal return of the same). We are speaking of a specific kind of *ana*-chronology that might repeat the moment forward. This process of repetitive return operates like a gyre or spiral that carries us through the same experi-ence for a second time, or a number of times, but at different alti-tudes, as it were—sometimes higher and farther, sometimes lower and closer. To repeat forward is, as Kierkegaard rightly insists, to reignite the possible in the actual. Eschatological repetition undoes the inevitable and deactivates (*katargein*) the actual by recovering the gracious seeds of possibility still lurking in our midst. It alerts us to the grace that can transmute each moment of linear time—past, pres-ent, future—into an instant (*kairos*) of eternity: timelessness in time, the not-yet in the now, the possible in the impossible, the word in the flesh. Thus while "recollection" may be said merely to reiterate the fixed actualities of the past, "repetition" retrieves the past in the pres-ent in such a way that it opens up possibilities for the future. Rather than simply remember what has been, qua fait accompli, repetition reorients time toward the possibilizing *eschaton* still to come. Repeti-tion, in other words, gets the world back, but as different—at an-other level in the spiral of eschatological time. *Vita mutata non tollitur*: life changed but not taken away. Life returned, turned around. As though life were experienced in reverse—ana-logically—so as to be lived forward! For the eschatological instant is the one (and it is po-tentially every moment) in which we receive the gift of the world anew. The same world, of course, but refigured. The inevitability of what-has-been suddenly transfigured into the possibility of what-may-be. Each instant, suddenly, a portal at which the possible knocks. And seeks to enter.

This recovery of the *eschaton* at the heart of things is nothing less, I suggest, than the rediscovery of *posse* in *esse*. I am speaking here of that *posse* which flows from the divine to the human and back again, like a river in endless flux. There is nothing new here, and yet it is an invitation to constant renewal. It is no secret; it has been recognized again and again by poets and sages (and countless ordinary people) throughout the ages. It is the river that the Dublin poet Patrick Kavanagh invoked in his passionate theopoetics of the common and contingent: "Leafy-with-love banks and the green waters of the canal / Pouring redemption for me, that I do / The will of God, wallow in the habitual, the banal. . . ." It is the river in the Taoist saying that "The best man is like water / Water is good; it benefits all things / and does not compete with them / It dwells in lowly places that all disdain / This is why it is so near to Tao."[8] And it is that same "river of compassion" which is celebrated by Bede Griffiths in his religious commentary on the *Bhagavad Gita*. For here in the confluence of diverse currents, possibilities crisscross and traverse, sounding an "infinite capacity for being."[9] In such times and places, the response "I am able" answers to the call "You are able." Divinity capacitates humanity and, in return, humanity reactivates divinity.

This is perhaps what Paul means by the "*dunamis* of the spirit" which outstrips all the powers of dominion (Ephesians 1). And it is surely what Nicholas of Cusa is intimating when he says that divine *posse*—his preferred name for God—is a "truth that shouts in the streets," something so obvious that even a child can hear![10] Such *posse* speaks in many distinct voices: *ebullutio, viriditas, sakti, lila, charis, gratia*. It is what in a previous work we have described as the *posse* of no-power capable of overcoming all powers.[11] This is why micro-eschatology begins, most simply, as a "poetics of the possible."

Conclusion

So why recommend a fourth reduction if all it does is bring us back to where we began? All the way back to the everyday universe? Why? Because without sundering there is no recognition. Some breaking down or breaking away from our given lived experience is necessary, it seems, for a breakthrough to the meaning of that same experience, at another level, one where we may see and hear otherwise. I do not wish to claim, however, that such a new optics and acoustics are only available through philosophical reflection. Epiphanies are already there "in the pots and pans." So what is it that triggers the shift of attention?

At its most basic it is, perhaps, the experience of death. The seed dying so that we may grow. Dying unto the world so that we may live again more abundantly. Being in the world still, more deeply than ever, but no longer of the world. No longer subject to the illusions and attachments of Habit. This is, doubtless, what Heidegger meant by *Angst*: an existential mood that "de-worlds" us, throws us off kilter, shatters our cozy preconceptions, so as to open us to the authentic possibilities of our being-in-the-world. But, for Heidegger, this experience seems to be the elitist prerogative of exceptional individuals who renounce life in community with others to bravely face the solitary instant. As he says in *Being and Time*, the traumatic experience of death "individualizes" each one of us in an authentic moment (*Augenblick*) in which one finds oneself utterly alone.

Such "existential solipsism" is not what we are after with the eschatological reduction. As a first step, it is true, such moments — which I would claim are available to everyone — can elicit a certain disenchantment which may then issue in a reverse moment of epiphany. This is an experience that, arguably, resides at the root of most great philosophical beginnings. One thinks of the moment of Socratic ignorance that precedes wonderment (*thaumazein*); the moment of Augustinian disillusionment serving as prelude to radical questioning (*quis ergo amo cum deum meum amo?*); the moment of "learned not-knowing" (*docta ignorantia*), which Cusanus and certain "negative" theologians saw as portal to a *visio dei*; the moment of Descartes's doubt, which precedes his recovery of the "idea of the infinite"; the moment of Husserl's suspension (*epoche*), which aims to return us, eventually, to a "categorial intuition" of the being of things. But my point is that epiphanies don't *have* to be exclusive moments of philosophical insight-through-detachment. The above are exemplary cases, and ones from which we can greatly learn. But they are not primary. They are no more than "repetitions" of more primordial experiences — aesthetic, mystical, spiritual, existential. I think Merleau-Ponty acknowledges this when he admits, in his preface to the *Phenomenology of Perception*, that there is nothing that the phenomenological reduction discloses that was not already laid forth, for example, in our cultural life-world. "The unfinished nature of phenomenology and the inchoative atmosphere which has surrounded it are not to be taken as a sign of failure, they were inevitable because phenomenology's task was to reveal the mystery of the world. . . . If phenomenology was a movement before becoming a doctrine or a philosophical system, this was attributable neither to accident, nor to fraudulent intent. It is as painstaking as the works of Balzac, Proust, Valéry, or Cézanne — by reason of the same kind of attentiveness and wonder, the same demand for awareness, the same will to seize the meaning of the world or of history as that meaning comes into being."[12]

In short, the philosophical reductions are doing no more than "repeating" at the level of reflective discourse what Cézanne, for one, was already doing in painting when he "exploded perspective" and solicited a more primordial way of seeing—enabling us to apprehend not just *natura naturata* but *natura naturans*. Or, by extension, what writers such as Proust and Joyce were doing when—in the pivotal "library scenes" of *Remembrance* and *Ulysses*—they showed their young authors (Marcel and Stephen) renouncing Grand Illusions in order to embrace epiphanies of the everyday.[13] Moreover, it is precisely this homecoming that the poet Patrick Kavanagh calls the reaffirmation of a "second simplicity" after the experience of skeptical loss. Such a moment is movingly captured in his poem "Hospital," which describes the poet's reentry to ordinary life after his recovery from a near fatal illness. Suddenly, almost posthumously, he sees the world again as he had never experienced it before—all the broken, battered, throwaway objects suddenly redeemed. "Naming these things is the love-act and its pledge," he concludes, "to snatch out of time the passionate transitory."

Does this imply that one must be either a philosophical initiate or an aesthetic connoisseur to have access to epiphanies? Are such insights confined to readers of Heidegger and Proust? Not at all. My argument has been, all along, that they are already available to the most simple of beings in the most simple of experiences—namely, in sacred moments of the ordinary aside from any grand leaps into Art or Metaphysics. They are there in the detritus of a Dublin canal, in stray cries of the street, in the mere "mereness of things" (Wallace Stevens). They are always already there. But we do not heed them unless, at some level, we have an experience of sundering. This can be registered in the simplest prayer of letting-go or in the commonest exposure to pain or disappointment. For dying unto oneself can happen in the most indigent and banal instants. If one follows the call of these dark ruptures in our natural attitude, one reaches a no-place from which one is invited to return to the place of life. One becomes a no-one called back to oneself. Though the world to which one returns is never quite the same. Just as the self to which one returns after such estrangement is always oneself as another.[14] The *moi* comes back to itself as *soi*.

So, we ask one last time, why bother with philosophical reflection at all if the end of our elaborate bracketings and retrievals is already accessible in the prephilosophical experiences of life and art? The reasons are, I think, twofold. First, philosophy is one of the most formative discourses of our culture. And even if the vast majority of people never actually read Plato or Aristotle, the Scholastics or Descartes our accredited ways of understanding ourselves are deeply marked by their thinking. This doesn't require us to buy into the Heideggerian notion that the entire world picture, governing our technological age, is determined by a forgotten destiny of Being. Suffice it to note that the long history of metaphysics has left indelible watermarks on our most basic forms of thought. (Just as the great texts of the Vedic or Buddhist traditions have profoundly informed Eastern ways of thinking, even if many adherents have no direct familiarity with the original Sanskrit philosophies.) If this be so, then it is incumbent on us to find ways of repeating these decisive philosophical maneuvers *forward*, by letting the flies out of the metaphysical bottles so that we may come back again from perplexity and skepticism to the "habitual and the banal." Though we acknowledge that after the Odyssean detour through the wandering rocks of reflective detachment, the same is never quite the same. One rediscovers oneself as "othered," as never before, as never again. One's life has changed.

But there is a second reason to embrace the philosophical journey of exodus and return. It is this: philosophy sometimes gives us special pause to review things at a more considered remove than is afforded by our usual nights of the soul or exposures to estrangement. This has something to do with that intellectual conversion that Plato called *periogoge* (turning around) and that Aristotle described as *anagnoresis-catharsis* (recognition through purgation). It refers to that peculiar sense of mental inversion that is signaled, today, by such terms as *epoche*, *Überwindung*, or *Kehre*. It is, in short, that indispensable loop on the hill path that enables us to climb higher before doubling back to the valley below. The step forward as step back. And vice versa.

In *Love's Knowledge*, Martha Nussbaum defends this philosophical countermove vis-à-vis our given experience. She makes the point that philosophical reflection on our primary lived experience, and even on our secondary literary experience, can help us "see" things that have gone unnoticed in our daily lives. At best, philosophical deliberation permits a second knowing, which returns us to experience for a second time *as if for the first time*. On occasion, writes Nussbaum, "I think the human heart needs reflection as an ally. Sometimes we need explicit philosophy to return us to the truths of the heart and to permit us to trust that multiplicity, that bewildering indefiniteness. To direct us to the 'appearances' rather than to some-where 'out there' or *beneath* or *behind* them." And she adds that in certain contexts it is the momentary detour through "sceptical uneas-iness," provoked by philosophy, which can "lead us back to and ex-press a respect for the multiplicity of the everyday."[15]

I would say, in conclusion, that the eschatological reduction aims to bring a second sight to bear on the hidden and often neglected truths of first sight. It seeks to offer a form of recognition newer than cognition and older than perception. And, so doing, it hopes to serve as a modest guide to terrestrial wisdom: "I am the necessary angel of earth, / Since in my sight you see the world again" (Wallace Stevens).

These questions call for extensive detailed investigation well beyond the limits of this brief outline. We can, for now, but sketch a menu and offer a preliminary taste. The essay "Enabling God," which fol-lows in part 2, is a small offering in this direction.

Toward a Fourth Reduction?

JOHN PANTELEIMON MANOUSSAKIS

In this essay we attempt a redefining of the phenomenological method as this has been developed mainly through three "reductions"[1] represented by three thinkers whose work advanced phenomenological research in novel ways: Edmund Husserl, Martin Heidegger, and Jean-Luc Marion. Our rehearsal of the phenomenological tradition aims at formulating a set of controversial questions: Is it, perhaps, time for a *fourth* reduction that would better serve the sensibilities of the so-called phenomenology of the apparent? And if so, what might be its guiding principles, its ways of operating, its scope and aim? Such a fourth reduction, we believe, would not seek to overcome or discard the preceding movements of reduction; rather, it would strive to complete them by rehearsing, retrieving, and repeating them. In some sense, a fourth reduction could be a corrective recapitulation of the transcendent, ontological, and dosological[2] reductions. In the following pages we will try to flesh out what the basic principles of a fourth reduction might be by clarifying further the definition of the *prosopon* and its pertinence for a phenomenology of the experience of God.

Husserl's transcendental reduction called for a return "to the things themselves," where consciousness refocuses on the phenomena as they appear in themselves and by themselves (eidetically), cutting through, as it were, the layers of preassigned signification that common usage has accumulated over them. Heidegger's ontological reduction guided consciousness's eye in seeing that phenomena, even before being the manifestation of this or that thing, simply *are*. This understanding of phenomena as beings led Heidegger's thought to a retrieval of the difference between beings and the horizon of Being. The dosological reduction disclosed a structure more ulterior than phenomenality and being, that of unconditional givenness.

The fourth reduction does not seek to overcome or discard the preceding movements of reduction; rather, it strives to complete them by rehearsing, retrieving, and repeating them. In some sense, the fourth reduction is a corrective recapitulation of the transcendent, ontological, and dosological reductions.

What, then, is the fourth reduction? As Richard Kearney has phrased it in the opening essay of this volume, the fourth reduction "leads us beyond the horizons of 'essence,' 'being,' and 'gift' *back to existence*, that is, back to the natural world of everyday, embodied life where we may confront once again the Other as *prosopon*."

We will try to flesh out the basic principles of the fourth reduction by clarifying further the definition (discussed elsewhere) of the *prosopon* and its pertinence for a phenomenology of everyday experience.

It could be relatively easy to accuse the fourth reduction of being partial, especially in comparison with the three preceding ones, since it either reduces phenomena to the experience of the Other as *prosopon* or it excludes phenomena (any other than the Other) by being applicable only in cases where another human being is involved — having little or nothing to say about an entire world of phenomena (things, feelings, events, etc.). Indeed, how does this tree that I see through my window, or this paper that I am writing on, "fit" in such a prosopic reduction? Would it not be absurd, by the very definition of *prosopon*, to subject this kind of phenomena to the fourth reduction, to the extent that they lack a face (and the capacity of relationship that only a face can offer) and, therefore, can never take the place of the Other? In other words, the fourth reduction is said to reduce the world to the Other as *prosopon*, who now becomes its privileged (and unique) example. Its partiality, in other words, would have been a humanism, or personalism.

As a way of responding to this objection, we need to go back for a moment and reexamine the three previous reductions in the history of phenomenology. What we come to realize is that in all of them (transcendental, ontological, dosological) there is always a predominant "structure" through which and by which each reduction itself takes effect and is occasioned. Even a casual reading of Husserl's work confirms that the operative structure in the transcendental reduction is *intentionality*. It is the intentional movement of consciousness that seeks and constitutes phenomena as objects. In return, the same structure elevates the I of the consciousness to the constituting I; intentionality, in short, holds the phenomenological scheme in place, since it is by means of it that the two poles of phenomenological operation are named and recognized for what they are: the constituting I and the constituted phenomena.

In Heidegger's *Being and Time* we witness how intentionality is replaced by *thrownness-into-the-World (Geworfenheit)*, which now becomes, if not the only one, then certainly the main operative structure of the ontological reduction. Indeed, it is through the existential experience of finding oneself thrown-into-the-World—and through the two sides of this experience, namely, anxiety and boredom—that one comes to see phenomena as beings projected against the ubiquitous and yet elusive horizon of Being. Our particular thrownness which brings about the disclosure of phenomena as beings (and Being as such) is a key characteristic of what Heidegger calls *Dasein*.

In Marion's *Reduction and Givenness*, both structures, intentionality and thrownness, are criticized as retaining something of the Cartesian/Kantian notion of subjectivity. Both the constituting I and *Dasein* retain characteristics of the old sovereignty of the subject. Against them, Marion suggests a new understanding of the self, beyond metaphysics and subjectivity, namely, the *interloqué*. The *interloqué* recognizes itself as the one to whom whatever givenness gives, is given. What, quite literally, calls the *interloqué* into existence is the gift that givenness gives. That giving, however, being absolutely unanticipated, is characterized by *surprise*. For Marion, surprise becomes precisely the operative structure by which the third reduction is effected.

What is *intentionality* for the transcendental reduction, *thrownness* for the ontological reduction, and *surprise* for the dosological reduction is *relatedness*[3] for the fourth reduction. I have shown in my "*Prosopon* and Icon" in this volume how relation is intrinsically connected with the etymology and conceptual genealogy of *prosopon*. We will see now how the understanding of *prosopon* as a relational structure can help us in formulating a fuller understanding of the ways the fourth reduction operates.

Richard Kearney's proposal for a fourth reduction summarized such a reduction under the imperative "back to existence"—but

[margin note: whitehead]

which "existence"? By "existence" do we mean "reality"? And what is real, the fundamental experience of myself as a unity *or* the experience of the world as a multiplicity? How can I have an experience (a discursive concept) of existence (an intuition)? Or, to put it differently, how can the sameness of *my* identity as consciousness be reconciled with the otherness of *my* experience of the world? And in which pole of the spectrum does reality ultimately lie? If the foundations of my ability to know are restricted by such rules as the law of identity, where every "I" equals itself, then how am I allowed to think of the other person, of you, as another "I," not identical with me? If everything is reduced to (some kind of) the One, how do we escape egotism? And if everything is reduced to the ever-changing manifold of the objective world (the world of experience), how does one escape reductionism? The Other and the Same, the One and the Many: such are the Cyclopes that await the philosopher in his quest. It is not easy to say "back to existence" without, somehow, deciding the matter at stake. The answers provided by the history of philosophy to this conundrum favor at some times the one end (the subject), at other times the other (the objective world).

We refuse to assign fundamentality or priority to *either* the experiencing I (rationalism, idealism) *or* the objects of its experience (realism, materialism). This refusal is our *epoche*. The experience to which the fourth reduction hails a return is that of relatedness. Before an experienc*er* and before an experienc*ed*, there is experienc*ing*. The relation between any two given *relata* is constitutive of them (with regard to their relationship) and, therefore, more primary and originary than their subjectivity or objectivity. For example, in viewing a painting, neither I (the viewer) nor the painting (the viewed) takes precedence (metaphysical, ontological, or epistemological) over the other. For it is our *relation* (the viewing) that reveals me as a viewer and the painting as viewed. Furthermore, I am a viewer *because of* the painting and *insofar as* the painting offers itself to my look; conversely, the painting is such (viewed as such, as a painting) *because of* me and *insofar as* I look at it. Strictly speaking, neither the painting itself nor I as a viewer "exist" outside this relation. There is an infinite number of such relations. *Existence* is this relational infinity.

Our position shows an affinity with two different and diverse theoretical systems that can provide us with examples: the striking conclusions of the Copenhagen School (Niels Bohr, David Bohm, and Max Born) in quantum physics and the theophilosophical work of the Russian theorist and scientist Pavel Florensky. The Uncertainty or Indeterminacy Principle, proposed by Heisenberg in 1925, boldly asserted that an electron "behaves" in reaction to its observer. Such a statement shattered both a static view of the universe, regulated by its universal and unchangeable laws (à la Newton) and by the certainty of the epistemological claims that scientists can make concerning our physical world. It was David Bohm, however, who radicalized the import of these changes toward an understanding of a desubstantialized (and consequently deobjectified) world. We read in his *Quantum Theory*:

> The properties of matter are incompletely defined and opposing potentialities that can be fully realized *only in interactions* with other elements. . . . Thus, at the quantum level of accuracy, an object *does not have any "intrinsic" properties* (for instance, wave or particle) belonging to itself alone; instead it shares all its properties mutually and indivisibly with the systems with which it interacts.[4]

Florensky presents a similar insight, only articulated in a philosophical language. In his attempt to ground Truth on a certainty more foundational even than that of the law of identity, he comes across the groundless ground of antinomy (very much like the *coincidentia oppositorum* of his predecessor Nicholas of Cusa). For Florensky, however, the contradictory character of an antinomy does not exclude either of the two opposite poles, but affirms each on the basis of the other. This leads him eventually to an understanding of contraries (such as sameness and otherness) as terms in relation. For Florensky, truth cannot be anything but relational, for it is defined as "the contemplation of Oneself through Another in a Third."

> If "another" moment of time does not destroy and devour "this" moment, but is both "another" moment and "this" moment at the same time; if the "new," revealed as the new, is the "old" in its eternity; if the *inner structure* of the eternal, of "this" and "the other," of the "new" and the "old," in their real unity is such that "this" must appear outside the "other" and the "old" must appear before the "new"; if the "other" and the "new" is such not through itself but through "this" and the "other," and "this" and the "old" is what it is not through itself but through the "other" and the "new"; if, finally, each element of being is only a term of a substantial relationship, a relationship-substance,

then the law of identity, eternally violated, is eternally restored by its violation.[5]

What Florensky calls "a substantial relationship," we call the *prosopon*. To understand the *prosopon* as only the person (and, thus, the other human being) is a misunderstanding. *Prosopon* defines a *tropos* (a way, a "how") as well as a *topos* (a place, a "who"). Person indeed becomes *prosopon*'s primary meaning, insofar as a person fulfills the description that *prosopon* signifies ("towards-the-face-of-the-Other"). A *prosopon*, therefore, is to be understood as a dyad of *topos* and *tropos*—these two meanings stand in a dialectical relationship with one another as "obverse" and "reverse." "All being is, by its very nature as being, *dyadic*, with an 'introverted,' or *in-itself* dimension, as substance, and an 'extroverted,' or *toward-others* dimension, as relational though action."[6]

I. The Extroversion of *Tropos*

The fourth reduction gives us indeed the totality of phenomena (every kind of phenomenon) through the prosopic relationship. The tree in front of me and the paper I am writing on, a text or a feeling, an event and a work of art, although they might radically lack a face, are still capable of appearing in a prosopic fashion. For they would never appear if they didn't relate themselves somehow back to a person. If this pen is not the pen that I use to write (or not write) to you, or for you, or about you, then what is it to me? The pen *in itself* (detached from any prosopic relationship) is meaningless. One could actually pose the question if I could possibly ever see the pen as a pure object (outside of the relational nexus). Only in relation to someone (you, the *prosopon*) the pen, or any other object, acquires meaning. The seed of relatedness is already contained in Husserl's breakthrough of 1900, the realization that, albeit in perception, imagination, or memory, consciousness is always a "consciousness of. . . ." For what else is this "of," which unites the intending consciousness with its intended world, if not the indication of a relation? To the extent that the consciousness is intentional, it is also relational.

Heidegger's analysis of everydayness had already revealed how the World is that referential totality of relations. We add to this definition only one more thing: the World is the totality of relationships that eventually take us back to a person (*reductio ad personam*); relationships with someone and toward the Other. For us, too, the World is this complex network of relations that become meaningful only through the presence or absence of a concrete Other (*reductio per personam*). In other words, the World (the totality of phenomena) appears only when it is reduced to my personal rapport with the Other. The fourth reduction reveals the things (emotions, thoughts, acts, events) that surround us and make up our World, as things-*for*-the-Other (*reductio pro persona*). Each thing falls into place by taking its place in this multifarious chain of relational connections that leads us to the Other, as the source of all relatedness. The Other is the implicit (and sometimes hidden) core of this configuration that reveals the World to me as such. Without the Other, this complex and elaborate scheme collapses.

With these remarks we have entered the order of the Platonic *exaiphnes*: that sudden, and perhaps urgent, emergence of the *aphanes* (the unapparent) into the "light" of phenomenality. The phenomena of the *exaiphnes* obey a different kind of logic: in the moment of the *exaiphnes*, the things that surround me have to retreat, and indeed "disappear," in order to allow that-which-is-not-seen to show itself. It is as if suddenly the things around me become transparent; as if the World is made of a see-through cloth, behind which I can still see you. And yet I know that it is not the things that withdraw but, rather, you that overwhelms them.

How, or rather what, do I see when I see you? A body? Isn't it the case that I see *you* only in your body? Are you totally exhaustible by your body? Then what is a gesture? The tone of your voice? Posture? The same questions can be asked concerning a painting. What makes this painting a Van Gogh and not a Rembrandt? What is the style? It is *in* the painting without, however, *being* the painting. It is the unapparent, the *aphanes* that somehow appears (without making itself as such visible). How does style "appear," since it is not visible? For what is visible in a painting—the colors, the shapes, the strokes of the brush—is precisely *not* the style. It is never the eye (as a physiological organ) or the ear that sees or hears, but "I"—this "I," however, cannot be seen, heard, or touched. That is why it (the I) can see and hear and touch what we call here the unapparent. This is not to deny embodiment and the flesh—quite the contrary. The "I" does not float in the air; it is always embodied—incarnate in my body (as style is in the painting), but it is not completely exhausted by the body understood as a physical, measurable (i.e., objectified) thing. Who would dare to say that the I is a thing? (That is, who else but Descartes, Leibniz, and Spinoza?) Strangely, then, the phenomenon of the unapparent duplicates itself on both ends of the phenomeno-logical spectrum: the *I* is as unapparent as the *you*.

The fourth reduction might be nothing else but this moment of the *exaiphnes*, when, looking at the things, we see the Other (or we be-come aware of ourselves as seen by the Other—for it is not so much that *we* see the Other; rather, it is the Other that shows itself through the World to *us*).

All of this is best illustrated in unique moments of one's life—as when one falls in love. When I am in love, the song that plays in an airport's waiting lounge (otherwise unnoticeable) comes forcefully to the foreground of my attention as soon as it reminds me of you. I am interested in the things that surround me only because I have been totally uninterested in them by being solely interested in you — however, to the extent that this World is also *your* World, the World *as yours* and only as yours, concerns me. Everything, absolutely ev-erything, becomes transformed by this manifold signposting that points back to you; or, failing to do so (and this is the only alterna-tive), everything remains utterly indifferent for me.

When the dreadful message of Patroclus's death reaches Achilles, the world around him is also lost: "I have lost the desire to live, to take my stand in the world of men" (*Iliad*, XVIII, 90–91); without him, Greece's greatest hero is nothing more than "a useless, dead weight on the good green earth" (104). What weighs on Achilles is the burden of an utterly indifferent world that, left unmediated by the Other, crushes him. The death of Augustine's friend, more than a millennium later, causes an equally severe break in the referential totality of his world: "My own country became a torment and my own home a grotesque abode of misery." The very things that had once defined what was most familiar to Augustine—his home, his homeland—suddenly appear strange. "I hated all the places we had known together, because he was not in them and they could no longer whisper to me 'Here he comes!' as they would have done had he been alive but absent for a while. . . . I had become a puzzle to myself" (*Confessions*, IV, 4).

It is in ways like these that the fourth reduction operates.

And yet, there is more to be said. For the *prosopon* in the fourth reduction is not only the Other, but also and equiprimordially *myself*. Here lies a key difference with Levinasian ethics, as Richard Kear-ney has already noted, for Levinas would have upheld "the asymme-try between self and Other," while the *prosopon* suggests a symmetrical reciprocity and mutuality. Let us rehearse once more the three reductions, so that we can see how through each one of them a new understanding of subjectivity or selfhood emerges.

In the transcendental reduction the "subject" assumes the role of the *constituting I*.

In the ontological reduction the "subject" is revealed as the locus of being's disclosure and, thus, *Dasein*.

In the dosological reduction the "subject" is turned into the *interloqué*—the one spoken to and called upon.

It might sound strange, but in the fourth reduction the "subject" is not—in terminology, at least—distinct from its "object." It couldn't be any different. Both poles of the relationship are the *prosopon* (*reductio ab persona*). We might note here that the prosopic relationship might prove to be the most successful overcoming of the subject/object dualism. And not only because the two, in some sense, have now "coincided" into a twofold one. What is more important is that it now becomes extremely difficult, if possible at all, to use the language of subjectivity and objectivity, that is, to still speak of someone "doing" or "acting" while another "suffers" or "receives" the action. We lose the ability to use language as grammar would command us, for it does not make any sense to use, say, transitive verbs. (Not an accident, for as Nietzsche reminds us, grammar is metaphysics.) This does not mean, of course, that we could not speak anymore. Rather, it forces us to use language differently, that is, reflexively.

To sum up, the fourth reduction is a fourfold reconduction (1) back *to* the person (*ad personam*); (2) effected *through* my relation with the Other's person (*per personam*); (3) where the world is revealed as the totality of things *for* the other person (*pro persona*); (4) from whom I receive back myself as a person (*ab persona*).

II. The Introversion of *Topos*

Another principle of the fourth reduction—perhaps the most obscure, but necessary—is the chiastic union of the phenomenality of the phenomenon with the phenomenon itself. This is a rather bold move that dares to bring together and think as one what in the terminology of classical philosophy we would have called the form (*Gestalt*) and the content (*Gehalt*). The fourth reduction makes room for a certain kind of phenomena that refer to nothing else but themselves, or rather to the fact that they appear—such are the phenomena of phenomenality. The paradox here, which the fourth reduction helps us to retrieve and rethink, is that every phenomenon, insofar as it appears, is first and foremost a phenomenon of (its own) phenomenality. Although to the extent that it carries or conveys other information (more than the bare minimum information of its appearance), it registers as a phenomenon of this or that. In exceptional cases, however, *which are no other than the ordinary*, phenomena can, even if it is only for a moment, fully exhaust themselves in their wondrous *phainesthai*. That means that, in exceptional cases (and what is exceptional here is not the sort of phenomena we are to encounter but our attitude toward them) we can let ourselves be enthralled by the extraordinary ordinariness of the things themselves. That is, I take it to be the case with what Kearney has in mind when he writes: "It is the divine itself manifest in the 'least of these,' in the color of their eyes, in the lines of their hands and fingers, in the tone of their voice, in all the tiny epiphanies of flesh and blood." When we let ourselves take notice of the unnoticeable manifestation of the divine in everydayness, we have arrived back at the original philosophical passion of *thaumazein*.[7]

There is, however, one phenomenon that adheres most strictly to this principle of the hypostatic union between phenomenon and phenomenality. Perhaps because it is itself the very ground of that principle, the archetype, the ur-phenomenon of all subsequent phenomena: *Incarnation*. One can already detect the structure of Incarnation in the passage by Kearney just cited. What else could be behind the divine that manifests itself in the flesh and blood of a concrete human being? Incarnation exemplifies (and with the same stroke also defies) the principles of phenomenology. If I want to offer a definition of the phenomenon of Incarnation, I would have to give an account of the singularity of Christ's epiphany. In His case, the "what" of the phenomenon *is* its "how." Its *Offenbarung* is nothing more or nothing less than its *Offenbarkeit*.[8] The "message" of the Incarnation is neither an "idea" nor a "system" (that would be an oxymoron), no matter how wonderful or lovely—it *is* flesh: body and blood.

Heidegger opens his magnum opus, *Being and Time*, with a particularly "blasphemous" statement: "The 'essence' of this being," he writes of *Dasein*, "lies in its to be. The whatness (*essentia*) of this being must be understood in terms of its being (*existentia*). . . ." What is provocative about this statement is the astounding fact that Heidegger defines the human being (*Dasein*) by assigning to it nothing less than the very definition of God. What Heidegger apparently had in mind was St. Thomas's definition of God, according to which *only*

God "is His own essence, quiddity or nature" (*Summa Contra Gentiles*, I, 21); and again "in God, essence or quiddity is not distinct from His existence" (*Summa Contra Gentiles*, I, 22). Of course, such a bold move was not meant as a tacit apotheosis of the human being; it was, rather, God who was sighted as its target. When we strive to redefine the person phenomenologically as *prosopon*, namely, as this coincidence of the phenomenon (essence) with phenomenality (existence), that is, a *hypostasized ek-sistence*, we have in mind nothing else but the event of the Incarnation. *Pace* Heidegger and St. Thomas, we do not think that God's self-hypostasizing of His existence should be mutually exclusive of man's potential of transcending his nature by choosing to be (and become) who he is. If man can exist as a person (which is what Heidegger claims concerning the *Dasein*), that is because God (the person par excellence) became man. To undermine God's incarnate person directly amounts to jeopardizing my own status as a person.[9] We have witnessed this principle throughout the history of philosophy: any distortion of God's personhood reverberates in man's selfhood.

The fourth reduction, then, precisely by being *prosopic*, has also to be *incarnational*. The event of incarnation has to be that center toward which all phenomenological analysis gravitates and against which each phenomenon (no matter how mundane) measures itself.

By being incarnational, the fourth reduction is also *eschatological*. For the Incarnation is the *eschaton* embodied in the incarnate Other, in the voice and visage of my neighbor. For if it were otherwise, if Incarnation were not the unsurpassable *eschaton*, one would have been justified in anticipating a time where I could have a more direct, full, unmediated understanding of the Other. In anticipation of such a time, however, one begins cheapening (relativizing) one's encounter of the Other as it is given in the here and now of everydayness. Such an *eschaton* beyond Incarnation would offer me the metaphysical excuse to overlook the Other in front of me, to ignore, neglect, or underestimate him/her in expectation of a more authentic encounter with another Other (perhaps the wholly Other, *tout autre*) at the end of History, conceived as some metaphysical totality à la Hegel.

III. The Departure from Religion

By speaking of the *prosopon*, Incarnation, and eschatology, one might wonder how the fourth reduction is not religion's most triumphal capture of phenomenology to date. Doesn't the fourth reduction confirm the fears of those who were speaking of "phenomenology's theo-logical turn" and even "philosophy's turn to religion"? Richard Kearney seems to be fully aware of such an objection when he notes: "Is the fourth reduction religious, then? Yes, but only if we under-stand here a religion *beyond* religion, *before* religion, and *after* religion."

We could take this statement a step further: what Kearney under-stands as "religion beyond religion, before religion, and after reli-gion" is in fact not religious at all in the strict sense. We might suggest, then, that the fourth reduction *has nothing to do with religion* if we recall Mircea Eliade's claim that all religions, pagan or monothe-istic, share a common emphasis on two things: *nature* (which they try to understand by providing a more or less mythic model of its gene-sis) and (as a result of that) *cosmology*. Contrary to this religious em-phasis on nature and cosmology, the *prosopon*[10] dramatically shifts the emphasis to *history* and *eschatology*. For this reason alone the related-ness of the *prosopon* cannot be and should not be confined to the strict limits of religion. When St. Paul experienced his conversion, he didn't change his religion for another—he abandoned religion alto-gether in order to offer witness to the event of the Incarnation, which surpasses religion.[11] That is why all the characteristics of religion (rit-ual, such as circumcision and sacrifices; observations of feast days; dietary regulations; the place of worship, such as the Jewish temple) lose their meaning and are not important anymore. They become "the shadow of the law" that has faded away or "the old order that has passed away" (2 Corinthians 5:17). Religion poses as great, if not a greater, a risk for the ecclesial event as secularization; for in the name of faceless love and justice it sacrifices the uniqueness of the *prosopon* by exchanging it for a fleshless ideology.

In fact, the entire objection against a "religious" *mis*reading of phenomena implies an alternative, second possibility: a nonreligious, secular reading. Therefore, such an objection reproduces the pagan (or "primitive," according to Levinas[12]) distinction between the sa-cred and the secular—a distinction rendered inoperative by the pro-sopic. To read the eschatological back in the ordinary of the everyday means to contaminate the temporal with the eternal; to blur the dis-tinction between a secular and a sacred world; to let the separation between the holy and the unholy collapse. It is, thus, in vain to raise the question of the "citizenship," as it were, of the phenomena: Is this face in front of me a phenomenon that belongs to the order of the secular (and thus the face of another), or is it a sacred phenomenon (and thus the face of God)? For the fourth reduction—precisely in its ability to overcome such a Manichaean view of the World—this is nothing but a pseudo dilemma; the face of the Other is essentially *both* the face of another and the face of God. Like matter in quantum physics, it can be both, either particle or wave. It depends on how I am able to receive the Other and on how the Other is able to give itself. Phenomenology should not and cannot decide a priori (i.e., prior to my relation with the Other and with the World) how to classify phenomena—as if she were an old librarian shelving books under the right call number. This chiasmus becomes the cross on which religion and secularism would have to sacrifice their logic. Religion, law, and ethics can, in the proper circumstances, play a crucial role in pointing us toward the *eschaton* of the Incarnation, but they are never more than ladders that must be left behind in time.

PART II

The Possible: Between Being and God

I. Philosophy Facing Theology

Enabling God

RICHARD KEARNEY

> You, God, who live next door —
> If at times, through the long night, I trouble you
> With my urgent knocking —
> This is why: I hear you breathe so seldom.
> I know you're all alone in that room.
> If you should be thirsty, there's no one
> To set you a glass of water.
> I wait listening, always. Just give me a sign!
> I'm right here.
> As it happens, the wall between us
> Is very thin. Why couldn't a cry
> From one of us
> Break it down? It would crumble
> Easily,
> It would barely make a sound
> **(Rilke, _Book of Hours: Love Poems to God_)**

The title of this essay—"Enabling God"—can be read both ways. God enabling us, us enabling God. As such, it affirms the freedom that characterizes our relationship to the divine as a mutual act of giving. So doing, it challenges traditional concepts of God as omnipotence. The notion of an all-powerful, autonomous, and self-sufficient deity has a long history ranging from the self-thinking-thought of Aristotelian ontology to the self-subsisting-act (_ipsum esse subsistens_) or self-causing-cause (*ens causa sui*) of medieval scholasticism and modern rationalism (Spinoza, Leibniz). It is a powerful lineage pertaining to a powerful concept of a powerful God. It will not be whisked away by wishful thinking or willful fiat. And even when we may think it has been deconstructed in recent phenomenological "overcomings"—Marion, Von Balthasar, Henri—it often resurfaces in drag. All too often the Omnipotence of Cause comes back in through the back door disguised as an Omnipotence of Love, or Beauty, or Self-Affection. Marion's cogent essay "God: The Impossible" is a good case in point. The omni-God of the philosophers (qua cause, substance, conceptual idol, logical proof) is indeed surpassed; but the God of Love who replaces it is, in important respects, just as overwhelming and invasive. One could say it is a God who gives up its "ways of making us talk" in favor of more subtle but no less coercive "ways of making us love." As Marion puts it in his reading of the Gospel scene of the Annunciation (where what is impossible to us is made possible by God), Mary's conception of Jesus is a matter of "when" (*lorsque*) rather than "if"(*si*). Marion does not consider the possibility of Mary saying "no" to the call by the Angel. And this for me profoundly modifies the "free" character of her "yes." In this very small textual point I see the reemergence of a very large intellectual presumption—that God's love is all-powerful, all-pervasive, all-knowing, regardless of how we act, think, or love in response. The gleaming back of the great white whale breaks the surface for a moment—reminding us of the ineluctable beast that continues to glide beneath: divine omnipotence. By contrast, I want to propose in this essay a God who needs and desires us, who dwells in the room next door, as Rilke so daringly puts it in "Du, Nachbar Gott," cited above, waiting for our signs, just as we wait in turn. Here is another kind of God—one who cannot come or come back, who cannot be conceived or become incarnate, until we knock, until we open the door, until we give the cup of cold water, until we share the bread, until we cry, "I am here. Where are you? Who are you? Why don't you come?" The wall between us is very thin after all. Rilke is surely right. And the signs that break it down are infinitely small and quotidian. As thin and as small as the voice that spoke in Elijah's cave, as the word that announced itself in Mary's room, as the loving hand that healed the withered hand, as the mustard seed that blooms into the kingdom. A million miles away from omnipotence.

In what follows here I propose to explore a hermeneutics of the possible God by moving through three concentric circles—

scriptural, testimonial, and literary. Traversing this threefold "variation of imagination," I hope to identify some key characteristics of
the God-who-may-be as it reveals itself to us poetically. So doing,
I seek the immunity of poetic license, with no claims to theological
competence, exegetical expertise, or confessional orthodoxy. I realize
that many were burned at stakes or put on the Index for far less in
centuries past, and I dedicate these tentative thoughts to their brave
acts of imaginative faith.

The Scriptural Circle

My efforts to rethink God as *posse* draw primarily from the biblical
message that what is impossible for us is possible for God. This latter
notion of messianic possibility is evident in many scriptural passages.
In Mark 10, for example, we are told that while entry to the Kingdom
seems impossible for humans, all things are made possible by God.
The exact text reads: "For humans it is impossible but not for God;
because for God everything is possible" (*panta gar dunata para to theo*)
(Mark 10:27). In similar vein, we are told in St. John's Prologue that
our ability to become sons of God in the Kingdom is something made
possible by God: "Light shone in darkness and to all who received it
was given the possibility [*dunamis*] to become sons of God." The term
dunamis is crucial and can be translated as either power or possibility—a semantic ambivalence to which we shall return below. Further
evocations of the possibilizing power (*dunamis pneumatos*) of the
Spirit are evidenced in Paul's letters to the Corinthians and Romans;
but perhaps most dramatically of all in the Annunciation scene where
Mary is told by the Angel that the "*dunamis*" of God will overshadow
her and that she will bear the son of God—"for nothing is impossible
[*a-dunaton*] with God" (Luke 1).
   In all these examples, divinity—as Father, Son, or Spirit—is described as a possibilizing of divine love and logos in the order of
human history where it would otherwise have been impossible. In
other words, the divine reveals itself here as the possibility of the
Kingdom—or, if you prefer to cite a *via negativa*, as the *impossibility of
impossibility*.
   A hermeneutical poetics of the kingdom looks to some of the recurring figures—metaphors, parables, images, symbols—deployed in
the Gospels to communicate the eschatological promise. The first
thing one notes is that these figures almost invariably refer to a God
of "small things"—to borrow from the wonderful title of Arundhati

Roy's novel. Not only do we have the association of the Kingdom with the vulnerable openness and trust of "little children," as in Matthew 10, but we also have the images of the yeast in the flour (Luke 13), the tiny pearl of great price (Matthew 13), and, perhaps most suggestive and telling of all, the mustard seed (Mark 4)—a minuscule grain that blooms and flourishes into a huge tree. The kingdom of God, this last text tells us, is "like a mustard seed that, when it is sown in the ground, is the smallest of all the seeds on the earth. But once it is sown, it springs up and becomes the largest of plants and puts forth large branches, so that the birds of the sky can dwell in its shade."

One might be tempted to call this recurring motif of the Kingdom as the last or littlest of things a _microtheology_ to the extent that it resists the standard macro-theology of the Kingdom as emblem of sovereignty, omnipotence, and ecclesiastical triumph. The frequent reference in the Gospels to the judgment of the Kingdom being related to how we respond in history, here and now, to the "least of these" (_elachistos_) (e.g., Matthew 25:40) is crucial. The loving renunciation of absolute power by Christ's emptying (_kenosis_) of the Godhead, so as to assume the most humble form of humanity (the last and least of beings), is echoed by the eschatological reminder that it is easier for the defenseless and powerless to enter the Kingdom than for the rich and mighty. And I think it is telling—as Dostoyevsky reminds us in the Grand Inquisitor episode of _The Brothers Karamazov_—that the greatest temptation that Christ must overcome, after his forty days in the desert, is the will to become master and possessor of the universe. This is a temptation he faces again and again, right up to his transfiguration on Mount Tabor when his disciples want to apotheosize and crown him by building a cult temple there on the mountain (Luke 9). Instead, Christ proceeds to a second kenotic act of giving, refusing the short route to immediate triumph and embracing the _via crucis_, which demonstrates what it means for the seed to die before it is reborn as a flowering tree that hosts all living creatures. As "King," he enters Jerusalem not with conquering armies but "seated upon an ass's colt" (John 12). He overturns the inherited hierarchies of power, fulfilling the prophecy of Isaiah that he would bring justice to the world, not by "shouting aloud in the street" but as a "bruised reed that shall not break, a smoldering wick that shall not quench" (Isaiah 42:1–4).

But in addition to these _spatial_ metaphors of the Kingdom exemplified by little things—yeast, a mustard seed, a pearl, a reed, an infant, the "least of these"—a hermeneutic poetics of the Kingdom might also look to the *temporal* figures of eschatology. These invariably take the form of a certain achronicity. I am thinking here of the numerous references to the fact that even though the Kingdom has *already come*—and is incarnate *here and now* in the loving gestures of Christ and all those who give, or receive, a cup of water—it still always remains a possibility *yet to come*. This is what Emanuel Levinas calls the "paradox of posterior anteriority," and it is cogently illustrated in an aphorism of Walter Benjamin that combines the spatial figure of the portal with the eschatological figure of futurity: "This future does not correspond to homogeneous empty time; because at the heart of every moment of the future is contained the little door through which the Messiah may enter."[1]

As "eternal," the Kingdom transcends all chronologies of time. Christ indicates this when he affirms that "before Abraham was, I am" (John 8:58), and when he promises a Second Coming when he will return again. In short, the Kingdom is both (a) already there as historical possibility and (b) not yet there as historically realized Kingdom "come on earth." This is why we choose to translate the canonical theophany of God to Moses on Mount Sinai (*esher ayeh esher*) not as "I am who am" (*ego sum qui sum*) but as "I am who may be." God is saying something like this: I will show up as promised, but I cannot *be* in time and history, I cannot become fully embodied in the flesh of the world, unless you show up and answer my call "Where are you?" with the response "Here I am." I explore this eschatological enigma of time in further detail in the conclusion.

The Testimonial Circle

Our second hermeneutic circle explores a poetics of the Kingdom in light of a number of testimonies recorded by religious writers down through the ages. This we might call the *testimonial* or *confessional* genre. Unlike "metaphysical" thinkers who presuppose an ontological priority of actuality over possibility, these more "poetical" minds reverse the traditional priority and point to a new category of possibility—divine possibility—*beyond* the traditional opposition between the possible and the impossible.

Let me begin with the pregnant maxim of Angelus Silesius: "God is possible as the more than impossible." Here Silesius—a German mystical thinker often cited by Heidegger and Derrida—points toward an eschatological notion of possibility that might be said to transcend the three conventional concepts of the possible: (1) as an epistemological category of modal logic, along with necessity and actuality (Kant); (2) as a substantialist category of *potentia* lacking its fulfillment as *actus* (Aristotle and the Scholastics); and (3) as a rationalist category of *possibilitas* conceived as a represention of the mind (Leibniz and the idealists). All such categories fall within the old metaphysical dualism of possibility versus impossibility. But Silesius intimates a new role for the possible as a ludic and liberal outpouring of divine play: "God is possible as the more than impossible. . . . God plays with Creation/All that is play that the deity gives itself/It has imagined the creature for its pleasure." Creation here is depicted as an endless giving of possibility which calls us toward the Kingdom.

I think the early medieval Jewish commentator Rashi also had something like this in mind when he interprets Isaiah's God calling to his creatures—"I cannot be God unless you are my witnesses." He takes this to mean "I am the God who will be whenever you bear witness to love and justice in the world."[2] And I believe that the Holocaust victim Etty Hillesum was gesturing toward a similar notion when, just weeks before her death in a concentration camp, she wrote: "You God cannot help us but we must help you and defend your dwelling place inside us to the last."[3] Both Rashi and Hillesum were witnessing to the *dunamis* of God as *the power of the powerless*. This, clearly, is not the imperial power of a sovereign; it is a dynamic call to love that possibilizes and enables humans to transform their world—by giving itself to the "least of these," by empathizing with the disinherited and the dispossessed, by refusing the path of might and violence, by transfiguring the mustard seed into the Kingdom, each moment at a time, one act after another, each step of the way. This is the path heralded by the Pauline God of "nothings and nobodies" (*ta me onta*) excluded from the triumphal preeminence of totality (*ta onta*)—a kenotic, self-emptying, crucified God whose "weakness is stronger than human strength" (1 Corinthians 1:25). It signals the option for the poor, for nonviolent resistance and revolution taken by peacemakers and dissenting "holy fools" from ancient to modern times. It is the message of suffering rather than doing evil, of loving one's adversaries, of "no enemies," of "soul force"(*satyagraha*). One thinks of a long heritage ranging from Isaiah, Jesus, Siddhartha, and Socrates to such contemporary figures as Gandhi, Havel, Dorothy Day, Jean Vanier, Ernesto Cardinal, Thich Nhat Han, and Martin Luther King, among others. The God witnessed here goes beyond the will-to-power.

Nicholas of Cusa offers some interesting insights into this eschatological God when he declares that "God alone is all he is able to be" (*Trialogus de Possest*).[4] Unlike the God of metaphysical omnipotence, underlying the perverse logic of theodicy which seeks to justify evil as part of the divine Will, this notion of God as an "abling to be" (*posse* or *possest*) points in a radically different direction. Let us pause for a moment to unpack the phrase "God is all he is able to be." Since God is all good, God is not able to be non-good, that is, non-God – defect or evil. In other words, God is *not* omnipotent in the traditional metaphysical sense understood by Leibniz and Hegel. The Divine is not some being able to be all good *and* evil things. That is why God could not help Etty Hillesum and other victims of evil. God is not responsible for evil. And Hillesum understood this all too well when she turned the old hierarchies on their heads and declared that it is *we* who must help God to be God.

Was Hillesum not in fact subscribing here to a long—if often neglected—biblical heritage? After all, if Elijah had not heard the "still small voice" of God in his cave, we would never have received the wisdom of his prophecy. If a young woman from Nazareth had said "no" to the Angel of the Annunciation, the Word would not have become Flesh. If certain fishermen, tax collectors, and prostitutes had not heard the call to follow the Son of Man, there would have been no Son of God—and no Gospel witness. So, too, if Hillesum and others like her had not let God be God by defending the divine dwelling place of *caritas* within them, even in those most hellish moments of Holocaust horror, there would have been no measure of love—albeit it as tiny as the mustard seed—to defy the hate of the Gestapo. For if God's loving is indeed unconditional, the realization of that loving *posse* in this world is conditional upon our response. If we are waiting for God, God is waiting for us. Waiting for us to say "yes," to hear the call and to act, to bear witness, to answer the *posse* with *esse*, to make the word flesh—even in the darkest moments.

I think Dionysius the Areopagite could be said to add to our understanding of this great enigma when he speaks, in Book 7 of *The Divine Names*, of a "possibility beyond being" (*hyperousias dunameos*) which engenders our desire to live more abundantly and seek the good. "Being itself," he writes, "only has the possibility to be from the possibility beyond being." And he adds that it is "from the infinitely good *posse* [*dunamis*] of what it sends to them [that] they have received their power [*dunamis*]."[5] I am tempted to relate this notion of an infinitely good possibilizing of God to another extraordinary passage in *The Divine Names* — this time Book 9, section 3 — where Dionysius writes of the God of little things: "God is said to be small as leaving every mass and distance behind and proceeding unhindered through all. Indeed the small is the cause of all the elements, for you will find none of these that have not participated in the form of smallness. Thus, smallness is to be interpreted with respect to God as its wandering and operating in all and through all without hindrance 'penetrating down to the division of the soul, spirit, joint and marrow,' and discerning thoughts and 'intentions of the heart,' and indeed of all beings. 'For there is no creation which is invisible to its face' (Hebrews 4:13). This smallness is without quantity, without quality, without restraint, unlimited, undefined, and all embracing although it is unembraced."[6] Is this extraordinary passage by Dionysius not a passionate invitation to embrace a microtheology of the kingdom? Is it not a solicitation to embrace an eschatology of little things — mustard seeds, grains of yeast, tiny pearls, cups of water, infinitesmal everyday acts of love and witness? It appears so.

Moreover, I think it is just this kind of microeschatology that Gerard Manley Hopkins had in mind when he records God's grace in small and scattered epiphanies of the quotidian — when he speaks, for example, of God's "pied beauty" being manifest in various "dappled things," from "finches wings" and "rose-moles all in stipple upon trout that swim" to "all things counter, original, spare, strange;/ Whatever is fickle, freckled — who knows how?" ("Pied Beauty"). For Hopkins, it is not the mighty and triumphant Monarch that epitomizes the pearl of the Kingdom ("immortal diamond") but, contrariwise, the court fool, the joker in the pack, the least and last of these. Here is Hopkins's take on the eschatological Kingdom:

> In a flash, at a trumpet crash,
> I am all at once what Christ is, since he was what I am,
> And
> This Jack, Joke, poor potsherd, patch, matchwood,
> Immortal diamond,
> Is immortal diamond.

Hopkins's deity is one of transfiguration rather than coercion, of *posse* rather than power, of little rather than large things.[7] An echo perhaps of Dante's deity in the *Paradiso*, who is described as a tiny, indivisible point of light in contrast to the towering figure of Lucifer in the final canto of the *Inferno*. But in our shift of registers from theology to poetry we are already embarking on our next circle of readings.

The Literary Circle

In our third and final hermeneutic circle—the *literary*— I include a number of passages that offer more explicitly poetic epiphanies of the possible. This amplification of our investigation to embrace a literary poetics extends the range of reference to take in soundings of *posse* which transcend the confessional limits of theism or atheism, enjoying as they do a special liberty of imagination—a "poetic license" to entertain an unlimited variation of experience. As Emily Dickinson rightly observed, "possibility is a fuse lit by imagination," a belief that informs her imaging of the eschatological possible:

I dwell in possibility—
A fairer house than prose—
More numerous of windows—
Superior—for doors. . . .
Of visitors—the fairest—
For Occupation—This—
The spreading wide my narrow Hands
To gather Paradise—

The French author Rabelais had his eye on a similar paradise when he affirmed the possibility of life through death, yea-saying to his last moments as he jubilantly declared: "J'avance vers le grand possible!" In his remarkable novel *Man Without Qualities*, the Austrian writer Robert Musil offers a further perspective on the eschatological *posse* when he claims that "possibility is the dormant design of God in man"—a design waiting to be awakened by our poetic dwelling in the world. Our true vocation in history, for Musil, is one of utopian invention. It involves an audacious surpassing of given reality toward imagined possibility. Here is the passage in full: "One might define the meaning of the possible as the faculty of thinking all that *might be* just as much as what is. . . . The implications of such a creative disposition are huge. . . . The possible consists of much more than the dreams of neurasthenics; it also involves the still dormant plans of God. A possible event or truth is not just the real event or truth minus the 'reality'; rather it signals something very divine, a flame, a burning, a will to construct a utopia which, far from fearing reality, treats it simply as a perpetual task and invention. The earth is not so spent, after all, and never has it seemed so fascinating."[8]

The metaphor of fire—with its allusions to both the burning bush (Exodus 3:14) and the Pentecostal flame of speaking tongues—is also explored by Wallace Stevens in a poem addressed to the philosopher George Santayana, "To an Old Philosopher in Rome." Here again the correspondence between the simple (indigent, small, inconsequential) and the eschatological (the Kingdom) is conveyed by the figure of a candle flame which illumines the real in the light of the "celestial possible." The pneumatological call to speak in tongues commits itself to a poetics of the poor and unremembered. Stevens writes:

> A light on the candle tearing against the wick
> To join a hovering excellence, to escape
> From fire and be part of that of which
> Fire is the symbol: the celestial possible . . .
> Be orator but with an accurate tongue
> And without eloquence, O, half-asleep,
> Of the pity that is the memorial of this room,
> So that we feel, in this illumined large,
> The veritable small . . .
> Impatient for the grandeur that you need
> In so much misery, and yet finding it
> Only in misery, the afflatus of ruin,
> Profound poetry of the poor . . .
> It is poverty's speech that seeks us out the most.

But it is doubtless the Prague poet Rainer Maria Rilke who composes one of the most inspiring invocations of the gracious power of *posse* in the conclusion to his *Letters to a Young Poet*. Here the eschatological promise of a coming God is combined with the erotic expectancy of a waiting lover. "Why don't you think of him [God] as the one who is coming," he asks his youthful correspondent, as "one who has been approaching from all eternity, the one who will someday arrive, the ultimate fruit of a tree whose leaves we are? What keeps you from projecting his birth into the ages that are coming into existence, and living your life as a painful and lovely day in the history of a great pregnancy? Don't you see how everything that happens is again and again a beginning, and couldn't it be *His* [God's] beginning, since, in itself, starting is always so beautiful?" Then Rilke poses this crucial question: "If he is the most perfect one, must not what is less perfect *precede* him, so that he can choose himself out of fullness and superabundance? — Must not *he* be the last one, so that he can include everything in himself, and what meaning would we have if he whom we are longing for has already existed? As bees gather honey, so we collect what is sweetest out of all things and build Him." Rilke ends this remarkable passage with a call to vigilant attention and expectancy. Messianism at its best. The metaphor of the flowering, flourishing mustard seed is brought to a new poetic intensity. "Be patient," Rilke counsels the young poet, "and realize that the least we can do is to make coming into existence no more difficult for Him [(God)] than the earth does for spring when it wants to come" (*Letters to a Young Poet*).[9]

Here we return, as it were, to the "pregnant sense of the possible"—the interweaving of the divine and the human in patient prayer and longing. And this eschatological desire, as Rilke vividly reminds us, is not confined to human existence but involves, by extension, the entire expanse of the terrestrial universe as it awaits, yearns, and prepares itself for the coming *prima vera*.

My daughter, who brought this passage to my attention, told me this was a God she could believe in! Could I disagree?

Conclusion

So much depends, then, on what we mean by the *possible*. If one defines possibility according to established convention, as a category of modal logic or metaphysical calculus—then God is closer to the impossible than the possible. But if one seeks, as I do, to reinterpret the possible as eschatological *posse*, from a postmetaphysical poetical perspective, the stakes are very different. For now we are talking of a *second* possible (analogous to Ricoeur's "second naiveté") *beyond* the impossible, *otherwise* than impossible, *more* than impossible, at the *other side* of the old modal opposition between the possible and the impossible. And here we find ourselves close to Kierkegaard's "passion for the possible" as portal to faith.

I think it is crucial to recall here the telling distinction between two competing translations of the Greek term *dunamis*. On the one hand, we have the metaphysical rendering of the term as *potestas/potentia*, that is, as a potency understood in terms of an ecomomy of power, causality, substance—what Levinas calls the economy of the Same (or Totality). On the other hand, we have an eschatological rendering of *dunamis* as *posse/possest*, that is, as a gracious and gratuitous giving which possibilizes love and justice in this world. It is this latter interpretation of *dunamis* that I have been seeking to promote in my three hermeneutic detours through the poetics of the possible (and, in more depth and detail, in *The God Who May Be*).

In triumphalist accounts of the Kingdom, the advent of the Messiah on the last day is often described in militaristic terms—as sublimely apocalyptic rather than lovingly vulnerable, as "almighty" rather than solicitous, as coercive rather than caring. By contrast, the divine *posse* I am sponsoring here is more healing than judgmental, more disposed to accept the "least of these" than to mete out punishment and glory. If God can prevent evil from happening by re-creating the historical past, as Peter Damian once suggested, He is by implication a God of theodicy: namely, a God who has the power to decide whether history unfolds as good or evil. To me, this sounds like *potestas* rather than *posse*. A far cry from the divine power of the powerless that Etty Hillesum invokes when she summons us to help God to be God in the face of violence and war. A world away from the God of little things.

Sometimes I wonder what would happen to the God of the Possible if we were to destroy the earth. How could God's promise of a Kingdom on earth be fulfilled if there is no earth to come back to? What might be said of the existence of God in such a scenario? There are a few observations I would like to make here by way of conclusion, surmises that claim the poetic license of a "free imaginative variation."

First, I would say that as eternally perduring and constant (that is, as faithful and attentive to us in each *present moment*), God would live on as an endless *promise* of love and justice. This would be so even if we fail or frustrate this covenant by denying its potential for historical fulfillment *on earth*. In this case, God would be like a spouse abandoned by a spouse—to take up the bride/bridegroom analogy from the Song of Songs. A lover forsaken. Or, to borrow a metaphor from Hildegard of Bingen, the *posse* would be like a tree deprived of its greening (*viriditas*).[10] If denied its ultimate incarnation in the last days, the possible God would be like a flowering seed arrested before it could come to its full flourishing and fruition on the earth. It would still be *adventurus*, but no longer *futurus*. The divine advent would be deprived of a historical, human future but would remain, in each moment, enduringly faithful in spite of all. It would still be a "yes" in the face of our "no."

Second, as eternal *memory* (past), the divine *posse* would preserve all those eschatological "moments" from the past where the divine was incarnated in the flesh of the world every time (as Christ and Isaiah taught) someone gave a cup of cold water to someone else. In kairological as opposed to merely chronological time, these instants would be eternally "repeated" in divine remembrance. This would take the form of the adage "The good that men do lives after them, the evil is interred with their bones" (to juggle with a line from Shakespeare's *Julius Caesar*). It would be in keeping with the repeated assurances of the biblical deity to remember the faithful who lived and died in history (e.g., Isaiah 49:15: "Can a mother forget her infant, be without tenderness for the child of her womb? Even should she forget, I will never forget you." And it would also be consonant with the contrary commitment to erase the memory of evil: "The Lord is close to the broken hearted/The Lord confronts the evildoers/To destroy remembrance of them from the earth" (Psalm 34). There is, then, a deeply eschatological character to the biblical injunction to "remember" (*zakhor*). And this character is what translates God's mindfulness of creatures into a form of "anticipatory memory" (the term is Herbert Marcuse's) that preserves a future for the past. As Psalm 105 tells us, "He remembers forever his covenant which he made binding for a thousand generations—which he entered into with Abraham." In other words, the promise made at the beginning of time is kept by the divine *posse* as an "eternal" remembrance of both the historical past and the present right up to the *parousia*.

Third and finally, then, qua eternal *advent* (future), we might say that even though we would have deprived the divine *posse* of its future realization as a Kingdom *come on earth*, we could not, by such an act of self-destruction, deprive God of the possibility of starting over again. Nothing *good* is impossible to God. And rebirth in the face of death is good. As in any nuptial promise or pledge, each partner can speak for him/herself only: God can promise only for God, not for us. We are entirely free to break off *our* part of the promise at any time. And if we do, if we engage in collective self-destruction (God forbid!), why should God not have a "second chance"? Is not *posse*, after all, the possibility of endless beginning?

Of course, the *posse* of the kingdom is not just a promise for humanity as a universal community (to be reassembled as the mystical body of Christ on the last day, according to the Patristic notion of *anakephalaiosis*/recapitulation). *Posse* is also and equally a promise for each unique self whose singular good—but not evil—will be preserved eternally in the recollection of the *deus adventurus*: like each glistening speck of dust in a comet's tail or each glint of plankton in the nocturnal wake of a ship. But if we destroy the earth, we also refuse the possibility of each of these recollected and resurrected selves returning to a "new heaven as new earth" on the last day. Such selves would return with *posse*—as part of the eternal promise—but without the *esse* of a Second Coming. That is why Dante had a great poetic insight into the character of divinity when he had the divine Beatrice descending from Paradiso to help her beloved (if errant) Pilgrim on his journey through the hermeneutic circles of faith.

Several of the above remarks and conjectures find textual support, I believe, in the "Palestinian formula" of eschatological memory (*eis anamnesin*) prevalent in late Jewish and early Christian literature. The formula finds one of its earliest inscriptions in Psalm 111, "the righteous will be for eternal remembrance"; and again in Psalms 37 and 69, where the memory of God refers not just to creatures remembering their Creator in rituals and liturgies but also to the Creator recalling creatures, making the past present before God in a sort of eternal re-presentation that endures into the future and beyond. Likewise, in Ecclesiasticus we find the repeated prayer that God will mercifully remember his children. As the biblical commentator Joachim Jeremias observes, such remembrance is an "effecting and creating event which is constantly fulfilling the eschatological covenant promise. . . . When the sinner 'is not to be remembered' at the resurrection,' this means that he will have no part in it (*Psalmi Solomonis* 3.11). And when God no longer remembers sin, he forgets it (Jeremiah 31:34; Hebrews 8:12, 10:17), this means that he forgives it. God's remembrance is always an action in mercy or judgment."[11]

The notion of eschatological memory is, as noted, also frequently witnessed in New Testament literature, where it takes the form of a double "repetition"—looking to past and future simultaneously. In the Eucharistic formula—"do this in remembrance of me" (*eis ten emen anamneisin*) (Luke 22:19; 1 Corinthians 11:24)—the proper translation of the repetition injunction, in keeping with the Palestinian memorial formula, is this: "Do this so that God may remember me."[12] The appeal to divine memory during the Eucharistic sharing of bread and wine may be seen, accordingly, as an echo of the third benediction of the grace after the Passover meal which asks *God to remember the Messiah*—a benediction that is followed with a petition for "the remembrance of all thy people": "may their remembrance come before thee, for rescue, goodness. . . ."[13] The remembrance of past suffering is thus tied to the hope for the advent of the *parousia*— for Jews the entry of the Messiah to Jerusalem, for Christians the return of Christ on the last day. The petition for repetition—in the kairological rather than chronological sense—may be translated as

"God remembers the Messiah in that he causes the Kingdom to break in by the parousia."[14]

This allusion to a bilateral temporality whereby divine memory recalls the *past as future* is further evidenced in Paul's gloss on the Eucharistic remembrance formula: "For as often as you eat this bread and drink this cup, you proclaim the Lord's death *until he comes*" (*achri ou elthei;* see 1 Corinthians 11:23–25). Indeed, the use of the subjunctive term *achri* refers often in the New Testament to the arrival of the *eschaton* (Romans 11:25; 1 Corinthians 15:25; Luke 21:24). The crucial phrase here—"until he comes"—may thus be read in light of the liturgical *maranatha* (come, Lord!) invoked by the faithful in their prayers for the coming of God. So, rather than remembering the death of God as no more than a historical event of the past, the remembrance formula can be said to celebrate it as an eschatological advent—that is, as the inauguration of a New Covenant. "This proclamation expresses the vicarious death of Jesus as the beginning of the salvation time and prays for the coming of the consummation. As often as the death of the Lord is proclaimed at the Lord's supper, and the *maranatha* rises upward, God is reminded of the unfulfilled climax of the work of salvation until [the goal is reached, that] he comes. Paul has therefore understood the *anamnesis* as the eschatological remembrance of God that is to be realized in the *parousia.*"[15] It is with this in mind that Luke speaks of the eschatological jubilation and "gladness"(*agalliasis*) that characterizes the mealtimes of the earliest Christian communities (Acts 2:46).

In sum, the close rapport between the Eucharistic request for repetition and the Passover ritual suggests that for both Judaism and Christianity the Kingdom's advent is construed as a *retrieval forward of the past as future*. The remembrance formula might be interpreted accordingly as something like this: "Keep gathering together in remembrance of me so that I will remember you by keeping my promise to bring about the consummation of love, justice, and joy in the *parousia.* Help me to be God!" Or, as the Coptic version of the formula goes: "May the Lord come. . . . If any man is holy, let him come. *Marathana.* Amen."

The above conjectures operate, for the most part, in the realm of hermeneutical poetics, which enjoys a certain imaginative liberty vis-à-vis the strictures of theological dogma, speculative metaphysics, or empirical physics. Though, I hasten to add, a fruitful dialogue remains open with all three disciplines.

Let me end with a final eschatological image from the poetics of the Kingdom—the invitation to the feast. "I stand at the door and knock, says the Lord. If anyone hears my voice and opens the door, I will come in and sit down to supper with him, and he with me." The great thing about this promise of an eschatological banquet is that no one is excluded. The Post-God of *posse* knocks not just twice but a thousand times—nay, infinitely, ceaselessly—until there is no door unopened, no creature, however small or inconsequential, left out in the cold, hungry, thirsty, uncared for, unloved, unredeemed. The Post-God keeps knocking and calling and delivering the word until we open ourselves to the message and the letter becomes spirit, and the word, flesh. And what is this message? An invitation to the Kingdom. And what is the Kingdom? The Kingdom is a cup of cold water given to the least of these, it is bread and fish and wine given to the famished and unhoused, a good meal and (we are promised) one hell of a good time lasting into the early hours of the morning. A morning that never ends.

Maybe, Maybe Not:
Richard Kearney and God

WILLIAM DESMOND

I.

Richard Kearney displays an enviable range of concerns in the embarrassment of riches that he offers to us with his three most recent books.[1] Each book asks for careful attention in its own right, though each contributes in a distinctive register to a larger project which goes under the title *Philosophy at the Limit*. Not unexpectedly, there is some seepage among the three books, for the sense of limit that emerges is a porous one. Thus the emphasis on stories is evident in all three books, while the themes treated in *Strangers, Gods, and Monsters* appear in some of the stories told in *On Stories*. His discussion of the nature and indispensability of stories often zones in on stories dealing with a kind of "between," and seepage is unavoidable in this porous middle. Then, further, the hermeneutical approach to religion adopted in *The God Who May Be* obviously bears on the storied character of biblical religion. It is not incidental that Kearney is a story-teller himself, and his fine novels are sometimes revealing in a richer vein of what academic commentary alone tends to make duller. So, too, his novels can be seen as religious quests, or quests of the religious. The space between these works and his more scholarly work is also porous. We find the desire not just simply to talk about the poetics of the possible but to enact something of it imaginatively.

Given present limitations of space, I will confine myself to some remarks on what I understand of Kearney's sense of the God of possibility that emerges from *The God Who May Be*. This is a complex and rich book, and not amenable to simple summary. There are many excellent things in it, among which I number a passionate engagement with the question of God; a subtle touch in his phenomenology of the persona, as well as his readings of Exodus and the Song of Songs; wide-ranging familiarity with and ease of reference to resources, especially in contemporary Continental thought. Needless to say, I am pleased that he aligns himself with something of the spirit of my own efforts to do philosophy in a metaxological manner. I have learned from his stress on eschatological possibility, for my own work tends more to stress a certain "archaeology." My conviction is that we cannot think last things without first thinking first things, there being no re-creation and eschatology without first creation. I put questions in friendship, and with immense admiration for his work. If I sometimes get a bit cranky with the question of God, maybe I need some penitential time on Croagh Patrick. I may have to get my ears scoured to hear the angel of Patrick's Hill.

In relation to the quest(ion) of God, one might broadly distinguish those who are "lovers" and those who are "theorists." When I mention love, I mean to call to mind, at least at first, *erōs*. When I say "theory," I mean something of its older meaning of "delight in seeing," not the modern sense of an instrumental hypothesis. The "theorists" often find themselves more at home with the God of the philosophers; the "lovers," with the God of religion (including the gods of paganism, as with Nietzsche). Many of the great philosophers were "theorists" in one sense, but one could also say that they were sometimes strange lovers. Often it is a matter of whether love or theory is in the ascendancy. A theory might well kill the love that is in it, a love at work without a by-your-leave from explicit rationality. Love, too, can be a kind of knowing, and most especially in being religious. We may love the divine, even if we do not know "theoretically." I mean delight even in not seeing, and even seeing in this sightless delight.

I think Richard Kearney falls first into the class of "lovers" rather than "theorists," evident in a number of ways. It is evident in his choice of the Song of Songs for special consideration. It is evident in his philosophical option for a hermeneutical approach rather than a philosophical way that is more in love with systematic strategies. It is evident in his agreement with those who are critical, sometimes too critical, of what they denominate, following Heidegger, as "onto-theology" or, following the process philosophers, as "substance metaphysics." It is evident, I suppose, supremely in the special place given to possibility. Who knows what might be, when one is in love? In love everything seems possible—at first. There are more fires in heaven and earth than are dreamed of in the systems of the more wintry "theorists." Of course, there is possibility and there is possibility, and some possibilities lead to the impossible; not always the impossible for us but possible for God, but just the madly impossible. Can love or theory then tell the difference between divine madness and mad madness? Worry about that difference is important for Kearney, but there is no doubt that his God of possibility is primarily and pervasively understood in terms of *erōs* rather than, say, *agapē* or *philia*. I will return to this question of possibility and *erōs*.

A philosophy, of course, is more often than not a hybrid of theory and love; in the best cases, a marriage. We can get gruesome distortions of love by theory (one worries sometimes about Spinoza's *amor intellectualis Dei* or Hegel's speculative *Gottesdienst*), or dreams of theory bordering on the incredible, perhaps because tangled around by strange love (I think of Kierkegaard and Nietzsche). The better practices of philosophy in the longer tradition seek a marriage of love and theory. My own sense of what I will call the longer Augustinian-Platonic tradition is one that seeks such a marriage (I demur concerning some of the cartoons of "Plato" that have occupied the ruminations of many anti-metaphysical metaphysicians and atheists of post-Nietzschean pedigree). Platonic philosophizing is erotic; Augustinian seeking is *erōs* transfigured by agapeic coaxing and interrupting. Lovers, of whatever stripe, from premodern to postmodern, do tell their stories rather than exchange theories or argue abstractions. And yet, one has to ask if philosophical love has a heart for *both* systematics and poetics. Love is not always green, and comes to thoughtfulness about itself and its beloved. The gray of theory awaits its aging. Might gray theory, too, come to a second spring of love, beyond the importunities of the first infatuations? So I would like to note a few systematic considerations that arise in Kearney's discourse. I will remark on three: how the question of God comes up; the question of the nature of possibility with reference to God; the *erōs* of God, and agapeic possibilizing power.

II.

How we raise the question of God can give us guidance to how we seek to address it. How, more generally, does the question properly arise in human life, and, more specifically, in a time of widespread godlessness, especially in the West? Many of the thinkers upon whom Kearney calls, Heidegger not least, have been touched, even blasted, by Nietzsche's "announcement" that God is dead. And yet here not much is said about this. Not too long ago quite a bit of Continental philosophy danced to the rhythms of Nietzschean dithyrambs. Some of those dancers have now, via Levinas, undergone a *metanoia* toward the ethical, and even an agonized worrying about transcendence and the divine. When I think of that *metanoia* from aesthetics through ethics and toward religion, I have to say: "Hats off to Kierkegaard!" But has the *metanoia* wiped the slate clean of Nietzschean traces, or perhaps imposed a Levinasian layer on the palimpsest where below the surface Nietzschean inscriptions still lie? My sense is that in much of Kearney's writing, the hot vehemence of Nietzsche's death of God does not figure, or is, rather, recessive. I am not saying it should figure, but if one goes for help to Heidegger, for instance, one cannot forget that here a certain ensemble of ideas goes to configure an attitude to metaphysics and theology that hinders one from a more fertile and generous appeal to longer traditions of reflection on the divine. When Kearney proximately refers to Heideggerian and post-Heideggerian resources, he is not rigoristic, and dips liberally in a number of rich sources in premodern philosophy. My mother used to say: "Show me your friends, and I will tell you who you are." Words worth considering for a philosopher, too. When it comes to God, I put on gloves when reading Heidegger. A sixth sense puts me immediately on guard as this bewitcher begins his incantations. I divine something truer in the tortured Kierkegaard, and not least with respect to the agapeic possibilizing power of God.

To ask how the question of God comes up is to be concerned with the matter of philosophical *protocols*, as it were. These protocols involve complex considerations I cannot elaborate here.[2] But how might we speak of God at all, if God is not a being among beings, albeit the highest, or even being itself? This is more complicated in that we find ourselves in the between whose immanence is defined by a network of interrelated beings. How think of a God of the between, from the between, without reducing God to the between? I put the question in these, my own, terms, since Kearney explicitly aligns himself with a kind of metaxological approach. In his terms the hermeneutical appeal to figurative language is obviously central. This is an old theme bearing on the efficacy of metaphor, symbol, analogy, hyperbole, and so on, in speaking meaningfully about God. I found it interesting that Kearney found in Heidegger the inspiration to talk about an analogy of proportionality between being and God. I swiveled in my chair for a moment as a silhouette of the dumb ox seemed suddenly to incarnate itself before my unbelieving eyes.

The issue of protocols is especially crucial in talking about *possibility*. God as possibility cannot be just finite possibility, for if so, one would produce that reduction that is quickly charged against "onto-theology": reducing God to a being among beings, or, here, possibility among possibilities. How, then, to speak of transfinite possibility? Kearney is not without a response, most especially in his understanding of desire. And yet there are categories used, such as possibility itself, or becoming, that remain defined by certain finite determinations, such that their attribution to God risks reducing the otherness of the divine. That otherness and transcendence is a great problem, and Kearney wants to find a middle way between a transcendence so high it vanishes, and then nothing can be said about it, and something abyssal that is so low or abject that God vanishes there, too (*The God Who May Be*, 7). I would say it is not a matter of finding a middle between these, as thinking about the meaning of middles, and of the God of the between that possibilizes the between without being reduced to it, whose otherness as creative is also a name for its being in communication with what it brings to be. But we have to find our way around that between in terms of the signs of this other transcendence and what they communicate concerning the God beyond the between, beyond as not itself being just the between, or the milieu of finite being.

Kearney is perhaps at his strongest in the reading of signs, not unexpected from a storyteller, and a thinker about stories and the telling of stories. Telling stories, reading stories, thinking about stories require the mind of finesse, and finesse is what the philosophical lover most tries to incarnate. In the present instance, figuration and transfiguration have always been linked in Kearney's writings since his early *Poétique du Possible*.[3] The need of religious imagination is here all the more important, when we are dealing with language at the limit, and perhaps beyond. The beyond of those limits is clearly at stake if one is to say anything with a more *eschatological* stress. Plato's myth of Er is an eschatological story or myth in that sense, drawing deep on the finesse of philosophical imagination—perhaps, indeed, prophetic imagination, though obviously in a pagan sense. The eschatological stress is the major emphasis to be found in Kearney's divine "may be"—he does mention an "onto-eschatology" (8). This does not exclude other emphases: his reading of the Song of Songs is also redolent of some signs of present enjoyment, and not only future-drawn longing. The point here is the importance of the religious imagination, whatever the dimension of time of which we speak.

Kearney has done much earlier work on the imagination, but tilted in the main, if I am not mistaken, toward an aesthetic understanding, with a concern for cultural and political matters, though there has always been a strong concern for the ethical imagination. The problem confronted by the religious imagination concerns the doublet icon/idol. Kearney is strong in insisting on the icon, but of course, all the agonies of being religious are concentrated in the question of the difference. What can we say about an icon, to the extent that it transcends all our autonomous knowing, for the divine communicates and we cannot predetermine, or even determine, what it will be? We are in the "may be." But what if we find ourselves not first concerned with a hopeful eschatology but, rather, overtaken by perplexity as to how to discriminate between God and the counterfeit doubles of God? The "may be" always drags along with it its mocking twin, "maybe not."

I say this as a theist. It is not only the atheist who might mock the theist with his "maybe not." The perplexed theist finds himself, mocks himself, in that equivocal space between idol and icon. I cannot quite understand the way some atheists take the trouble to testify to their atheism, lest, as it were, you might get the wrong impression. They seem so contented with themselves, even superior, when they tell you that, yes of course, they are atheists. What self-satisfied witness this? I should qualify: there are atheists who are the more self-satisfied heirs of the Enlightenment, some of whose numbers we find more often on the analytical branch of contemporary philosophy. On the Continental side, it is the dissatisfied atheists whom we seem to find more and more. And yet there can be a superior satisfaction in such dissatisfaction. The dissatisfaction does not find itself in deep enough despair about itself to drive it to God. It exists between the counterfeits of God and God, tempted by a more finessed idol whose mouth is verbosely muzzled when it comes to uttering the name "God."

Obviously one cannot count Richard Kearney among either the self-satisfied theists or atheists, whether self-satisfied or satisfied in dissatisfaction. He makes no bones about calling himself a "Judeo-

Christian theist" (5). I find the forthrightness refreshing. But he is deeply aware of the problem of discrimination. The need for discernment returns again and again. Indeed, some of his most effective discussion bears on the questions he brings to such thinkers as Marion and Derrida. What are we finally left with? Monsters or nothing? Or a God who is either monstrous or nothing? How tell the difference between God and these possibilities? I wonder if the same difficulty of discernment applies to the idea of the possible as such.

III.

So I turn to the question of the possible, and the "possible God." The book opens with a stark statement of Kearney's view (1):

> God neither is nor is not but may be. This is my thesis in this volume. What I mean by this is that God, who is traditionally thought of as act or actuality, might better be rethought as possibility. To this end I am proposing here a new hermeneutics of religion which explores and evaluates two rival ways of interpreting the divine—the *eschatological* and *onto-theological*. The former, which I endorse, privileges a God who possibilizes our world from out of the future, from the hoped-for *eschaton* which several religious traditions have promised will one day come.

Richard Kearney's earliest work was the *Poétique du Possible*, and he returns to the themes of this work extensively here, while deepening the insights he earlier pursued. On the nature of possibility, two major sources of inspiration are evident in the earlier work: Heidegger and Cusanus. In *The God Who May Be*, the sources from which he draws are perhaps wider, and there are illuminating critical discussions of Husserl (84–87), Bloch (91), Derrida (93–99). Nevertheless, one senses the continued influence of the Heideggerian claim that possibility stands higher than actuality. This is a view Heidegger "borrowed" from Kierkegaard, where the thought is intimately connected with the human being in its religious relation to God. One might see Kearney's book as an attempt to return Heidegger's "borrowing" to an earlier, and perhaps even more rightful, "owner," even though the name of Kierkegaard—surprisingly, I thought—does not figure very prominently.

I reiterate my own diffidence about Heidegger. I find him riddled with equivocation on the question of the religious, playing a pagan game which yet resounds with echoes borrowed, without being cleanly acknowledged, from the biblical tradition. Kearney takes a double attitude to Heidegger. In a discussion of Heidegger's "last god" in *Strangers, Gods, and Monsters* (213–28), he is quite critical. In *The God Who May Be* he does refer to "the intriguing use" (119, note 11) Heidegger makes of the "last God." I think there is much bogus prophecy in all of this. In *The God Who May Be*, Kearney is more benign to Heidegger on the issue of the possible. For instance, he accepts, without severe enough qualification, the translation of Heidegger's *Vermögen* as "loving possibility" (91ff.). I balk at the loving, and while there may be some kind of loving in Heidegger, the whole question is what kind. He may talk about the quiet power of the possible, but malice and raging also belong to being. I think that Heidegger is, on the whole, an underdeveloped thinker when it comes to the ontology of love. John Caputo has very effectively drawn this to our attentions in relation to *caritas*.

I know that the later Heidegger was working toward a vision of release and serenity, but the issue remains as to what right he has to such a vision, given other terms that loom so large in his discourse. Are the intellectual resources of that discourse rich enough to do justice, for instance, to the event of agapeic love and its free release of the other as other, or toward the other? I doubt it. In "The Origin of the Work of Art," how does "peace" come out of strife, if *polemos* is the father of all things?[4] How the *metanoia* from war to peace? It is analogous to the reversal from will to will-lessness in Schopenhauer, who speaks of art as offering the *Sabbath* of the will. But how can there be *any* Sabbath at all on his terms; or released serenity, if *polemos* is the father of all things? If we are concerned about eschatological desire, we must take this question of peace and sabbatical being most seriously. In Heidegger, pagan *polemos* is more original than peace, and peace is an outcome of *polemos*; there is no vision of an original ontological peace in being, such as we find in the vision of sabbatical being in the biblical religion. What Heidegger himself says about creation, with reference to the latter, I find close to inexcusable. This has tremendous implications for how we conceive the original creative possibilizing power of the divine. I will suggest below that we need more overt agapeic resources to think this.

But Richard Kearney is not Heidegger, and he cannot be charged with Heidegger's sins, even if the company he sometimes keeps raises worries in an old mother hen like me. I hope I will be forgiven my friendly, if worried, clucking. I find myself breathing easier when the name of Cusanus is sounded. He is a bold and brilliant and singular speculative thinker, who has to be honored in high terms for his finesse with respect to the protocols of approaching the question of God. His famous *coincidentia oppositorum* is itself instantiated by the *possest* which, in ways not easy to explain, is *esse* and *posse* together, and hence beyond the binary oppositions that can mar the thought of divine being. True, the *coincidentia oppositorum* can be put to different pan(en)theistic uses, for instance, in the hands of a Hegel. But the major concern here is to find a way beyond all finite ways in finite thinking, such that the very otherness of God is respected in thought—nay, revered. Richard Kearney worries about a kind of identity in the divine with Cusanus which is too predetermining of what is to be in finite creation (103–5). This is perhaps a genuine worry to the extent that the ghost of Parmenides may not be laid to rest in some strains of Cusanus's thinking. I would worry far more about Hegel on this score than Cusanus, perhaps because the latter's sense of thinking always happens in familial communication with meditation and prayer. Intriguingly enough, whenever Cusanus speaks of the *non-aliud* (not-other), I can think of nothing but the *aliud* (other). The *non-aliud* seems so *aliud* to finite determinate ways of thinking that we cannot fixate God as other or not-other in any univocal way. This is perhaps an instance of being beyond binary oppositions such as determine more usual finite thinking, offering us a sense of the *aliud* that strains against any univocal pan(en)theistic reading of the signs or figures of God.

This sense of the otherness of divine *possest* to finite possibility is absolutely crucial. This otherness is such that divine *possest* possibilizes without univocally determining finite possibility, and most intensively in the case of the creative possibility of the human being. I find in Cusanus a feel for the immense difficulty of thinking the difference of the divine *possest*. At the least this must be freed from potentially idolatrous identifications with different forms of finite possibility. It may be true that much traditional metaphysics in its use of the potency/act distinction did not pay enough attention to this other, one might say, hyperbolic sense of *possest*, and hence risked an idolatrous reduction of the divine. I tend to be a little more generous to the so-called tradition of metaphysics than most Heideggerians, or those too bewitched by Heidegger's rhetoric; generous, if not with respect to the performance, at least with respect to the intention. If I am not mistaken, in premodern thought the difference of the divine constitutes a nonnegotiable concern, while from Descartes onward, finesse in approaching this difference in philosophical thought becomes seriously eroded. The erosion of that finesse is really the defect of modern ontotheology; it is unfair to attribute it totalizingly to the entire tradition since Plato. Richard Kearney's realignment with Cusanus is with the hope of the resurrection of that finesse, a finesse Kearney practices more in the hermeneutical register than in the systematic, and yet we need finesse in systematic considerations also. The "theorist" needs finesse, just as the "lover" does. Indeed, the finesse the "theorist" needs may be something he can learn only from the "lover," letting the delicatesse of love seep into, steep, the very texture of thought.

Kierkegaard is a religious thinker who has finesse enough to draw our attention to the hyperbolic sense of possibility with respect to the human being. This sense of hyperbolic possibility is finally embedded in a vision of creation and human life as given to be by the goodness of God, a God who reserves its transcendence even while communicating to and with immanence, a God of hyperbolic possibilizing power that now hides in the incognito of powerlessness, that now astonishingly offers possibilities to human beings that to human beings alone are utterly impossible. I would say this is true also of Richard Kearney's God, except there is perhaps more of the erotic sunshine of the south in his vision than in the sometimes too overcast Dane. We find this in Kearney's less negative view of the aesthetic, here in the full robustness of bodily being such as is caressed and kissed and aroused in his delighted, fleshed reading of the Song of Songs; in a less Kantian view of the ethical, still there in the good Protestant Kierkegaard; in a more ecumenical appreciation of the pagan whose splendid vices were, after all (and did not the great Augustine say it?), splendid.

Here are some of my worries about the sense of the possible in Kearney's "may be." He gives a strong ethical determination to the meaning of the "may be." Hence the future and eschatology assume the dominant place in his consideration. This is consistent with a kind of modern privileging of futurity. It is consistent with a desire to draw the divine into the temporal process itself—signaled by the Christian claim of the entry of the divine into time with the incarnation, secularized in modern progressive ideologies when the absolute completion will be also intrahistorical. This is a big theme, I know. My worry is that what I will call the archaeology of possibilizing power is given shorter shrift than it deserves because of the primary stress on the possible as pointing to a future of more perfected realization. For Kearney this is not a teleology in the immanent sense we know from Hegel and Marx, and some other "grand narratives." But I would like more inoculation against the idolatries of certain historicisms, inoculations built more intimately into our understanding of divine *possest*.

There is no question that Kearney, like many postmodern thinkers, eschews these idolatries. But idolatry, in whatever form, becomes a meaningless idea if there is not a true God, and if we cannot in some way, granted always failing, do justice to the true singularity of the divine. We come back to the first command, which in effect says: God is God and nothing but God is God. Our philosophical destruction of one idol may be itself the construction of another idol. This is why we need the sifting of the counterfeit doubles of God. Our temptation as philosophers is that our idols can be as much wrought from concepts and words as from wood and stone; and the very words and concepts used to deconstruct one idol may themselves be the seeds of another usurping idol. My point: I think there are seeds in the notion of possibility that do contain the germs of idolatrous growths. Do we have to wait until the end of time to see which are the wheat and which are the tares? Maybe. But also maybe not.

We need a stronger "archaeology" of possibility to guard against some of the temptations of an eschatology of possibility. By an archaeology of possibility I do not mean a first principle in the sense attributed to so-called ontotheology. A true first principle (if we were to talk that way) would not be homogeneous with the series it generated, but put that aside. It would be a first, but in a hyperbolic and heterogeneous sense. We ask: What makes possibility itself possible? Finite being is defined by possibility and actuality, but actualizing is itself a possibilizing; hence both finite possibility and actuality are dynamic through and through (a dynamatology would not be completely new news even to Aristotle).

Further again, dynamic possibilizing power could not be just the logical possibility as defined by the laws of identity and contradiction. This sense of possibility has been immensely attractive to philosophers, and invested with a certain eternity, or a least timelessness (not quite the same thing). Timeless possibility creates all the problems of how anything arises in being at all, for timeless possibility is not creative. The question What makes possibility itself possible? is addressed to a sense of the possibilizing of possibility, itself hyperbolic to finite possibility/actuality; and also to logical, or indeed ontological, possibility understood as formal in a kind of quasi-Platonic sense.

What makes such possibility possible? I don't think we say enough if all we say is just possibility again. We would, rather, have to talk about creative possibilizing power that itself gives rise to possibility as form, whether logical or ontological; and, more, gives rise to finite being as itself defined by the doublet possible/actual. Hyperbolic possibilizing power is not just possibility; it *must be* (not simply may be) in some other hyperbolic sense.

I do not share the anxieties about "being" that some thinkers evidence, though I do share a perplexity about the meaning of being, and the different senses of being that have to be distinguished. I do not see why we cannot find something suggested of this hyperbolic sense in the traditional translation of the Exodus name as "I Am Who Am." Kearney is right to resist here any objectification and determination of God in terms of finite presentness that can happen. I concur entirely with his efforts to keep open the surprise of the divine — more than surprise, the rupture, the excess of the hyperbolic in the "may be." I still think, in a stronger regard, that the "may be" cannot be divorced from the "is" — granting again that the "is" is as deeply mysterious and perplexing as the "may be." I think this is what Cusanus was trying to get at also. But the "is" here has to be referred to creative power, creative power which itself possibilizes possibility in a more than determinate and finite sense, and to which we are more drawn in the given world.

It may be the case that human possibilizing gives us some image of what this hyperbolic possibilizing power is. I believe this is so: that an imaging of the ultimate possibilizing power in terms of the potency/act of finite determinate things is not at all adequate; that human possibilizing is a more intensive image of the ultimate power. But it is not more than an image, even though it is marked by original power. We can be dazzled by this image. One of the dazzlements bears on the intoxicating temptation to think too much in terms of futurity as the privileged modality of time. Kearney might say that eschatological futurity is not historicist futurity with its immanent teleology; very well, but then we cannot be dealing with just temporal "futurity." We are addressing, so to say, time's other, what the premoderns called eternity. A God of the future is not God, if that God is not also the God of the past and the present; not by being the *hyper* temporal "now" but by being *hyper* the temporal now, whether in its modality of the to come, or the coming now, and the already having come now. We are pointed to the hyperbole of the eternal possibilizing power, and no modality of time exhausts its excess.

In my view, an eschatology without a robust sense of creation, hence without an adequate archaeology of coming to be, always risks collapsing into the historicist idolatries of holistic immanence. Kearney wants to avoid such a collapse. Yet when he says, "For *possest* may now be seen as advent rather than *archē*, as *eschaton* rather than *principium*" (110–11), the "rather than" implies an exclusion that is too overdrawn. If *archē* is understood in the hyperbolic sense here intended, the need for the more robust sense of creation would be evident. Am I right to notice a hesitation in the way Kearney refers to "eternity" in quotation marks (81–82). A thorough rethinking of eternity may be needed to counteract the idolatries of holistic immanence, though it is just the one notion that has been tabooed in modern historicist consciousness and in all talk that tends to give to "futurity" the temporal laurels. Kierkegaard reminded us that eternity is the one thing we most need when we most think we need it not at all. Heideggerian handbooks will not guide us. Fortunately *The God Who May Be* is not such a handbook.

IV.

I think we need to distinguish at least the following six different senses of possibility or (creative) possibilizing.

First, possibility with respect to *origin* — origin as *hyperarchē* (do not think of "archē" as a determinate beginning in time). Does the idea of the possible even arise here, properly arise? Can we know what is possible for this *hyperarchē*? If anything, only from what is given by it. But this is defined by what derives from it; hence our knowing can never be absolute, even if that origin communicates with us, reveals itself to us. We are and know in the "lag" derived from it, the "lag" being the given between of the finite creation. Hence any knowing of its "possibility" must be indirect. But what we know of the possible is derived from what here and now is actual/possible, itself derivative vis-à-vis the origin; hence, again, what "possible" means relative to origin *must* remain *reserved*. Most of all, we must guard against identifying immanently available senses of the possible with it; for its "possibility" is "*hyper*-possibility" — above the possible: sometimes facing us as the absolutely necessary, sometimes as the seemingly impossible (again, when our sights are kept on finite possible/actual). A wiser agnosticism is needed here.[5]

God in self—hidden in inaccessible light. In light, but light that terms such as possibility and actuality darken; darken, if we forget that what meaning we give to these notions comes proximately to us from finite creation. Here we are trying to address something that is unsurpassably other, hyperbolic to finite creation in that regard. The mystery of the Godhead: we should worry about the applicability of temporal terms derived from finite becoming. Ought these to be applied at all here? Our reserve is entirely proper about the ultimate reserves of God. The point, of course, is not to deny *dunamis*, as if the most intimate being of God were some dead stasis. We are not addressing the frozen autism of some catatonic God. Not at all. Here we have metaphors, symbols, analogies, hyperboles, each of which should be crossed out, even as it may perhaps help us cross over, or rather be crossed by something that exceeds us exceedingly. If we use the language of becoming, and we cannot avoid this if we speak of "may be," we should not take ourselves too seriously. Should we speak of an eternal becoming? Hegel here lost his sense of metaphysical humor in thinking that he had the categories necessary to account for "eternal becoming" in the Godhead itself. He fell into conceptual idolatry before his logical sticks and figures. I have spent too many years keeping watch on the magic of Hegel's dialectic, and when anyone speaks of the "becoming" of God, I find myself getting vexed. I wonder if any language of the "may be" is applicable here.

Second, possibility with respect to *creation*. This is not the same as origin, but the giving to be of finite being by the origin. Creation can refer to either an "activity" or an "outcome" of activity, and I refer here primarily to the "act" of creating, rather than the "product" created. This is a possibilizing, but it is more than that, since it is not just the reduction of possibility to actuality, but the bringing to be of possibility and actuality; with these latter then further showing the dynamism of possibility and actuality in a more finite sense. Again there is something hyperbolic here about creative possibilizing, since without this, nothing finite would be or become. I think the traditional doctrine of creation *ex nihilo* is very important here. I only mention it without expanding on the kind of nothing, creation, and related notions at issue here.[6] The origin is not creating itself in creating finite being: it is bringing to be the finite other as genuinely other and endowed with promise, ontological, aesthetic, ethical, and religious. I think creation is best thought in terms of the hyperbole of agapeic bringing to be. We might respond to this suggestion by saying "may be, may be not." Very fair, since we glean something of this agapeic bringing to be from the finite creation as already given. In that given creation, we are always tested between a "maybe" and a "maybe not." But if there is a more primordial creative possibilizing that itself makes possibility possible, it is not clear if we can use the language of "may be" in dealing with this more primordial possibilizing.

Third, possibility with respect to *coming to be*: this is what creation effects. I would say: not first a becoming, but a coming to be, a bringing to be. I would say that all becoming presupposes a coming to be. I say it, for instance, because process philosophy (to which Richard Kearney refers sympathetically) does not advert to this, and hence collapses difference, and hence also different senses of possibilizing. It worries me in the case of Kearney whenever he tends to counter-pose being and becoming, as if derogation from the latter and fetish-izing of the former were the defining sins of the so-called ontotheological tradition. Process philosophers should beware here of offering us more slogans than thoughts. I do not say that of Kear-ney, but it is certainly too one-sided to think that we can just substi-tute becoming for being. In any case, coming to be refers us to a primal givenness of being, what I call a *passio essendi*, prior to the be-coming of any and all *conatus essendi*. *Passio essendi* is as much an onto-logical notion as it is applicable to the determinate forms of being we find in the middle world of creation (in the sense of the produced world). Original creation is a bringing to be and a coming to be (inti-mated to us sometimes in our astonishment at the "that it is at all" of being there).

Fourth, possibility with respect to *becoming*. Becoming refers to a more determinate process of transition from possibility to actualiza-tion, a transition granted on the basis of the more primal coming to be given in creation. In my view, becoming is an intraworldly cate-gory, and should be applied to God with great caution. God may be in solidarity with becoming, but in the more precise sense of the term, we should be extremely diffident in speaking about God as becom-ing. Process philosophers often lack that caution, in my view because they univocalize the difference between God and every other reality. Hence, when they talk of God, they do not talk of God. So I think. I grant their good intentions to think a God involved with creation, but their way of talking produces a counterfeit double of God, and a philosophical sin against the first command: God is God and nothing but God is God. The difference implied by this command is blurred by the *homogeneity* of categorial determinations that the process philosopher says must be applied to all being and processes, God included. Including God thus, is excluding God.

I think Kearney's attraction to the language of becoming is not well enough qualified here, though when one takes into account his book as a whole, it is the hyperbolic character of divine possibility that is crucial, and hence he cannot be placed in the same camp as the process univocalizers. Is "becoming" too thin to preserve the difference of God and finite creation? Why apply "becoming" to "origin," to "creation," to "bringing to be," none of which suggest any dualistic opposition of "being and "becoming"? One might rather speak of the divine as being in communication with creation; being in excess of the finite between, and yet in intimate rapport with it, though the difference of divine transcendence is not conjured away.

Fifth, a further sense of possibilizing might be connected to *self-becoming*. This presupposes the other senses, and you might venture that all forms of being are marked by this. (I do not like to identify self-becoming with "self-creation," a quite widespread tendency, not least by process thinkers; such a use of "creation" has to be done more circumspectly.) But if this is so, with human self-becoming, there may be something *more* emergent—what one might term a more creative moment: a self-becoming that is always endowed with creative possibilizing, such as we find with great artists, but not only there. If this is here a kind of "self-creation," there is also more. Ethical self-becoming offers us a sign of the unconditional: something unconditional about our being as ethical suggests something of the absolutely unconditional good, hyperbolic to the terms defining the possibilities of finite becoming. (Kant's doctrine of the *summum bonum*, and his postulation of immortality and God, might be seen to approach this hyperbolic ethical possibility. That said, I have my reservations about his way of approach. Kant himself hated everything hyperbolic.) We are at the boundary of possibility that can be defined in terms of becoming. In human terms (I say nothing of God), it calls for an ethical constancy in full communication with becoming, a constancy not quite a becoming, more a certain fullness at the ready for the practice of human becoming.

Sixth, and finally, a sense of the possible emergent *beyond self-becoming* in which the *other* possibilizes a freedom released beyond our own powers of self-determination. This enabling of release makes possible a transfiguration of our own efforts and claims to be self-determining. Since the openness to the other comes to form for us here in this release, there emerges a more radical possibilizing of self-becoming that is creatively there for the other in an ethical and religious mode. But this possibilizing is not first what we do; it is received by us as gift from the other. The surprise of the generous other is in this gift—itself calling forth our "being generous." It is here, more than anywhere else, that I think Kearney's notion of the eschatological "may be" finds its opportunity of greatest moment. What here emerges as possible and possibilizing? The most intimate and often incognito creativity which does not insist on itself, in that it is in the image of the origin and the first creation. This is the communicative creativity whose generosity of being is agapeically released beyond itself, making way for the other. There is no circle that is closed here; rather, the between is defined as an open space of porosity. In that porosity, communication is enabled, possibilized, sparked between humans, and between humans and God. (Prayer happens in the intimacy of this porosity.) Kearney, if I understand him, and some other important modern thinkers, can be seen to search here for a transcendence more ultimate than human self-transcendence. I am in accord. And I have learned much from Kearney's search in terms of his understanding of the eschatological God. I still think we need more firm discrimination of the above different senses, to avoid reducing possibility to a too indeterminate and homogeneous notion, in the process losing both the distinctiveness of finite possibility and the difference of the divine.

Richard Kearney and John Manoussakis have recently spoken of a fourth, an eschatological, reduction. This would require more extended treatment, but among other things, I appreciate the spirit of their coming back to the extraordinary in the ordinary. Should this be called an *eschatological* reduction? I take eschatology to bear on last things, and what is to come, beyond the present order of things. If we are coming back, or being led back, to the extraordinary in the ordinary, how do we connect with what is to come? We are the beneficiaries, so to say, of godsends here and now, hinting to us of a hidden promise of what is to come, beyond the present order which is passing. If these godsends are what is intended, well and good. But should one speak of a *reduction* in regard to them, since we do not take the initiative? Godsends grace us. Grace us with perhaps eschatological signs that ask our finesse.

I also have some hesitations, given that their way of formulating this eschatological reduction takes its sights from concerns immanent to the entire phenomenological movement, its method(s), and its diverse developments. Suggestions in relation to previous reductions are intriguing, but I worry about something too scholastic about this way of seeking release toward the ordinary in its extraordinary promise. The phenomenological movement cannot be entirely separated from its origins in terms of trying to make philosophy as scientific as possible. Though one might find in some of its better intentions something like a release to the "ordinary," perhaps named as the *Lebenswelt*, I wonder if we create a whole new school jargon which risks screening us from the ordinary in its extraordinary promise.

My own practice of philosophy comes from a different direction, though I would like to nod in ecumenical recognition toward other practices of philosophy. One can philosophize more directly from life itself. My efforts to practice a metaxological metaphysics has always been in the middle, in the midst. Indeed, the word *"meta"* itself has a certain doubleness, in that it can be taken as what is "in the midst," but also as what is "over and above," what is "beyond." There is the promise of the extraordinary in the ordinary itself. I would not be worried about going directly to the poets and the religious figures rather than to the scientists, since metaxological philosophy is first and foremost a practice of finesse, not of geometry, to borrow Pascal's terms. Even where it meets certain systematic requirements, these are informed by the priority of finesse to geometry. And when I say "the religious figures," I do not mean the theologians, but the singular figures of sanctity, the holy ones, who live to the fullest our human porosity to the divine. This porosity cannot be attained by any "reduction" we could devise. What we need as thinkers is what elsewhere I have called a new poverty of philosophy.[7] If necessary, all school languages and technical jargons have to be jettisoned where they clog our porosity to the divine.

V.

I offer some final remarks on the erotics of Kearney's God. This is related intimately to the theme of the possible, but also allows us to return to the theme of the "lover" and the "theorist." The love that draws Kearney is erotic, and he is at pains to celebrate the divine *erōs*. I have no objection to such a use of *erōs* in a suitably qualified metaphorical, even hyperbolic, sense. We are dealing with different figures of the divine, of course. Kearney defines his project as dealing in "metaphorology" (7–8). Once again, as with the possible, I do think these discriminations between different loves are needed. Kearney does mention *caritas*, and *kenōsis* once or twice (74, 108); nevertheless, the other forms of love tend to range themselves around his understanding of *erōs*, though not all of them are just erotic. I would prefer myself to be overt on the different possible forms of love, such as the self-affirming, the erotic, the philial, the agapeic. Why? Because different forms of transcending, of relation to the other and of self-relation, are present in these different forms. In thinking about what God might be, utmost lucidity about different relations, and different forms of transcending, is extremely important. I find nothing adequate in the discernment of different loves in Heidegger, and not enough in Hegel.

There is also the fact that there have been developments in modernity that put the emphasis on a certain erotics of the divine, leading to one or other version of what I call an erotic origin or absolute. Such an erotic God is often found attractive by contrast with the allegedly dead "impassible" God of "metaphysics." An erotic God "needs" man, and hence is defined as what it is or may be in terms of its relativity to us. I think this matter of relativity is crucial, but once again, if we take our sights by different forms of love, we will be guided by different forms of relativity or "being in relation," and not all of these are entirely appropriate when trying to think of God. On the whole, with an erotic God we tend to find this: a God that is not truly what it may be in the beginning, but has to become itself, fully realize what it might be, or may be, in a process of becoming or self-becoming, in which it is teleologically, or eschatologically, more fully itself or complete at the end of the process. I think this way of thinking runs a grave risk of producing counterfeit doubles of God, even if it gives to some the satisfaction of being needed by God. The most evident of the great eroticists of spirit in modernity was perhaps Hegel, and he was also a master in the counterfeiting of God.[8] I would argue: a God that has to become God, must first *be* God to become God; that has to create itself, must first be itself to create itself. But why become itself, if it is itself; why create *itself*, if it is? And perhaps *is* as the hyperbolic possibilizing origin of all creation? To do justice to this hyperbolic possibilizing, I think we need an agapeic origin. There is a divine possibilizing in excess of the erotic.

Then there are forms of *erōs* that lead to godless gods, such as Schopenhauer's will, itself strongly marked by a form of *erōs turannos* (tyrannical *erōs*), and the residues of that *erōs* are not at all expurgated, but accentuated, in Nietzsche's will to power and the erotics of his Dionysian god. Hegel's *Geist*, Schopenhauer's will, Nietzsche's will to power all give evidence of being an erotic absolute: the rational *erōs* of Hegel becomes the *erōs turannos* of a darker origin prior to reason in Schopenhauer, exploding into a self-affirming monstrous energy in Nietzsche's Dionysian will to power. How in thinking of divine erotics do we avoid loss of *erōs uranios* (heavenly *erōs*), and the mimicking of the agapeics of being, or diverse counterfeit doubles of it? Heideggerian *polemos* does not give us the way out; his later equivocal mixing of *polemos* and something more released tends to add to the ambiguation of being and dissimulates its agapeics. Kearney himself, I think rightly, puts the question of discernment to Derrida's monstrous desire of god (see 77, 94). Could not the question also be put to "possibility," if this, too, is also too indeterminate between good and evil? Kearney's God is playful, a *deus ludens* (106), but there are darker plays, as when Gloucester in *King Lear* says: "As flies to wanton boys are we to the gods, they kill us for their sport." The wantonness of Kearney's God is not that wantonness. Its *erōs* is good. Yet there are ways of privileging possibility that end up making no possibility privileged. We risk ending with an indeterminate possibility hard to distinguish from a blank check drawn on nothing.

Kearney wants to avoid this ending. I do not have the space to develop the point, but I think he needs to give more attention to the agapeics of the divine: excess of love that, in exceeding self, can give itself over to a poverty of being to make way for the other as other; and so making way, that it looks to be in one sense erotic, but in fact the *erōs* is possibilized by a surplus, superplus enabling power that lets be, in order that the good of the other may come to be. God is a lover, God may be an erotic lover, but the *erōs* of the divine, and the porosity of love between humans and the divine, are possibilized by God as agapeic servant. The agapeics of the divine would call for an entire restatement of the erotics of the divine. Without some sense of the superplus of this agapeic good, even *erōs uranios* is too easily tempted by its own tyrannical twin.

The company of Hegel is not company Kearney would like to keep, but there are things he says connected with the erotics of God, perhaps innocently, that sound to me too like things Hegel said. What are some of them? Speaking at the outset of a promised Kingdom, he says: "God can be God only if we enable this to happen" (2). Sentences like these could be parsed in such a way that we risk idolatry. We are human. God is God, and only God is God. We do not make, or enable God to be. God makes us to be. God must be to enable to be. God is not the Kingdom of God. God is God. God enables the Kingdom to be, and we may be co-operators, perhaps even creative contributors, but God is not the Kingdom of God. Kearney is aware that the unconditional nature of God might evaporate without us taking due care in how we speak. So he asks (37): "Does all this amount to a *conditional* God? No. For if God's future being is indeed conditional on our actions in history, God's infinite love is not. As a gift, God is *unconditional* giving. Divinity is constantly waiting." God's future being? Conditional on our actions in history? God a being in time, then? Hence one being among others? If so, how God? And if you even say "a being among beings"—suppose you say "the incarnation"—then this is *not* "possibility."

Kearney does not overtly say, as Hegel does, that God is not God without the world, though he does imply that God could not be God without us enabling him to be God. I have perhaps grown oversensitive to this kind of talk. But a God who needs us to be God would be pitiable. The most difficult and the most terrifying of the commandments is the first. We secrete idols, even when we call them icons. Maybe the God who may be is another idol. Maybe not. Kearney would be amazed to be included with such as Hegel, I know. But equivocations in what I call the erotic absolute are not entirely put to rest (in my mind, anyway) by his work as a whole.

Just ask: Could you *love absolutely, love unconditionally,* a beloved who may be? With your whole heart and your whole mind and your whole soul? A beloved who, in some sense, seems not yet to be? Maybe, maybe not. And if you love only what may be, are you then truly loving? But if the beloved is, then we love the may be of the beloved because of what the beloved is now and not just what it may be, even what it will be. To love is the unconditional yes to the beloved now: no if or buts, no maybes. Think if one were to say to one's beloved: "I love you *maybe,* my dear." Why, then my dear would surely reply: "You do not love me, you love your dream of me." And would she be right? (Think also of Mr. Micawber offering his solicitations concerning "Mrs. Copperfield *in esse* and Mrs. Traddles *in posse.*"⁹) We love most genuinely the "is" of the beloved—an "is" that no doubt may be full of promise, but full of the promise of the "may be" because full of that promise now, not empty now, and not only deferring or detouring to an always other future to come. Come now. Otherwise, as the White Queen said to Alice in *Through the Looking-Glass*: "The rule is, jam tomorrow, and jam yesterday—but never jam today."

At the close of the book, we are promised a new heaven and a new earth. Kearney is aware of the hyperbolic nature of the promise. He asks (111): "Is such a thing possible?" He answers: "Not for us alone. But it is not impossible to God—if we help God to become God." I agree: God can create a new heaven and a new earth, but because God is not heaven and not earth but maker of heaven and earth. But such a God could not be just a God who may be. I must also confess astonishment at the thought that we must help God be God. God is God, and nothing but God is God. God does not need help to be God. If I must help God be God, God help God—and God help me. I know I cannot do it. Maybe others think they can. I count on God. If God had to count on me to become God, I would worry for God. But maybe I am getting cranky.

(The sun will rise tomorrow, and tomorrow, an absolutely new day, under a new heaven and over a new earth. The sun will rise, and I will not make or help it rise. To think so would be reversion to an idolatrous blurring of difference.)

A God who could not be God without us is hardly a God of possibility, more an impossible God, or not a God at all. If God possibilizes, God possibilizes us; but if God could not be God without us, somehow we possibilize God. Would it be so, then, that the God who may be would be impossible if *we* did not possibilize God? But if God possibilizes us, how can we be said to possibilize God? Either God is possibilizing Godself in and though us (Hegel), or we are possibilizing ourselves in God and through God (Feuerbach and sons). There is an impossible possibilizing in thus speaking of God.

I fear again a derogation from the first commandment: God is God, and nothing but God is God. Here we have the stark statement of the transcendence Richard Kearney knows is necessary and for which, I think, he also asks. That is first, even though *how* God is in relation to what is not God is all the mystery of the creation of the finite being, and the promise of human life as ethical and called to be godlike. I do not underestimate the second at all, and would say something like this.

I could say to you: "I am depending on you to . . . ," and what is meant is that I am entrusting you with a promise that I wait on you to realize. This is very evident in human life: we depend on others, others depend on us, in this mode all the time. And this depending is something profoundly positive, because profoundly promising (it is much richer than a mere insufficiency on my part or your part). If Kearney means something like this, in implying that God depends on us, is depending on us, I think there is truth to this. Here this means that as created beings, we are entrusted with promise: God's promise. This is the endowment of creation.

But there are other senses of "dependency" that are not so admissible. There is an *asymmetry* in the relation of endowment that is the source of different senses of depending/dependency. That I am depending on you may be part of the promise of the endowment; but I am not dependent on you in deriving what I am from you. If I were, I could give no gift, in the radical sense of creation, and in the sense of releasing this gift to the other as other. In fact, in creation the release is a bringing to be, and in this giving, the finite recipient comes to be: the primal ontological endowment. This releasing creating may show itself, in one sense, as "depending on us" to realize the promise of the endowment. But in a more fundamental sense, it is not dependent on us, for we are radically dependent on it: without it we would be nothing. And God would be God, no matter what.

If God were to say "I am depending on you," it would not mean "I am dependent on you" in this primal ontological sense. It might have the qualified meaning implied above, in an eschatological sense. We might imagine God saying eschatologically: because I am, and because of what I am, and because you are, and because of what you are, I am depending on you to realize the promise of the endowment. If Kearney means to draw our attention to creative possibilizing in this sense of endowment and depending, I completely agree. Endowment is promise, and the real possibilizing of the future. But the possibilizing of the future is not the same as the endowing possibilizing. This is hyperbolic, and one wonders if speaking of dependence and independence is helpful, since again we fall into binary oppositions appropriate to determinate finites. Endowing possibilizing is more than possibilizing: it is agapeic creating. But again the asymmetry comes back: we are, because first given to be by God. God is not given to be, but giving qua giving; and as creativity creating, God is other to the given creation. And even then, origin is not the same as creation. Eschatological desire waits in hope on that hyperbolic origin that is neither in the beginning nor in the end, but gives the beginning and the end. We human beings are in the middle of that hopeful gift—never quite univocally sure of what God might be . . . or might not be.

Hermeneutics and the God of Promise

MEROLD WESTPHAL

In *The God Who May Be*, Richard Kearney has given us a gift whose power to provoke thought is out of proportion to its small size. Its opening sentences read as follows: "God neither is nor is not but may be. That is my thesis in this volume. What I mean by this is that God, who is traditionally thought of as act or actuality, might better be rethought as possibility. To this end I am proposing here a new hermeneutics of religion which explores and evaluates two rival ways of interpreting the divine — the *eschatological* and the *onto-theological*."[1]

Before turning to the central thesis about "is" and "may be," about actuality and possibility, I want to look at its corollary, the "new hermeneutics of religion." We can call this Kearney's methodological thesis if we notice (1) that it is a substantive and not merely a formal commitment, and (2) that as such it belongs to the human theory being set forth; it is not a kind of Prologue in Heaven, spoken *sub specie aeternitatis* from some neutral, transhuman (non)point of view. In other words, the new hermeneutics we are to explore seeks to exempt from the hermeneutical circle neither the hermeneutical stance in general nor the particular commitments that make up this specific hermeneutic.

The new hermeneutics revolves around the distinction between the eschatological and the ontotheological. With Kearney, I want to affirm the importance of the eschatological. I believe our God talk should be at once future-oriented and metafuture-oriented.[2] Such eschatologically oriented God talk should inform our epistemology, our ethics, and our spirituality. However, that means it must inform our metaphysics as well. If in faith we are to be a people of hope, God will have to be the God of hope (Romans 15:13).[3] Moreover, I think that overcoming ontotheology is an important task for theology and the philosophy of religion, the disciplines that inform and critique our God talk.[4] So it would seem we are in the same ball park.

But perhaps not on quite the same page, if I may mix my metaphors. Kearney has told me he suspects that I, the Protestant, will be more sympathetic to Aquinas than he, the Catholic; and, as we shall see, he was right. However, perhaps he did not suspect that I would be more Hegelian than he. It seems to me that Kearney treats the eschatological and the ontotheological as mutually exclusive. Over against his Kierkegaardian *either/or*, I wish to suggest a Hegelian *both/and*, which of course signifies not addition but *Aufhebung*, or, to revert to Kierkegaardian language, not either/or but teleological suspension. He himself hints at such a possibility when he labels his position "onto-eschatology," but he leaves this possibility undeveloped (*GMB*, 8).

Unlike so many who bandy the term "ontotheology" about without giving it any precise meaning, Kearney tells us quite clearly how he uses the term. In the first place, "ontotheology" signifies "the old deity of metaphysics and scholasticism" (*GMB*, 2). The coin of the realm for this theology is the "abstract" categories of "pure being," such as *ousia, hyperousia, esse, essentia, substantia, causa sui, ipsum esse,* and *actus purus* (*GMB*, 2, 23). Second, the use of these categories is motivated by a desire for a "plenitude of presence," the untrammeled vision that would be "absolute knowledge" (*GMB*, 2, 61). Third, the result is a "disembodied cause, devoid of dynamism and desire," or, in other words, an impersonal God (*GMB*, 3). Kearney's brief but splendid phenomenology of *persona-prosopon* as *eschaton* not as *telos* (i.e., a fulfillable, predictable, foreseeable goal) reflects his own desire (no pretense of disinterested reflection here) to preserve the biblical sense of a personal God, "an eschatological God who transfigures and desires" (*GMB*, 9).[5] There is a distinct echo here of a Lutheran, Pascalian, Kierkegaardian, and Heideggerian preference for the God of Abraham, Isaac, and Jacob over the God of the philosophers.

As a matter of fact, all three dimensions of ontotheology so far presented correspond to the account Heidegger gives in his own critique. First, ontotheology revolves around such categories as ground, *ratio, causa prima, ultima ratio,* and *causa sui.*[6] Second, for ontotheology, "the deity can come into philosophy only insofar as philosophy, of its own accord and by its own nature, requires and determines that and how the deity enters into it" (*ID*, 56). God talk is in the service of philosophy's project, which Heidegger articulates in terms of representational and calculative thinking.[7] Informally, this project can be described as the desire to make the whole of reality intelligible to human understanding, a notion which can easily enough be developed in terms of sheer presence and absolute knowledge.[8] Third, Heidegger joins Luther, Pascal, and Kierkegaard when he writes:

> Man can neither pray nor sacrifice to [the god of philosophy]. Before the *causa sui,* man can neither fall to his knees in awe nor can he play music and dance before this god. The god-less thinking which must abandon the god of philosophy, god as *causa sui,* is thus perhaps closer to the divine God. Here this means only: the god-less thinking is more open to Him than onto-theo-logic would like to admit. (*ID*, 72)

Heidegger notes that ontotheology involves a certain marriage between Greek metaphysics and Christian theology, but whether this is "for better or worse may be decided by the theologians on the basis of their experience of what is Christian, in pondering what is written in the First Epistle of Paul the Apostle to the Corinthians. . . . Has not God let the wisdom of this world become foolishness?" After linking the "wisdom of this world" to what Aristotle calls first philosophy, Heidegger asks, "Will Christian theology one day resolve to take seriously the word of the apostle and thus also the conception of philosophy as foolishness?"[9]

Happily, at least from my own point of view, Kearney omits one aspect of Heidegger's account of ontotheology and replaces it with another. Heidegger derives the term from the fact that Aristotle's *Metaphysics,* which sets out to be an ontology, a theory of being qua being, ends up being theology, a theory of the highest being and thus ontotheology. This opens the door to his *Seinsvergessenheit* critique of ontotheology. By focusing attention on the highest Being, ontotheology neglects to think being, the primary task of philosophy as Heidegger understands it. This objection will carry force only with those who share this conception of philosophy, those whose religion is Heidegger's *Seinsmystik* or something very close to it.

Following Marion rather than Heidegger, Kearney adds a fourth element to his description of ontotheology. He notes that it involves granting "priority to being over the good" in our thought about God.[10] He finds an ethical significance in this insofar as the human correlate to this God is our own *conatus essendi*, which, as Spinoza and Levinas have shown us, yields at best a therapeutic ethic in which the self concentrates on itself, and not an ethic of responsibility for others (*GMB*, 19). This is why he contrasts "the eschatological relation of one-for-the-other with the onto-theological relation of one-for-one, or if you prefer, of the one-for-itself-in-itself" (*GMB*, 15). Although there is an "ethical" dimension in Heidegger's account, insofar as he links ontotheology with Nietzsche's will to power or will to will and to its expression in modern technology, it is an ethics concerned with the relation of humankind to being, not an ethics about my relation to my neighbor. It is the latter that Kearney wishes to retrieve.

There is an intimate connection between Kearney's third and fourth points about ontotheology. An impersonal God involves at best an impersonal ethics. A God personal enough for one to worship will also be personal enough to give rise to a personal or, if you prefer, interpersonal ethics. Invoking the language of Patristic Trinitarian theology, Kearney points to "the promise of a perichoretic interplay of differing *personas*, meeting without fusing, communing without totalizing, discoursing without dissolving" (*GMB*, 15). If his hermeneutics is to be called a "new or quasi-phenomenology," it will be one "mobilized by ethics rather than eidetics" (*GMB*, 16). He calls our attention to the etymology of *prosopon*, the Greek term rendered in Latin as *persona*.

> The term is made up of the two parts: *pros*, meaning "in front of" or "toward," and *opos*, as in optics, meaning a face or more particularly an eye, countenance, or vision. More precisely, *prosopon* refers to the face of the person as it faces us, revealing itself from within itself. . . . So to be a *prosopon* is to be a-face-toward-a-face, to be proximate to the face of the other. And, tellingly, the term rarely appears in the singular but almost always as a plural noun . . . signaling that the *prosopon-persona* can never really exist on its own (*atomon*), but emerges in ethical relation to others. In this sense, the *prosopon* may be said to be radically intersubjective, invariably bound up in some ethical vis-à-vis or face-to-face (*GMB*, 18).[11]

Heidegger's two paradigms of ontotheology are Aristotle and Hegel. Doubtless they fit Kearney's fourfold account as well as Heidegger's own. Their practice of the first two aspects results in the third and fourth, an impersonal deity who gives rise to no personal ethics, whether of duty or virtue, a task that is left to society.[12] The four elements in Kearney's definition sometimes come as a package deal, but not always, for there is no necessary link among them. In particular, there is no necessary link between the first and the second, which means that there is also no necessary link between the first and the third and fourth. The point can be put quite simply in terms of a distinction from some older systematic theologies between the metaphysical and moral attributes of God, or, as we might put it in the present context, between the impersonal and personal aspects of God. By themselves, categories such as *causa prima* and *causa sui*[13] don't give us more than "some spectral woof of impalpable abstractions, or unearthly ballet of bloodless categories."[14] But the God of the Bible is the creator of heaven and earth, and as such is the first cause. Moreover, the notion of being self-caused could be interpreted as a way of expressing the biblical theme that everything else is created, but God is not. This would place these "metaphysical" aspects of God in the context of a very personal God who is, in the context of biblical faith, at once worthy of worship and the ground of an ethics of personal (or interpersonal) responsibility. There is no necessity for putting this kind of God talk in the service of the desire for pure presence or absolute knowledge, and it doesn't need to take the form of representational/calculative knowing, which is in the service of the desire for power and control, both conceptual and practical.

No doubt there is an either/or relation between ontotheology as a fourfold package deal and the kind of God talk Kearney and I desire to preserve. But there is no such relation between that kind of God talk and the employment of abstract, metaphysical categories. God is more than *causa prima* and *causa sui*, to be sure, but not necessarily less. By being placed in the service of a particular philosophical project, abstract, metaphysical categories become the end, the *telos* of thought. God becomes nothing but what is articulated in a system, and Kearney and I are in agreement that such a God is way too small. The *Aufhebung* or teleological suspension referred to earlier means that instead of fleeing from this kind of God talk as from the plague, we recontextualize it in the service of speaking biblically about God. Whatever gets *aufgehoben* or teleologically suspended ceases to be a self-sufficient whole and becomes part of a whole of which it is not the first and organizing principle. Its *telos* is outside itself, which means, in this case, that the metaphysical discourse about God must be in the service of moral, personal discourse about God.

Karl Barth is a good example of what I have in mind. If we allow ourselves a slight anachronism, we can say that his theology opposes ontotheology as the fourfold package deal on virtually every page, from the *Epistle to the Romans* to his *Church Dogmatics*. His God, the God we know only through the free decision of divine grace to reveal Godself to us as Redeemer and Reconciler, is an intensely personal God.[15] Moreover, Barth insists that theology and ethics are inseparable. "Ethics so-called I regard as the doctrine of God's command and do not consider it right to treat it otherwise than as an integral part of dogmatics, or to produce a dogmatics which does not include it."[16] By virtue of his view not only that theology rests entirely on God's self revelation but also that God remains paradoxically at once hidden and manifest in that revelation, he has no room whatever for any theology that would aspire to pure presence or absolute knowledge.

This is the context for Barth's well-known opposition to natural theology. The appeal to a natural capacity for the knowledge of God and the corollary notion that philosophy can give this to us means that, at least for this branch of theology, our God talk is in the service of philosophy's project and must play by its rules. But this God is an idol and no God at all, so it is not surprising that in spite of his own theological realism,[17] Barth does not accept Thomistic realism.

What is surprising is that precisely in a critique of Thomistic realism and its appeal to natural theology, Barth not only insists on the realism of his own theology—"Indeed, if we are here presupposing revelation, won't we immediately have to add, how could God be anything other than real in the preeminent sense?"—but puts this in language Kearney would relegate to ontotheology: "As the preeminent reality God is *causa prima*, *ens realissimum*, and *actus purus*, the reality of all reality."[18] However, what keeps this from being a lapse into ontotheology is the context in which it occurs. Although Barth considers these to be legitimate ways of speaking about the God whose gracious love is revealing, redemptive, and reconciling, they are at once *independent*, not in the service of philosophy's ideal of autonomous and adequate knowledge, and *dependent*, having their *telos* outside themselves in the God at whose deepest nature and love they cannot even hint.

And now comes a second surprise. Aquinas isn't an ontotheologian either. No doubt he would be if his natural theology were left to stand alone. But it most decidedly is not. In his *Summa Theologiae*, his natural theology, establishing the existence and (abstract, metaphysical) nature of God (I, Q.2–11) is sandwiched between two radically qualifying claims. It is doubly inadequate. First, it is inadequate for salvation. There are truths necessary for salvation not accessible to "the philosophical disciplines investigated by human reason," but only to faith through "Scripture, inspired by God" (I, Q.1, A1). Unlike the sciences, "which proceed from principles known by the natural light of the intellect . . . sacred doctrine accepts the principles revealed by God" (I, Q.1, A2). Second, our knowledge of God, whether by reason or by revelation, philosophy, or theology, is inadequate in another sense. We are not able in this life to have a vision of the divine essence, but only an indirect, analogical knowing based on our direct acquaintance with creatures. Far from being a matter of sheer presence or absolute knowledge, our knowledge of God is true, strictly speaking, but only in a secondary, derivative way, since it does not meet the criterion of adequation between the intellect and its object. Even when, in rapture or in the life to come, we are enabled to see the essence of God, God remains incomprehensible (I, Q.12–13).[19]

The first of these two inadequacies comes into clear focus if, like Thomas himself, we do not let the Five Ways stand alone as if they were the Alpha and Omega of his theology. If, instead of stopping after the first eleven questions of the First Part, we read the whole of the *Summa Theologiae*, a strikingly Hegelian pattern emerges.[20] Just as in the *Phenomenology of Spirit* and the *Science of Logic*, the movement of thought is from the most abstract, least adequate (but nevertheless indispensable) forms to more concrete, richer, and ultimately more fundamental forms of experience or thought.[21] As such, Aquinas's theology moves from the Prime Mover to the very (tri)personal God to whom one relates in terms of law, grace, faith, hope, and charity.

Thomas Merton puts the Thomistic position succinctly: "For although I can know something of God's existence and nature by my own reason, there is no human and rational way in which I can arrive at that contact, that possession of Him, which will be the discovery of Who He really is and of Who I am in Him."[22] Barth is so eager to refute the first part of this claim that he fails to give sufficient attention to the second, namely, to notice how, in spite of their quarrel over natural theology, he and Aquinas end up as comrades in arms in the battle against ontotheology.

Barth does not make this mistake in the case of Anselm. He complains that most commentators on his work "have completely failed to see that in this book on Anselm I am working with a vital key, if not the key, to an understanding of that whole process of thought that has impressed me more and more in my *Church Dogmatics* as the only one proper to theology."[23] How can Barth possibly say that about a theology that revolves around such abstract and (apparently) impersonal notions as "that than which a greater cannot be conceived" and "that which cannot be conceived not to exist"? For it is above all Anselm's ontological argument, not *Cur Deus Homo?*[24] that concerns Barth. The answer is quite simple: he recontextualizes not only these conceptual abstractions but the whole process of seeking understanding in the life of faith. Far from being an attempt of autonomous reason to make itself master of the whole of being, this desire for understanding has its origin in a faith informed by Scripture and the creeds to which it relates as servant, not as judge. Moreover, the entire exercise is addressed as a prayer to God, whose help is invoked in worshipful awe. The faith that seeks understanding with the help of abstract, metaphysical conceptualities precedes that search and is a personal relation to a personal God. As belief, it is "belief in" and never merely "belief that." Anselm never forgets, and never lets his reader forget, that the search for understanding has its origin in praise and prayer, and has these as its goal as well. This is not ontotheology. It looks like ontotheology at the first stage, but at the second, third, and fourth, it reveals itself to be its antithesis.

By decoupling the first element of ontotheology as a fourfold package deal from the second element, Aquinas and Anselm, like Barth, keep it from having the third and fourth elements as its consequences. In order to have a biblical, personal, eschatological, and ethical God, the goal Kearney and I share, it is necessary to overcome ontotheology. This does not require that we abandon abstract and impersonal metaphysical categories in our God talk, but only that we put them in their proper, subordinate place. After all, you and I are material objects and organisms. While it would surely be dehumanizing to treat us as nothing but material objects and organisms, it is not necessary to denigrate the study of these dimensions of our being to affirm that we are first and foremost persons capable of responsibility and of love. It is necessary only to demote such reflection to its proper, subordinate place.

I turn now to Kearney's central thesis: "God neither is nor is not but may be" (*GMB*, 1). The "is" he associates with ontotheology; the "is not," with negative theology rather than with atheism; and the "may be," with the eschatological God talk he wishes to defend. Kearney sometimes speaks of the latter as a "third channel" or a *"via tertia"*

(*GMB*, 8, 34). But he says little about negative theology,[25] and in the "Prologue from History" he speaks of "*two* rival ways of interpreting the divine": the ontotheological, which thinks of God as act or as actuality, and the eschatological, which thinks of God as possibility (*GMB*, 1; emphasis added). It's the God who is versus the God who may be.

As a *hermeneutic* phenomenologist, Kearney does not try to think God directly, but through the mediation of texts. The hermeneutical circle within which he operates is one committed to taking biblical texts seriously.[26] As such, it is no surprise that he directs our attention to the God who promises (*GMB*, 2–4, 22, 25–28, 36–37). Of course, only a God who can perform speech acts can make promises,[27] and this ties in directly with Kearney's concern for a truly personal God. Essences and substances do not, as such, make promises.

But when he speaks about the God who promises, the emphasis falls on the future orientation of promises. Our texts privilege a God who "possibilizes *our* world from out of the future . . . the God-who-may-be offers *us* the possibility of realizing a promised kingdom by opening *ourselves* to the transfiguring power of transcendence. . . . This capacity in each of *us* to receive and respond to the divine invitation I call *persona*. . . . [The God of promise is] the *posse* which calls *us* beyond the present toward a promised future" (*GMB*, 1–3). I have added italics in the above quotations in order to emphasize the way in which the divine promise is about *our* future. In this context, we get a clear meaning of what it is to oppose the tendency "to subordinate the possible to the actual" (*GMB*, 1). Such subordination would put us in what Marcuse calls a "one-dimensional" world, one whose only dimension is the status quo.[28] "Realists" know that the empirically observable way things are is the limit within which possibilities can be thought. But "for God all things are possible" (Matthew 19:26; Mark 10:27; cf. Luke 18:27). Neither the laws of nature as we discover them, nor the laws of society as we devise them, are ultimate. With God on the scene, there are possibilities undreamed of in those worlds.

Without disputing such a reading, Kearney wishes to go beyond the physical and the social to the metaphysical in resisting the tendency "to subordinate the possible to the actual." He sees the biblical God as "*posse* (the possibility of being) rather than *esse*[29] (the actuality of being as *fait accompli*)" (*GMB*, 4). The title of *The God Who May Be* is meant to express this central theme, which he formulates in various ways: "God can be only if we enable this to happen" (*GMB*, 2); God is "someone who *becomes with us*, someone as dependent on us as we are on Him" (*GMB*, 29–30); God says, "*I am who may be if you continue to keep my word and struggle for the coming of justice*" (*GMB*, 37–38).

Such statements clearly take us beyond the horizon of the "for us" to the horizon of the "for God." Accordingly, we must add to them statements which otherwise might be given a weaker "for us" interpretation. When we read that "the promise remains powerless until and unless we *respond* to it," this is a statement about the being of God[30] and not just about us (*GMB*, 4). In a similar vein, we must read the claims that "if we say no to the kingdom, the kingdom will not come" and "God commits Himself to a kingdom of justice if his faithful commit themselves to it too" (*GMB*, 5, 29). All this strikes me as a triple non sequitur.

First, from a logical point of view, it seems clear that there can be no promises without an actual promisor. The possibilities opened up by the promise have their ground, at least in part, in the actuality of the promisor, which of necessity precedes them insofar as they are not reduced to mere logical possibilities. The very logic of promising requires us "to subordinate the possible to the actual" in this sense (*GMB*, 1). Only an actual God can make promises. From the fact, affirmed in faith, that the possible exceeds the horizons of the actual, as defined by the natural and social orders as we are familiar with them, it does not follow that it exceeds the horizon of the actuality of the God who promises. It is, rather, the very *act* of promising that opens up those excessive possibilities and thus precedes them.[31]

Second, there is a textual as well as a logical sense, as it seems to me, in which Kearney's conclusion does not follow from his premises. In the process of talking about the God of promise, he often speaks, both directly and by citation, of the God who *will be* (*GMB*, 3–4, 21, 25, 30). Surely the God of promise is the one who will be there "for us" in keeping with the promise. It may well be, as we shall see, that we should think of God as having a future as well as ourselves. It is precisely in the middle of these God-who-will-be contexts that Kearney shifts to his may-be mode (*GMB*, 3–4, 30). But it is entirely unclear what the textual warrant in Kearney's text for such a shift might be and what keeps it from being hermeneutically arbitrary.

Third, Kearney is likely to respond that the textual basis for his may-be talk is the covenantal character of the divine promises. He appeals to the covenant between God and Israel mediated by Moses, which clearly has a conditional character: Here are the blessings that are yours if you obey, and here are the curses that are yours if you don't. But he fails to take account of the unconditional character of the covenant with Abraham[32] and with David.[33] The promise of a new covenant, made through Jeremiah, is not conditional.[34] Neither is the promise made to and through Peter: "I will build my church, and the gates of Hades will not prevail against it" (Matthew 16:8).[35] None of these texts suggests that the God of the Bible is as dependent on us as we are on God. Taken as a whole, the Bible does not offer warrant for privileging the God who may be over the God who will be. Kearney's conclusion does not follow from the text he is interpreting any more than from the text in which he presents his interpretation.

Thinking here about human promises may be helpful at this point. Suppose I promise my son to take him to a chain store where his favorite superstar (athlete, pop singer, poet) will be signing autographs. "Be sure to come home right after school. I'll come home early and we'll go right over, since (s)he will be there only from three to four o'clock." Let us assume that I make this promise in good faith: "I *will* be there and I *will* take you." In spite of this intention, my *will-be* might very well be a *may-be* in some obvious ways. I might get caught up in my work and simply forget, or I might be in an accident on the way home, and be both unable to be there and unable to let anyone know why. Happily, I see no evidence that Kearney seeks to warrant his move to may-be with the help of such contingencies in the case of divine promises. I may forget or be in an accident, but God will not.

There is, of course, another way in which my promise may remain unfulfilled. My son may not show up. He might get caught up in conversation after school with his latest heartthrob, and he may either forget our date or decide that walking her home is a better way to spend his time than standing in line for an autograph. But neither my actuality as promisor nor my actuality as promise keeper is compromised by his failure to show up.

Kearney is clearly not working in a context where grace is irresistible or divine foreknowledge renders future contingencies certain. Setting these possibilities aside for the sake of argument and focusing on the case where my son fails to show up, we have a genuine analogy to the relation between God and those to whom God makes conditional promises. Blessings promised can fail to become actual *for us* if and when we exclude ourselves by our own behavior; this is true *for God* as well. Just as I *may be* the father who takes his son to the autograph party at the book store only if he shows up after school, so God can be the Savior only of those willing to be saved (on God's terms). But this is no reason to convert *will be* into *may be* across the board or to invert the order of actuality and possibility. For, as we have just seen, the actuality of the one who makes and keeps his promises both precedes and is the condition of the possibility that what is promised will actually occur.

Given his (one-sided, as it seems to me) emphasis on the conditionality of divine promises, Kearney asks whether he ends up with a conditional God. "No," he replies to his own question. "For if God's future being is indeed conditional on our actions in history, God's infinite love is not. As a gift, God is *unconditional* giving. Divinity is constantly waiting" (*GMB*, 37). This would seem to confirm the argument just given, namely, that even if (bracketing irresistible grace) we can say that aspects of God's being, such as *being* my Savior, are what God *may be*, depending on my response to the promise and command of God, other aspects of God's being, including the love that is the condition for the possibility of this *may be*, are unconditional. God *is* love. If we are to express this in relation to time, we will have to speak of the God who will be there as promised, not the God who may be.

In the background of Kearney's discussion is the question of how our God talk should relate God to time. As Wolterstorff puts the relevant issue, "All Christian theologians agree that God is without beginning and without end. The vast majority have held, in addition, that God is *eternal*, existing outside of time. Only a small minority have contended that God is *everlasting*, existing within time."[36] The classical definition of God's eternity is provided by Boethius: "Eternity is the whole, perfect, and simultaneous possession of endless life."[37] This notion is closely intertwined with that of God as *actus purus*, and we have seen that Kearney relegates such a notion to "the old deity of metaphysics and scholasticism" (*GMB*, 2). Clearly his sympathies are with Wolterstorff, who promises to "take up the cudgels for that minority [who affirm everlastingness over eternity], arguing that God as conceived and presented by the biblical writers is a being whose own life and existence is temporal" (*GE*, 77). So, for that matter, are mine.

The question comes up especially in Kearney's discussion of the burning bush incident, in which the name of God is given to Moses as *'ehyeh 'asher 'ehyeh*, translated into Greek as *ego eimi ho on*, into Latin as *ego sum qui sum*, and variously into English as "I am he who is," "I am that I am," and "I am who I am" (Exodus 3:14).[38] Against these "ontotheological" translations, Kearney suggests that we should hear promise and the future tense in this name, favorably citing the following translations: "I shall be what I shall be" (Rashi), "I am as I shall show myself" (Gese/LaCocque), "As the one who will always be there, so shall I be present in every time" (Buber), and "I will be there as I will be there" (Rosenzweig) (*GMB*, 25–27). Hebrew is rather vague about tenses and leaves a good bit to contextual determination. My view is that the issue is properly decided on contextual, and thus hermeneutical and theological, rather than grammatical, grounds, and that the context favors such future-tense renderings as Kearney cites.[39]

The contextual cues are abundant. God's first self-identification to Moses at the burning bush is as "the God of Abraham, the God of Isaac, and the God of Jacob" (Exodus 3:6), that is, as the God of covenantal promise. Then, in response to Moses' "Why me, Lord? Why not send someone else?" God replies, "I have observed . . . I have heard . . . I know . . . I have come down . . . I will send you . . . I will be with you" (Exodus 3:7–12). It is immediately after this that Moses asks for God's name and he is given the crucial words whose translation we are discussing. Then God tells Moses to convey the following promise to the elders of his people: "I declare that I will bring you up out of the misery of Egypt, to . . . a land flowing with milk and honey" (Exodus 3:17). To this he adds a further promise: "I will stretch out my hand and strike Egypt with all my wonders that I will perform in it . . . I will bring this people into such favor with the Egyptians that, when you go you will not go empty-handed" (Exodus 3:20–21). Much later, as Moses and his people are about to leave Sinai for the Promised Land, God reaffirms his promise: "My presence will go with you, and I will give you rest." Moses responds, "If your presence will not go, do not carry us up from here," to which God patiently replies, "I will do the very thing that you have asked" (Exodus 33:14–17).

All these indicators point to a future-tense reading of the name God gives to Moses and of the Tetragrammaton, YHWH, that is so intimately linked to it (Exodus 3:15). But they also point to speaking of the God who will be rather than the God who may be. The conditional character of the covenant at Sinai does not render God's actuality conditional. The subordination of conditionality to unconditionality, and thus of possibility to actuality, can be seen in this summary of the Sinai covenant: "I will be there for you. Whether I am there in blessing or in judgment is up to you. But one way or the other, I will be there. That is certain. You can count on me."

One could, of course, read this future tense as only "for us" (who are "in" time) and not also "for God" (who is eternal). But let us suppose, as both Kearney and I are disposed to do, that Wolterstorff is right in suggesting that we are more faithful to biblical texts if we speak of God as everlasting (and thus temporal) rather than eternal (and thus "outside" of time). It will still be the case that the personal, promising God of the texts will more appropriately be described as the God who will be than as the God who may be.

But what about traditional renderings of the name of Exodus 3:14 in the present rather than the future tense, those that restrict the future of God's promise to the "for us" and retain a pure (eternal) present "for God," who is conceived as *actus purus*? In the first part of this chapter, we saw that Karl Barth sees no conflict between such language and the language that portrays God as a fully personal lover whose future Kingdom we await in hope. Among similar cases to which Kearney points us is Augustine. In his "quasi-Parmenidean" reading of Exodus 3:14, there is "no fundamental difference between [the biblical] *ego sum qui sum* and the *esse* of metaphysics," or the latter's *ipsum esse, ousia, substantia*, or *essentia*. In each case, we are dealing with "an a-temporal, immutable essence" (*GMB*, 22–23).

It would be foolish to deny the influence of Greek philosophy on the Christian theology of God as *actus purus*, immutable and eternal. At the same time, we should not fail to note that many who speak of God this way have thought that they were thereby preserving something important about the biblical revelation of God, that this is, for example, one way of expressing the infinite, qualitative difference between God as Creator and the whole of the created world. Augustine would surely be surprised to hear his reading described as "quasi-Parmenidean." Like Aquinas, he is keenly aware of the limitation of pure philosophical insight, calling attention to what "I did not find" in the books of the Platonists, in particular the Incarnation and Atonement, making it necessary to turn from the Platonists to the apostle Paul.[40] Christian "confession" is thus to be contrasted with platonic "presumption," namely, the presumption that philosophical speculation is all we need (VII, 20). Accordingly, when we speak of God as "I am that I am," God is not merely *ipsum esse*, but the very personal "voice from on high: 'I am the food of grown men.'" Or, again, "You cried out to me: 'I am that I am'" (VII, 10). The abstract metaphysics of being is *Aufgehoben* in the theology of the personal

God who speaks.[41] Similarly, God may well be "That Which Is" (VII, 17), but in the Word flesh, wholly unknown to Parmenides and Plato, we know God as "Truth in person" (VII, 19).

Another example of such a teleological suspension is found in Augustine's commentary on Psalm 9:10:[42]

> *Let those who know your name hope in you*, when they have ceased to hope in riches and in the other allurements of this world. When the soul which is being turned away from this world is looking for somewhere to place its hope, the knowledge of God's name welcomes it at exactly the right moment . . . knowledge of that name exists only when he is known, whose name it is. . . . Scripture says, *The Lord is his name* (Jeremiah 33:2; Amos 5:8).[43] This means that whoever has willingly subjected himself to God as a servant has come to know this name. *And may those who know your name put their trust in you.* The Lord said to Moses, *I am who I am. Thus shall you say to the children of Israel, HE WHO IS has sent me* (Exodus 3:14). *Let those, therefore, who know your name put their trust in you*, to avoid putting it in things which flow past in the swift flux of time, things that have no being other than "will be" and "has been." What in them is future is instantly past as soon as it has come; it is anticipated with eagerness, and let go of with sorrow. But in God's nature there will not be anything which does not yet exist, or anything that was, which is not now; there is only that which is, and that is eternity itself. Therefore those who know the name of the one who said, *I am who I am*, and of whom it was said, *The I AM has sent me*, should stop hoping for and loving temporal things, and instead should devote themselves to the eternal hope.[44]

Three things to note about this striking passage. First, it employs the traditional, "ontotheological" translation of Exodus 3:14 and speaks of God as *actus purus*, and not merely as eternal but as "eternity itself." Second, the God who is the bearer of these metaphysical attributes is a personal God, to whom we relate as servants of a Lord and in whom we can rightly place our hope and trust. While the promises of God are not explicitly mentioned, they are the implicit presupposition of the notion that we can put our hope and trust in this Lord. Finally, the purpose of the eternity talk is not to provide an essence to gaze at, much less to have a first principle in terms of which we can achieve the goals of a certain philosophy, pure presence, or absolute knowledge. The purpose is, rather, ethical, instructing us where to look for the Good, the proper object of our desire. To be sure, this is the ethic of the First Commandment, You shall love the Lord your God, and not the Second Commandment, You shall love your neighbor as yourself. But for Augustine, as for Jesus, the First is never an alternative to the Second, but always its indispensable presupposition. Only those who have learned not to put their hope and trust in the fleeting goods of this world will be free for the divine call to responsibility toward their neighbors.

We are miles away from Parmenides.

Wolterstorff and Kearney might argue that this is incoherent, or at least that there is a poor fit between the Greek, philosophical and the Jewish, biblical dimensions of the God talk of thinkers such as Augustine, Anselm, and Aquinas.[45] And they might well be right. God everlasting may fit the biblical accounts better than God eternal. But we should notice two things. First, the debate should not be between ontotheology as a fourfold package deal and the attempt to speak biblically about God as everlasting rather than eternal. Augustine and Aquinas do not fit the first alternative, and they become straw men when we treat them as if they do. The debate should be between those who abandon immutability and eternity for change and everlastingness and those who retain the former attributes but teleologically suspend such metaphysical categories in the moral or personal attributes that give us a God of love, whose unchangingness is faithfulness to covenant promises.

Kearney's Wager

PATRICK BURKE

In a 1991 essay, Dominique Janicaud lamented a "turn" in recent French phenomenology "toward the theological," toward the question of the nature of postmetaphysical divinity. In 1984, Richard Kearney had published *Poétique du Possible*: *Phénoménologie Herméneutique de la Figuration*, in which he had already mapped a new eschatological hermeneutics of God as possibility in critical comparison with Heidegger's ontological hermeneutics of being as *Vermögend-Mögende*. Kearney continues to situate his own work within this turn, arguing that the dialogue between postmodern philosophy and religion is "one of the most burning intellectual tasks of our time." In *The God Who May Be*, Kearney makes a wager, namely, that the God of the possible, *posse*, is much closer to the God of desire and promise than scholasticism's old metaphysical God of pure act, *esse*. This wager is in response to the question raised by the "turn toward the theological," but is framed here to reflect Kearney's own variation of the postmodern project: How may we overcome the old notion of God as disembodied cause, devoid of dynamism and desire, in favor of a more eschatological notion of God as possibility to come, the *posse* which calls us beyond the present toward a promised future? The wager takes more specific forms, namely (a) that *it is wiser* to interpret divinity as a possibility-to-be than as either pure being in the manner of ontotheology or as a pure non-being in the manner of negative theology; (b) that *it is wiser* to take "the mediating course of narrative imagination" between two polar opposites in contemporary thinking about God, that of Levinas, Marion, and at times even Derrida, and that of Campbell, Zizek, Lyotard, Kristeva, and Caputo. Both sides claim that God is utterly unthinkable, unnamable, unrepresentable—that is, unmediatable.

The wager character (rather than proof character) of Kearney's analyses is indicated throughout the book not only by many direct claims to be offering a wager, but also through expressions of uncertainty such as "my ultimate *suggestion* is that we might do better" (*GMB*, 22); "let me conclude with the following *surmises*" (*GMB*, 37); "I propose to *hazard* something of a hermeneutical *guess* in what follows" (*GMB*, 60); "to say something, however hesitant and provisional, about the unsayable" (*GMB*, 7); "I conclude with a tentative summary *hypothesis*" (*GMB*, 79); "my *conjecture* that God neither is nor is not but *may* be" (*GMB*, 80); and "my aim here, as throughout this volume, is to break open new sites and sightings of the God-who-may-be" (*GMB*, 101). A master of the art of conjecture joins the tradition of the scholarship of the compelling hypothesis celebrated, for instance, in the writings of Ernst Gombrich. In his essay "Botticelli's Mythologies," Gombrich argued in the preface to the second edition that what he presents about Botticelli's *Venus*, rather than being a proof, is no more than an interpretive hypothesis—one relative to which none better has yet been offered. Pascal's wager was framed too narrowly: either God exists or he does not exist, and we are unable to determine which alternative is true. It seems that, for Kearney, we are lost if we accept that wager as stated, especially if its attendant presupposition is a double abyss, namely, God as pure being or pure non-being, since our narrative experience is gutted to the core by either alternative. He frames the wager in terms of a third alternative, a *via tertia*, which, if we accept it, can greatly affect our present lives and our possible future. The path of the ontotheologians, such as Thomists, and that of postmodern deconstructionists, such as Caputo and Derrida, present unreasonable risks. His path toward the profoundly personal God-who-may-be is the reasonable gamble.

What is at stake in this wager? What do we gain or lose by accepting Kearney's wager? Biblical narratives are finally rooted in an ontology that preserves their richness. God becomes *prosopon*, person, in the dynamic sense described by John Manoussakis as facing toward a face, as being profoundly for-and-with-the-other.[1] We gain the historic responsibility for completing creation: through and because of our freedom, we help God bring forth the kingdom of love and justice. God depends upon us to make the Word flesh. Like the Mary of the Annunciation in Christian Scripture, we must through our "yes" enable this to happen, to make the hitherto impossible possible. If our response is "no," social evil is then exclusively our responsibility. As such, our actions matter, and have meaning and value.

The reason for the language of wager has to do with the overall character of Kearney's project within which this book is situated. *The God Who May Be* is the second work in a trilogy titled Philosophy at the Limit, which begins with *On Stories* and is completed by *Strangers, Gods, and Monsters*. The first work argues for the place of stories and their interpretation in a postmodern world: stories as open-ended invitations to ethical and poetical responsiveness, stories as spiritual guides and mentors of wisdom, helping us to practice what Ignatius calls "discernment of spirits." Faced with frontier experiences of strangeness, whether in the form of strangers, gods, or monsters, the last work argues for a "diacritical hermeneutics" of alterity beyond the romantic hermeneutics of Hans-Georg Gadamer, which seeks to recover some lost original consciousness by way of a "fusion of horizons," and beyond the radical hermeneutics of John Caputo, which invokes an irreducible dissymmetry of self and other and insists on the unmediatable and ultimately "sublime" nature of alterity. More radical and challenging than the hermeneutics of either Caputo or Gadamer, Kearney's diacritical hermeneutics of discernment and hospitality argues for the dialogical interbeing, intersignification, interanimation, and mutual traversal between ourselves and strangers, gods, and monsters. Each volume of the trilogy contributes to an overall hermeneutics of narrative and deals, in its different way, with "experiences of extremity which reside at the edge of our conventional understanding, seeking to address phenomena beyond the strict frontiers of reason alone in efforts to imagine new possibilities of saying and being. The three volumes share an abiding conviction that when "we are confronted with the apparently inexplicable and unthinkable, *narrative matters*" (*OS*, 157). According to Kearney, the radical otherness of God requires that we take the path of narrative and the interpretive wager if we are to maintain a personal relation with the divine. The narratives taken up by *The God Who May Be* include the Hebrew Bible (Exodus 3:14, The Song of Songs), the New Testament (Luke 9 and Mark 10), and Holocaust literature such as Etty Hillesum's *An Interrupted Life*. These narratives call for a hermeneutics beyond traditional cataphatic ontotheology or apophatic postmodern negative theology. Kearney calls for an onto-eschatology, the God of the Possible, so that these narratives' rich meanings are more fully revealed and embraced.

Generally speaking, the occasion and a necessary condition for a wager as a particular species of decision making is a certain *present undecidability*, which in most cases can be equated with an appropriate level of uncertainty and a conflict of apparent evidence regarding (a) a future empirical outcome such as a horse race, which is nevertheless decidable, for instance, by fixing the race or merely waiting for the outcome; or (b) textual and/or moral ambiguity based on competing meanings, values, or evidence, unresolvable by ordinary strategies of clarification but resolvable nonetheless, for instance, by taking some unsuspected middle path or by compromise. De facto undecidability calls for decision, even in the ordinary form of a wager or the extreme form of a leap of faith. Although Kearney situates us at or beyond the limits of theoretical reason—the concern with discovering proofs of truth claims and evidence of truth—and thus beyond the domain of decidability by theoretical reason, Kearney never claims that the question of God is essentially or in principle undecidable; this, as Pascal so well knew, would obviate the very ground of the wager. The matter can be decided by practical reason or by religious faith, for instance, although in the case of the latter, it still remains a question of which faith and in what God is the wiser, the more reasonable. If one of the competing alternatives is a sure thing, then we don't make a wager. There has to be reason for entertaining or believing the alternatives, otherwise the wager situation collapses; the alternatives have to exhibit rough epistemic parity. Kearney, the gambler, has to shoulder the responsibility for making a case for the reasonability of each alternative. Indeed, he generally does this throughout his work, for example, in his presentation of the virtues of the deconstructive reading by Caputo and Derrida.

The alternatives that Kearney entertains in *The God Who May Be* are many. He looks at mutually exclusive ways of reading Exodus 3:14, thus leaving undecidable on their account the question of who is the God who speaks to Moses; he looks at competing and often conflicting ways of reading the Christian narratives of transfiguration on Mount Tabor (Luke 9) and the paschal apparitions in Emmaus, Jerusalem, and Galilee. He also looks at metaphysical readings, phenomenological readings, and deconstructive readings of desiring God, each competing with or in conflict with the other and thus, taken together, leaving undecidable God's desire for us and ours for God. Given such de facto undecidability, and the consequent lack of a sure thing, Kearney, employing several categories of evidence, wagers that there is a way out, via an unanticipated and unprecedented dark horse: the onto-eschatological reading. However, not everything is in the mode of the wager. Kearney offers philosophically tough arguments pro and con relative to the alternative positions, especially relative to the postmodern readings by Levinas and the deconstructive readings of Derrida and Caputo. In other words, he has to demonstrate that although no particular reading is a sure thing, it is at least reasonably believable; otherwise, it is excluded from the wager. In the last analysis, Kearney is not saying that Derrida and Caputo, for instance, are wrong, just that they are not wise enough. Let us look at his reading of Derrida and Caputo to see if Kearney is justified in wagering on his dark horse.

Kearney makes a favorable case for the reasonability of Derrida's a-theism as a radical openness to an alterity that knows no name, beyond the revealed deities of Islam, Christianity, or Judaism, utterly indeterminate and undefined. And Kearney cites Caputo's analysis of Derrida's "desire beyond desire" as being more respectful of singularity and alterity than the narratives of specific messiahs. Caputo likens Derrida to those anchorite Desert Fathers who desired a God "without being, beyond being, otherwise than being" (*GMB*, 77). Such openness/renunciation, Kearney rightly claims, makes a place for the possibility of his own God, the God of the possible, a God still to come. Kearney, in a sudden and noble burst of generosity, writes that Derrida and Caputo have "done more than most contemporary philosophers—theist or atheist—to make us sensitive to the three calls of God: *donne, pardonne, abandonne*" (*GMB*, 79). But are they a good bet? The virtue of their openness would also seem to be their Achilles' heel: freed from all narrative traditions, it is undecidable on Derridean/Caputian terms whether the voice I hear in my tent is that of the God of love or of some monster. The risk of such undecidability is too terrifying for Kearney, who wants recourse to the evidence of narrative imagination, to the eschatological tradition whereby the voice can be *recognized* as that of the God we desire. Caputo rejoins that the virtue of deconstruction is that it genuinely engages this undecidable, which provokes in us "the urgency and passion of decision" to overcome it through faith or, for that matter, hope and charity, and Kearney acknowledges that such engagement is what Derrida is after when he says that the desire beyond desire is a desire for justice. In order to distinguish the messiah from the false prophet, Derrida says we have to listen to and closely read the other. Well and good, Kearney notes, but how is alterity to be *experienced* as other, to be listened to and read as other, if it is outside the light of our phenomenal horizons of experience? This is the famous question Derrida had put to Levinas, and so Kearney puts it to him, and closes by asking of both Caputo and Derrida: "How do we read in the dark?" Yes, the Derridean/Caputian alternative can be held rationally, it would seem, and I find its radical openness to alterity enormously attractive but, like Kearney, at too great a risk—dancing with the devil. Kearney's onto-eschatological account would seem to presume and rest upon several categories of evidence long embraced by various faith traditions and certainly by Christian biblical scholarship, such as the reliability of biblical documents, the moral profundity of the Christian message, the veracity of apostolic testimony to Christ, the supernatural origin of biblical prophecy, the divine status of Christ, the truthfulness of Christian accounts of divine-human interaction, and the path to human salvation. For Kearney, these become canons of evidence if and only if they yield the right fruit, "fruits of love and justice, care and gift" (*GMB*, 48). Yes, God speaks in stories, and responding to his voice is a case of love responding to love, a love that is self-liberating, enriches the other, and is honest, faithful, socially responsible, life-serving, joyous, and genuinely transformative for both lovers. Rather than Jacques's (Jack's) blind leap, Kearney traverses the narrative bridge into the sea reaches of alterity.

Relative to the "non-God" of deconstruction, Kearney has, in my judgment, stronger reasons, by virtue of his conception of narrative, for wagering on his dark horse. I place my bets with him. But is it so with the God of ontotheology? Has this God received a fair chance? Has a case been made by Kearney for the reasonableness of this alternative? If not, he should exclude it from the framing of the wager in its first form above. But to do so makes the wager less interesting, since he could well be excluding the best horse from the race. Kearney's depiction of the God of ontotheology seems to be a rehashing of postmodernism's caricature of the God of Augustine and Aquinas as devoid of dynamism, desire, and possibility, since He is eternal, immutable, simple, self-sufficient, and the disembodied cause and principle of every creature. Now the latter four properties are indeed ascribed to God as pure *esse* by Aquinas. But staggering back into the gray ruins of my memory, back to those catechism days in Dublin

Gulch in Butte, Montana, back to those school days at Gonzaga University and St. Louis University (not unlike Kearney's school days in Dublin, mind you) where Thomistic Scholasticism was pounded without mercy into the tangle of our brains, it seems that God was indeed presented in terms of dynamism, possibility, and desire. Dynamism was ascribed to God because he was the source of all actualization and, in his providence, the present, actual sustaining force of all that exists and can exist. Possibility was assigned to God insofar as he was all-powerful. Power is related to the possible: what *can be done* is what is called possible, and God was said *to be able to do* all logical possibles. Potency was thus predicated of God, not passive but active potency, the power to be the active principle of something else. Finally, if real memory, rather than fantasy, serves me here, God was said to desire or wish the perfection of all creatures, to love all created things freely and contingently. God desired that all persons be saved on the condition that, through a responsible exercise of their freedom, they keep his commandments, cooperate with his grace, and so on. The kingdom of God, the kingdom of love and justice, was indeed at hand, but we humans had to achieve it, freely choose it, and work fervently toward it. Our profound dignity as persons rested upon the fact that we were able to do this. Thus it was said that God depended upon us, albeit contingently, to realize the Kingdom. During those eternal scholastic afternoons, our Jesuit professors told us not to be discouraged by God's silence; it was simply his love for our freedom. The postmodern notion of the God of the scholastics comes out of Heidegger, who was educated in the dreary German scholasticism of the Suarezian type, namely, metaphysical essentialism. If Kearney is to keep the ontotheological god as a competitive alternative to his wager, then he would do well to return to what Etienne Gilson calls Aquinas's "existentialist" account.

Let's get clear about Kearney's use of the word "God" and his description of God as *posse*. Kearney is addressing the God of Exodus 3:14, who speaks to Moses through a fiery thornbush. It is not, he tells us, the traditional God of the philosophers, the pure *esse* of ontotheology or the pure non-being of negative theology. When Kearney writes that this "God neither is or is not but may be" (*GMB*, 80), is he denying God every mode of being except that of possible being? This is an important question since in ordinary language, the intelligibility of a possible lies in its relation to being. Can it *be*, that is, is it a real possible, an existential possible? Can it *be* thought, that is, is it a logical possible, an essential possible? In ordinary language, being would seem to be logically prior to possibility. Kearney tells us that the God-who-may-be is something "before, between, and beyond the two" (*GMB*, 34), beyond pure being and pure non-being. Kearney proposes a "nuptial chiasm" (*GMB*, 110), a "nuptial nexus" (*GMB*, 8), or a "middle space" (*GMB*, 6) between these extremes:

> The divine possible takes its leave of being having passed through it, not into the pure ether of non-being, but into the future which awaits as the surplus of *posse* over *esse*—as that which is more than being, beyond being, desiring always to come into being again, and again, until the kingdom comes. Here at last we may come face to face with the God who may be, the deity yet to come. (*GMB*, 4)

The astonished reader may find something intensively counterintuitive in this quotation. How does God take his leave of being, that is, his own being, without ceasing to be? How can God desire anything if he has a taken leave of his own being? After all, isn't being logically fundamental to and a necessary condition for the desire for being? Kearney steers his way through this Scholastic morass by means of a nuptial chiasm between ontology and eschatology. With an emphasis on the latter, Kearney effects a "radical alteration of the metaphysical use of the copula" (*GMB*, 31) where *to be* is transformed into *to become, to be able*. With this, the whole framework of God talk shifts from substance and syllogism to function and narrative, from abstraction and conceptuality to relation and covenant. The eschatological focus is principally on the ethical, not the ontological, on the God who is responsible for having made promises to the human person and the human person who is responsible for fulfilling the promise made to God to trust his promise. The promise of God transforms God into the promised God, a very different sort of "god of the gaps," in this case meaning that there is a gap in the divine, a *"free space* gaping at the very core of divinity, the space of the possible" (*GMB*, 4). The surplus of *posse* over *esse* would thus appear not to deny the *esse* of God but to defer God's full *esse* to the promised future. God takes leave of his full being in order to make us partners in achieving the Kingdom. Thus, he is not all-powerful, because he takes from himself and confers upon us the power to bring forth his being freely as the reign of love and justice.

With this move, he also surrenders any knowledge of future contingencies. The shift to the exclusively ethical side takes the scandal and scare out of the claim that God is the God-who-may-be. But to keep the scandal and scare alive, Kearney dances between the two, shifting from the ontological meaning of being to the ethical and from the ethical back to the ontological, from ontological *esse* to ethical *posse*, and from ethical *esse* to ontological *posse*. But this is understandable: when primacy is given to the narrative sense of the being of the ethical, then ontology must follow upon it, that is, rendering its categories sufficient to it. In other words, there is an ontology embedded within the narrative of the Promise. Kearney's eschatological/ethical interpretation of the God who spoke to Moses as the God-who-can-be who was promised to Moses, if only he will carry to his people the message of liberation and redemption and teach them to keep the commandments, is a fascinating piece of biblical exegesis that, when properly understood, does not offend either logical or ontological sensibilities. The mistake, and Kearney is right about this, occurred when Exodus 3:14 was read exclusively from the perspective of an ontology of presence, making God of "I am who am" into the pure *esse* of the philosophers, ignoring the God who enters history and who suffers with his people as depicted in various biblical narratives. Kearney makes a convincing case that, when read as an ethical narrative, Exodus 3:14 requires that God be the God who may be, and to make this possible, there must be some ontological concession to the primacy of potency over actuality within God. This drives us to ask how Kearney understands possible being and, consequently, how he understands the impossible. This is important if we are to understand his wager.

Taking up the notion of *dynamis* as possibilizing power invoked in the New Testament, Mark 10, and reading it in terms of messianic time, Kearney interprets the divine *posse* surpassing divine *esse* as the ever surprising loving possibility that "comes to us from the future to redeem the past" (*GMB*, 82), whose possibilizing is actualizing and whose actualizing is possibilizing. This eschatological notion of possible being exposes or generates the eschatological notion of the impossible, not as the logically impossible in principle, but as the phenomenologically unanticipated and unpredictable, as (to borrow a phrase from Pessoa) the radical surprise of being. In fashioning his notion of possible being, Kearney also draws selectively upon and integrates/transforms various twentieth-century philosophical notions of the possible, such as Edmund Husserl's teleological notion of the possible (which motivates the development of reason toward a universal goal), Ernst Bloch's dialectical notion of a possible future society of revolutionary justice and peace (which functions as a "mobilizing catalyst" for our present behavior), Heidegger's notion of the "loving possible" as the giving of Being itself, and Derrida's notion of the impossible-possible (which lets the future come as future, that is, as unpredictable otherness), in which the "perhaps" that is the very condition for the possibility of present events.

Of all the twentieth-century notions of the possible analyzed by Kearney, Derrida clearly comes the closest to stating what Kearney is after. Examining Derrida's *The Politics of Friendship* (1994), Kearney notes that, for Derrida, friendship, decision, invention, interpretation, and the pardon are all categories of futurity as unpredictable otherness, which is what he and Derrida mean by the impossible of the possible. These are also categories of *faith* and *commitment*. Each category is intelligible only against the background of the undecidability of the future. If the future is decidable as one of my possibles, then it loses its very futurity, and with it what Derrida and Kearney will call (but with different emphases and substance) the faith structure, the messianic structure, of all experience, thus becoming a mere entailment or unfolding of what is already present. Although Derrida names no God, names no messiah, his paradox of the impossible-possible marks for Kearney "an invaluable opening to a new eschatological understanding of God as *posse*" (*GMB*, 98), and here Kearney's onto-eschatology effects a nuptial nexus with deconstruction and belongs, in its own way, to the history of deconstruction. His wager depends intrinsically on this.

Is the Possible Doing Justice to God?

DOMINIQUE JANICAUD

Actus justitiae est reddere debitum. Sed Deus nulli est debitor. Ergo Deo non competit justitia.

Thomas Aquinas, *Summa theologica*, Q. XXI, Art. I

I would have preferred not to speak *of* God. I don't deny the possibility of speaking *to* God; the great Judeo-Christian tradition has done it and still does. But speaking *of* God is particularly risky in philosophy, by using ideas, concepts, and categories that might turn out to be irrelevant to God (or not worthy of Him).

I hope He will forgive me nevertheless, for speaking *of* Him in this chapter, taking into account the fact that this is a reply to a friend of mine whom I like and sincerely admire. Long before Heidegger asked, "How does the deity enter into philosophy?"[1] Pascal opposed the God of Abraham, Isaac, and Jacob to the God of the philosophers. In the wake of these great forerunners, Richard Kearney in *The God Who May Be* suggests thinking of God not as an actuality, but rather as a possibility, and initiating a hermeneutical-poetical approach to the divine, rather than seeking Him through the ontotheological determinations of standard metaphysics.

My goal in the following pages will not be to refute this highly respectable position that Kearney maintains with a great deal of talent and with such poetical insight. It would be preposterous to negate the possibility of religious faith. It would be even more dangerous and illegitimate to claim God is an absolute impossibility. Even the most determinate and coherent atheism is erected within the framework of a possibility it rejects, on the ground of arguments in favor of a more valuable thesis, namely, God *might exist;* but we also have sufficient arguments against this possibility.

Abraham, Job, David, and the prophets speak directly *to* God. They don't speak *of* God as theologians and philosophers do. This being admitted, are philosophers guilty of arguing and seeking reasons in regard to God? Certainly not. Kant demonstrated once and for all that the search for argumentation in the metaphysical domain is unavoidable, for it reveals the very structure of pure reason.

But how is it possible to advance beyond classical metaphysics? Is a discourse on the possible opening up new horizons? Is the possible doing justice to God? My first reply will be negative: the possible as a philosophical category cannot do justice to God. Does it completely preclude the possibility of the impossible, this new kind of possibility which Kearney suggests? I shall eventually answer *maybe*—how could I be expected to exclude any kind of possibility?—provided certain methodological precautions are taken.

The Possible as a Philosophical Category

As the first category of modality, the possible is defined by Kant as "that which is in accordance with the formal conditions of experience."[2] These formal conditions of experience being given by space and time, it is impossible that I suddenly become a pure spirit or an angel, or that I have an unchanging intuition of eternal presence. I can move from one place to another, but I cannot be everywhere at the same moment. On the contrary, God, who is not submitted to the formal conditions of experience, is not potentially here or there, now and then; He is potentially and actually everywhere at once and the same time. The possible, thought as deprivation, a lack of form or potentiality, is not in conformity with the notion of the supreme being. Kearney is right in stressing that the God of metaphysics is a pure actuality, *purus Actus essendi* (a pure act of Being), as Thomas Aquinas puts it. As such, we agree that the possible cannot do justice to God, neither from the viewpoint of classical metaphysics nor if it remains within the framework of the (metaphysical) first category of modality.

Now one might argue that, for the very same reason, actuality as a category should not benefit from the privilege of characterizing

God's supreme nature. If God is simply actual, would He be deprived of possibility and of necessity? Would He be limited to the self-offering of His very presence and to an ontologically static sovereignty? Is actuality rich enough to express God's infinity and transcendence? By criticizing the ontotheological conception of God, Kearney picks up on the same kind of objection against the exclusion of other qualifications, such as openness, dynamism, and teleology, in what he calls "standard metaphysics."

The problem is nevertheless more complex, primarily because it is not clear where the limits of "standard metaphysics" are located. Kearney also speaks of a "metaphysics of the Possible," which in comparison with "standard metaphysics" would not suffer from its limitations, and he further initiates "post-metaphysical readings of the possible" (including Husserl's teleology of reason). A clearer view of the distinctions between "standard metaphysics," the metaphysics of the possible, and postmetaphysical discourses is needed. I shall return to this point later.

The second difficulty is to be found within the metaphysical conception of the actuality of God. I would agree with Kearney in protesting against the highest metaphysical insights regarding the essence of God, in the cases where these reduce God's actuality to a plain actuality, as we would find within the conditions of experience. But this is not at all the case. The "pure act of Being" is not equivalent to actuality in the ordinary sense. It does not preclude our understanding of the possible, since it goes far beyond any human, limited representation, or category. Let us take the example of a great metaphysical intuition, namely, Malebranche's conception of the immensity (*immensité*) of God. No idea is sufficient to lead us to God's immensity. No material infinity could do this either. A materially infinite extension is not yet God's immensity, that is to say, "being without any limitation" (*l'être sans restriction*). The possible is not omitted here, since the divine Being includes everything created as well as possible. Malebranche adds, "All beings, created and possible, with all their multiplicity, cannot fill up the broad extension of Being."[3] God as Being par excellence, the God of Exodus (3:14), who is the "who He is," is actuality as well as possibility.

How could He be deprived of the possible? I suppose that Kearney would concede that the possible is formally included by classical metaphysics within the attributes or qualities of God, but that he would object that it has not been thought *as such*, as that openness to the unpredictable, which is the "possible-impossible" of the promise and an open eschatology. Provisionally accepting this answer, I can take it into account under the following condition: if the meaning of the possible has radically changed, let us not give the impression that this change is the replacement of one category with another.[4] Let us eliminate any reversal of this kind. We should not try to retrieve a metaphysical category. Instead, we should turn toward this radical innovation which takes place in (and with) *The God Who May Be*.

The Eschatological May-Be

The new direction of the possible is not given by abstract theological or metaphysical considerations regarding the essence of God, but is illustrated through phenomenological descriptions and inspired by the presence of the Other, as a person (*persona* or *prosopon*) in epiphanic moments, such as the burning bush, the transfiguration of Christ, or the rereading of the Song of Songs. Are these glimpses purely phenomenological? They are already hermeneutical in that they refer to the text of the Holy Bible, especially in chapter 2 of *The God Who May Be*, in which Kearney proposes an exegesis of the famous quotation of Exodus. The reply of God to Moses, "*ehyeh 'asher 'ehyeh*" is first understood according to the traditional ontological reading, "I am the one who is." The second reading is eschatological and stresses the future mission of Moses as well as our possible commitment to the promise of God: "God does not reveal himself, therefore, as an essence *in se* but as an I-Self for us" (*GMB*, 29). Beyond any negative theology, this reading is completed with the attempt of a *via tertia*, inspired by Eckhart's interpretation of God as *passage*. How is this third way the "possibilizing" of God? It is through a paradoxical "possibility of the impossible," a desire beyond desire. Such a deconstructive hermeneutics of the would-be may lead to a poetics of the possible God in the conclusion of *The God Who May Be*.

I hope that this too-brief summary of Kearney's approach to a new sense of the religious (in terms of a radical may-be) sufficiently shows that phenomenology and hermeneutics are intimately united and can work together in this way, provided that their "object" is revealed, or inscribed within our experience, through texts, traces, words, poems, and so on. But is it really satisfactory to claim that all these figures or symbols of the divine are immanent? Classical metaphysics had already made a distinction between the essence of God and his human representations or images. One could claim that the possible God is not God at all, but just an announcement of His absolute transcendence. A hermeneutical phenomenology might pave the way for some kind of genuine faith and true theology. But is it truly continuing in this direction?

In fact, the novelty of Kearney's attempt lies perhaps more in the appeal to deconstruction than in the rearticulation of a hermeneutical phenomenology. The very heart and the aporia of this attempt is a retrieval of Derrida's "impossible-possible." This is the reason why we have to pause, in order to make a closer examination of this kind of paradox.

It cannot be denied that the "perhaps" is the condition of possibility for any experience, insofar it is open to an unpredictable future. An event would not be an event without this kind of radical indeterminacy of what happens and of what *might* happen. But should the acceptance of this assumption lead to Jacques Derrida's thesis[5] that there is, in this way, an anticipation of the possible *as* impossible? This kind of double bind was already suggested by Levinas, who wrote, "The impossible does not vanish as that which contradicts itself. It is impossible in the sense that one says: this life is impossible; this life is impossible, even though it is. Being works the impossible out."[6] In this way, Levinas makes it clear that the impossibility at stake here is not formal or literal; it is a very personal way of protesting against the injustice of misfortune. When one says, "This day is impossible," it is just a way of speaking, without giving any precision on the level of empirical possibilities or impossibilities. I concede that the possible advent or coming of the Messiah might be considered both as a possibility and as an impossibility. However, are these two terms on the same level in the strict sense, even in this very exceptional example? It is not true that, strictly speaking, any scientific or technological invention challenges the impossible. It challenges, rather, our usual conceptions and the overly mental framework that we have of the possible. It is not true either that a genuine "pardon" in the sense of Levinas and Derrida occurs as an impossible; its unpredictability is not to be confused with a strict impossibility. Should not a difference be maintained between the "impossible" and the "unlikely"? Blurring this distinction could lead one to lose the sense of the very limits of every experience that we try to undertand in its richness. It could also allow an overly simple rhetoric of undecidability. To this first objection, one may add another that more clearly indicates Kearney's return to Derrida's point of view, namely, is not this phenomenology of the "perhaps" both too loose and too general to fit with the approach to God? What *might be*, or happen to occur, in general is so wide-open that it includes just about anything you want to put there. One does not need to be a theologian to understand that the God of Abraham, Isaac, and Jacob remains a distant figure, if we start our analysis from the position of an indeterminate "may-be."

But Kearney does even more than this, since he eventually recalls the great hermeneutical insights of God as possible within our Western tradition, the Aristotelian understanding of *dunamis*, the magnificent conception by Cusanus of a coeternal union between actuality and possibility in God, and Schelling's interpretation of Exodus 3:15 as *Seyn-könnende* (*GMB*, 101–106). Are these hermeneutic retrievals nothing more than reinstitutions of metaphysics under the pretext of its transfiguration? Kearney does not really deny this. He claims that the overcoming of the old metaphysics of presence unfolds a new teleological metaphysics of the may-be (*GMB*, 110). This means that a determinate metaphysics ("standard metaphysics") is replaced by another, better one; let us call it a "hermeneutical metaphysics." At any rate, is not the very gesture of "transfiguring" being highly metaphysical (as well as looking for a "desire beyond desire," as Levinas does)?

These remarks are not intended to blame metaphysics or to prevent any retrieval of its greatness, provided that one makes clear what the methodological stakes are. Such a return would imply dropping or seriously correcting the Heideggerian conception of metaphysics as ontotheology. What puzzles me is that Kearney seems to accept this (since he alludes to it without questioning it)[7] while at the same time claiming that the possible God he is aiming at is "postmetaphysical."[8] But how can one be both highly metaphysical and beyond (or after) it? Is not the very notion of a "postmetaphysical" era extremely historicist? Furthermore, the possibility of an overcoming of metaphysics proves to be a much more difficult task than many postmodern discourses assume it to be.

Is the possible doing justice to God? I shall not answer as negatively as I did at first, provided that one avoids using the Possible as a metaphysical category and that one respects God's *quant à soi*, which is perhaps the key notion of the crucial passage in Exodus 3:14. I find it fascinating to build upon a "poetics of the possible," as Kearney has and continues to do. My point is that when the project becomes *philosophical*, trying to "adumbrate a philosophy of God," more methodological requirements should be required (*GMB*, 6). Therefore, I would prefer that (1) the difference was clarified between a phenomenology and a hermeneutics of the may-be, which would not yet be theological nor religious, since the may-be is open to everything possible; (2) one would have to take into account the various possible versions of a hermeneutical phenomenology of faith and religion, inasmuch they would rest on the reading of sacred texts, above all the Bible; and (3) while considering the legacy of metaphysics, it does not seem illegitimate either to look for a retrieval of the highest tradition of ontotheology (such as Ricœur does in his later work) or to perform the unceasing deconstruction of metaphysics in the manner of Derrida. In my view, all these attempts are possible, but not necessarily compatible. The solution does not lie in the notion of anything "postmetaphysical," since the desire for an overcoming of metaphysics does not guarantee a complete "success."

How can we escape from such a methodological dilemma? I don't possess a magic wand to help us get out of this labyrinth. I simply want both to profess my empathy toward Kearney's attempt and to present my methodological objections, without excluding the possibility of one day reaching a complete agreement, provided that we can continue with our most friendly dialogue. Let us hope that this *may be* the case![9]

The God Who May Be and the God Who Was

CRAIG NICHOLS

In the context of the reductive paradigm inspired by Husserl's phenomenological method, Richard Kearney proposes a return (*reducere*)
to the face-to-face encounter with *existence* through, after, and indeed
even in the preceding reductive stages that have highlighted a return
to essence (Husserl), being (Heidegger), and the pure gift (Marion
et al.). This "fourth reduction" advocates a new vision of transcendence (qua *eschaton*) in ordinary experience—but not simply a generic form of transcendence that cares not which finite forms it
assumes. Rather, it makes an ethical claim through the face (*prosopon*)
of the other revealed in every encounter with finite being(s). Further,
while necessitating a plurality of interpretations, guaranteeing hermeneutics as the alpha and omega of every attempt at knowledge, the
ana-theism or ana-religion of Kearney's wager affirms the incarnate
reality of lived history wherein the interpreter is no longer able to
suspend judgment concerning the truth, or meaningfulness, of phenomena. A complex pluralism results, one in which, as Kearney contends, "Jesus and the Buddha [can] converse without seeking to
convert each other," since an open space of compassionate dialogue
is opened and "let be" to presence between competing traditions.
However, the alternate historical contexts of such competing paradigms of transcendent compassion do in fact force the interpreter to
choose between different, perhaps even irreconcilable, finite paths,
since the finite forms of traditional experience must be reaffirmed

and reappropriated—for that is precisely where we are brought by the fourth reduction. Hence, we must ask whether all the epiphanies of the *eschaton* in quotidian experience have the same transcendent source (i.e., an absolute identity). But we must pose this question in the context of historical tradition, for it is this very tradition that has opened the possibility of asking the question at all. More to the point, we must understand Kearney's prosopic fourth reduction, which potentially reveals an onto-eschatological God-beyond-God, to be made possible by the strange phenomena of the "closing" of the Western metaphysical tradition (Hegel) and the consequential "death" of the Judeo-Christian God as a result of this metaphysical closure (Nietzsche). In this context I here explore what might be called the incarnate historicity of the phenomena of the "life," "death," and potential "rebirth" of the "Same" God of the Western ontotheological tradition. For the multivalent advent concepts, or in metaphysical parlance, *parousia* concepts, of the Western tradition are the very *conditio sine qua non* of a present return (*reducere*) to the God-who-may-be through the God-who-was.

In his recent book *The God Who May Be*, Richard Kearney proffers a historical response to the Nietzschean madman's proclamation concerning the "death" of the "last God."[1] In so doing, Kearney situates himself within the deconstructive and reconstructive problematic of key postmodern thinkers, among whom Heidegger, Levinas, and Derrida figure most prominently. Particularly sensitive to Levinas's censure of ontology's history of subordinating *otherness, plurality, difference*, and so on to *sameness, unity, identity*, or other names for Oneness, Kearney develops an innovative, eschatologically focused discourse defining the irreducible, ethically distant "persona" of human existence (i.e., that which lies beyond all being and knowing as the final arbiter of the good, in contrast to the sameness which unifies and identifies all "persons" with one another). What seems most compelling in Kearney's discourse, and a significant contribution to postmodern discourse, is the potentially fruitful manner in which Kearney brings the cosmological *nothing*, lying beyond the totality of being, into the practical sphere of individual moral existence.

Kearney reminds us that the no-place, or nothing, which in my own terms provides the "con-text" of being,[2] is instantiated in each individual, each *person*, as an ethical frame, or guideline, and provides more (although, it should be noted, *not less*) than the conceptual parameters for understanding the fateful rise and fall of cultures and societies.[3] The appearance of persona through the face of the other, or the mandate from beyond being *to be* in certain ways as one projects oneself into the future, is, for Kearney, a transfiguring event experienced through the present encounter with other persons as well as through the encounter with otherness encoded in traditional religious symbolism. It is this latter encounter through language, furthermore, which allows us to conceptualize and communicate the ethical value of persona radiating from the face of the other. Via symbols, spoken by way of traditional religious narratives—whether as myths, legends, epics, poems, histories, doctrines—a voice is given to the ineffable silence surrounding the event of persona. As Kearney puts it, referring specifically to the eschatological transfiguration of the face in the "persona-visage" of Christ on Mount Tabor: "Indeed it is, paradoxically, the very silence which surrounds the event that in turn provokes a plurality of competing and often conflicting interpretations. Its ineffability becomes the motor of its *fability*—its translation into a variety of accounts, testimonies, fables, narratives, and doctrines."[4] Kearney, however, reminds us that his Christocentric reading of messianic time does not necessarily exclude other messianic, *or even nonmessianic*, religions in the name of a Christocentric triumph.[5] This seems to suggest a pluralistic approach to religious symbolism, wherein no single set of cultural symbols is afforded priority. But how, one might ask, can a particular reading of messianic time, that is, qua eschatological transfiguration, not place itself *above* its conceptual peers (i.e., other messianic conceptions) and those conceptions it seeks to instruct, or explain in *higher* terms of clarity (i.e., specifically nonmessianic conceptions), insofar as it seeks to schematize all other schemata? Such questions stand as a defining challenge before any postmodern attempt to conceptualize divinity insofar as such an attempt is concerned to avoid the specter of either traditional ontotheological dogmatism (ontological objectivism) or its more recent counterpart, postmodern egalitarian dogmatism (relativistic subjectivism). Let us pursue the point.

Kearney goes on to say that a repudiation of the multiplicity of interpretations of religious symbolism—"the excess of fantasy generated by the very *figurative* character of the transfiguration itself"[6]—is not warranted. Rather, the point is "to enter the conflict and *take sides*. And the choice of sides," he suggests, "is determined ultimately by which interpretations we deem more faithful to the ethico-eschatological import of the Christ-event. Which readings, in other words, best testify to the transfiguring (i.e., singularizing-universalizing) power of the *persona*?"[7] We must enter the fray and take sides, but how are we to know which interpretation should be considered more faithful to the import of the Christ event than another? That is, by what standard, if any, are we to judge the situation? To put the point more starkly, is there any *law* governing what is contained in the conceptual content of the persona, even though it may only be heard as an echo emanating from around the language of the narrated symbol? Why, for instance, is the nothing lying beyond being an *ethical* no-place rather than a monstrous, violent, all-consuming blackness, held off only by the *reasonable* behavior of persons obedient to the moral law of pure reason, as Kant would have it, or even preserved in the "authentic existence" purported by the early Heidegger? Why, again, is persona inclusive and not exclusive in its messianic quality? It seems, in fact, to be held up as the one concept, above all others, capable of *redeeming* the various symbols, narratives, doctrines of its conceptual "others." How can the appearance of persona—here understood as messianic-eschatological in origin and transforming in character—be *universally* indicative of the value of symbolic interpretation without appealing in some measure to a hierarchical structure of concepts and a systematic construct of being to house those concepts?

Kearney points out that the bottom line is *testimony*: "Faithful and discerning testimony—known by its fruits. Fruits of love and justice, care and gift. We have to try to tell the difference, in sum, between narrative testimonies that transform or deform lives. The rest is indeed silence."[8] The appeal of this criterion is immediately evident. But let us assume with Nietzsche that the traditional meanings of such terms as love and justice, care and gift have passed into oblivion through the same nihilistic twilight that has engulfed the God who *was* and now *is not*. At the heart of Kearney's argument, aphorized in the provocative phrase "God neither is nor is not but may be,"[9] lies, in my estimation, a Nietzschean rhetorical move wherein the traditional conceptions of God (qua pure *esse*, absolute *causa sui*, *ens realissimum*, *noesis noeseos*, *ens increatum*, etc.) no longer provide thinking with a transfiguring event of meaning—although, perhaps, the underlying symbolism that led to such conceptions may still retain some latent potency. But what ground do the terms *love*, *justice*, *care*, *gift*, and others have apart from some historical reference, however obscured, to the symbolization of these notions in the tradition of ontotheology? Nietzsche suggested a complete revaluation of all traditional values, which lends itself, at least potentially, to a monstrous ethical/political theory lying beyond the boundaries of good and evil as they have hitherto been known. Kearney clearly does not want a monstrous God, a point he emphasizes repeatedly in *The God Who May Be* and much more so in the sequel, *Strangers, Gods, and Monsters*[10]; and this has caused him to search for a new hermeneutical approach between *radical hermeneutics*, which treads headlong into the abyss beyond the logocentric tradition (cf. Levinas, Derrida, Blanchot, Lyotard, Caputo) and *romantic hermeneutics*, which searches with nostalgic hope for a new path beyond logocentrism by revitalizing and reconceptualizing the old logos and its potentiality for speculative, systematic thought (cf. Schleiermacher, Dilthey, Heidegger, Gadamer, Ricoeur). In *Strangers, Gods, and Monsters*, Kearney calls his new approach *diacritical hermeneutics*, which he describes as a somewhat unsystematic attempt to build "tentative footbridges" and throw out "rope-ladders reaching across the chasms separating old ontologies from new heterologies."[11] This is an enormous task for thinking, and, as Kearney himself points out, this is a middle way that is actually "more radical and challenging"[12] than either extreme, since this new dialectic has raised the bar for hermeneutic discourse one new level, both forbidding and demanding a resolution at the same time. When Kearney at times seems to fall to one side or the other in his attempt to define a radically new, yet comfortingly old, conception of God, we must with due charity recognize the virtual impossibility of his task, as well as that this is in fact the vanguard of thinking in the postmodern situation, and hence we are led down this new path with a sense of urgency and necessity, happy that a rough-hewn path has begun to emerge from the thickets and brambles. In what follows, my primary concern will be to lend a hand in helping to clear the path of the middle way of diacritical hermeneutics he envisages—and (pardon my straining the metaphors) perhaps add a few footbridges or rope ladders of my own.

Qualifications and Critique:
Onto-eschatology as Eschatological Theogony

Kearney puts the reader of *The God Who May Be* in a tense situation. On the one hand, Kearney's conception of the fruits evidencing a transformation toward "the good" are none other than those that have only recently been shaken from the tree of ontotheological symbolism *and* speculation—and we must not forget that the absolute of ontotheology and the symbolism that clothes this God are intimately intertwined and cannot be easily separated (and perhaps not at all). And, of course, Kearney makes repeated appeals to the traditional symbolism of the divine. On the other hand, Kearney's proposal of a God who "neither is nor is not" at least rhetorically draws us into the Nietzschean "death of God" paradigm in a most radical way. Given the occasional rhetorical extremes of Kearney's argument, we are led to ask why he holds himself back from the more radical implications of Nietzsche's death of God pronouncement.

Let us assume, for the sake of argument, that Kearney's negative assessment of the God-who-was and the God-who-is, is in fact the lens through which we should view the entire work (and, one might add, this is suggested by its placement as line one on page one). One would thereby be led to question whether this position can rightfully be deemed an *onto*-eschatology without giving greater deference to the ontological nature of the claim that God should no longer be spoken of in ontological terms, for such a negation (again, God *neither* is *nor* is not) necessarily depends in its conceptual formation upon the very ontology being negated. But Kearney's discourse assumes the Judeo-Christian God in most of its facets *to be* not *dead*, but ready-to-hand for retrieval. But we might ask whether this assumption gives the God of ontotheology its due as the One, the *causa sui*, which itself *makes possible*, historically and hermeneutically, the God-who-may-be in advance, as it were. In response to Kearney's ontologically exclusionary formulation of the God who "neither is nor is not but may be,"[13] and acknowledging the death of God scenario suggested by this rhetoric, I offer for consideration a new hyperbolic metaphorical formulation of the God-who-may-be as a God whose possibility for meaningfulness arises as an *eschatological theogony* from out of the *chaos* (confusion *and* openness) "generated" by the deconstructive, or "forensic," analysis of the textual corpus, or "corpse," of the onto-theological God. The phrase "eschatological theogony" may be yet another introduction of rhetorical excess, but perhaps pursuing this line of rhetoric will shed some new light by helping us to situate such rhetorical excesses (both mine and Kearney's) vis-à-vis the more modest definition of Kearney's position as an "onto-eschatology." But, in my estimation, such a radical conception—eschatological theogony—must be tempered and given meaning through reentering and reaffirming ontotheology itself, albeit in a qualified, that is, hermeneutical, sense. My goal is thus to heighten the tension between romantic and radical hermeneutics even farther, and in so doing, I hope to reveal with greater clarity the nature of the abyss, the ontological void, that has opened beneath us in the absence of a traditional ground. To that end I suggest three clarifications of Kearney's position that point toward the emergence of a God of *posse* that simultaneously seeks to renew the traditional ontotheological possibility of maintaining normative constraint, a sense of necessity, and conceptual universality (*esse qua essentia*). These three points will then serve as a basis for a discussion of our greatest present concern: the relationship between the potential, deconstructive God-who-may-be and the actual, constructive God-who-was.

First, the *via tertia* suggested by Kearney[14] should not be understood as a *standpoint* per se, fixed between the system-building venture of traditional metaphysics and the radical deconstructionism that has followed in its culmination and demise. The point is not to exclude either of these two poles, and forge a position in between, but rather to embrace them both *hermeneutically* and allow the *via tertia* to emerge "in between" through its own revelatory capacity. Because this middle ground must emerge between the final constructivist system of ontotheology and the definitive deconstructivist collapse of every metaphysical system, one could "reasonably" expect to find this middle ground (or *quest* for a ground) through a demonstrated hermeneutical correspondence between Hegel's understanding of systematicity as the closure of metaphysics and Heidegger's ontological-hermeneutical attempt to reopen thinking to a new infusion of meaning from the revelatory nature of being, understood as the nothing that contextualizes every revelation of/from being. Insofar as he leans very close to Levinas's vision (in defining persona) for his definition of the God-who-may-be, Kearney's readers may be encouraged to close themselves off too quickly from the possibility of a *real* (i.e., ontological) ground for thought rather than the aporetic play of fantasy—which is clearly not his intention.[15]

Second, Kearney's approach in *The God Who May Be* does not make altogether clear why human beings in a postmodern world should revive a conception of *God* at all. "God" *could* be interpreted here—especially since we are dealing not with what *was* and *is*, but with what *may be*—as little more than a unifying Idea around which human beings can rally in promotion of ethical behavior and new poetic imaging. But truly embracing such an Idea would mandate finding a way to reenter ontotheology rather than attempting to leave it behind. Again, Kearney does not want simply to leave it behind, but he does not specify just how we are to reenter the ontotheological tradition. What ground, for example, other than a hermeneutically retrieved ontotheological one, can justify the idea that even though "God's future being is indeed conditional on our actions in history, God's infinite love is not. As a gift, God is *unconditional* giving."[16] Such an ontological statement implying the *esse/essentia* of the God-who-is (cf. God as pure *esse* in Aquinas or as the *Unbedingt* in German idealism) can be guaranteed and justified only by first defining the relationship between the postmodern God-who-may-be and the traditional God-who-was. Furthermore, if the eschatological God of possibility is to obtain meaning as a *present* reality—a *real* hope—rather than an illusion receding endlessly into the future, the need for such a revelation must be established on the inability of human beings to take over God's job of establishing peace and justice in the world. We would do well, therefore, to heed Heidegger's caution against forcing a revelation of being (learned all too well from his own political mistakes), insofar as it points to the need for a retrieval of Augustine's conception of human nature as incapable of establishing the good from our own finite resources (*non posse non peccare*) over against the ubiquitous Pelagianism of modernity; and this again requires a further degree of clarity with respect to the hermeneutical correlation between the God of *posse* and the God of *esse*.

Finally, the hermeneutical relationship between system and deconstruction, or *esse* and *posse*, that Kearney is aiming at—and that I will subsequently sketch in terms of a Hegel-Heidegger counterpoint—necessitates a hermeneutical correlation between the revelatory capacity of being/nothing and the symbolism of the divine. The clue for which side to take upon entering the semiotic play of postmodern theogonic mythmaking is ultimately to be found within the horizon of this correlation. I will lay out the basic parameters of such a correlation by defining the relationship between the eschatological theogony of the absolute ontotheological God-who-was and the potential eschatological theogony of a present, or future, God-who-may-be.

The Eschatological Theogony of the God-Who-Was

Heidegger's early lectures on Pauline eschatology and Augustinian original sin[17] (winter semester 1920–21 and summer semester 1921, respectively) reveal that his retrieval of Greek and medieval modes of ontological thinking included an orientation to the history of nature that extends beyond the primal notion of *physis* as *ousia/parousia* to include the Christian transformation of these Greek ontological notions as they fused with and transformed the foundational Hebrew eschatological myth of a paradise lost and to be regained—that is, the first real possibility of something like an ontological history that arose in the Hellenistic intertestamental period. This breakthrough to ontological history (i.e., the breakthrough to ontotheology) came as a resolution to the Greek impasse that obtained after Plato and Aristotle had thoroughly circumscribed the possibilities inherent in the uniquely Greek concept of ontological circularity. The Greeks of antiquity first began to resist the violent sway of *physis* (as Heidegger would describe it),[18] and hence placed themselves conceptually into the "rift" (*Riß*) of protohistorical self-awareness, by subsuming all of nature, including therein the gods and human beings, under an abstract form of the absolute: *moira* (Fate). This provided the initial horizon for the directionality (*telos*) the Greeks themselves were able to discern in *physis* for the manner and shape the emergence of beings ought rightly to assume (*ethos*). *Moira* thus functioned as the a priori, tragically abortive *telos* of the speculation-revelation, reason-mysticism, *techne-dike* circle that provided the catalyst for early Greek thought. The primal-religious, sacred ritual vision of reality gradually transformed itself into the tragic vision of Greek artistic/poetic reflection.[19] The primal-Dionysian, fundamentally mystical circularity of time revealed in the ritual-tragic orientation eventually combined with the ontic duality of Orphism, but ultimately failed thereby to resolve the resulting dualism of *moira-dike*, sacred space-sacred time, destiny-emergence, and so on,[20] on the anthropological plane toward which it had gravitated; and it thereby failed to yield a true conception of *historical* human freedom. By the time of Aristotle, the poetically conceived *moira-physis*, or destiny-emergence, relation had become crystallized in the *hyle-morphe*, or matter-form, interpretation of *ousia* (i.e., Aristotelian hylomorphism/hylozoism). Specifically Greek thought ultimately foundered on the inability to get beyond the circularity of a ritual-tragic view of humanity (as can be seen in the fatalistic sentiments of the post-Aristotelian cynics, stoics, skeptics, and hedonists). The cycle of being was no longer seen as a dynamic emergence-process; it had hardened into substance ontology in the process of searching for a means to calm the tempest of the violent self-consumption of the primal revealing-concealing event. The original *telos* provided by *moira* in the Homeric epics, in Hesiodic theogony, and in philosophy as early as the Anaximander fragment emptied itself into an atomistic compartmentalization of being devoid of any future drive toward the realization of human destiny.

Christianity effected a breakthrough of Greek ontology to a truly historical sense of freedom insofar as it was able to combine and transform both Greek ritual-tragic ontology and Hebrew eschatology in the context of a single metanarrative: the death and resurrection of the absolute God. Stories of the death and resurrection of gods can be found throughout primal mythologies and stand as archetypal symbols of primal circularity. Judaism's Adamic myth—the archetypal ancient myth of freedom, following Ricoeur—provided the key for breaking beyond such a circularity by suggesting, implicitly, that the absolutes of life and death are not merely stories, but have absolute consequences for existence, and hence provide absolute moral directionality to existence—that is, mythology, in the Hebrew worldview, was not about ideal images that circle about the heavens as mere exemplars, but about real history, spiraling through its seasonal recurrences in a *direct line* toward the reestablishment of the Edenic paradise lost at its primal (cyclical) beginning. Ancient Judaism conceived of this direct historical line genealogically and politically, but was unable to mediate its own inner tension between the absolute, transcendent source of the divine law, the unspeakable apophatic "I am" (YHWH), and the concrete realization of the divine law as an immanent temporal reality, the equally absolute, kataphatic inscription of directionality—Torah—actualized historically in the nation-state. The two poles of Hebrew religious leadership, prophets/mystics (emphasizing the former oral law tradition) and the priesthood (emphasizing the latter written law tradition), further reveal the tension that the Jewish messianic sect that came to be known as Christianity sought to resolve through the introduction of Greek ontological categories.

Greek substance ontology provided Christianity with the tools it needed to concretize the absolute *apophatic-kataphatic* tension inherent to Hebrew messianism and, further, to introduce a principle of developed identity between the two, a resolution of the ethereal and substantive conflict within the dual Hebrew legal absolute. It did so by fusing the uniquely historical directionality of Hebrew messianism (the promise of a fulfillment of lived historical existence) with a concrete, ontological death of God narrative (an absolute heightening of the ideal-real tension) in order to produce the concept of an absolute revelation in time: the ethereal absolute negated entirely through incarnation and death.[21] However, because this duality had taken on an ontological structure, it was able to conceive of the reunification of the absolutely separated components of the Hebrew dual absolute, now narratively expressed through resurrection of the dead God and outpouring of the Holy Spirit, that is, as the unity of eternity and history instantiated in the living reality of the community of faith. Of course, this conceptual resolution (likewise a conceptual revolution) had yet to be worked out historically. Thus, the ontological formulations arising from the early Church's Trinitarian and Christological controversies did not come to a full determination of their content, that is, a full determination of the revelation of the absolute, until Hegel's doctrine of Spirit brought pneumatology, the "orphan doctrine" of Christian theology, as Adolf von Harnack put it, to full expression as the concrete absolute.[22]

The Eschatological Theogony of the God-Who-May-Be

We find ourselves again today struggling to comprehend the possible contemporary meanings of terms such as *resurrection, renewal, rebirth, regeneration,* and so on, within the context of a new death of God narrative—this time, not the death of a God conceived through an absolute expression of mythopoetical dogmatism (crystallized in the Christological and Trinitarian controversies), but the death of the religiophilosophical discourse into which this mythopoetical symbolism found its absolute expression. The God of the philosophers has been crucified, if you will, because the promise of an eminent *parousia* (the promise of future revelation—the very essence of eschatology) was turned into an immanent appearance of the Godhead through the completion of an absolute system encompassing every last possibility of thought. Every possible meaning of "the rational"—that is, every possibility for thought—was reduced to the actuality of a self-contained system—"the real." The fundamental clue, I suggest, for conceiving the future God-who-may-be must be sought, therefore, in a postmetaphysical conception of *parousia*, albeit one that gives due recognition to the necessary entanglement of such a concept with the ontological tradition that first gave birth to it. In other words, like the two conceptions of Christological presence identified in the New Testament—that is, the first and second advents of Christ—we must not lose sight of the fact that the dogmatic-mythopoetical God who died on the cross and the speculative-philosophical God who died in the absolute metaphysical system are inexorably, albeit opaquely, "the Same." And it is this *Same* God that is offered up for regeneration, for how could any finite god possibly outreach the absolute shadow cast by the "last God"? The possible meaning of an eschatological *parousia* of a contemporary or future theogony—for here the concepts of *resurrection* and *theogony* coalesce—is hinted at by the later Heidegger in his treatment of Hegel's self-resolving, or, as he insightfully puts it, self-"ab-solving," conception of the *parousia* of the divine essence.

Drawing, at least latently, upon his early deconstruction of Pauline eschatology in the winter semester of 1920–1921 and setting it in a new context vis-à-vis Hegel, Heidegger argues in his 1950 reading of Hegel's *Phenomenology of Spirit*[23] that the ungrounded (i.e., non-foundational, or self-grounding) forward propulsion of the Hegelian system, its very possibility of presence, in fact finds its hidden ground in an unjustified will to power of the absolute: absolution as presence via the sheer will to be "with us"—that is, traditionally, "God with us" (*Emmanuel*) in the messianic appearance.[24] In Hegel's thought, this presence of the absolute appears in the context of the self-detachment and reconstitution of the relation of self-consciousness to its object (i.e., in the end, the absolution of all relations); Heidegger comments:

> Unconditional self-certainty thus is its own absolution. The unity of *absolving* (detachment from the relation), *its completion* (the achievement of full detachment), and *absolution* (the freeing acquittal on the strength of full detachment) are what characterizes the absoluteness of the Absolute. All these elements of absoluteness have the character of representation. In them there *is* the *parousia* of the Absolute.[25]

The difference between Hegel's conception of the self-revealing of being as absolving *parousia* and Heidegger's parallel, deconstructed conception of the same (or, should we say, "the Same") turns upon the mode of receptivity governing the possibility of appearance respective to each perspective.[26] Heidegger's earlier discussion of the Pauline "waiting" "before God"[27] for the *parousia* becomes transformed in the later Heidegger into the expectational stance of letting being be, a view both within and without Christianity at the same time. It stands outside the tradition insofar as it provides the directional parameters of the possibility of systematicity in general qua *abgrund* of presence.[28] On the other hand, the fundamental clue to the structure of the directionality thus provided was first revealed in the primal Christian conception of the *parousia*. Heidegger's critique of the will to power of the absolute in Hegel—modeled, for Hegel, after the Trinitarian will of God to reveal and redeem his absolute other (fallen nature and humanity)—thus highlights the opposing perspective of the believer who awaits for the full revelation and appropriation of this will to manifest itself, the believer whose *hope* is fulfilled thereby. But, of course, neither Heidegger nor Hegel embraces the dogmatic-theological perspective per se. In terms of the movement of the concepts themselves, or the deconstruction thereof, Hegel's will to power of the absolute allows for the possibility of resolving the inner Christian conflict by transmuting the individual ego that (dogmatically understood) awaits the presence of the absolute as the full instantiation of the Trinity in actual history (i.e., as Spirit) into the "Same" super-*on* (or Absolute Being) as the *theos* (God) that originally willed to reveal itself. This makes possible an absolute resolution of the tension within the Christian conception of presence by making God (qua Concept, or absolute Idea) fully present in lived historical existence (thus Hegel's "inverted world").[29]

Heidegger, by contrast, reopens a new potential for the absolute's self-revelation, highlighting the fact that for the presence of the absolute to manifest itself, that which is to be revealed is not known until the revelation occurs, even if the destiny of such a revelation has already been laid down in advance. In terms of Christian doctrine, this amounts to saying that even though the absolute, God, had already been fully manifested "in time" through Christ (first advent), the full actualization of that revelation had yet to appear universally, and hence, the meaning of the absolute's presence as the fulfillment of time itself (second advent) cannot be comprehended until the latter manifestation takes place. The two advent concepts feed upon one another and remain in tension within Christian dogma. Heidegger's philosophy of "letting be" seeks to balance Hegel's resolution of the conflict by reinstituting the tension, albeit nondogmatically (i.e., deconstructively).[30] It waits for the revelation of a meaning of presence (*parousia*) that might deliver the resolution of Hegel's system from the unresolved nihilating abyss underlying the system. This, Heidegger thinks, is the only oppositional possibility for movement remaining once the system has closed itself off and receded into the (internally differentiated) "monism" of a final, absolute circularity— that is, has peacefully reposed (ironically) in the violent circularity of pure will. Heidegger's thinking seeks to save the system (as much as destroy it!) from this fateful possibility by reopening the circle to a new forward movement, a new climb up out of the darkness of the abyss, but this time directed by the awareness of the need to resist the absolutization of the will in the interpretation of being.

One must ask, of course, whether the postmetaphysical manifestation of the ground of system is a *real* possibility for historical human existence, or merely a groundless hope, a false ghost rather than a real *Geist*. That, Heidegger would say, has yet to be revealed (or, in Kearney's terms, this possibility *may be*). The danger, however, would be to end the search and rest content with either of the following extremes: cessation of movement in the closed, circular totality of being (Hegel) or the absolute opposite, cessation of movement in the closed, circular totality of the nothing (antifoundationalist Derrideanism). Rather, following Heidegger—and, I think, remaining true to Kearney's intentions in *The God Who May Be*—I believe that we must remain in a new tension between these poles, for in the postmodern "rift" (*Riß*) between the circular violence of these two necessary components of being there lies—*perhaps*—the possibility of something like a poetic dwelling that saves humanity from either extreme of such an absolutely contextualized *techne-dike* circle.

In this ambiguous "between," we await a revelation of/from the "Same" "God" who *was*, *is not*, and *may be*, to put it in the Nietzschean rhetorical frame I have sketched. All of these modes of being, of course, like Augustine's analysis of time and memory in the *Confessions*, and Heidegger's in *Being and Time*, refer to modes of being *present*. In short, they refer to the *distance* of the God-who-is—such as seemingly very far in the past, qua systematic *ousia*, yet perhaps very near, in the future, qua symbolic *parousia*. The death of the "last God" in Hegel's system (through the systematic closure of metaphysical categories) already contained within it the seeds of a symbolic, or metanarrative, eschatological theogony due to the implicitly hermeneutical manner in which it subsumed the history of determinate religion (culminating, for Hegel, in the Christian *Trinitätslehre*) under the methodology of speculative metaphysics. To guarantee the internal movement of the System, what I would call its *hermeneutical pull* forward (which works in conjunction with its *logical-dialectical push* from behind, as it were), Hegel had to reach out "ahead of himself" into the mythopoetical conception of the Absolute qua imminent *parousia* (a conception necessarily resistant to closure) and subsume this into the System as a moment of the System (albeit a penultimate one). Heidegger's thought, at least potentially, liberates the God-who-may-be (qua imminent *parousia*) from this position of subordination. But it does so only to the extent that it acknowledges the identity, or essential "Sameness," of the ontotheological God-who-was (and who "died") with the imminent God-who-may-be. The two concepts are hermeneutically co-constitutive, whether conceived dogmatically as two advent concepts, or metaphysically/deconstructively as two ontological concepts. These parallel pairings (dogmatic adventisms and ontological adventisms) likewise stand in a hermeneutical coreflexivity. Hence, we come to the realization that there are at least four aspects of presence/being that each turn upon each other bidirectionally and also cross in the middle. It is this "between" that forms the condition of possibility for an open site of presence, a clearing of being, in which a potential God-who-may-be could in fact emerge. Will such a God emerge again as a real Being for collective—and objective—human imagination? Who can say? One must await such a revelation. But at the very least, we can acknowledge the present being of the God-who-may-be as a phenomenon of hope through an onto-eschatological (or alternatively, an *eschatologico-theogonical*) retrieval of the traditional ontotheological *parousia* discourse.

Conclusion

By recasting Kearney's project in the terms of a Hegel-Heidegger, or system-deconstruction, tension, and by defining this ambiguous middle place as an eschatological theogony, I have attempted to clarify in some measure the tension necessarily remaining in Kearney's own "onto-eschatological" discourse. I have attempted both to heighten the tension, experimentally defining it as an "eschatological theogony," and to relieve the tension a bit. I would also suggest to those who enter the orbit of Kearney's discourse that his diacritical hermeneutics, despite the attempt to remain "in between" romantic and radical hermeneutics, must necessarily lean more closely to the romantic side if it is to retain the possibility of having a *real* God-who-may-be. One could even say that diacritical hermeneutics *is* a version of romantic hermeneutics, but one that strives with incessant vigilance to remember its own potential for violent domination (an ideal Heidegger set forth in his notion of *Seinlassen*, "letting be," but at times "forgot" in the practical sphere). Withdrawing ultimately from the Derridean, and even Levinasian, reservation of judgment with respect to the radically open question of the postmodern God-who-may-be (i.e., a question we—or God himself?—are warned by the radicals should never be answered), Kearney demands a God of absolute goodness, strange perhaps at times, but never ultimately monstrous. Such a demand necessarily appeals, with all the romantic nostalgia we are cautioned against in the critique(s) of logocentrism, to a rebirth (an "eschatological theogony") of "the Same" God-who-was. Kearney insists that if the God-who-may-be turns out to be a monster (or monstrous system) when expectation turns to realization, or possibility to actuality, then we have ultimately taken a wrong path. How do we *know* this? As Kant intimated through the sober vision of Enlightenment rationalism, reason must finally give way to *faith* if we are to have a God of beatific vision rather than a revelation of horror. The deconstructionists may well be right to insist that we cannot *know* that God is good. And yet, we must *believe* it or despair. And this necessity brings us back into the orbit of traditional theological symbolism (mythopoeisis) and its necessary correlation with speculative doctrine (dogma).

If this is so, can Kearney finally avoid a Christocentric triumph, as Hegel proudly trumpeted? Not entirely, since onto-eschatology requires, at least in some sense, a romantic overture to the traditional ontotheological conception(s) of the Christian advent—traditionally thought as a *parousia*. But perhaps the concept of triumph is diffused by the new possibility that this romantic overture may allow for a revitalization of positive religion across the religious-phenomenological spectrum. Christological adventism has provided Kearney with the clue he needs to enter the fray and take sides, but perhaps it grants non-Christian religions the same gift. And yet, we cannot assume this in advance—we must in fact enter the fray and take sides, yet with the vigilant caution always in place to "let be," so as not to become monsters in the process.

Christianity and Possibility

JEFFREY BLOECHL

I.

We do not yet know what it means to speak of the death of God, and not only because those who speak of it do not always have the same thing in mind. The simplest controversy is also the weightiest, and still the most painful: Is it only a persistent idol that dies, or must it be religion itself, as the practice of idolatry? Do the fires of suspicion only purify, or do they consume everything that touches them? What religion, if any, survives the fever of Sils Maria and Turin?

Even while many of us struggle with that sort of question, there arrives another way to understand the death of God, and another debate about its consequences and limits. The problem, one hears, lies not so much with ontology as with politics, and specifically with the politics that accepts without further question the principle that each of us acts constantly from self-interest, and therefore inevitably in conflict with others. This of course would mean that war is prior to politics, which for its part could bring only a peace that consists of compromise. It would also mean that whatever interest a person has in a God who is alleged to transcend the political sphere must be treated first of all as precisely that—interest—and as such submitted to the rule of common order after all. To be sure, none of this quite banishes the possibility of religion or even religious faith, but it none-theless does restrict its meaning in a manner that the believer may well resist. The God that can be comfortably kept in the margins of civil society is no longer evidently God; the end of the theologico-political will also have been the death of God himself. One thus understands the strange solidarity, seen already in some of the Jewish Scriptures, between a prophetic voice claiming access to a dimension beyond the reach of earthly politics and an embracing critique of how politics treats the human dimension it is able to reach. For a certain tradition, the refusal of totality is at same time an affirmation of infinity. And faith in the true God would be the source of ceaseless revolution.

Much of contemporary philosophy of religion is drawn toward one or the other of these debates, either affirming the glory of a God beyond every idol, or demanding a demonstration of the mercy and justice of a God opposed to every totality. Of course, one would like to think that these two efforts are complementary or even mutually supportive, but with few exceptions the arguments to that effect have been only suggestive, fragmented, or incomplete. Of those few, in recent memory only Richard Kearney's *The God Who May Be* assigns that task specifically to hermeneutics.

The founding principle, it turns out, must be ethical. "Religiously," says Kearney, "I would say that if I hail from a Catholic tradition, it is with this proviso: where Catholicism offends love and justice, I prefer to call myself a Judeo-Christian theist; and where this tradition so offends, I prefer to call myself religious in the sense of seeking God in a way that neither excludes other religions nor purports to possess the final truth. And where the religious so offends, I would call myself a seeker of love and justice *tout court*" (*GMB*, 5–6). We may note in passing that this ready criticism of the traditions is at first sight ambiguous. Are their offenses rooted in the heart of essential doctrine, in which case one must watch against the religious as such? Or are they rooted only in certain corruptions of doctrine, in which case the prescribed vigilance would lead to a rediscovery of the truly religious? There is no easy answer to this question, since one and the same argument says almost nothing at all about cult and ritual, and dedicates considerable energy to mining neglected insights of a tradition that otherwise reserves a place for them. Are we then to think that the insights which genuinely matter—in this case, the thought of a God who is possibility exceeding actuality, and of a soul defined by its own futurity—are not merely outside mainstream "Judeo-Christian theism," but also at best indifferent, and perhaps even alien, to the mainstream commitment to worship? Kearney does not say so. But the unity of an argument that never feels compelled to address this complication makes the thought unavoidable.

This sort of thought also occurs in response to the frank confession of fundamentally ethical criteria that opens the book. Whatever religion still animates the choice for love and justice against all else has no need to express itself in prayer and worship. One thus thinks of the ethical monotheism of someone like Herman Cohen, but only until recalling that Kearney's God is plainly somewhat more than Cohen's guarantor of an eternal world. The God who is surplus of possibility over actuality—or, as Kearney prefers, of *posse* over *esse*—is a God who constantly pours into actuality from beyond, disturbing the tendency of acts to seek conclusion and thus, at least by design, stability. This is a God who both transcends all the names and images by which we humans reach toward God from within this world, and transforms consciousness otherwise inclined to accept closure in its own world; it is a God who refuses every idol and a God who defies every totality precisely by coming to us from outside and, in that sense, ahead of them. The ethical principle guiding Kearney's reflection thus reveals its deeper ground in eschatology. In *The God Who May Be*, eschatology supplants ontology just as surely as ethics supplants politics. The God who is *posse* calls each of us out of immersion in this world, to awareness of a futurity that the time of being and act can never contain.

This points the way to the proper meaning of Kearney's expression "may be." It is obviously not, to begin with, the logical "maybe" by which we suppose that a thing may possibly exist but also possibly does not. It is also not the "maybe" by which Bergson envisioned the past moment and condition in which an event that is now present was once only possible. When Kearney speaks of a God who "may be," he invokes a God who is not contained in being but is also not opposed to being, as if the other of being is simply non-being. The God who may be is a God who does exist and does enter human experience, but without submitting to comprehension in and through the concept of being, understood in its fully verbal or active sense. Here, then, is the source of an inevitable polemic against ontotheology on terms remarkably close to, of all possible works, Jean-Luc Marion's *God Without Being*, where it is also said that "God is, exists, and that is the least of things."[1] With this in mind, we ought to not mistake Marion's English title for unqualified allergy to being (as Kearney does at *GMB*, 31), but attend closely to the other possible translation of Marion's French title, *Dieu sans l'Être*, God without being It—that is, without being "God," or, more precisely, God without *having to be "God."* At this point, it is no longer clear just how much separates the God who *may* be from the God who *does not have* to be.

Of course, the two conceptions do meet in their opposition to the God that Heidegger has led us to recognize as the linchpin of what he calls "ontotheology," the God who is *ground*. Whereas the Marion of *God Without Being* responds to this with a defense of the theophantic God of the Eucharist, Kearney now contends that it must be the eschatological God, the God who overflows being and acting from beyond their reach, from a moment always yet to come, that truly eludes Heidegger's determinations. And he considers this to express more than a difference of focus. What he misses in the notion of theophantic excess, with its presence beyond being, its hyper *esse*, is the possibility for intuition to yield determined meaning and in turn give rise to ordered thought (*GMB*, 117, n. 25). It must be asked whether this is quite the right worry to have about a work that restricts theophany to sacramental presence (on this count, the Marion of *God Without Being* may be less troubling than the Marion of later works), and, moreover, in a manner that makes it all too clear that a certain kind of thinking can and should result, yet Kearney's objection is nonetheless in keeping with the nature of his own ethical concern: any encounter with the God who is truly God must assuredly—that is, directly and without possibility of confusion—open the way to sensitivity and care for one's fellow human beings.

Given Kearney's associations of being with act or actuality and of God with possibility, it is understandable that he sees drama in this encounter. The God who arrives from beyond and ahead of any act of comprehension must certainly strike us in surprise. At one moment, there is the relative stability of a world and things presenting themselves to an existing subject who comprehends them as beings. At the next moment, there is an opening to what comes from beyond incorporation into the world and things, which is to say from a future that always already outstrips any not-yet projected in the anticipation of factical existence. Such a God would be eschatological, and since it would thus absolve itself of any and every manifestation called divine—from any and every actualization, in other words—it would also be what Kearney means by possible, or *posse*.

This surprise would be revelatory not only for the God who becomes knowable as eschatological and possible, but also for the human being who may come to a new and deeper understanding of its own condition. Both as eschatological and as possible, the God who may be is a God who is always already approaching from beyond the range of what gets settled in the comprehension of things and a world—a God who is always already with us, but without becoming visible in any here and now. And this is to say that we are turned not only into the world, though indisputably this, too, but also, and first, toward God.

This is where eschatology flows back into ethics, for the surprise that Kearney describes has now become a potentially transformative event. To know oneself as being-toward-God while, or perhaps even before, one is being-in-the-world is to be awakened from any thought of relating to oneself as the locus of what offers itself to comprehension; it is to be opened out into the world and to others met in the world, without immediately gathering them around oneself. It is to be liberated from a heavier materiality, though not from material concerns altogether. The surprise is grace, and grace comes as a surprise, Kearney sometimes says. This grace renders us sensitive to the other person beyond what may be contained in a material understanding. By grace, we are sensitive to the soul of the other person, to his or her *prosopon* (or *persona*). It is by this grace, therefore, that love and justice become possible.

II.

It is here, where Kearney's argument for a particular conception of God and a particular conception of humanity meet in a well-defined event, that one is most entitled to expect the patient and nuanced treatment rightly associated with the approach promised in his subtitle, *A Hermeneutics of Religion*. Yet there is curiously little of this in the book, at least if the word "hermeneutics" signifies close attention to distinct forms of expression and their various linguistic, conceptual, and historical horizons. Of course, Kearney is extremely adept at navigating the passages from one field of thought to another, and indeed at discovering passages hitherto unknown to most scholars and their readers. This, however, cannot take the place of an analysis of the event or events that those fields undoubtedly interpret in any number of overlapping ways. In this latter sense, there is precious little hermeneutics of the grace event so plainly crucial for the rest of Kearney's argument. But the reason for this has in fact already been argued.

To begin with, at the moment being is been aligned with act and actuality as opposed to possibility, it becomes essential that the grace by which the God who may be would enter human experience and history occurs from outside the domain of act and actuality. It is not easy to measure the depth of this reservation about being and act, but the sheer notion of "surprise" seems to imply a previous closure into monotony. It is as if first there was experience closed from what breaks into it and deserves to be called grace, and then there is the event in which something new and other thus arrives. However, if such a surprise may be interpreted, it must first show up in its effects; and if it is thus to be understood as "graced," then those effects must be of the particular sort Kearney would have us associate with justice. Is this to say that grace deserves to be called grace only if those to whom it is offered actually recognize and act on it? *The God Who May Be* provides no answer to this question for the simple reason that it does not attempt an account of the disposition and the capacities of the person who may indeed do those things. A phenomenologist wants to know how it is—on what existential condition—that an event of grace goes beyond the surprise itself, into the possibility of that transformation. A good classically minded theologian thinking along the same line misses much talk of the grace that is infused. Whichever the case, the argument that passes over them moves toward the view that nature acts independently of any support from the divine, and the divine for its part intervenes in nature, if at all, to correct it—and not rather, as Augustine has preferred, to perfect it.

One therefore anticipates great pressure on even the best-intentioned acts. Even acts of love and justice, as acts, are in need of immediate correction by further events of grace which give rise to new acts of love and justice, and so on *ad aeternum*. The best among us sometimes do great things, but no act is sufficient to perfect goodness: this means, more deeply, that no exercise or expression of being is sufficient to what grace alone permits to come to pass. Being, understood primarily as act, is invested with a fault that can be amended or at least supplemented only from elsewhere or beyond. Kearney thus stops short of saying that being is simply evil, but it is not clear that he can avoid concluding that it alone contains the *potential* for evil. This, too, will have been virtually assured the moment he aligned being with act and actuality, and indicted it with closure from the God who is possibility. If being is the source of any eventual idolatry, as forgetfulness of God, then being is also the more distant source of the dark things that may transpire in that forgetfulness.

Left to itself, without surprises, being seems without any inclination to goodness.

In this way, Kearney's approach to the concept of grace invites reflection on the theme of theodicy just as he himself turns instead to a critique of ontotheology. The God of ontotheology would be a God made present—a God projected to fill a lack, and thus a God drawn into being (*GMB*, 61). This would also be a God contaminated by the source of every potential for evil, a God whose goodness has been rendered all too available to human grasping. Conversely, when Kearney therefore withdraws his conception of the true God from the horizon of being as act, he likewise also withdraws that God from the potential for evil that we should think is rooted in our very existence. In *The God Who May Be*, both of these steps are taken in the appeal to eschatology.

It is true that Kearney engages the theodicy problem only briefly (*GMB*, 5, 104–105), just as it is true that he never openly reduces being to the source of all potential evil, yet these thoughts are nonetheless visible behind some crucial turns in his account of some of the history of philosophy. Two of these will suffice. (1) Turning toward the eschatology that would free God and us from ontotheology, he casts a last look back at the latter, and objects above all to its foundation in a God who is *ens causa sui* and thus implicated in a thought of totality that leaves no room for the otherness of the other person (*GMB*, 15). It is one thing to say this of the *causa sui* interpreted according to efficient causality, which does indeed trace all individual beings back to a first being that is the principle of their movement; it is quite another—or would be, if the question were envisaged—to say it of the *causa sui* of formal causality. One finds such an effort in the fifth of Plotinus's *Enneads*, where, moreover, the One is defined by a potency perhaps not far from Kearney's *posse*. (2) Likewise, his opposition to the active and actualizing sense of being is sometimes extended all the way to a refusal of Aquinas's conception of God *actus purus* (*GMB*, 23, 83), where it no longer makes much sense to equate being with closure or idolatry, and where, at any rate, Aquinas himself is plainly concerned with avoiding those dangers. Of course, so long as this sort of complication is suppressed, it appears quite reasonable to divide the Western tradition, as Kearney does, between a thinking of God as pure act that is in fact projected from within being, and a thinking of God as possibility that always already withdraws from being and act. There can be no doubt that it is on the authority of Heidegger that Kearney conceives of much of the tradition in the former terms (*GMB*, 24), but in the latter he charts a new course, with positive and determined statements about a God who has not come to be.[2] By all appearances, everything is guided by an unwillingness to associate God and goodness with being in any primarily active sense.

From this perspective, it is one and the same thing to reject any religious claim that "offends justice" and to reject any such claim that defines God within the horizon of being as act. For Kearney, we do not have access to justice unless we are open to the true goodness that surprises us from a God who is *posse*, and if we are so open, then at last justice has a chance. Such a God would enter experience directly, touching us as we already are, here and now. Kearney reminds us of how distant this is from ontotheology: the God who is self-sufficient in the manner of Aquinas's *actus purus* but also of Augustine's *ipsum esse* is therefore also a God who is withdrawn and distant, a God who does not share in human suffering and human joy. He also observes that this self-sufficiency is a mark of the failure of theodicy (*GMB*, 5): the God who is self-sufficient is easily a God who is therefore free of any lack and, in that sense, omnipotent. We are all familiar with the sort of question that this always raises: Is it still possible to attribute omnipotence and supreme goodness to one and the same God? Doubt about this is also doubt about the theodicy that is woven into the ontotheology that promotes a God who is pure act, and now at least we may recognize the precise site of their inner relation. When the concept of divine omnipotence is introduced, the God who is principle of all things becomes a God who is their origin. Under this second determination, *though not necessarily the first*, an understanding of God's being and action grounds an explanation of the being and action of all that is not God. Under this second determination, in other words, God is submitted to the principle of sufficient reason, and thus appears accountable for suffering and evil. One cannot fail to sympathize with Kearney's attempt to free God from all of this, but one also suspects that there might be other avenues toward doing so.

III.

The God who may be is thus a God who comes alive in Western thought after the death of the God who is *actus purus* and *ipsum esse* at the hands of a philosophical critique of ontotheology and an existential revolt against theodicy. If we follow all of Kearney's argument, this would mean not only the emergence of a new and better idea of God, but also the discovery of greater intimacy with God. In what we have been led to understand as the surprise of grace, the God who is *posse* comes to being without having to submit to being, and this surprise makes possible human action that transcends the economy of self-interest to the surplus of justice, in which each of us respects and serves the other as *prosopon* or *persona*. This surprise, we know, defies the usual hermeneutical investigations of horizons of meaning for reasons essential to its definition, but this does not prevent Kearney from locating its privileged revelation in Jesus Christ, *"prosopon par excellence"* (*GMB*, 40). It is in and through Jesus, he says, that we may catch sight of the spiritual dimension of a humanity thus irreducible to physical and material concerns—the dimension that opens each of us to his or her own future beyond the limits of this world. In this Jesus, we are opened *"to the father through the features of man's face"* (*GMB*, 40; Kearney's emphasis).

This would be the Jesus of the transfiguration, and not necessarily the Jesus of the transubstantiation, the passion, the crucifixion, or the resurrection. Kearney's Christology, let us then note, does not need Jesus to have actually died in order to fulfill its role within his eschatology. This would be the precise moment where he parts ways with the theology of Dorothee Sölle, who shares his interest in a God of justice and his love of the eschatological elements of Jesus' teaching, but turns instead to a meditation on the suffering of Jesus with whom God also suffers. It would also be his moment of departure from the philosophical anthropology of Rene Girard, who supposes that an acute sensitivity to victims of injustice defines the Christian religion, but contends that it is explicable only if we take seriously the sacrificial character of Jesus' life, passion, and death. For Kearney, justice depends wholly on us, even if the way to justice has been opened for us by the approach of God. In this respect, and indeed in many others, he is closest of all to Levinas, for whom ethical commitment constitutes the labor of redeeming creation.[3]

It would probably be going too far to say that Kearney's Christology is fundamentally ethical, but it does seem to assign a primarily ethical meaning to a phenomenon that one might rather call "supernatural." In that line, one can only infer from his treatment of the passages describing events on Mount Tabor that the unique revelation of Jesus opens us first and most directly to sensitivity to the properly human nature of each and all of us as *prosopon*. This is somewhat different from the lesson of kenotic humility described by much of the Christian tradition. On this point, Bernard of Clairvaux is particularly unambiguous: self-scrutiny and the cultivation of humility must precede any movement toward sensitivity to one's neighbor and the cultivation of compassion.[4] And while he is quick to observe that the very desire to become humble exhibits the work of grace already in us, infused in creation, he is also quick to repeat that the only sure way forward in this has been made plain in the example of Jesus—beginning in the self-emptying of God into human flesh.

This difference among Christologies is not without consequence for some of Kearney's more urgent concerns. The more classical position, let us simply remind ourselves, reserves a unique messianic role for Jesus Christ, whereas Kearney prefers to envision Christ as a unique *example* who invites, or at least makes possible, a role for each of us that might instead, in his philosophy, be called messianic. Here again what he only comes close to saying, Levinas has argued openly and often: each of us who has learned what it is to be truly human may, by word and deed, bring that good news to the others. This would be a labor against the natural tendency of our being, which in itself does not incline to goodness, and this difficulty only underscores the importance of community and solidarity. Yet if we are to take seriously the proposition that a human being can nonetheless respond to the surprise of grace with new acts that are truly more just than before, then we must also ask whether it can indeed be the case that being is wholly without goodness—wholly fallen, closed from God, and interested generally in itself. Even if being does *incline to* this condition, the sheer notion that it might reform itself, albeit with important help, supposes that a certain help has already come to it. And this would mean, as a matter specifically for metaphysics, reconsidering the idea that being, as act and actuality, is necessarily without a positive relation to God and goodness. As a matter for Christian theology, it suggests the thought, anything but new, of a first and unique messiah who has already saved being from death and darkness. What the classical theologian therefore misses most is an account of the Christ of sacrament, where all of this is anchored at the heart of Christian thought.

This notion of sacrament, it seems to me, is suspended from the metaphysics that results from what Kearney and Manoussakis call the "fourth reduction" to possibility, notwithstanding their insistence on a return to existence, embodiment, and the necessity of frequent hermeneutical mediation and detour. For only a Christianity that does not know the sacramental Christ—only a Christianity without the Christ who has always already come to us in our fallenness—could ever find itself calling on a God who needs our help to enter being and transform it. The God of Kearney's Christianity, the God who remains after the "eschatological reduction" back to ordinary things, is thus also the God of Etty Hillesum in the transit camp at Westerbork: "If God does not help me go on," she writes, "then I shall have to help God"[5] (GMB, 107–108; see also GMB, 2). Kearney's evident sympathy with Hillesum's conception of God should not surprise. What has been (quasi-)phenomenologically reduced, if not the very God of sacrament and promise that Hillesum and others assumed has died, or perhaps withdrawn, with the rise of the Nazi terror?

Indeed, much of Hillesum's diary and letters record the drama of awakening to a God very like the God who may be. As the traditional God of order and power loses credence (a God to whom, at any rate, one was never able to pray),[6] she writes increasingly of a heightened sense of freedom that nonetheless bears a great responsibility: a plaything who has now slipped from God's preoccupied hand, it is up to her to shape her own response to the situation that confronts her.[7] Henceforth, God must be experienced within, as the source of her otherwise incomprehensible desire to suspend every personal concern in favor of service and compassion. The knot between who she is and what she does, on one hand, and who God is and what God wants, thus tightens. Life itself is "an uninterrupted dialogue with You, oh God, one great dialogue,"[8] and in the final account the desire to serve others, reversing every selfish impulse to serve herself, is "God hearkening to God."[9]

These are moving thoughts, and considered in their terrible context, they are not incomprehensible. Still, one may well hesitate before any move to transform them into a general principle in every situation. Without the terrible clarity of the evil witnessed in places like Westerbork, who among us can always be sure that what one wishes to do is also what God needs accomplished? How, in other words, may we today be sure of the remarkable equation of human action and divine salvation underlying Hillesum's determination to remain true "to that in me which [thus] fulfills its promise."[10] From the notion that grace surprises and interrupts being, which for its part inclines away from grace, it follows necessarily that grace simply announces itself, arrives with its own horizon, and administers its own criteria by which to be recognized. One may be forgiven some hesitation before embracing this thought: Hillesum's experience, however uplifting it seems to have been, is conditioned by imposed suffering. In her situation, there was neither a reason nor the means to ask whether this was truly unavoidable. In Westerbork, where the God of order and power has died, care for others and fidelity to the true God must encounter, and indeed shoulder, constant pain. It seems far from evident that the resultant "art" of suffering[11] can and should become the model for all human behavior. But it is also unclear that an eschatological reduction to the God who may be can easily prevent this—even if, I concede, it does not necessarily require it.

This final concern notwithstanding, Christian thinking may be well served by a critical response to the complacency that leads all too easily to a vision of what theologians sometimes call an "achieved eschatology." As a concept or a proper name, the "God who may be" is a God who is always still to come even while also already present. Yet, as we have seen, this is not the only God capable of bearing that thought, since it is far from alien to the same tradition that it is now said to disrupt. Perhaps, then, Kearney is right to look for the differences that matter in the lives that embody them. The God who may be, he tells us, is a God who needs us to indeed *be* God. It remains to be seen whether or how this God, better than the God of the great tradition, not only survives the deaths promised by ontotheology and theodicy, but also serves human flourishing. In the meantime, in all of these matters one may only hope. And in this much one rejoins the mood and outlook even Nietzsche recognized in a properly Christian life. "Christianity," he wrote, "is still possible at any time."[12]

Quis ergo Amo cum Deum Meum Amo?

BRIAN TREANOR

I. *Quid ergo Amo cum Deum Meum Amo: Khora* or **God?**

Continental philosophy, since the work of Emmanuel Levinas, has been marked by a particular concern with otherness. Although this concern is expressed in a variety of ways—the Infinite, the Other, the impossible, and so on—each of these expressions orients itself around the absolute incommensurability of the other (*autre*) with the self:

> [It] is of importance to emphasize that the transcendence of the Infinite with respect to the I which is separated from it and which it thinks it measures (so to speak) its very infinitude. The distance that separates the *ideatum* and idea here constitutes the content of the *ideatum* itself. Infinity is characteristic of a transcendent being as transcendent; *the infinite is the absolutely other.*[1]

The other, qua other, cannot be accounted for by the same. Unlike the patterns of Kantian, Hegelian, Husserlian, or Heideggerian accounts of the other, each of which ultimately returns to the self in a movement of comprehension, the postmodern account of the other is concerned with encountering the *otherness* of the other, not the other as comprehended or categorized by the same. This concern for otherness manifests itself in both ethical and theological thought.

In the course of thinking about otherness, postmodern thinkers have recently availed themselves of the rich tradition associated with

Augustine of Hippo, in particular the Augustine of the *Confessions*.[2] The retrieval of Augustine's question "What do I love when I love my God? [*quid ergo amo cum deum meum amo*]" has proven to be fertile ground for the postmodern consideration of otherness, impossibility, faith, and religion. The concern with alterity has considered a variety of archetypal encounters with otherness: Levinas's *visage du autre*, Derrida's *différance*, and Marion's *eikon*. However, in considering Augustine's *quid ergo amo*, postmodern thought is particularly indebted to the work of Jacques Derrida and John D. Caputo in discussing "the impossible."[3] Deconstruction's passion for the impossible constitutes, it is claimed, a strange "religion without religion," one in which "I do not know who I am or whether I believe in God," "I do not know whether what I believe in is God or not," and "I do not know what I love when I love my God" (*PT*, 331–332).[4] The "undecidable" nature of the impossible leaves us with *khora*, undecidability, and aporias, even when we choose, as we must, a historically determinate position with respect to God (the impossible).

However, while the deconstructive retrieval of Augustine's question has undoubtedly been philosophically rich, as retrieval it has also sparked intense debate regarding the hermeneutic legitimacy of its interpretation and its pretension to the status of religion. The objections come from a variety of sources, but often focus on the notion of undecidability. For example, Graham Ward of the "radical orthodoxy" movement objects that deconstruction's questioning of the impossible is different from an Augustinian questioning of God, which Derrida and Caputo acknowledge, and that this difference casts doubt on the claims of deconstruction to be ethical, hopeful, or religious.[5] In its trenchant insistence on the impossible as impossible, undecidability, and that *tout autre est tout autre*, deconstruction is left not with religion's *relation* to God, but with "regulative ideals," the "tyrannous demand for infinite responsibility," and "the logic of Camus' Sisyphus" (*QG* 285). Religion allows us to relate to God. However, "a God who is wholly other cannot be God at all" (*QG*, 281).

In reply, Caputo claims that Ward and those with similar objections have misunderstood deconstruction and that, in creating a caricature of it, they have failed to acknowledge its essentially religious character. This is often the result of positing a "disjunction between faith and undecidability" (*DRO*, 296). However, rather than creating an opposition between undecidability and faith,

> Derrida thinks that, precisely because of his notion of undecidability, everything begins and ends in faith. Deconstruction is

filled with faith . . . but it always maintains a certain ironic distance from and alertness to the *specific* or determinate messianisms. . . . But that is *not* to say deconstruction leaves us stuck in undecidability. . . . We are always responding and at the same time always asking what we are responding to, always choosing and at the same time asking what we have chosen or has chosen us, what we are doing in the midst of the concrete decisions we always make. ~0/

Deconstruction is not undecidability pure and simple. Undecidability is the condition for the possibility of decision and attends any decision even after it is made. With respect to the question of God, undecidability does not mean that we cannot accept any of the confessional faiths. On the contrary, it leaves us with nothing *except* concrete confessional faiths among which we must choose. Undecidability merely maintains that such decisions—hospitality, responsibility, belief in God—are acts of faith, not acts of knowledge. It acknowledges the necessity of deciding, but maintains that decisions are always haunted by undecidability.

Undecidability, in turn, leaves us in the desert of *khora*. Reading Plato's *Timaeus* in light of Heidegger's *es gibt* and Levinas's *il y a*, *khora* is a word that signifies the ineffable, irreducible, and atheological no-place of absolute alterity (*tout autre*).[6] Undecidability, however, is the condition for the possibility of decision, and for faith. Faith comes into play precisely where we cannot know. According to Caputo, Ward is the one who has done injustice to faith, not by deciding—that is, choosing a particular, determinate, historic messianism rather than the messianic—but by assuming that such a commitment would do away with the undecidability that it presupposes.

Thus, at stake, among other things, is the legitimacy of our claim to knowledge concerning God, our relationship with God, and even our ability to know that it is God with whom we are confronted. In light of these questions surrounding the contemporary retrieval of Augustine's question "quid ergo amo cum deum meum amo," one might rephrase this question as *"khora* or God?" That is, when we love God, whom we certainly do not understand, can we at least say that it is God that we love, not another *tout autre*? In saying that we know anything about God, even that God is God, have we already reduced the divine to terms that are merely human?

Kearney's recent work is inscribed within the dialogue surrounding the postmodern retrieval of Augustine's question, offering a *via tertia* between what have become two entrenched positions on this topic. The deconstructionists, following Derrida and Caputo, focus on Augustine's question qua question, that is, on the question as unanswered, even unanswerable. We do not know what we love when we love God, and that is precisely the point. To answer this question would be to limit God, the impossible.

> Everything about deconstruction requires that we let the *tout autre* tremble in undecidability, in an endless, open-ended, indeterminable, undecidable *translatability*, or *substitutability*, or *exemplarity*, where we are at a loss to say what is an example of what, what is a translation of what. (*PT*, 25)

Members of the second group, a diverse coterie whose members are identifiable by their objections to deconstruction rather than any unified philosophical agenda, argue that our answer to Augustine's question, and its modern variant, is exactly what is important. They maintain that the notion of a "religion without religion," to which the first group subscribes, is incoherent as religion insofar as it never knows if its questioning is directed to God. The opponents of deconstruction also claim that it is too rigorously indeterminate, leaving us with no way to distinguish, even provisionally and imperfectly, between God and *khora*, the divine and the diabolical. As Kearney notes, "The danger of God without being is that of an alterity so 'other' that it becomes impossible to distinguish it from monstrosity—mystical or sublime" (*GMB*, 34). To put it in ethical terms, if *tout autre est tout autre*, how can we distinguish between the widow, the orphan, and the stranger (Exodus 22:21) or the murderer, the rapist, and the terrorist? Deconstruction answers that we cannot, that any more determinate claim already betrays *the* impossible. Augustine's question forces us to confront the relationship between questioning and faith, both of which seem to require a certain ignorance. We question that which we do not understand. We have faith in that which cannot be proven. What, then, do I love when I love my God? Caputo maintains that we do not know, and as soon as we think we do know, we can be sure that it is no longer God that we love.

Kearney is typically considered a member of the second group because he objects to a strict deconstructive view that "[compromises] God's unique transcendence" and gives us "no way of telling the difference between the demonic and the divine other" (*GMB*, 74, 75). Kearney asserts that God is a unique *autre*, which calls into question the assertion that *tout autre est tout autre*, and holds that we must undertake a hermeneutic inquiry regarding encounters with alterity, which challenges the strict version of undecidability. However, while Kearney is an opponent of the strict deconstructive position, he is no friend of philosophies that claim to have certain, clear, and exclusive access to divine truth. In my view, Kearney's achievement is precisely that he avoids both the dogmatic fixity of those who claim unique, privileged, or certain access to the word of God and the ultimate sterility of a purely deconstructive religion without religion. "*Khora* or God?" By asking *who* God *may be* rather than *what* God *is*, Kearney points the way toward a faith that calls us to an active relationship with God (not *khora* or monstrosity) without allowing us to lapse into the dogmatism of an already accomplished or established truth.

Seems reasonable

II. *Prosopon:* The God Who Promises

Kearney accomplishes this through his claim that otherness is encountered as *persona.* "*Persona* is that eschatological aura of 'possibility' which eludes but informs a person's actual presence here and now . . . another word for the otherness of the other" (*GMB*, 10). Contrary to "person," which refers to the similarities between myself and the other, *persona* "is all that in others exceeds my searching gaze, safeguarding their inimitable and unique singularity." As such, *persona* lies beyond my "intentional horizons of re-tention and pro-tention," outstrips the "presenting consciousness of my *perception* . . . and the presentifying consciousness of my *imagination*," and even "defies the names and categories of my *signifying* consciousness."

Because *persona* is beyond consciousness, we never encounter others without also configuring them in some fashion. In the case of other people, we encounter them as person-*persona* and, in so doing, we configure them as both present and absent, paradoxically both incarnate and transcendent. To ignore either aspect is to disfigure the other: "We disregard others not just by ignoring their *transcendence* but equally by ignoring their *flesh-and-blood thereness*" (*GMB*, 11). Kearney, unlike fellow apostles of the impossible such as Levinas, Derrida, and Caputo, does not feel that such a configuration necessarily implies violence, although the potential for violence (or idolatry) requires an "acute hermeneutic vigilance."

Kearney's account of *persona* does justice to the irreducible singularity of the other without placing the other on the hither side of an abyss across which no relationship is possible. This eschatological relationship of one-for-the-other is one in which the *persona* of the other takes an asymmetrical priority over the person in me, allowing for a relationship between persons that preserves otherness while allowing for intimacy (what I have elsewhere called "relative otherness").[7] The asymmetrical nature of this encounter does not necessarily mean that it is nonreciprocal (Levinas) or absolutely foreign (Levinas, Derrida). The self can relate to an other without compromising alterity and can recognize something in the other without comprehending the other. For example, while one's spouse is no doubt other than the self, it would be strange to say that he or she is entirely foreign, utterly other. Rather, both similarity and (absolute) difference characterize the other person; there are aspects of similarity and aspects of otherness. In other words, not every unity is a totality, and the eschatological universal in which the other and I encounter each other is *not* a totality.

> We might say that the eschatological universal holds out the promise of a perichoretic interplay of differing *personas*, meeting without fusing, communing without totalizing, discoursing without dissolving. A sort of divine *circumin(c/s)ession* of the Trinitarian kingdom: a no-place which may one day be and where each *persona* cedes it place to its other (*cedere*) even as they sit down together (*sedere*). (15)

The *eschaton*, however, is a promise, not a possession. The eschatological *persona* is beyond my power, and "to the extent that I avow and accord this asymmetrical priority to the other, I am transfigured by that particular *persona* and empowered to transfigure in turn—that is, to figure the other in their otherness" (16). By affirming the otherness of the other, I move beyond merely configuring the other to be transfigured and to transfigure in turn.

But what is this otherness in the other? The *persona* is never present and accounted for. Rather, we encounter the otherness in the other (*persona*) only by way of a chiasmus with the same in the other (person), namely, the infinite other in the finite person, the trace of God in the face of the other, and the icon.[8] Even absolute alterity must somehow show up—as icon, *visage*, saturated phenomena—if I am to encounter it. Complete alterity or impossibility would, so to speak, remain under our radar, go wholly unnoticed; therefore, we would be incapable of a relation with it.

Although *persona* is never present, always deferred, and encountered only chiasmatically in the person, Kearney is able to recover, significantly, *persona* as *prosopon* (the face of the other as she faces me). The otherness of the other is a face. *Persona*, encountered chiasmatically in a person, shows itself as a *prosopon*. *Prosopon*, as Kearney uses the term, refers to fact that, phenomenologically and ethically, *persona* appears in and through a person, "transcendence in and through, but not reducible to, immanence" (*GMB*, 18).

The etymology of *prosopon* is illustrative here, as John Mannoussakis points out in this volume. To be (not to have) a *prosopon* is to be a face-toward-a-face: *pros-* (in front of or toward) *-opos* (an eye or countenance).

> Tellingly, the term rarely appears in the singular but always almost as a plural noun (*prosopa*), signaling that the *prosopon-persona* can never really exist on its own (*atomon*), but emerges in ethical relation to others. In this sense, the *prosopon-persona* may be said to be radically intersubjective, invariably bound up in some ethical vis-à-vis or face-to face. (18)

I am a *prosopon* in facing the other, and the other is reciprocally (though not symmetrically) a *prosopon* in facing me. The other is proximate but distant, present but absent, given but not possessed, like me but irreducibly other. God is also encountered as *persona*. God speaks through (*per-sona*) a burning bush. Jesus reveals the divine *persona* of Christ during the transfiguration. Both God and other persons are *prosopon*, which distinguishes the otherness of *persona* from the otherness of monstrosity.

If *persona* refers to this radical otherness—*la trace d'autrui*, alterity, *Geist*, *pneuma*—it refers to our encounters both with other persons and with God. However, while both the other person and God are *persona*, the *prosopon* of other persons are given to us phenomenologically, in contrast to the *prosopoetic* encounter with God, which is only hoped for (*GMB*, 61). It may seem that the deferral of God as *prosopon* confirms the deconstructive position, which asserts that there is no phenomenological difference between the experience of the monstrous and of the divine. However, this is not the case. While the encounter with divine *prosopon* may be (infinitely?) deferred, God is encountered as *persona*, which secures the personal nature of God as one who gives and promises.

God speaks to us as a God who promises, a God-who-may-be, leading Kearney to characterize God in terms of *persona* (and, eschatologically, as *prosopon*). Thus, while we cannot understand or comprehend God or God's ways, we do "know" something about God.

The God who gives and promises must be a who (*quis, persona*), not a what (*quid*). This is significant because to speak of God in terms of gift, promise, or fidelity, which Continental philosophy does, requires that God be a "who" rather than a "what." It is precisely an encounter with God qua *persona* that ensures that there is in fact a difference between the divine and the monstrous, or at least some senses of the monstrous.

Although deconstruction allows that there is a conceptual difference between the divine and the monstrous, it denies that there is any phenomenological difference.[9] The impossible is undecidable, endlessly substitutable, and infinitely translatable. To the question "*khora* or God," Caupto answers: "Our experiences of the two are not necessarily so widely divided, for in both cases we experience a certain confusion (Levinas), a kind of bedazzlement (Marion), or what Derrida and I . . . would call an 'undecidability'" (*RKE*, 92). However, we cannot simultaneously maintain that we are in danger of confusing God and the *il y a, khora*, or *'ehyeh 'asher 'ehyeh*, and maintain that we relate to this indeterminate otherness in terms of gift, hope, and promise, which Derrida and Caputo do.[10] Gifts and promises are made by and to "whos," not "whats."

III. *Posse*: The God Who May Be

Although thinking God in terms of *quissity* (who-ness) rather than *quiddity* (what-ness) allows us to avoid confusing God with *khora*, the characterization of God as *posse* rather than *esse* avoids dogmatism or programmatic preordination.[11] The challenge is to think transcendence without making it impossible to experience or encounter transcendence. Moving beyond ontology, phenomenology, negative theology, and deconstruction, Kearney, drawing on Meister Eckhart and Nicolas of Cusa, reads Exodus 3:14 as revealing God's *esse* as *posse*: "*I am who may be if you continue to keep my word and struggle for the coming of justice*" (*GMB*, 37–38).

Although the problems associated with a strictly ontological or ontotheological God have long been noted by Heidegger and others — the reduction of God to the "highest being," reduction of the infinite to the terms of the finite, idolatry, understanding God conceptually in terms of substance (*ousia*) — eschatological readings can also err in making transcendence too transcendent. Negative theology — and, I might add, deconstruction — tends toward a theology of absence that construes God as "so unknowable and invisible as to escape all identification whatsoever" (31). These two extremes, which reduce God to the status of a being and put God out of reach, respectively, do injustice to God and our ability to relate to God.[12]

IV. The God Who May Be

In the wake of these ways of thinking, Kearney attempts to speak of God in a manner that accounts for the transcendence of absolute alterity while giving an account of how that alterity might appear phenomenally. If thinking of God in terms of *persona* and *prosopon* gives an account of a personal God who "appears" in some way, characterizing God as *posse* ensures that such appearances can never become the locus of a programmatic, definite, or fully accomplished truth. Thus, following Levinas and Derrida, Kearney's God-as-*posse* seeks to protect the hoped-for-but-always-deferred character of God, otherness, and the impossible.

According to Kearney, thinking God in terms of *posse* rather than *esse* has several benefits: "the presuppositions and prejudices that condition our everyday lives are put into question in the name of an unprogrammable future"; "since no die is cast, no action is preordained, we are free to make the world a more just and loving place, or not to"; and, we are reminded "that what seems impossible to us is only seemingly so" (*GMB*, 4–5). The future is not preordained, and we are not acting in a programmatic manner. Rather, we are free to fulfill, or fail to fulfill, what God has told us is possible; and, thus, our responsibility to struggle to make the world a just place—that is, our responsibility to others—takes on a singular urgency. If we do not struggle for justice, the world will not be just. However, if we do struggle in this way, the world can become a just world, for "all things are possible with God" (Mark 10:27).

Ontological philosophies of God—either ontotheology or mystical ontologism—think God in human terms and thereby limit God's transcendence. Apophatic philosophies—negative theology and deconstruction—tend to place God utterly beyond human understanding. Kearney attempts to chart a course that can "respect the otherness of the Exodic God without succumbing to the extremes of mystical postmodernism" (34). In other words, Kearney tries to account for the postmodern concern with otherness while retaining the ability to say something determinate about the human relationship to God.

Kearney questions, against the repeated objections of Caputo, whether deconstruction backs itself into a corner in which it is committed to a kind of indiscriminate relation with otherness. "If every other is wholly other, does it still matter who or what exactly the other is?" (73). If every other is wholly other, then my relationship with any other is the same as my relationship with every other, for they are *all* wholly other. Although Kearney questions if this position confounds "the otherness of God with everything and everyone that is not God, thereby compromising God's unique transcendence," I would take this objection one step further (74). Does such a blanket application of absolute alterity not compromise *every* unique transcendence? The *quissity* of the other is lost if the alterity of the other is absolute. If *tout autre est tout autre*, what distinguishes the otherness of my wife from the otherness of my death? The widow, orphan, or stranger from the murderer, rapist, or terrorist? The Holocaust from the Resurrection? If every other is wholly other, otherness does not protect singularity, but subsumes it as surely as totality.

Although phenomenology, negative theology, and deconstruction offer correctives to the ontotheological conceptions of God as the highest being, they tend either to fail to provide an account of how the absolutely other or the impossible might appear as phenomena and still maintain alterity or, at the other extreme, to err by supposing that we can encounter that which never appears at all. Absolute otherness has to arrive on the scene (though not necessarily appear per se) as person, *prosopon*, *visage*, *eikon* in order for me to encounter it in bedazzlement, hope, desire, or love. But doesn't this sort of admission lead directly to the compromising of alterity that Caputo fears? Not necessarily.

Because Kearney thinks of God in terms of *posse* rather than *esse*, the kind of faith he advocates *cannot* be programmatic, as Caputo claims (*RKE*, 90). "Refusing to impose a kingdom, or to declare it already accomplished from the beginning, the God-who-may-be offers us the possibility of realizing a promised kingdom by opening ourselves to the transfiguring power of transcendence" (*GMB*, 2). In thinking of God's *'ehyeh 'asher 'ehyeh* as a promise that "I Am Who I Will Be" or, better, that "I Am Who May Be," any claim to comprehension or apodictic knowledge is put out of reach. The programmatic, thematized, fixed, and achieved faith that Caputo accuses Kearney of is inimical to the God-who-may-be.[13] *The God Who May Be* reveals Kearney's own prayers and tears, which are symptomatic of neither archive fever nor teleological fever, but of eschatological fever.

V. (Im)Possibility, Undecidability, and Taking Sides

If Kearney's reading of God as *posse* safeguards the alterity of the divine—and his characterization of other persons as chiasmatically person-*persona* does the same for other persons—is there any difference between alterity as described by Kearney and alterity as described by Caputo and Derrida? If so, what do we gain by thinking of God in terms of *posse* and *persona*? As Caputo notes, Kearney's meditations on possibility and impossibility in *The God Who May Be* bring him very close to Derrida's account of the impossible, which "does not mean a denial or negation of possibility but something that propels us into the most radical of all possibilities, the possibility of the impossible" (*RKE*, 90). However, as we have seen, Kearney's work discusses God not only in terms of possibility and impossibility, but also in terms of *persona* and *prosopon*. Herein lies the crux of the difference. Caputo and Derrida maintain that the impossible is subject to endless substitution, translation, and reinterpretation. However, on my reading, *The God Who May Be* says one very critical determinate thing about God, and that is that God must be a *who*. This divergence is clear in the difference between *khora* as *tout autre* without a face and God as *persona* and *prosopon* (i.e., with a face).

Caputo notes that the messianic dissociation of deconstruction is always matched by a historical association with a concrete tradition that it "disturbs from within," and further allows that life in the desert of *khora* would be "unlivable and that messianic hope cannot live apart from the 'determinable faiths'" (*PT*, 150). Moreover, he acknowledges that the "faith" of deconstruction is "a determinable faith [and] something like a certain messianism." It is significant that deconstruction is characterized as "a certain messianism" rather than the "messianic" per se. Deconstruction, qua faith—if we allow it that status for the moment—is as guilty, or innocent, as (nonfanatical) examples of Judaism, Christianity, or Islam of sinning against the impossible.

How so? One may ask on what basis Derrida and Caputo think the impossible in terms of hope, justice, hospitality, forgiveness, gift, and responsibility. Why not, if *tout autre est tout autre*, in terms of despair, injustice, horror, or tragedy, which are equally capable of confronting us with an otherness we cannot comprehend? There must be some difference between the bewildering alterity of monstrous injustice and the dazzling alterity of messianic justice and, if so, "surely it is important to tell the difference, even if it's only more or less; and even if we can never *know* for certain, or *see* for sure, or *have* any definite set of criteria" (*GMB*, 76). I think Kearney is on to something when, citing Simon Critchley, he asks how, if the deconstructionists are right, we can affirm that *alterity is ethical.* "Why is it not rather evil or an-ethical or neutral?"[14]

Strict deconstruction must either acknowledge that both interpretations of the impossible (justice and injustice, for example) are equally legitimate or admit that there is something that distinguishes the two and, therefore, something different about the way we are confronted by each. If the former is the case, then Ward is correct in pointing out that deconstruction per se is neither ethical nor hopeful, although Derrida and Caputo, as individuals, may be. If the latter is the case, then the notion of undecidability has to be reworked in order to explain why one ought to seek the impossible (God) in justice rather than injustice, which comes down to explaining, or attempting to explain, how the impossibility of messianic justice differs from the impossibility of monstrous injustice. This point is significant, and worth elaborating. Ultimately, my claim will be that a deconstructive religion without religion falls short on both counts, that it is neither religion nor without religion.

Assuming for the moment that we agree that there is in fact a difference between choosing justice and injustice, love and hate, what is the basis for this choice? If the events, equally impossible in themselves, are infinitely translatable and substitutable, am I left with *only* the good fortune to have been born into a family and culture that values tolerance rather than one that propagates racism? I suspect that many people are good (or try to be so) for less arbitrary reasons, although such reasons might be difficult to articulate in the face of the impossible. Some people certainly follow their tradition blindly, even to the point of fanaticism. However, many others do not choose good and avoid evil simply because they were raised—as Jew, Christian, Muslim, Buddhist—to do so. Rather, they choose the good, I trust, because they think it preferable to evil. On what basis am I to make this choice if not on the basis of something that differentiates (even imperfectly) good and evil or justice and injustice, making them nonsubstitutable (or at least not infinitely so)? As Kearney notes, the point is to "enter the fray and *take sides*. And the choice of sides is determined ultimately by which interpretations we deem more faithful" to the transfiguring power of God (*GMB*, 48).

The difference seems to turn on the notion of undecidability. Undecidability is clearly an important contribution to the philosophical debate surrounding the other, but this contribution is problematic if taken in a strict sense. Such a strict reading follows from "undecidability characterizes faith" and "everything is a certain faith," leading to the conclusion that everything is, in some sense, undecidable.[15] This seems a bit extreme. There is certainly a significant role played by undecidability, especially with respect to questions of faith. However, undecidability does not apply to all things or to any one thing absolutely—that is, we cannot engage undecidable questions without some way of undertaking a hermeneutic process of discernment.

Caputo asserts—and reasserts in answer to the objections of Kearney and others—that "undecidability is not indecision" (*PT*, 338; *RKE*, 93). In the same vein, he clarifies that infinite translatability "does not say that everything can be translated but that translation cannot be stopped" (*PT*, 54). Thus, infinite translatability does not mean that anything can mean anything else, that good can be evil, or that justice can be injustice, but that the messianic justice of the impossible is always open, subject to never-ending translation. However, if deconstruction is concerned with an open-ended translation of justice, but one that, nevertheless, will never be translated into injustice, it has fallen into the very "double bind/double save" of which it accuses apophatic theology (45).[16] Just as negative theologians know very well that it is God of whom they can say nothing, that all their negations are in the service of a higher affirmation, so deconstruction is already oriented toward justice, hospitality, and generosity when it sets about deconstructing the Grand Narrative. Deconstruction's "religion" is not really "without religion" after all.

Undecidability, says Caputo, is not indecision. However, I am not sure that undecidability, as deconstruction has it, does not result in lukewarm decisions, which lack resoluteness and, therefore, are not really decisive. Questions of faith are indeed defined by or characterized by their undecidability or indeterminacy. However, faith itself is defined by its commitment and decisiveness. That is, faith qua faith is decisive and certain, although this certainty does not extinguish the (possibility of) doubt that haunts all faith. Any faith that is not fanaticism must be theoretically open to doubt, modification, and further questioning. However, qua faith, it is a leap that is made unconditionally, or at least one that aspires to be unconditional. This decisiveness differentiates faith from belief. While belief and faith both admit of doubt insofar as they are not knowledge, faith aspires to unconditionality and belief does not. Deconstruction believes in the impossible, but does not have faith in it.

If fanaticism is not faith insofar as it pretends to know the impossible and, thus, confuses faith and knowledge, is it equally true that deconstruction is not faith because it pretends that faith is nothing more than a decision made without knowledge? The first errs in thinking too much, so to speak, of faith (by thinking that faith is, or even needs to be, equivalent to knowledge because only knowledge is true); the second fails by thinking too little of it (and implying that all unverifiable beliefs are faith). While deconstruction is right to make a distinction between knowledge and faith (and in so doing, distinguishes faith from fanaticism), it fails to make the equally important distinction between faith and belief.

This is not a blanket rejection of deconstruction's project or its applicability to theological questions. Contemporary philosophy owes too much to Derrida and Caputo. However, in the movement from speaking of *différance* to speaking of God, deconstruction has encountered some problems that demand either further elaboration or qualification of that position. I am inclined to agree with Caputo and Derrida that our faith, qua faith, has to do with something undecidable, if by that they intend to say that one can never be *unreservedly* sure, never *completely* know, never *fully* comprehend the object of one's faith (*RKE*, 94). However, deconstruction goes too far when it claims that *tout autre est tout autre* and that the impossible is infinitely translatable and substitutable; to claim this is to say that one cannot have even partial certainty concerning one's faith or know anything about it (except that it is impossibly bewildering). Faith in God takes place "through a glass darkly," not in the absolute darkness of the blind (1 Corinthians 13).

In the final analysis, deconstruction's "religion without religion" is neither. In simultaneously insisting on the hopeful and just character of the impossible and on its undecidable nature, deconstruction exhibits the shortcomings of historical messianisms—belief in a determinate version of the impossible, in this case a hopeful and just version—without having recourse to their strengths and benefits, that is, faith, belief that aspires to be unconditional while remaining humble regarding its limits. As an essentially apophatic movement, deconstruction alone is ultimately sterile. Deconstruction's negative movement must be wedded with a positive movement, and Kearney's hermeneutics is an example of one attempt to do so. "Supplementing" deconstruction's excessively apophatic movement with a diacritical hermeneutics of discernment is one way of describing what Kearney and Manoussakis have come to call the fourth reduction of phenomenology. This fourth, eschatological reduction aims to return philosophy *"back to existence*, that is, back to the natural world of everyday embodied life where we may confront once again the other as *prosopon"* (Kearney, "Epiphanies of the Everyday"). This fourth reduction does not "abolish" the first three *epoche*, but "radicalizes and supplements them" (ibid.), exhibiting structural similarities to both the second naïveté of Kearney's mentor Ricoeur and to the *réflexion seconde* of Ricoeur's mentor Gabriel Marcel. All three philosophers take pains to ensure that the abstractions and hermeneutic detours that characterize their philosophies are followed by a return to the embodied subject that acknowledges the abstractions and detours as abstractions and detours. The *epoche* that characterizes deconstruction causes it to think otherness in absolute, all-or-nothing terms. But otherness is relative. Any other we actually hear, to whom we actually respond, with whom we have a relation of any kind is, as Kierkegaard illustrated, not absolutely other. Otherness is made absolute only by an artificial abstraction, detour, or *epoche*, and while this abstraction, detour, or *epoche* can be worthwhile, it must be supplemented by a move that reconcretizes the abstraction, follows through on the detour, or removes the brackets in order to return us to the everyday embodied life we live, which is exactly what the fourth reduction does.

Quid ergo amo cum deum meum amo? "What do I love when I love my God?" The way in which one asks this question and the kind of answer one hopes to find are central to understanding the philosophical schism discussed above. When I love God, do I know anything about the God I love, or even that it *is* God that I love? When I respond "Here I am," how do I know if I am responding to God or the devil? "What," for Derrida and Caputo, asks, "what do I love?" "For what do I grope blindly in the desert darkness?" The impossible. What is that? God? *Khora? Il y a? Tout-autre?* The sublime? The monstrous?

However, for Kearney—and for Augustine, whose question inspired these remarks—"what" (*quid*) asks, "What is God like, this God whom I love? What about my God do I love when I love my God?" and, ultimately, "*who* (*quis*) is my God whom I love?" Augustine's questioning of the "earth . . . the sea . . . living animals . . . wind

. . . heaven, sun, moon and stars" in Book X of his *Confessions* is a rhetorical move, not the result of ignorance concerning the recipient of his love.[16] Augustine's question, certainly made in prayer and with tears, is nevertheless certain of its addressee, which is God, not *khora*. Faith is frequently haunted by doubt and, even in times when it is not explicitly wrestling with doubt, it should maintain a healthy sense of humility with respect to the limitations of human knowledge and understanding. Nevertheless, the religious question is not *quid ergo amo*, but *quid (quis) ergo amo cum deum meum amo?*

Divinity and Alterity

FELIX Ó MURCHADHA

Divinity and alterity have haunted phenomenology since its beginnings. At phenomenology's margins Rudolf Otto described God as
the "wholly other."[1] This otherness of God and the divinity of otherness came into sharp relief in Husserl's transcendental phenomenology, where God's transcendence is bracketed as much as the alterity
of the other in the reduction of intentional consciousness.[2] This is a
move replicated in Heidegger's "reduction," to use the vocabulary of
Marion which is employed in this volume by Kearney and Manoussakis, where the question of God depends on the analytic of *Dasein*.[3]
Arguably in both Husserl and the early Heidegger the otherness of
appearance is reduced to the sameness of the subject of that appearance, and as a consequence the phenomenality of that which breaks
through and disrupts that sameness cannot appear. If this is the case,
then both these reductions fail in their aims: namely, to bring the
phenomenality of appearance itself to appearance. The alterity of appearances understood as those of the divine brought the question of
god or gods to the fore of phenomenological research. The route
taken by Heidegger was that of a return to a putatively Greek, pre-
Christian, experience of the divine in the sacredness of things. This
route, however, has been subject to sustained criticism starting from
Marcel in a line of phenomenologists who draw from Judeo-Christian accounts of the divine. Phenomenology has given a new twist to
the question of Athens or Jerusalem. Richard Kearney's recent work

responds to both of these issues—two sides of the one issue in fact—and does so by a reinvigoration of a hermeneutical approach that seeks to respond to the question of alterity/divinity in a manner that is open to different and conflicting accounts of the divine. His latest attempt to formulate his position is in terms of a fourth reduction, a guiding principle of which is, as Manoussakis puts it, "the chiastic union of the phenomenality of the phenomenon with the phenomenon itself."[4] It shares with the preceding reductions the motif of a return to what is always already there. For Kearney what is already there is the *eschaton*, that is, the reserve of possibility in the simplest of things. Although he does not use the Husserlian term "bracketing," I take it that what is bracketed is the everyday indifference to things. As already with Husserl, this amounts to a change in attitude (as Manoussakis puts it).[5]

This fourth reduction seeks a middle road between a Husserlian phenomenology of the same and a Levinasian phenomenology of the Other. It seeks this through an appeal to a hermeneutic of the *eschaton*, one which is guided by the practical interest in discernment. In this way the fourth reduction draws on themes already to be found in Kearney's *Strangers, Gods, and Monsters*. In this article I will deal with the latter work before returning again at the conclusion to the question of the fourth reduction.

"This volume," Kearney says of *Strangers, Gods, and Monsters*, "is an attempt to reinvestigate practices of defining ourselves in terms of otherness."[6] The pivotal element here is ourselves: Kearney's goal is to understand ourselves in relation to otherness. More specifically, his concern is how in practice we can and how we should deal with otherness both in ourselves and in the others who confront us. The relation between these is of course a complex one: the otherness in ourselves can often be projected onto others, in the most extreme case as scapegoating. He talks in this context of Girard's famous thesis of the scapegoat. He is broadly supportive of Girard's analysis, but finds his privileging of Christianity in this respect problematic. Kearney's task is to understand how we can deal with the alien within and outside of ourselves without practicing scapegoating. Central to this is the practice of discernment, of understanding the alien; more specifically, of discerning between positive and negative aliens. Such a practice of discernment lies at the heart of Kearney's critical hermeneutics. Hand in hand with this goes a strategy of finding the middle road. He wishes to avoid either a subordination of the same to the other or of the other to the same (*SGM*, 77). Instead, following Ricoeur, he wishes to understand the self as an other. This practical task also concerns the encounter with god or gods. In this encounter discernment is necessary because the monstrous can often be confused with the godly. Furthermore, while god opens himself up to human beings, becomes indeed like us, the alterity of *différance* or the *khora* is unmediated, is an alterity which leaves us bereft of appropriate action. Throughout, the fundamental issue is how to act. Hence, although there are some experiences of the *khora* or *il y a* as the "horror of the night," for Kearney the point is to find one's way out of such darkness to a god, which is neither the same as nor wholly other than ourselves (*SGM*, 204).

In what follows, I will pose three questions of *Strangers, Gods and Monsters*. The first is methodological, concerning the place of philosophy in the project of the book. If, as I will suggest, in this regard Kearney's hermeneutics is committed to a concept of philosophy as practical, then I would propose that this colors his debate with Levinas and Derrida. My second question concerns the basis on which he criticizes these "prophets of absolute alterity." My third question concerns the account of Heidegger's last gods. If Kearney sees philosophy as having practical efficacy, he does so in the light of extraphilosophical commitments, commitments to some version of the Judeo-Christian god. This commitment, I wish to claim, is assumed rather than defended in his critique of Heidegger.

I.

In his introduction Kearney, having stated that for Julia Kristeva there are three main ways in which we may respond to our "fundamental experience of estrangement"—art, religion, and psychoanalysis—goes on, "I will . . . be suggesting a fourth way of response: philosophy" (*SGM*, 6). This response involves a "certain kind of understanding" (*SGM*, 7). This understanding turns out to be exemplified by a "hermeneutics of discernment." Now in what sense is philosophy a fourth way of response? Is it just one more mode of responding to estrangement? But what does response mean here? I sense it means something like coping, dealing with—something, in short, akin to therapy. The experience to which it responds is that of limit situations, limit phenomena both within and outside of ourselves. But this response is one that seeks not disinterested understanding but, rather, an understanding "closer to phronesis than to *theoria*," which seeks to answer the question What is to be done? But

Isn't that Jamesian pragmatism?

on what basis does Kearney suggest that the touchstone of philosophy in regard to these issues should be its capacity to answer this question?

The question here concerns the place of philosophy itself. Is philosophical reflection to be judged on the basis of its capacity to cope with situations, to offer us practical help in making political and moral decisions? This question obviously has particular urgency when dealing with the issue of otherness. The other is that with which we have to deal, with which we have to come to terms. But can such questions be decided philosophically? My suggestion is that while religion, psychoanalysis, and art have—among others— therapeutic ends, philosophy does not. In that case, philosophy is not on the same level, but rather is on a metalevel, is a reflection on religious, artistic, and psychoanalytical phenomena. Levinas says that religion and philosophy are fundamentally different because philosophy does not offer consolation. I sense that Kearney sees philosophy as consoling, as itself a narrative that gives us understanding of our lives. But to see philosophy in this way is to abandon the ideal of *theoria*—that of disinterested observance of human life. It is here that despite Kearney's closeness to phenomenology, he departs significantly from it. His hermeneutics is one guided not so much by the things themselves as by *hope* in the things to come. It is—as is made clear in the opening essay/manifesto of this volume—an eschatological hermeneutics tied to the Christian promise of redemption and forgiveness.

II.

Levinas and Derrida are in certain respects more phenomenological than Kearney. While Kearney presupposes the biblical ideals of justice and love, and the goals of forgiveness and redemption, Levinas is more concerned to show how justice is phenomenologically grounded in the claim of the other. This claim is one which obliges me *before* I will or act. "Before" here is not to be understood chronologically, but rather as a prestructure, as that past that is never present. Kearney is in a temporal position different from that of Levinas: he is concerned with what I have to do, how I am to act, directed toward the future, which to some extent depends on my decisions, and toward the future past of the narration and remembrance of that action. Levinas, on the other hand, is concerned with what no action of mine can undo. The ideals and goals of the Bible may aid me in acting, but they cannot be presupposed in the description of what it is to be faced with the other. And Levinas does not presuppose them; rather, in my understanding, he is seeking the ethical moment in ontology: he is seeking to show that the discourse on being is interrupted by a moment of alterity for which it cannot account. This ethical moment is described in the Bible, but it is the phenomenological warrant for this description that it is at issue.

Kearney and Levinas are often at cross purposes. A case in point is Kearney's discussion of Levinas's claim that I am "responsible for the persecuting by my persecutor" (*SGM*, 71). For Kearney this leaves us without the possibility of discernment: we are left in an indifference between the other as persecutor and the other as benefactor. He does not so much reject Levinas's insight here, as attempt to "supplement" it by a "hermeneutics of practical wisdom." It seems, though, that such a hermeneutics is based on different premises. The account Levinas gives of vulnerability from which the above quote is taken attempts to think passivity not from activity but, rather, from sensibility. Suffering from and for the other—indeed, the merging of both in the figure of maternity—points to an original, premoral "gestation of the other in the same,"[7] which is not, *pace* Kearney, a nonjudgmentalism, but rather a description of a *pre*judgmental moment. It is not a question of suspending "all criteria of ethical discrimination" (*SGM*, 72), because it comes before, not after, any such discrimination. Ethical discrimination depends on a prior otherness in the same.

Kearney's view is that this must then be supplemented by discriminating criteria. But this means turning to that issue that phenomenologically is undecidable, namely, discerning "the other in the alien and the alien in the other" (*SGM*, 67). This is undecidable *phenomenologically* because there is nothing in the other that can decide the matter. The other is that which silences, which cuts off our discourse. Once we discourse again, once we talk and judge, we are dealing with the same. This is a case of *tertium non datur*. In effect, I am questioning Kearney's distinction of other and alien. Can we act toward an other without treating him as an alien? If I give water to a thirsty person, am I not *also* doing a violence, placing him in my debt even if I never ask for anything in return? To act toward an other is to insert myself into her narrative, and no such insertion is without injury. Practically, morally, it makes a difference—a world of a difference—whether I give water or pass by. But does it make a difference philosophically? Only if we presuppose a practical goal for philosophy.

Decisions as to how to act have their own discourse. Derrida, I take it, seeks to reflect upon that discourse. In discussing everyday concepts such as hospitality, he is not exhorting us *in practice* to open our homes to the Charles Mansons and Idi Amins of this world. Rather, he is attempting to show the latent contradictions in our practice of hospitality. This we may say, following Kearney, is the problem with deconstruction: that it leaves us only halfway, does not give us the instruments to decide. But is not the point that we decide all the time and always will, and that philosophy's task is to reflect upon such decisions? And this is not peculiar to deconstruction: is it essentially any different from Socrates discussing piety and beauty?

Can philosophy help us in making practical decisions in a way which religion, art, or psychoanalysis cannot? Or does it reflect upon what is going on when we make such decisions? I tend toward the latter view. Do we just leave it at that, two separate views of philosophy? No, because these different views can themselves come into debate.

My argument is that when, as Kearney does, a philosopher attempts to decide the matter in relation to the other, he relies on pre-philosophical and philosophically unjustified commitments. This seems inevitable, for to make practical decisions requires commitments, but philosophy understood as *theoria* requires the suspension and reduction of them. (Whether Kearney's "fourth reduction" can escape from this requirement is another question.)

"If the divine becomes sublime to the point of becoming sadism it has, in my view, ceased to be divine" (*SGM*, 95). But what is the basis of that view? Was the god who called Abraham to sacrifice his son not sadistic? Are not the Homeric gods often sadistic? Are these not gods, or are they the wrong types of gods? But wrong in what way and for whom? Is there not here an implied paradigm of the Christian idea of the good and loving god? But if so, what justifies this paradigm? It is of course one that finds a counterpart in the metaphysical god, already coming to the fore in Plato's moral critique of the Homeric gods. With god or gods. Kearney does not wish to turn to the god of metaphysics, but rather the god of Christian revelation. Why this privilege? I suggest that the phrase "in my view" in the above quotation is significant, and it, or variants of it, dot Kearney's text. The commitments are personal. That is not to say subjective, but simply that these are decisions for certain values for which personal commitments are necessary, such a freedom, human rights, and so on. Is faith a name for such commitments? Not surprisingly, Heidegger becomes for Kearney the main opponent in the final part of the book.

III.

Kearney suggests that Heidegger's attitude to theology is to be understood in terms of the medieval debate regarding faith or reason. But while Heidegger does understand theology as the science of faith, the vital point is that faith—not god—is a *positum*. Hence, it is not the case that philosophy and theology are two truths, but rather that theology is a positive science—with as much and as little privilege as, say, physics—and as such is different from philosophy. Crucially, the question of god is not dismissed, but rather that of the god of faith. The methodological atheism of Heidegger's work is an a-*theism*, a bracketing off of the theistic interpretation of god as a philosophically ungrounded one. Hence, what is at issue for Heidegger is not—*pace* Kearney—a question of god *or* being, but rather an interpretation of god from the question of being. This explains why during a period of "aggressive atheism" (Caputo, quoted in *SGM*, 214), Heidegger could again begin to explore the question of god and gods. For Kearney, though, there are three possible candidates for god: the god of revelation, the god of metaphysics, and the god of the poets. Heidegger's is the last. But first, this is not a choosing of poetry over prose: the god of thought is—given Heidegger's distinction of the sciences—ipso facto not the god of faith. And second, the god of the poets is not simply a poetical construct, but rather one that reflects a profound religious sensibility that comes to poetry first in the works of Homer. The polemics suggested by Kearney's opposition between monotheistic revelation and Greek paganism (*SGM*, 36, 216) are Christian polemics—"paganism" is a Christian term of abuse. But while Kearney himself admits that it is not at all clear that "perverse sacrificial practices" are absent in monotheism, he implicitly maintains its privilege over "paganism." What gets lost in such a view is the question of the different characterizations of the relation of gods and humans in, say, the *New Testament* and the *Iliad*. These differences, I submit, motivated much of Heidegger's thinking on the gods, not "antagonism" toward Christianity (Caputo, quoted in *SGM*, 286).

Following Walter F. Otto,[8] Heidegger criticized the common dismissal of the Greek gods as anthropomorphic. It is rather the case that human beings gaze into the uncanny (*Ungeheur*), that the human is that entity which sees into the unconcealment of being. Gods and humans are understood as different beings who, however, both receive being. Both humans and gods are subject to *moira*, destiny. Unlike the Christian god, which can will the world to exist and will it to end—whether that will is a loving or a malicious will is here irrelevant—the Greek gods are limited by the world in their actions. Hence, while they are immortal, they are powerless to hinder the death of a human being they hold dear, when he is destined to die. Indeed, death is anathema to them; at the hour of greatest need they must abandon their beloved heroes.

The gods in this sense do not hold up an ideal of human action and human willing, but rather point to the limits of all action. Arguably the gods of Homer reflect more, not less, of the limits of human experience than the god of the New Testament. They reflect above all else the limits of human action. Could it not be that within human action itself there is an estrangement, a moment of unwilling, of impossibility and impotence; that perhaps at the heart of the Greek experience of divinity is an awareness of this impotence, of mortality in the face of the immortals? It is such an insight that I think Heidegger is reflecting in his account of the last god. The last god is a god that, as Kearney says, is "utterly subordinate to the destiny of being" (*SGM*, 218). Kearney is right to oppose this to the Christian god. He is right also to link this to Heidegger's general account of destiny. But it is only if we implicitly or explicitly assume the Christian god and the human in the light of that god that Heidegger can be accused here of "extreme quietism" (*SGM*, 220). Furthermore—to allude to Heidegger's Nazi engagement (see *SGM*, 253f.)—where might we best find a model for the actions of Hitler and Stalin in the Greek notion of *moira* or the Christian notion of *creatio ex nihilo*? The answer to this question is not self-evident. Is Kearney's assertion of the capacity to "legislate a new understanding of being" (*SGM*, 224) not a restatement of Christian voluntarism, which above all Heidegger opposed? This despite Kearney's endorsement of the "'step back' from the metaphysics of the will" (*SGM*, 227).

Kearney neglects the context here in Heidegger's critique of technology. In the light of this critique, action is itself problematic. Not that we should not act, but rather that we should reflect on what it is to act, and pose the question whether what we understand as our actions are not simply perpetuations of a forgetting of being. The flight of the gods is symptomatic of that forgetting. The point in this context is precisely to act. What Heidegger takes from the Greek gods is the thought that our actions are not in our own control. They are not in our control because they respond to a sending of being, to which humans and gods are subject. Waiting, in this context, is not the antithesis of action; it is the essence of action. Action—if it is to act upon something—must first wait upon it to show itself in an appropriate way. Pathos is not dumb suffering, but that for which it is necessary to be ready. Patience is essential if action is to be possible. What shows itself to our acts does so not only as it is, but also in terms of what it is to be, in terms of being. That is beyond our making or willing.

The believer may, as Kearney quotes Richardson as saying, find the god in which this is reflected "a rather impoverished god" (*SGM*, 288), but the believer is perhaps not the best judge in these matters. The believer, after all, has already answered the question as to the nature of god and, by implication, the nature of human action.

IV.

The fundamental question that emerges here, particularly in the light of the "fourth reduction," is what the phenomenal basis of divinity is. Of what do we speak when we speak of god and gods? It is not by accident—and it is an important contribution that Kearney makes here—that we speak of strangers and monsters and of god and gods in the same breath. For Kearney the divine here is the possibilizing, the transforming in the possible, the transfiguring. The divine is the moment, the *kairos*, of repetition and the opening of the future. But the moment of truth—as we call it—can be a moment of incapacity, of denigration, of death (real or metaphorical) as much as of rebirth. Taken to its kairological ultimacy, the difference here cannot be fully discerned, or discernment is prestructured in hope. Does the fourth reduction, then, arise out of the experience of hope? Certainly this is not stated. Yet, it seems implicit. Indeed, hope has been a theme of Kearney's since his reading of Bloch—precisely with regard to possibility—in *Poétique du Possible*.[9] While Kearney begins with a wager, let me end here with a suspicion. The question that troubles all previous three reductions is what motivates the reduction: Is it an act of will in the face of the strange, or the experience of nothingness in anxiety, or radical boredom (*ennui*)? Kearney does not explicitly state what motivates the fourth reduction, but let me wager the suspicion that it is the experience of hope. If this is the case, there is an urgent need to show that hope is more than a theological virtue, and has a philosophical relevance in line with the methodological reserve Kearney rightly characterizes philosophy as requiring.

II. Theology Facing Philosophy

On the God of the Possible

STANISLAS BRETON

Under a title that captures our attention and puts a question that will not go away, Richard Kearney offers a conception of the divine and of divinity that immediately strikes the reader by its extraordinary youthfulness. For youth, not only in its most current sense, but in its most philosophical as well, could be defined precisely by the two words in his title that open the new perspective to which he summons us: *may be*. How should we translate—in a way that allows us to dream, as if finding ourselves on Celtic ground—the "potency to be" indicated by this expression, which is a common one in our different Western languages? At the simplest level, the possible at once calls up various paths of thought. In the first place, it suggests the lightness of taking wing or exceeding the speed limit, so as to leave behind both the finished matters of the past and the actuality of the present. Thus understood, the possible breaks the bounds imposed by memory, with its often burdensome weight, and by attention, with its sometimes fixated rigor. While not denying memory and attention, the possible in its youthfulness is essentially the theme of a creative imagination that has no concern with reproducing things or jealously possessing them.

A second path of thought is suggested if we take the possible in the adverbial form of the perhaps. In French at least, the perhaps (*peut-être*) invests the possible with a connotation of doubt that cools its fervor. But it is a peculiarity of this word that it can also carry connotations of eager hope, or of a courageous hope against hope, as in the sentence attributed to Rabelais: "I make my way to the great perhaps." Here hope of the impossible is shadowed by fears that the best of what ought to be and *could be* (in Latin, *posset*) will in the end fail to be. Yet the desire that it be so, an aspiration carrying all the force of Eros, seems to overcome these fears of a negative end result. Kearney offered a first phenomenology of these poetic and existential overtones of the idea of the possible in *Poétique du Possible*. Now, in *The God Who May Be*, he continues to explore the transfigurative dynamics of the possible, with the focus on its religious dimension. In order to bring out the originality of what he is proposing, I should like to clarify, under the heading of "preliminaries," a number of presuppositions, or what may be called a quasi axiomatics, shaping the climate and texture of his thinking.

Preliminaries

First of all, I think it will be found helpful if we begin by ruling out senses of the possible with which Kearney is not concerned. When I hear the word "possible," I spontaneously tend to give it the meaning conferred on it by logicians. Perhaps this reflects my age. In logic the possible figures among the alethic modalities, under two forms: "possibly the case" and "possibly not." These are related, in a square of opposition, with the necessary and the impossible. Needless to say, this is not what is in question in Kearney's usage. Though he does keep up a discourse of the impossible, there is no place in his inquiry, if I am not mistaken, for the idea of the necessary in its rigorous logical or scientific sense. This means that what Pascal calls the spirit of geometry will be of little help to us in our attempt to bring into focus the transfiguration that haloes God and the person set in relation to this God. Instead, we must draw on the other term of the Pascalian antithesis, the spirit of finesse.

Also very remote from Kearney's concerns is the account of the possible worked out by Bergson, a quite original, even revolutionary, one in its own way. Bergson saw the possible not as the opening of a future but as the bitter product of a retrospect that would palliate the scandalous novelty of the present by finding it already inscribed, as possible, in the past. For such a projection of the present into the past there would be a twofold motivation: on one side, the need, when confronted with some major rupture, to recall the conditions that must have prepared the event; on the other, the slothful or traditionalist tendency to explain away the emergence of the new by identify-ing it with a claimed analogue of reassuringly ancient date. Bergson's orientation in thinking the possible is clearly opposed to that of Kearney.

Moving on to the enunciation of Kearney's positive presupposi-tions, we note first that he advances a new idea of God,[1] a God no longer enclosed in his being and in the immutable plenitude of his actuality. The basic concern here is to recover the God of the Bible and of the Gospel, the God of the promise and of a coming kingdom, a God whom we may call *eschatological*, in clear opposition to the God of ontology or of a metaphysics of presence and, more precisely, of ontotheology. Despite the oft-proclaimed "death of God," the God of the promise comes to us anew today, but under the form of the *posse* and the *may be.* This is a living God, whose "dynamism and desire" cannot be confined within the "I am who I am" of a scholastic exege-sis that dooms God to an abstract subsistence (*GMB*, 2–3).

This new idea of God carries significant implications for a new conception of our relation as humans to God. If I have correctly grasped the import of these presuppositions, we can no longer think of ourselves as passive witnesses to the being of God and his actions in history. As one who believes in a God who descends with us into history, and who makes himself historical above all in "the Word made flesh and dwelling among us," I feel we should take seriously one of Kearney's most resonant affirmations: "God depends on us to be" (*GMB*, 4). The very being of God depends on us;[2] such is the unheard-of reversal here proposed. God as power-to-be remains nonetheless the "burning bush" whose flame inspires us and entrusts to us the mission of making him exist in the human world. This has consequences for the theological problem of evil, a tormenting ques-tion to which the theodicies respond in exhausting efforts to acquit the Creator. It is wrong to discuss the problem of evil in relation to some divine predestination of the world, for that would presuppose "a God of pure act and necessity," remote from the biblical God who enters human history. Rather, we should think of evil as something for which we all bear responsibility in solidarity. Thus, "interpreting God as *posse* rather than *esse* is a final 'no' to theodicy" (*GMB*, 5). Kearney asks himself whether there is a suitable name to designate this kind of "philosophy of God." He suggests various titles, such as *dynamatology* or, preferably, *metaxology,* before finally opting for the French term *milieu,* which indicates, as regards the conception of God, a middle term between the two extremes of the *trans-ascendance* expressed in negative theology and a *trans-descendance*[3] that would consign the sacred to an underground of abyssal depths. The two extremes have the same upshot: whether one opts for the extreme of height or for that of depth; God remains in either case the unthinkable and the unnameable. The hermeneutic approach Kearney adopts is a middle position between them, to which he gives the title "metaphorology." The term is well chosen, because it invites us to draw on all the resources of a language of the imaginary, resources so abundant in the Bible, whether in the prophets or the Song of Songs, and because it also has an affinity with Kearney's cherished theme of transfiguration.

Contrary to what is often thought, negative theology is equally prodigal of images and metaphors. If "negation is more divine than addition," it is because it exerts a critical function on all the denominations of the Principle, thus despoiling them of their ontological validity. For the Principle, whether one calls it One or Good, is "beyond being and essence," to use hallowed Platonic language. It has been said with truth that negative theology can be just as garrulous as theologies following the *via eminentiae*. But that criticism is beside the point. In prohibiting ontological reference, negative theology leaves the field free for every kind of naming, in virtue of an axiom known to tradition and taken up by Eckhart: *"the unnameable is omninameable."* By the same token, what is beyond being *is made to be* in an infinity of manners in the human sphere, and by humans themselves whose energies are inspired by the Principle.

In a very different context, what St. Paul would have us understand by the sign of the Cross of Christ is also a new God of "foolishness" and "weakness," a God beyond wisdom and power, the two attributes that at that time defined being as the being of the divinity. The crucified Word thus shows us a God "beyond being and essence" whose weakness and foolishness urge us, by the inspiration breathed forth from the Cross, to make him exist on our earth, among human beings, especially among the most disinherited. The *nothingness of the Cross*, that "seed of non-being" as it has been called, has become, in all of us, a potency of being (*dunamis*), enabling us, in a continual exercise of creative imagination, to hasten the coming of the kingdom of heaven on "our oblique earth."

The reader will notice that the God of the possible, the *God who may be*, is not very distant from the God of the Cross. In both discourses, "God depends on us," and it is our responsibility that is engaged in the transfiguration of the world. In addition, though not necessarily in the same style, the language used in the two cases has to appeal to creative imagination, in view of the fact that what surpasses every name has the right to all names.

I Am Who I Am

On the ample horizon opened by Richard Kearney, I have chosen, regretting that I cannot choose everything, the chapter dedicated to the oracle of Exodus 3:14. This text is a summit of our Scriptures, impossible to ignore, and lends itself, by reason of its thoroughly enigmatic character, to a multiplicity of interpretations. It has often been observed that the name, especially among the Semites, does not serve merely to indicate an individual who is "that man." It exerts a real power over the one whom it names. Now the true God who speaks to Moses cannot be subjected to such powers. It is because God eludes all claims of power that God transcends all naming and is thus called ineffable. The same exigency that forbids making of God "a graven image, or any likeness of anything that is in heaven above, or that is in the earth beneath, or that is in the water under the earth" (Exodus 20:4), forbids as well all naming. Image and name are equally idolatrous, and thus subject to the iconoclastic imperative.

Meanwhile, it has been established that the title "Yahweh" is derived from the verb *to be* in Hebrew. It appears that between the impossibility of naming God and the necessity of naming him if the relation of the people to their liberator is to be possible, a compromise solution was found in a title as indeterminate as *to be* yet as concrete as the first-person pronoun. Thus "I am who I am" figures as the ceremonious designation that best respects the conditions of possibility of an authentic liberation of Israel and ourselves from "the bondage of Egypt." A God so human that he would scarcely mark himself off from our limits would be incapable, suffering the same misery, of liberating us. Inversely, a God isolated from the world by his transcendence would be condemned to the same impotence. Thomas Aquinas, in his commentary on the Exodus text (cf. *S.T.* I, Q. 13, A. 11), shows a keen grasp of the first condition. The choice of the name "He who is" is justified by the "universality of being" in virtue of a principle he enunciates as follows: "the less names are determined" (or limited), or again, "the more they are common" (or universal), "the more appropriate they are to a speech about God."

The problem, then, is to find an authentic translation of the Exodus text that would satisfy this double condition. That ideal eludes us, however. The known interpretations of the text fall into three orientations: the ontological option, negative theology, and the circumstantial or relational interpretation. On the ontological flank, one should distinguish the Thomist position from the dynamic version of Meister Eckhart. On the steep negative side, we have the already mentioned opposition between those who advocate vaulting toward the heights and those who prefer the untamed depths of the monstrous or the horrible (which are indeed always fascinating). The third approach, the relational exegesis, which Kearney follows, itself leaves a great place to a variety of nuances that are not necessarily incompatible. I note especially distinguished versions that insist, for grammatical reasons, on the future "I will be," rather than "I am." The future expands the horizon of the promise far beyond the present. And this translation makes more sense than to suppose that the people to whom Moses had to deliver the divine name would have been asked to decipher an ontological enigma. The name had to be at once sufficiently indeterminate not to suggest a magical significance and yet very close to a humanly audible and promising voice. The stress on the relational gives space to the different kinds of relation. Biblical language is generous in this respect. It seems to me that the most plausible nuances speak of the fidelity of God to the people he has chosen. The fidelity of active presence is expressed in a language of prepositional inflections: Yahweh is *beside* his people; he watches *over* them; he does not cease to belong *to* them; he is always *with* them (the Emmanuel); and he goes *before* them, thus showing that he is always *for* them.

I cannot summarize the rich pages Kearney has dedicated to this problem of translation. The abundance of notes signals a concern for precise information that is very useful to the reader. Before turning to his development of the third exegetical approach, I should like to return to the exegesis of Meister Eckhart.[4] I have referred to its *dynamism*. Eckhart clearly brooded on the reduplication of the "I am" in the Exodus formula. It could not be a mere tautology or repetition that would issue in the insipid formula A = A. Between the first and the second "I am," there is a distance that is not, and could not be, one of separation. How are we to understand this gap and this proximity? Eckhart's masterstroke is to respect both, no longer in an inert coincidence of opposites but in a movement of self-generation articulated by the verbs that remain (in oneself), proceed from oneself, and effect a return or conversion to oneself. Being, in this translation, is the *act* of being, living, and thinking. God is no longer supreme being and fully constituted; or, more precisely, if one speaks of entity or being in connection with God, it is on condition that both the one and the other are seen as the trace and the result of a fecundity that, following the image of the burning bush, will be named "ebullition": "internal ebullition" on one side and "external ebullition" on the other. This ebullition signifies the springing up of the inner fecundity in a creative expansion. Eckhart transferred to God the two aspects of that bush that burns internally and projects on the world surrounding it the light and heat of its effervescence. Kearney, from his eschatological point of view, seems to have retained two features of Eckhart's exegesis: the themes of the gift and the passage (*GMB*, 36). God gives himself to the point of sacrifice and self-emptying; he is also in continual passage among us, and thanks to us. On that point, the text of a Latin sermon adds what seems to me a very useful detail to the Eckhartian exegesis: "Given that the intellect resolves [all that it grasps] in the light of being, this must be nothing more than a passage [or transit]. . . . For the soul must make a place of transit of God himself, under that name, and indeed under any name, whatever it be."[5] All the names, then, are only sites and occasions of passage for the coming of God on our earth. These names are not only elements of a discourse *on* God. They are of a performative order and not merely constative. Their real task is to "do the truth" by coming "to the light." It is important to conceive of them as historical acts that make God to be, because they *actualize him* as so many events or dynamic emergences of our human and divine becoming. In Kearney's terms, they are active metaphors that inscribe in each epoch of history not just a trace of God, but the exultant emergence of a feast of the Transfiguration.

The third way, as Kearney adopts it, goes beyond both the onto-theology of the theologies of eminence and the meontology of negative theology in its two aspects of trans-ascendance and trans-descendance. Today we are supposed to learn a new fervor from the latter aspect, which arouses a kind of devotion toward monsters or the monstrously excessive. For the more horrible the monsters, the more they fascinate us. Kearney crosses over the ontological and the meontological in a traversal that constantly promotes "eschatological" against the "ontological." If this is accepted, then what will be our final interpretation of the Exodus text, "Ego sum qui sum"?

I wish to note clearly a radical alternative: either one maintains in its full value the "I" of the various translations of the text, or one decides to eliminate it. The first strategy risks taking us back to the radical ontology of which Thomas's *esse subsistens* is the most famous philosophical manifestation. For the "I" of the "I am" expresses, in terms of ontology, the highest degree of being, that is, the person who realizes maximally the perfection of substance as "being in itself and for itself." If one accepts this substantialist interpretation, which is not that of the medievals alone, then it seems that, at the very least, the ontological has priority over the eschatological. For only a being who says "I"—who is a person, in short—can promise and assure for all time a future of liberation thanks to an "I can" of high power, inseparable from an *eminent* "I am," given that action is proportional to being.

In the other approach, the accent is shifted to the eschatological and the divine condition of possible *esse* or *may be*, which tends to minimize the importance of the personal "I." In this case, one might say that the eschatological has devoured the ontological in its highest expression, which is the person implied in "I am," itself accompanied by an unavoidable and dynamic "I can." The person then becomes "persona" in the original literal sense: no longer a being in itself, by itself, and for itself, but a mask to be gone beyond by passing through it, a mask that asks to be treated as a mere place of transit in the energetic sense of Meister Eckhart. Person as mask is a kind of name or enigmatic icon characterized by a *being-toward* incapable of subsisting in itself, and pointing to a distance beyond.

The rejection of the ontological in its eminent form of personhood can in its turn retrieve various strands in tradition. Neoplatonism has accustomed us to transcending the ontological threshold of the person. The One is not someone. One can call it *personne* in the French sense of "nobody," recalling the wiles of Ulysses in his dealings with Polyphemus: "My name is nobody" (in Greek: *outis onoma mou*). Unnameable and omninameable, like "the human soul which has no nature because it is capable, through knowledge, of having all natures,"[6] or like Diderot's actor: "the actor is nothing and everything; and it is because he is nothing that he is everything par excellence."[7]

One can envisage another solution that would make God no longer the personal principle at the origin of the world, but the goal toward which the movement of history would tend. Husserl, dealing with the question tentatively, sketched his own notion of an eschatological God, a purely teleological one, in which God is envisaged as the final goal of human becoming (*GMB*, 84–87, 99). Kearney reviews various positions of contemporary philosophers. But what most interests him is the *possest* of Nicolas of Cusa, which is so close, in appearence at least, to the possible or "may be" God. He affirms anew that God "surpasses and transfigures being," and he sketches a rapid conclusion which I resume in its essentials: a God of radical transcendence; possible in the measure of our faith, but also actively *possibilizing* the messianic events he inspires; a God who never ceases to call us, urging us to personal engagement in the service of his cause; a God whose power-to-be is also his ought-to-be; a power-to-be that has nothing to do with the infinite power of long ago but that nonetheless, *as power of the powerless*—I allow myself to add "weak and foolish," like the crucified Messiah of St. Paul—remains an indispensable factor of the human and divine history that permits his coming; and, finally, a God who "bids us remain open to the possible divinity whose gratuitous coming—already, now, and not yet—is always a surprise and never without grace" (*GMB*, 100), the grace of surprise and the surprise of grace.

What these last remarks reveal is a God who is quite close to the Neoplatonic One-Good, beyond being, and *nothingness par excellence*,[8] which "gives what it has not and what it is not." It is by this withdrawal of kenosis or distance that what is to be becomes possible. Being is the trace of this withdrawal. To illustrate these difficult ideas, we can take the image of the child who says no to its mother, taking its distance toward her and giving itself, by that distance, a being of position and self-position, which is the trace of the distance taken. The paradox of this "power without power" is vividly exemplified in the nonviolence proclaimed by Gandhi, as the withdrawal or emptiness of a distance taken and which has produced liberation as its trace and result, namely, the finally liberated being of India. This nothingness par excellence will have achieved more than all imaginable revolutions. Likewise, a certain silence in face of injury, criticism, or aggression can be more effective than the "tooth for tooth" riposte. The Gospel Beatitudes (cf. Matthew 5) are from this point of view the best illustration of this "power of having no power."

1 *Poetics of the Possible*

The project then, to conclude, is to bring about the arising in our refractory world of a poetics of the possible, which would itself embrace an ethics and, more than that, a spirituality. In his closing chapter Kearney first seeks a "hermeneutical retrieval" of philosophical precedents that might come halfway to meet his own purpose. He examines first the Aristotelian distinction between *nous poietikos* (one dare not translate the Greek adjective by *poetic*) and *nous pathetikos*. The agent's intellect is the source both of the thinkable and of active thought, though it is an anonymous intellect, a kind of universal that cannot exist, because the generic abstraction is a pure abstraction of the mind. Only the singular exists. Moreover, as Thomas Aquinas points out, when there is thinking, it is always *this man (hic homo)* who thinks, who knows, and who judges. One does not think by proxy or in virtue of a "One thinks" or "it thinks" in us, as "it rains in my house." Kearney is, I believe, allergic above all to the receptivity of a purely passive intellect, which would not be very available for active service of the possibles to come from the God who can be (*GMB*, 101–103).

He turns next to Nicholas of Cusa, whom one would have thought more useful because of his *possest,* but who actually blunts the point of it by the fact that he projects onto his God, under the *name* of possibles, all the beings of creation *in the form of possibles*. Existence is anticipated in preexistence, with the effect that the radical newness of the world is diluted into a phenomenon of redoubling (*GMB*, 103–105). Such a possible recalls Bergson's critique summarized above. Kearney takes aim at the idea of predestination or an exemplary plan of things because such a conception annuls the novelty of the world and the creativity of the human subject.

Last comes the Schelling of the *Philosophie der Mythologie*, who discovers a becoming of the divinity in virtue of the passage, thanks to freedom, of essence to existence. The "I am" of Exodus is here in the future tense: "I shall be what I shall be." But the self-causing God, to realize this goal, must conquer, like a hero of mythology, a monstrous resistance, a substrate of dark nature that recalls Plotinian ideas of matter as radical evil. Kearney is only slightly interested in Schelling's exegesis of Trinitarian dogma, and he rejects the abyssal transdescendance toward the monstrous and horrible. However, we should be wary of neglecting the other side, in an apophatic style, which owes much to Plotinus (cf. *GMB*, 159, note 18).

All in all, these references to the past are of less account to Kearney than the recent theme of the divine play or the "play of being" in writings influenced by Heidegger. The cosmic play is not an absolute novelty for those who have read, in the Bible, the book of Wisdom or the writings of the Prophets. The Fathers of the Church did not forget that it is wisdom that, at the beginning of the world, played and danced before the Eternal. The play is not separate from the joy of dancing which is its very essence, of which the generality of philosophers seem ignorant. But the steps of this dance of joy in the play of the world, which formerly celebrated creation as the work of the Father, have become increasingly oriented to the Son and the Spirit, as the Father retires from view. The children that we are, are invited to join in the play and this dance. "This recurring motif of Creation as 'child play' epitomizes, I believe, the eschatological *posse* as both promise and powerlessness" (*GMB*, 107), a powerlessness well marked by Etty Hillesum in *Interrupted Life*: the essential is less to have the assistance of God than to assist God himself. Such is the ultimate meaning of this cosmic and human play, which is the becoming of the Kingdom of justice. The dancing God or Lord of the Dance invites us to enter the *perichoresis* of "an eschatological game of which we are neither the initiators nor the culminators" (*GMB*, 109). "If we cannot master the divine play of the possible, we can partake of it as a gift given to us, a grace that heals and enables" (*GMB*, 110). The *possible*, we recall, is less principle and *arche* than *eschaton* or end in the twofold sense of the word. The possible, thus understood as a humano-divine play, can exist only as poetry in a world become poem.

On the God of Little Things

There are several ways of responding to Kearney's description of the "return to the God of little things," facilitated by what he and John P. Manoussakis call the fourth reduction.

Let me begin with my response as a Christian. I speak first at a prephilosophical level before moving on to some philosophical observations. Jesus' exchange with the Samaritan woman, described in John 4, is for me a revolutionary intervention. Although she would have been considered, in her time, as something of a fallen or marginalized woman, Jesus does not hesitate to engage her in conversation. In answer to her question as to whether one can worship God in a Samaritan temple, Jesus replies that there will come a time when there will be no need to worship in any temple, even in Jerusalem (John 4:23–24). For the "God of spirit and truth," he suggests here, is greater than the God of the Bible in the strict sense, greater than any single tradition. Here he signals to a God beyond the "unique

God" of the Abrahamic tradition—which still functions as a bearer of qualifications and attributes, that is, plays a mathematical role of unicity. Jesus points to the enigma of the Cross, the same enigma that Paul refers to in Philippians when he speaks of the act of "kenosis," wherein God empties himself in order to open up and liberate a new space of relation. In order to become man, God resists the option of paternal divinity out of deference to the son made flesh in the world. The more bows to the less. I would say, then, that the "God of spirit and truth" is less the God of Religion than what I call the God of the Cross—or the God of Faith.

This God—what Kearney calls the eschatological God of little things—resists the attribution of absolute plenitude habitually associated with divinity. We might speak rather of a divine "void" (*vide*) whose very act of emptying creates space for the other. This represents a radical challenge to the traditional theologies of Eminence which viewed God as omnipotent perfection and fullness. The God who renounces eminence no longer lays claims to attributes, to properties, to a nature as such. And it is because it is dispossessed of any determinate nature that we can say that this new God is "beyond every God." Thus what the Cross teaches us, as *kenosis*, as dispossession of every possible possession, is that we must move to a new way of experiencing God beyond God—or, as Kearney and Manoussakis put it, "after God." In this manner we may read the Gospels as a story of God's "mad love" (*amour fou*), as a total renunciation of power for the sake of the least of these, the "void" now expressing itself as *agape*.

At this point, we can point to overlaps between this Christian notion of *kenosis* and certain metaconfessional notions that are, properly speaking, philosophical—such as Platonic and Neoplatonic notions of the Good beyond Being.

This emptiness or self-emptying, which is operative in God from the beginning, is not to be conceived as a pure "lack." It is in fact the *most real* of things. To say this divine void is beyond being is simply to say that it is not an "object" of religion, but rather an event of faith. I understand this distinction as follows: while religion seeks to represent God as a being of plenitude and determination, faith goes beyond religion to the extent that it empties God of all natural or human properties. Faith takes us beyond the religious imaginary. And it is insofar as the Cross responds primarily to faith rather than religion that we can say that it bears witness to an absolute that is, so to speak, "beyond God and Gods."

The *kenosis* also has a very *practical* expression. As we learn in the Gospel according to Matthew, the "last judgment" is the overcoming of religion for the sake of love. It is, remember, not because one went to the temple or recited the credo to a Unique God that one is saved on the last day, but because one loved the least of these. The love of eschatological faith, witnessed here, refers us to an active void—not the passive void of lack or absence or nothing at all—a void which says that "I am beyond being and beings in order that being and beings may be." And here again I rejoin Kearney's reading in *The God Who May Be*. Sometimes I have identified this "unknowable beyond" with the One who is known not by attributes but by effects. It is an act of unifying not to be confused with the "unique" (which, I repeat, is a mathematical function of attributing properties). The One can never be reduced to the "only one." That is the error of unicity setting itself up as an idol of exclusivity and power. An error that is the greatest inner temptation of monotheism. Eschatological faith, by contrast, surpasses being not to abandon or abolish it, but so as to bring it about (*pour le faire advenir*). That is how I read the last words of Matthew 25, in line with Kearney's eschatology of the everyday: namely, as a disclosure of the fact that the true absolute is one that refers us, in total modesty, to the quotidian, which brings us back to the most ordinary and simple acts of feeding the hungry, clothing the naked, giving a cup of cold water to the least of these. It is God himself who says "I was hungry . . . I was naked . . . I was thirsty," and so on. What you did to the least of these you did to me. So what we encounter here is the paradox of a "emptiness by default (*néant par défaut*)—I was hungry (etc.)—revealing itself as an "emptiness by excess" (*néant par excès*)—I go beyond all being so that being may be! Divine emptiness thus becomes identical with divine excess in an act of total self-forgetting and self-giving which enables others to be, to be with one, to be with one another.

Being may be reinterpreted, accordingly—borrowing from Plotinus—as the "trace" of a mysterious presence that cannot be approached conceptually and that expresses itself in the word "I"—an "I" that inhabits every single human being. This is, I believe, the last word of the Cross. That the emptiness of the One, of the absolute, of God, inhabits the deepest interiority and "thisness" of each and every being—to echo Kearney's terms—down to the very last and least of these. Every "I" may thus be said to be the trace of the divine One in every single human other. It is at once an "I" that individuates and an "I" that universalizes, at once particular and exemplary, someone and no one. As when St. Paul confesses, paradoxically, that when this "I" speaks and lives, it is no longer the ego which speaks and lives but "Christ who dwells in me" (Galatians 2:20). One's very self-possession—in the spirit—is a dispossession.

When we say—in keeping with Kearney's micro-eschatology—that God is beyond God, we simply mean that the term "God" has become too human a word, too metaphysical and mathematical a function to capture this sense of the beyond, of excess, of surpassing. That is why faith operates as a perpetual critique of all religious attempts to define and determine the divine in terms of anthropomorphic qualifications. That is what I call the Cross.

The resurrection, which I am sometimes accused of forgetting, might in turn be read not as a sign of metaphysical omnipotence but as part of the cycle of existence lived by Jesus. Jesus died and rose again. And his resurrection should, I suggest, be understood less as a "fact" than a construction. A construction founded on the announcement by a group of women confronted by the disbelief of the apostles—a disbelief based on the fact that the messengers were women (therefore deemed unreliable witnesses in those times). An old wives' tale! And it is also telling that the second "evidence" of the mysterious event of resurrection is to be found in the "touch" of Thomas. The resurrection is witnessed by a double phenomenon of woman's "vision" (nodular) and Thomas's "touch" (corpuscular). A crossing of the optical and the tactile. A double interpretation through sight and touch which already implies a surpassing of these habitual modes of access to material events. Matter, it seems, must be understood in a new way.

The enigma of the resurrection prompts us to ask "What is the real?" What is matter that manifests itself to us—to speak analogically—through the double visage of wave and body? Through the very different registers of nodular frequencies (such as light in air or eddies in a river) and three-dimensional space (solid stuff). The resurrection signals the crossing over and the surpassing of these two indices of matter. For here matter is glimpsed as something still unfinished, as an eschatological mystery beyond all given determinations. In philosophy and science we find recurring echoes of this enigma, for example, in Bergson's insights into matter as *élan vital* or in quantum physics. But as long as we live and think in historical time, we will not have the "last word" on matter.

The resurrection will always be an open book, a question of interpretation. Is the risen Christ a reality or a phantom? For if the Christ who returns from the dead reveals himself according to two ostensibly incompatible representations—through waves that traverse doors and walls and, on the other hand, through the massive presence of a tangible body that sits and eats with his disciples and whose wounds can be touched—we are left with the question, Who or what is this resurrected being? That is why, for me, the crucified and risen Christ remains not a solution but an enduring critical function that puts both theistic and atheistic dogmatisms in doubt. Going beyond both Greek and biblical religions, beyond all claims to omnipotence and knowledge, this is a call to a new faith in a God at once infirm and mad, beyond being and essence—a faith nourished by a *néant actif* that exceeds and defies all worldly powers and puts them into question.

Paul seeks to respond to the enigma of the resurrection by speaking of a "spiritual" or "germinal" body. But a body nonetheless. There are several bodies. First, the "empirical body," which corresponds to our commonsense experience of eating, walking, growing, dying. Second, the "psychic body," which corresponds to what the Greeks understood by *psyche* or *anima mundi*, which links each self to the ensemble of the world. This is related to the idea of a "cosmic body," where an infinity of lines traverse a single point. Finally, we have the "spiritual body," which traverses but transcends beyond both wave and particle, beyond the ondular and the corpuscular, to communicate a radically new kind of experience: a resurrected body. Here we might borrow from the Buddhist notion of the individual trace of someone as a singular "perfume." Not a substance but a scent. The spiritual body of the resurrected Christ might thus be described (again analogically) as the scent left by the acts that Jesus performed during his passage through the world. His residual but real presence which endures after his departure. This is what Paul refers to as the "good scent" of Christ. The balm. The aroma of God after God. And here I am reminded also of the "perfume" of divine love celebrated in the Song of Songs and so powerfully commented by Kearney in the third chapter of *The God Who May Be*.

This raises the question of the "individuality" and "reality" of the risen Christ. He cannot be an individual in the normal sense of the word since he lacks an empirical body. The tomb is empty, after all. But the stories of Christ that remain after him, the *effects* of his acts, the remainder of his life, still left behind him in his wake, comprise a particular scent or signature that is individual and unique and enduring. This is the residual "scent" of the Cross, the enduring aroma of the Beatitudes, the fruit of all those acts of healing and love performed for the least of these. In short, the enigma of the resurrection invites us to think the body—and by extension matter and reality and individuality—in new ways. And what applies to Jesus in this special way, applies to all creatures eschatologically. The resurrection of our bodies on the last day is a way of saying—imaginatively—that after we leave our empirical and psychic bodies behind us, the acts of love and justice that we performed in our lives may live on after our lives—eternally—as an individual scent or signature that endures, as a "spiritual body."

The void of the Cross may be read, in this light, as the signal of a new God, as an invitation or provocation to think the divine differently, otherwise. So that when we think of divine kenosis, we should not think of a God who is full who then decides to empty himself, as if he were stripping off his attributes like articles of clothing—but rather as an attempt to rethink God as before and beyond all determinations. Religion tends to think of fullness where faith thinks of emptiness. Religion always thinks in terms of images, myths, rites, doctrines, whereas faith operates a critical function with respect to religion, an "active no," as it were, which puts all such attributions and qualifications into question and clears a new space for the advent of the divine, ever anew. Not a *passive no* of absence, lack, abolition but an *active no*, like the child who revolts against its parents in order to create space for growth, for a new liberty in which life can flourish again. This is why we might say that the *eschaton* is a way of retrieving the *proton* that religion institutionalizes in rites and laws. The eschatological notion of resurrection may be interpreted as a redemption of original creation, a new return to the beginning, the ever anew. Moreover, the eschatological perspective also links our individual providence to that of the world; it reconnects each unique person with the larger body of community and universality, with humanity as a whole. This is at the root of all the positive utopias that dreamed of a radical transformation of the world, from the early interpretations of the apocalypse to the visionary images of the "Kingdom of the Spirit" envisaged by people such as Joachim of Fiore and Thomas Munster, images that inspired the optimism of revolution and the messianism of hope down through the centuries. But here again we need to temper the zeal of apocalypse—which animates so many religious movements—with the questioning of faith, with that critical vigilance inspired by the emptiness of the Cross. The social body needs to be perpetually interrogated by the spiritual body. The "everybody" of the resurrected mystical body needs to be accompanied by the "nobody" (*nemo/personne*) of the empty tomb. The glorification of the Messiah, in the final resurrection of the last day, can never forget the *nihil* of the crucified one, the shadow of the least and last of these—what Kearney calls the empty space at the heart of God.

To return to philosophy, it is arguably this same tension between the universal and the individual which we find recurring in the famous disputation between Averroës and Thomas on the role of the "active intellect," the latter's position being that universal truths always require to be mediated through the judgments of an individual. It is never "one" that thinks: it is, in each instance, an "I" that thinks. A subject. *Hic homo*. But a *hic homo* who is also potentially a *nemo*. A person who is also a *persona*. A particular somebody who can become a nobody by universalizing his or her particular judgment to embrace truths outstripping the limits of a unique person. This is how the human self can surpass the individual toward the universal without abandoning the former. So the passage to the universal is a way of saying, with Ulysses, "I am no one"—meaning that the objects and aims of the active intellect go behind what is simply "mine" in this particular context here and now to assume a universality which is translatable into a plurality of other languages, contexts, and cultures very different from my own.

The notion of God also epitomizes this interplay between "person" and "persona," a fortiori. The God of Exodus 3:15 who says "I am" is also and at the same time a God who says "I am no one"—I am the one still to come, who will be, who may be. I am someone here and now in the flame of this thornbush but also no one (*nemo*) in the sense that I surpass the specific determinations of this time and place to open up a space for the future, a promise of the possible. "There are many mansions in my father's house" (John 14:2). This is the paradox of the eschatological God explored by Kearney in the second chapter of *The God Who May Be*.

So, I repeat, this eschatological perspective invites us to rethink the *nihil* of divine creation not just as a passive nothing but as an active nothing, not as a mere absence but as an act—an act that creates a space in itself for the other. The God beyond being thereby makes room, from its own void, for all creatures to dwell, to be, to exist. The God beyond being creates being and lets being be.

To return, finally, to the question of the relation between the One and the Unique which has so preoccupied me throughout my intellectual career, I would say this. An eschatology of the Cross might be said to reopen monotheism to polytheism. (And I say this as someone who hails from Christian monotheism.) By recalling the active void at the heart of the divine, and linking this with the Neoplatonic notion of the One that unifies in an absolute sense beyond all particular entities (including the monotheistic concept of God as a sole and unique divine entity), we may liberate theology and religion into an infinity of names. My own theology of the Cross seeks to remind monotheism that God is always in the plural. It argues that God is not just a matter of arithmetical attribution or metaphysical determination, but an operation that unifies itself even as it liberates others into being, allowing each being to be different and unique, individual and specific. This is why I am so taken by John's descriptions of the divine as a "living breath" (*souffle*). We hear its voice but do not know where it comes from or where it goes; and so it is for everyone born of the spirit (John 3:8). For this sees God not in terms of attributes but in terms of effects: those residual perfumes of loving acts. God as breath, breeze, scent.

In this perspective, and it is one that I believe is very close to Kearney's, the kenotic act of God is not conceived as a prior plenitude that annihilates itself but, on the contrary, as a self-emptying of the One—understood as an active void beyond being— into a universe of multiple entities, names, and plentitudes. A positive nothing (*néant actif*) that creates all things. A breathing that gives life to being.

God as breath, breeze, scent

Questions to and from a Tradition in Disarray

JOSEPH S. O'LEARY

"Of all points of faith, the being of a God is, to my own apprehension, encompassed with most difficulty, and borne in upon our minds with most power" (Newman, *Apologia*, chap. 5). The biblical idea of God as Judge and Redeemer is borne in on our minds by moral experience, our sense of sin and desire of forgiveness, and also by religious experience. But the old sturdy confidence in the reality of God as creator of heaven and earth, attested by cosmic order and the very movement of the rational mind, has been depleted. If God cannot be spoken of in a way that chimes convincingly and powerfully with contemporary cosmology, then the notion of God has to be rethought. Some have proposed that God is just another name for "cosmic serendipity" or "creativity." Others invoke a kenotic vision of a God without sovereignty, power, or presence. Others see God language as but one among the conventional paths of traditional discourse that can serve as traces of an ineffable ultimate. Others, in reaction, give up on any effort to think of God apart from the data of biblical revelation, to be received in faith. Since the 1960s, students of theology have acclimatized themselves to a meltdown in talk of God, notoriously exemplified in Thomas Altizer's "death of God theology" and Don Cupitt's "taking leave of God." Now, with the theological turn in French phenomenology, philosophers are venturing where theological angels fear to tread. Unconstrained by exegesis or critical history of dogma, some of these have indulged a hybrid gnosis, best represented by Michel Henry, which has been prejudicial to the integrity of both disciplines. Meanwhile, in the camp of Radical Orthodoxy, theologians have rewritten the history of philosophy with comparable results.

In view of these postmodern phenomena, many lay the blame on those of us who have followed Heidegger in calling for an "overcoming of metaphysics" in theology. This overcoming was variously pursued by Luther, Melanchthon, Schleiermacher, Ritschl, and Harnack, long before the young Heidegger, who—under a strong influence of Luther and Harnack—undertook the "destruction" of metaphysics within philosophy itself in order to recover the integral phenomenality of human existence and of Being. All of these thinkers have sometimes been unjust and contemptuous in their attitude to classical metaphysics. But their project is not necessarily linked to such disrespect, and can, I believe, be retrieved as a "countermetaphysical" rather than antimetaphysical tradition of thought. The diagnosis they share is that metaphysical thinking has overshadowed a more primary kind of thinking, and that the latter needs to be restored to its due prominence. It need not mean that metaphysical theology rested on a mistake.

Taking the first forty-three questions of the *Summa* as the ripest expression of the Christian metaphysical determination of God, the product of a thousand years of disciplined thought, there is no "step back" from metaphysics that could consign this achievement to the dustbin of history. A firm determination of the nature of God, culminating in the Trinity, seems to be a necessity of Christian thought. It is tempting to rest content with the apophasis of Gregory of Nyssa: "It is before all beginning; it provides no tokens of its own nature, but is known only in the impossibility of comprehending it. For this is its most characteristic mark, that its nature is superior to every concept" (*Against Eunomius*, I, 373), which chimes so well with a Buddhist sense of ultimate signless emptiness. But pushed too far, this apophasis makes God indistinguishable from a *khora* of pure indeterminacy of which nothing whatever can be said. The dogmatic tradition, luminously clarified by Aquinas, gives God a profile and anchors talk of God in firm propositions. Hegelians and process thinkers offer an alternative theistic metaphysics, and the intrametaphysical argument can be extended to the dialogue with Islam or Vedanta. But no more than the overcoming of metaphysics can this intrametaphysical debate lead to a radical delegitimization of the orthodox Christian metaphysical determination of the divine.

We can come to a keener awareness of the concrete historical em-beddedness of Christian theistic metaphysics, as "a product of the Greek mind on the soil of the Gospel" (Harnack), and we can regard it as a cultivation of the field of "conventional truth" rather than the ineffable "truth of ultimate meaning," according to the Buddhist the-ory of the twofold truth. Nonetheless, its robust rationality is very well defended both against any challenge on its own terms and against any simple escape from it by a gesture of stepping back to the primary existential phenomena. Metaphysics, as Heidegger well understood, clings to us and will not let us go. Biblical language has considerable countermetaphysical potential. The "I am who I am" of Exodus 3:14, for example, positively repels the classical Platonizing reading that found in it eternity, the truly existent, and so on. The biblical God is primarily one who comes, a saving presence, and con-signs metaphysical definitions to a clumsy, secondary role. Yet a purely biblicist language about God would become rigid and sterile, as happens even in Karl Barth. Metaphysical thought provides a res-ervoir of critical awareness that is useful when, in response to new situations and encounters, we reinterpret or give an altered accent to biblical language about God. It serves as a guard rail against inspired arbitrariness and allows religious innovation to negotiate a responsi-ble continuity with the tradition it disrupts.

When Newman talked of the idea of God as "encompassed with difficulty," he registered the mismatch between the biblical and clas-sical picture of God and contemporary experience, a gulf between the fideistic enclave of the churches and the godless world outside. Intellectual objections increase this malaise, suggesting that the very notion of God in any traditional sense is an impossibility. Apart from the problem of evil, or problems arising from the relation of God to finite beings, the very idea of an eternal, simple, immutable being is difficult to sustain. The riddles introduced by the doctrine of the Trinity are of little account beside the basic riddle of divine simplic-ity, which allows almost nothing to be said of God and which seems incompatible with most of what we do in fact say of God. Divine simplicity was defended by Eleanor Stump in a memorable paper at the 2002 Castelli colloquium on negative theology. Though her de-fense of Aquinas's logic met a chorus of Heideggerian objections, on reading her text in the proceedings (*Archivio di Filosofia*, vol. 70), one has the sense that the austere claims of Aquinas do far more justice to the mystery of God than any of Heidegger's evocations of the divine.

The crisis of classical metaphysical theism can be handled in two ways—by a revisionist metaphysics that attempts to do more justice to the nature of reality as apprehended in contemporary science, or by an existential phenomenology nourished by a hermeneutics of religious traditions. Richard Kearney's discourse is primarily of the latter kind, and like that of his fellow Ricoeurian, Jean Greisch, it has been progressively drawn to the realm of philosophy of religion, a discipline that enjoys a rather amphibolous status between theology and pure philosophy. There is another amphiboly in Kearney's thought insofar as its existential hermeneutics spills over into metaphysical speculation, notably in his ontology of the possible, without the status of the resulting discourse being adequately clarified.

Existential phenomenology offers to "save" God by highlighting certain phenomena that anchor God in human experience—the phenomena of the sacred, of givenness, of the face of the other. But if allowed to unfold on their own terms, without theological interference, these phenomena do not necessarily point to the God of Scripture. Phenomenology places us in contact with a network of numinous phenomena and relations, which may partially confirm and accord with the languages of various religious traditions, but which do not assure any prominence to the idea of God. The space that the plurality of religious languages opens up is what appeals most to phenomenological awareness, and language about God need not have a hegemonic role within that space. There can be religions without God, or with a diffused conception of divinity, or with a virtual God that one can reach out to without affirming as truly existent.

Phenomenology tends to a certain immanentism, "bracketing" any reality that goes beyond the phenomenal, reducing Being to phenomenality, to givenness. The theology it favors is one of event rather than substance, and its God is an existential presence rather than the author of the cosmos. Its "reductions" may be methodological necessities, but they also carry the negative overtone of reductionism. Curiously, the word "reduction" is nowadays used to mean bringing the phenomenon into view in the integrity of its phenomenality; thus Marion's "erotic reduction" signifies the authentic emergence of love between two people. Kearney desiderates what could be called a Zen reduction, whereby one comes in touch with ultimacy by attending to the least of things in its "thusness." I use the word "Zen" here in a nonsectarian sense, to indicate a universal possibility of perception, in the sense in which R. H. Blyth was able to discover Zen in the poetry of Blake and Wordsworth. Heidegger himself, on reading

D. T. Suzuki, claimed that his own thought aimed at the same goal. In the humblest of things, Being comes into play. The Christian will add that in the humblest of things, viewed in its derivation, as a creature, and in its goal, as striving forward to the *eschaton*, the divine comes into play, creatively and redeemingly. But whether this Christian perspective has a nonsectarian, purely philosophical equivalent is unclear. A "reduction" in the Husserlian sense is a founding gesture of "first philosophy," and as such it must be an autonomous philosophical procedure, and cannot draw on extraneous sources, such as the Christian doctrine of the Incarnation. Moreover, a reduction requires rigorous methodological grounding, such as Jean-Luc Marion supplied for his reduction to givenness in his two major works, *Reduction and Givenness* and *Being Given*. Religious vision, whether Buddhist or Christian, may offer an integral view of phenomena that philosophy as such cannot attain. Hegel and Schelling confiscated religious vision lock, stock, and barrel for the cause of philosophy, but the methodological justification of this, both philosophically and theologically, remains controversial. A dialogic relation between philosophy and religious tradition, which constantly marks the distances between them, as in Ricoeur and Marion, is still the most promising way forward.

Khora

Kearney has well identified the major threat to theistic belief today in what postmodern thinkers call the *khora*. This notion, derived from Plato's *Timaeus*, has become the emblem of the postmodern vision, or lack of vision. It represents a world of indeterminacy, with no room for a founding *arche* or an ultimate *telos*. It does not allow, either, a Zen emergence of phenomena in their thusness, much less a Christian vision of phenomena from their origin in divine creation or in their straining toward the eschatological Kingdom. "God" figures in such a world only as the uncanny other or the monstrous. If the *khora* is "after God," it is also "after strange gods." The postmodern sublime is closely associated with the breakdown of meaning. Even when postmodernism becomes pious, the virtual God it reaches out to is not an abundance of possibility, but the Impossible. What the postmodernist means by hope is less a trust in the possible than a wistful fascination with the impossible.

Khora is a catchall expression that evokes such realities as the following: the nocturnal unconscious explored in texts such as *Finnegans*

Wake; Derrida's "archi-writing" in which all efforts to formulate truth are reabsorbed in a milieu of inescapable indeterminacy and undecidability; the Lacanian Real that is repressed by the constructions of the Symbolic order, but that always threatens to reemerge as a blank, mute denial of meaning; the desert of melancholy and ennui. This unmasterable pluralism of associations does not weaken the impact of the notion, but conveys the sense of a convergence of forces, all resulting in a primal landscape that is radically atheological.

Khora is redolent of the ashes of the Holocaust, conceived as a Holocaust of the very idea of God. Some religious thinkers want to cling to a gracious ultimacy, conceived perhaps as "Holy Nothingness" (Richard L. Rubenstein), but feel that after Auschwitz this can be thought only as an elusive possibility, withdrawing as soon as it is glimpsed. They prompt us to ask if all religions were not born of such glimpses of ultimacy, taking a false step when they built doctrines on this basis. The ultimate was borne in on the mind with power, but the step to the noumenal God thought to lie *behind* this encounter led to a barren realm encompassed with thorny difficulties. Philosophers reviewing the Jewish and Christian religious tradition may feel that what they are left with is the ashes of God, a God who cannot be blatantly, brutally affirmed, but who cannot be denied either.

For Julia Kristeva, as Kearney explains in *Strangers, Gods, and Monsters, khora* infuses the signifying process of language with "instability"; it threatens to return the conscious ego back to "its source in the abominable limits from which, in order to be, the ego has broken away" (quoted *SGM*, 195)—namely, the non-ego realm of archaic drive. Perhaps the threat of such regression has a salutary role, and perhaps even the regression itself could have a regenerative function. But basically, the God of Scripture comes into view as confronting this realm, under the appearance of the Law of the Father, and as sustaining the ego (or, rather, the subject a divine call summons into being) in its escape from the dominance of drives.

Slavoj Zizek claims that it was the great breakthrough of German idealism to outline the precise contours of this preontological domain of the "spectral Real": a domain that preexists and evades the ontological constitution of reality. While Kant identified this as the blind, uncanny X which preconditions the transcendental construction of our world, it was Schelling, ghosting Hegel, who took the dilemma by the horns, identifying the *khora* zone as the "divine madness" of the Ground of Existence itself, of that which "in God himself is not yet God." One could put an edifying gloss on this by supposing that this creative indeterminacy within God, the reserve of possibility that is sublated in his actuality, can allow God to be present to the primal chaos, less now as the Law of the Father than as the Spirit "brooding on the vast abyss." God does not treat this realm as abject but reveals an affinity with it insofar as it throbs with creative promise. Joyce's descent to that realm in *Finnegans Wake* could then be seen as a dark path to God.

But Milton's lines continue with the words "and mad'st it pregnant." It is the Spirit that draws out the creative potential of chaos, which otherwise lies waste. *Khora*, writes Kearney, "is neither identical with God nor incompatible with God but marks an open site where the divine may dwell, illuminate, and heal." In the midst of *khora*, God, whether conceived as actual, or virtual, or actual precisely because virtual, is insistently present in the voice of conscience, in the eschatological call of the Kingdom, present as an enabling, empowering May-be.

This affirmation is rather modest, as if tailored to the world of *khora*. Yet it is likely to meet resistance:

> *Khora* is a-theological and a-donational. It eschews the contemporary retrievals of transcendence and mystery—be it the Levinasian idea of infinity (otherwise than being), the Marionesque gesture of donation (God without being), or the Heideggerian principle of event (the gift of being). It is not even a third kind (*genos*) beyond the alternatives of being and non-being. No, it is not a "kind" at all, but a radical singularity of which one might say—what is your name? But then again *khora* cannot even possess a proper name. It is unnamable and unspeakable. And yet, both Derrida and Caputo keep repeating, it is the very impossibility of speaking about *khora* that is also the necessity of speaking about it! (*SGM*, 200)

That sounds rather grim, yet all the writers about *khora* convey the message that the descent to *khora*, like Faust's descent to "the mothers," is a creative process. There is something refreshing and rejuvenating about the encounter with ateleological drives, the raw material of the cosmos, scandalous as they are to all one's conceptions of order and purpose, of articulation and phenomenal presence. Is *khora* not palpable in erotic experience, in dream, in anxiety, and are not all of these domains matrices of creativity? These corners of our existence offer access to a subversive freedom that has an obscure affinity with the highest realms of spiritual freedom, as though one cannot be open to the heights without a proportionate openness to the depths. That is why Derrida, for all his concentration on atheological *khora*, comes across as a religious thinker, and why he feels an affinity with Eckhart and Angelus Silesius, both of whom had mystical transcendence chime with what is closest to hand, with the ebullition of life and desire. For Kearney the issue is one of hermeneutics: "The theistic leap construes our experience in the desert as 'a dark night of the soul' *on the way towards* God," while the despairing postmodernist "sees it as a night without end, a place where religious prayer, promise and praise are *not* applicable" (*SGM*, 203). But the leap of faith must surely be based on recognition of a firmly identified divine dimension that overcomes *khora*. Otherwise it is only a vague reaching after a virtuality, easily reabsorbed in *khora*. Faith may be traversed by moments of doubt where we rejoin the *khora* in its most desolate aspect. Faith, as a perpetual overcoming of doubt, is a perpetual graced decision to view the *khora* as the place where the Spirit of God is at work, a decision confirmed and substantiated by experience of the Spirit's calming and illuminating presence. Some biblical poems delight in evoking the untamed sea monsters writhing about in the primordial dark, in order to celebrate the power of the divine word to bind them.

Kearney refuses to disjoin the life of faith from the "pre-religious and atheistic" experience of the dweller in *khora*. But perhaps a consciousness of *khora* always already entails a certain religious stirring. Religion at its most primordial tunes into such consciousness, sometimes with the use of dreams, drugs, stupefying noises, and erotic images. One could argue that even the most fearful *khora* experience—when murderous drives are allowed to run their course in genocide and other atrocities—is atheistic only in interpretative choice. Certainly, atheism may seem to impose itself, as the fall of a black curtain. But the rhetoric of apocalyptic that evokes the anger of God, the withdrawal of God, God veiling his face, the hour of the powers of darkness, suggests that the total breakdown of meaning can carry a religious overtone. The numbing "banality of evil" resists religious interpretation more sturdily, but it equally resists the abyss of *khora* as "that pre-original abyss each of us encounters in fear and trembling when faced with the bottomless void of our existence" (*SGM*, 204).

Exploration of this realm, seen as corresponding to Lacan's Real, keeps religious thinking from complacent immurement in the Symbolic. Surely there is truth in the suspicion that Aquinas and even

Augustine were "victims of some kind of ecclesiastical closure," as Caputo suggests. That closure was the condition of their powerful role; in deconstructing it today we may release buried virtualities of their thought. However, Derrida seems to resist any such ultimately edifying economy of the relations between *khora* and the vision of faith: "*On one side,* on one way, a profound and abyssal eternity, fundamental but accessible to the messianism in general, to the teleo-eschatological narrative and to a certain experience or historical (or historial) revelation; *on the other side,* on the other way, the nontemporality of an abyss without bottom or surface, an absolute impassibility (neither life nor death) that gives rise to everything that it is not" (Derrida, *On the Name,* 76–77). Kearney comments: "What we have here, in sum, is nothing less than the abyss of God facing off against the abyss of *khora*" (*SGM,* 210). Derrida, however, delights in foiling attempts to lure him into such face-offs. Any choice he would make is immediately stymied by scrupulous remembrance of its apparent alternative. He is open to some aspects of the first way, in that he harbors a certain spirit of Messianic expectancy. But he believes that this cannot be sustained authentically without constant reference to the second way. His "messianicity without messianism" is "a form of vigilant openness to the incoming events of *all our experiences.*" He "refrains from responding one way or another to any particular God-claim." He speaks of the "'spectral' rather than 're-vealed' structure of such incoming" (*The God Who May Be,* 98). It is hard to deny that language about God has become spectral today. It has lost its rocklike status as revealed word or metaphysical fundament and has become something that hovers suggestively, sending out resonances in every direction. This spectrality could be read as the contemporary mode of presence of the Spirit. Yet faith scans the spectrum more fruitfully than a neutral vigilance can, tracing in it a new economy of revelation that goes beyond traditional closures without dissolving the truth those closures preserved.

Phenomenological Aspects

God, the Future

Deconstruction wants to be a dynamic radical opening up of futurity, as if the future were the temporal dimension that best matched its notions of radical undecidability. But if one's present and past coordinates have been thoroughly scrambled, one has no frame of reference within which to interpret the future as a source of novelty or surprise. Teleo-eschatological aspirations are unarmed against the pull of a nontemporal abyss, in which by forsaking the delusions of temporal construction one lives each moment in a perpetual now, savoring the uninterpretable thereness of things as they arise and pass away. This could be mysticism, but could also be mere vacancy and paralysis. Derrida wants to think the future not as a space of abstract possibilities, but as the arising of a concrete ethical challenge, which is at every moment something individual and unprecedented. But like Heideggerian resolve, this attitude is too formal, and what gives it concrete content, such as hospitality to the other, seems arbitrary.

For Kearney, the future is the call of the possible as concretized in the face, or the *persona*, of the other human being, with the aura of future destiny, the promise of transfiguration that it bears. Behind this lies the call of a gracious ultimate, the God who holds open the realm of the possible and promises transfiguration (*GMB*, chap. 1). Kearney's attempt to reimagine God as the Possible appeals to the divine self-designation in Exodus 3:14: "I am who am" (*Ehyeh asher ehyeh*). This echoes *ehyeh chimmak*, "I will be with you" (Exodus 3:12), and can be read as a refusal to give the name that Moses demands, providing instead the redoubled assurance, "I will be as I will be," where "be" has the overtone "be with you." The words *"Ehyeh* has sent me to you" (3.14b) transform the refusal of the name into a name in its own right, suggesting, on the part of the redactor of the biblical text, an (implausible) interpretation of the name *Yhwh*, prominent in the following verse, as the third person of the same imperfective tense of the verb *hayah*, "to be" (see H. Cazelles, in *Dieu et l'Être*, 31, 42–44). If "being" retains throughout this conjugation the overtone "being with you," then both the so-called *nomen essentiae*, *ehyeh*, and the Tetragrammaton itself would here be *nomina misericordiae* like the name that immediately follows: "the God of Abraham, the God of Isaac, and the God of Jacob" (Exodus 3:15).

Eschatology was one of the best-studied topics in twentieth-century theology. The palette of biblical conceptions was thoroughly investigated, and the existential, social, and—to a lesser extent—cosmic significance of biblical eschatology for contemporary Christians was exhaustively discussed. Nothing seemed better to lend definition to the idea of God in the 1960s than talk of "God, the future of man" (Schillebeeckx). A certain eschatological fatigue has befallen the Christian churches of late, confirmed by the regressive hype about the third millennium. Jewish thinkers have imported the

structures of messianism, apocalyptic, eschatology, and the principle
of hope into philosophy, but here, too, these themes seem to have
grown stale. The eschatological imagination now seems to flourish
only in fundamentalist sects. To reground eschatology in the face of
the other, in the tender hopes a father invests in the promise of his
child's future, could be a fruitful way of renewing this tradition.
God's eschatological designs could be rethought from this humble,
human point of departure. The divine fidelity, "I shall be with you,"
takes its sense from our fidelity to one another as we strive toward
the future.

The Advent of Grace

I would like to venture a further step, in the spirit of such biblically
inspired reflection and of the discipline of phenomenology as well,
by suggesting that the phenomenon of God is indiscernible from the
phenomenon of grace. God does not settle into a fixed figure of
being, but is the unobjectifiable power of grace present as creative
possibility in each moment. The withdrawal of God as being opens
up a space of emptiness, of possibility, which empowers and frees our
actions. In *Moses and Aaron*, Arnold Schönberg consigns to a choir the
words God speaks to Moses from the burning bush, as if to consume
rigid, substantial conceptions of divine identity and to free the divine
as Spirit, which moves where it wills and cannot be defined or confined. What mystical writers suggest is that opening up to the presence of the divine, far from bringing an ever tighter grip on God's
identity and on one's own, entails relinquishing the securities based
on conceptual mastery in order to enter into the immediacy of life,
wherein it may seem equally valid to say with the Vedantists: "Atman
is Brahman" and to say with the Buddhists: "No Atman, No Brahman." Here the divine simplicity is not a metaphysical conundrum
but a phenomenological evidence. Metaphysical definitions of God
are a hedge of negative prescriptions set about this encounter. Necessary as they are, they do not close in on the phenomenality of God as
grace.
    Kearney sights the phenomenon of grace in dialectical terms: "the
eschatological May-be unfolds . . . less as a power of immanent potency driving toward fulfillment than as a power of the powerless
which bids us remain open to the possible divinity whose gratuitous
coming—already, now, and not yet—is always a surprise and never
without grace" (*GMB*, 100). The sense of God as one who calls God's

people to action and makes that action possible, underpinned by the phenomenology of *persona* (*GMB*, 9–19) and desire (*GMB*, 53–79), brings God into focus as enabling grace. The focus is sharpened by the biblical paradox that God's strength is manifest in human weakness. "For God everything is possible" (Mark 10:27) is interpreted as follows: "When our finite human powers—of doing, thinking, saying—reach their ultimate limit, an infinite *dunamis* takes over, transfiguring our very incapacity into a new kind of capacity" (*GMB*, 81). Perhaps the best New Testament account of this phenomenon is found in 2 Corinthians: "We have this treasure in earthen vessels, to show that the transcendent power belongs to God and not to us. We are afflicted in every way, but not crushed . . . always carrying in the body the death of Jesus, so that the life of Jesus may also be manifested in our bodies" (4:7–8, 10). God "empowers our human powerlessness by giving away his power, by possibilizing us and our good actions—so that we may supplement and co-accomplish creation" (*GMB*, 108).

This idea takes on a tragic hue in Etty Hillesum: "You cannot help us, but we must help You and defend Your dwelling place inside us to the last" (quoted *GMB*, 108). God's grace works through the freedom of the creatures, never interrupting or suspending it. God's powerlessness is itself enabling, empowering grace (see 1 Corinthians 1:25). The message that "God depends on you" can be an encouraging and empowering one, but if it is misstated, it can conflict with the biblical proclamation of the sovereignty of God. To suggest that God will triumph at the *eschaton* only if we do our part is to undermine the divine promises and lay a crushing burden on humanity. Levinas hails the idea that since God wishes to be dependent on humans, "*I* am responsible for the universe. . . . The world is, not because it persists in being . . . but because by the mediation of the *human* it can be justified in its being" (quoted *GMB*, 135). This way of talking no doubt inculcates a deep sense of responsibility. But is it really empowering and liberating? There is tranquillity at the heart of the life of believers, precisely because they know they do not carry the whole weight of the world on their shoulders. Despite its gloomy history, the doctrine of predestination (especially as rethought by Barth in *Church Dogmatics*, II/2) offers powerful reassurance that God's plans cannot miss their fulfillment: "Those whom he predestined he also called; and those whom he called he also justified; and those whom he justified he also glorified" (Romans 8:30).

Augustine's writings against the Pelagians have made theologians acutely conscious of the dangers of any turns of speech that might suggest that justification and salvation are a matter of human effort rather than divine grace. Even the statement that evil is purely our responsibility would be viewed askance by Augustinians as underestimating the bondage of the will to sin and the need of grace in order to be released therefrom. A synergy between humans and God is not excluded in Augustinian and Lutheran theology, but there is no synergy *in loco justificationis.* Cooperation in God's saving work is a blessing consequent on the free gift of justification. (That the strictures of the Tridentine Decree on Justification do not signify major discord on this point is confirmed by the 1999 Catholic-Lutheran agreement, whatever its theological merits.) Proverbs such as "God made the sea, we make the ship" (*GMB,* 4) could easily lead one to the Pelagianism that says: "Christ has done his part, now you do yours!" or, even more depressingly, "Christ cannot do his part unless you do yours!"

Defining grace has been a matter of life and death for Christian theology, for without a clear and telling account of how God is present as a saving God, the entire Christian discourse would flounder in impotent indeterminacy. The Lutheran dialectic of divine judgment and mercy gave a powerful account of how God works in our lives, and the Tridentine system also established a concrete profile of the operation of grace in Roman Catholicism. We lack any comparable concrete understanding of grace at present. The idea of an empowering God, who works through weakness, could be extended to embrace the course of evolution and the tragedies of history, bringing the confidence that at every moment humans face the divinely sustained horizon of the Possible, and can find therein resources of strength to tackle their cocreative task anew.

The Quiet Power of the Possible

Kearney seeks to accord the "power of God" with the Heideggerian idea, expressed in the third paragraph of the *Letter on Humanism,* that Being is to be thought of as the "quiet power of the possible," which is higher than actuality. This loving potency is that whereby beings are able to be. "From this loving, being has the capacity of thought. The former makes the latter possible." (*Aus diesem Mögen vermag das Sein das Denken. Jenes ermöglicht dieses*). Heidegger explains that "to be capable of something" (*etwas vermögen*) means to produce it in its essence, that is, to allow it to be. It is being that allows thought to be, and only when it abides in being does thought attain its essence. Whereas Heidegger stresses thought's dependence on being, Kearney asserts a reciprocal dependence of being on thought: "to love-possibilize Being in return by thinking things and selves in their authentic essence" (*GMB*, 92). Heidegger talks of a double genitive, the thinking of being, as referring to the fact that being owns thought and that thought thinks being, as it accords itself to that to which it belongs. Kearney's double genitive introduces an inflection that goes beyond Heidegger: "The possibilizing of being . . . refers both to Being's loving-possibilizing of thought and thought's loving-possibilizing of Being. . . . Being possibilizes thought which possibilizes Being" (*GMB*, 92). This mutual dependence is less disturbing than in the case of the biblical God, since the phenomenon of being cannot become manifest unless there are thinkers to apprehend it. Nonetheless, while the idea of a reciprocity between being and human *Dasein*, as with the idea of a reciprocity between God and humankind, is attractive, in both cases one should not gloss over the asymmetry of the relationship, the primacy of being over thought, and of divine initiative over human response.

In Heidegger, the graciousness of being as what enables the essence of humanity needs to be recognized if we are to think worthily of the gods or of the supreme God when they make their appearance. All philosophers who deal with religion formulate imperatives and criteria, which they claim that religion and theology must meet, be they rational, ethical, or, in this case, phenomenological. The gracious givenness of being is a phenomenon recognized by poets such as Hölderlin and Wordsworth and by Zen meditators (who often express themselves in poetry or painting). It does not preempt or forestall the biblical God's eschatological call. There is nothing pagan or idolatrous in Heidegger's insistence that this is a reality that any religious vision must respect, and which will help assure the integrity of religious vision. What is unacceptable, and justifies Marion's Barthian strictures, is the edict that God cannot be known until the sacred emerges, and that this emergence requires a long preparation in which we learn to experience being in its truth. While I do not think that Heidegger sacralizes being as such, in "a sacred-sounding liturgy of love and grace" (*GMB*, 92), or "equates the essence of Being with the 'sacred' and the 'divine'" (*GMB*, 93), there is an interference of the ontological and the sacral that is deleterious to both. Kearney cites Heidegger's "analogy of proportionality" between ontology and theology as evidence for the crypto-theological character of his thought, but this is not such a good target, since it is intended to mark the autonomy of the two disciplines: "A is to B as C is to D. As philosophical thinking is related to being, when being speaks to thinking, so faith's thinking is related to God, when God is revealed in his word" (Robinson and Cobb, *The Later Heidegger and Theology*, 43). Heidegger assumes that there must be an analogy of some sort between the quest for Being and the quest for God, as indeed the entire Western tradition does, but he seeks to differentiate the two for the welfare of both. Kearney sees Heidegger as dismissing any idea of a saving God, but in reality, when Heidegger speaks of a "last God" who does not "redeem" us (for that would reduce human dignity) but restores us to the authenticity of our being, he remains in dialogue with Christianity, calling on it to formulate its doctrines in a manner more respectful of the texture of human existence and of Being as his philosophical thinking apprehends it.

The Open

It should be possible to give a phenomenological account of the mode of God's presence in human existence and in history, as registered exemplarily in the Bible. Such an account finds a more promising basis in "the quiet power of the possible" or in a Blakean sense of God as "a shout in the street" than in rigid representations of the divine substance or hypostasis. If we empty out the inherited God languages of all delusory stabilities and identities, then that to which we reach out in using the word "God" becomes a space of potentiating withdrawal. To say that "God deconstructs" (*GMB*, 124, n. 32) means that the ultimate sets off a deconstructive ferment in our thinking and imagining, one in which received notions of God are relativized. In addition, it would suggest that we know God only in the constant deconstruction of our language about God, a deconstruction always already afoot in language itself, for instance, in the taut simultaneity of advent and withdrawal in the statement "I will be who I will be." Much of this mirrors the Buddhist apprehension of reality as an emptiness that leaves the grasping mind no place in which to settle (least of all by fixating on the notion of emptiness itself). Many have seen Buddhist emptiness as coming to the rescue of our tottering Western conceptions of God, and it may be augured that a comprehensive phenomenology of divine presence as a space of possibility will be increasingly informed by Buddhist themes.

Metaphysical Possibilities

Although *The God Who May Be* is an essay in phenomenological hermeneutics, there are many points at which it offers statements on the nature of God that ask to be read as metaphysical. Even the basic thesis of a God who "neither is nor is not but may be" can scarcely be confined to the level of phenomenological observation. Even interpreted as a straightforward metaphysical statement, "God may be" can produce quite a respectable lineage in classical metaphysics, and if we teased out the phenomenological potential of the statement and its analogues in the tradition, we could reconstitute a rich phenomenology of divine possibility that has been quietly brewing over the centuries in classical metaphysical texts, at least since Plato's meditation on the Good "beyond being."

A certain precipitation in Kearney's essay may limit its power to stimulate such a research project. The subversive potential of Eckhart, Cusanus, and Schelling is not enhanced by denunciations of mainstream metaphysics, as in the claim that the idea of divinity as pure act involves the characterization of evil as "the pre-established will or destiny of God" (*GMB*, 5). A classical metaphysical answer to this objection might begin by pointing out that being is inherently good, and that evil is a mere privation of being. When Augustine defines evil as the privation of good, that is a strictly ontological statement. It does not refer to "a *lack* or *absence* of God" who "removes mayhem and misery from the eternal design" (*GMB*, 104). That would be a lack of providence (which is never lacking in Augustine's world). But neither providence nor the divine omnipresence removes evil. The role of providence is not to eliminate evil, but to order evils to the good. To say that evil "is the absence of God, the lack of divine goodness (*privatio boni*), the consequence of our refusal to remain open to the transfiguring call of the other *persona*" (*GMB*, 5) is to read a metaphysical statement as an existential or phenomenological one, in a way that short-circuits the reception of the metaphysical tradition. A question stirring beneath the surface is whether phenomenology is best located within the horizon of metaphysics or whether the realm it opens is intrinsically irrecuperable by metaphysical reason. Perhaps Kearney would make the latter claim, while at the same time calling for a reformed metaphysics that would have a valid secondary role.

One metaphysical interpretation of the phrase "the God who may be" is the agnostic one: God may be and he may not be; we just don't know. When Kearney uses Kantian language about the conduct of the ethical life in view of a teleological Good that is only "a postulate of reason" realized in a "possible kingdom of ends" (*GMB*, 85), it looks as if ethical conviction is in inverse proportion to metaphysical certitude, as if one can be truly responsible only if one has no independent assurance that the postulated grounds of one's responsibility have, or will have, any solid existence. However, the manner in which the notion of God presents itself in Kearney's thought excludes simple agnosticism. When he says that God "may be," he is not using the expression in the way one would use it of an ordinary thing ("there may be scissors in the drawer") or even of such things as ghosts, life on other planets, black holes, or subatomic particles, in regard to which the category "really exist" may begin to wobble slightly. Rather the "may" is intrinsic to divine being as the very mode of its presence as empowering call. In general, the question whether or not God exists is a very unsatisfactory one to anyone who has reflected on the ideas of "necessary being" or "infinite being" or "transcendent ground of being" or "being itself subsisting." To ask whether such realities exist seems almost a contradiction in terms; such "essences" seem to imply their own "existence." It is on that unease that the various forms of the ontological argument have thrived. The question of God's existence changes under our gaze into the question whether these designations of ultimate reality make sense; once we become involved in that question, we can never come back to the "yes or no?" mentality of the conventional believer or the village atheist.

Plotinus can count as a source for a metaphysics of God as *posse* if we translate the *dunamis pantôn* of *Enneads* V, 3, 13 as "potency of all." The supreme power of the One would reside in the fact that it is the possibility of all else. Plotinus might thus agree that "it is divinity's very potentiality-to-be that is the most divine thing about it" (*GMB*, 2). However, it is unlikely that Plotinus is using the word *dunamis* in the Aristotelian sense, for this would entail that the One is somehow lacking or incomplete, and needs the lower orders of being for its full actualization. If there is a hint of potentiality in the One, it is a potentiality fully realized, for the One is supreme actuality (*energeia*), albeit an actuality beyond being, a *hupostasis* without *ousia*. A Neo-

Kantian, such as Paul Natorp, whom Heidegger revered, might say that it is more *Sollen* than *Sein,* and that supreme reality is not the crass thereness of the "is," but the dynamic attraction of the "ought." With some hermeneutic violence, then, one might dragoon Plotinus into the camp of the May-be God.

Enneads VI, 8 is the paradoxical pinnacle of Plotinus's apophatic thinking, paradoxical in that it offers a positive teaching on the self-relation of the One, characterized as *causa sui,* a teaching qualified by the recurrent expression *hoion* (so to say). In this tractate, the *causa sui* is primarily associated with the autarchy of a supremely free agent, but the warrant for this is found in the idea that he is as he wills to be: "If then there is nothing random or by chance . . . in the things which have their cause in themselves, and all things which come from him do have it, for he is the father of reason and cause and causative substance . . . he would be the principle and in a way the exemplar of all things which have no part in chance . . . cause of himself (*aition heautou*) and himself from himself and through himself" (*Enneads* VI, 8, 14 [35–42]). Though "it is impossible for something to make itself and bring itself into existence" (*Enneads,* VI, 8, 7 [25]), nonetheless "it is he himself who makes himself and is master of himself" (*Enneads* VI, 8, 15 [9]); "he gives himself existence (*hypostêsas hauton*) . . . he is an actualisation (*energêma*) of himself. He is not therefore as he happens to be but as he acts (*energei*) . . . he as it were makes himself and is not as he chanced to be but as he wills . . . he brought himself into existence . . . he is as he woke himself to be . . . his being comes by and from himself. He is not therefore as he happened to be, but he is himself as he willed" (*Enneads* VI, 8, 16). In Proclus, the concern with self-grounding becomes systematic to an almost Hegelian degree, but it concerns entities below the One, and Plotinus's talk of an *absolute* self-grounding is rejected: "If the Good be self-constituted (*authupostaton*), producing itself it will lose its unity. . . . The self-constituted must exist, but posterior to the First Principle" (*Elements of Theology,* prop. 40, trans. Dodds).[1]

The discourse of the *causa sui* is an attempt to give some definition to the idea of God. The ineffable, ungraspable One had become a blank space into which the Gnostics could project all sorts of fantasies. Despite the firm rejection of this idea in Christian philosophy— Augustine begins his *De Trinitate* with an attack on it—it plays a role similar to that played by the Trinity in fixing the identity of God. Both ideas confirm the sovereign self-sufficiency of God. However, it is a mistake to use "self-causing" as a synonym of "self-existent," as in the reference to "the Aristotelian and scholastic deity" as "a self-causing, self-thinking Act lacking nothing and so possessing no 'potencies' which might later be realized in time" (*GMB*, 83). In fact, the effort to find a dimension of possibility in God can be aligned with the *causa sui* tradition, not in its crudest form, wherein God is his own efficient cause, but in the sense that God's essence is the formal cause of his existence, his possibility the precondition of his actuality.

Kearney sees the metaphysics that banishes potency from the pure act of divine being as sterilizing the idea of God. However, those repelled by the starkness of Aquinas's thesis, *Deus est purus actus non habens aliquid de potentialitate* (I, q. 3, a. 2), may find some comfort in the fact that Aquinas's discourse on the divine simplicity proceeds under the sign of the negative. "Because we cannot know of God what he is, but what he is not, we cannot consider the manner in which God is, but rather the manner in which he is not" (I, q. 3, prologue). Questions 3 to 11 of the *Prima Pars* offer, then, not a positive account of divine attributes but a denial of any attributes that would imply lack of simplicity, perfection, goodness, or unity in God or the limitations of temporality, location, or change. However, Aquinas treads a narrow rope, perhaps falling into self-contradiction, for he rejects Maimonides' view that the names of God are "devised rather to remove something from God than to posit something in him" (I, q. 13, a. 2). A biblical retrieval of Aquinas might relocate these philosophical wrestlings within the phenomenology of the individual or collective encounter wherein God is addressed by or announces the divine name. Some argue that a Thomist may speak of God's *active*, as opposed to his *passive, potentiality*. Barth, in *Church Dogmatics*, paragraph 29, corrects the rigidity of the doctrine of divine simplicity and attempts to retrieve it for a biblical account of God as "the one who loves in freedom" (perhaps having his cake and eating it, too).

Reminiscent of Plotinus's supreme *dunamis*, which is also supreme *energeia*, is the *possest* of Cusanus, "absolute possibility which includes all that is actual." The One is the power/possibility of all things, just as Cusanus's God is "all things *complicite*," "all things are enfolded (*complicari*) in the *possest*" (*De Possest* [1460], 9 and 16; ed. Steiger). Aristotelian and Scholastic traditions forbid Cusanus to call God *causa sui*, but he captures some of the dynamic of that idea in teaching that God "is what he is able to be" (*GMB*, 37). Every being is first of all a capacity to be, and God's being is his fully realized capacity to be. Cusanus sees God as the conjunction of opposites: absolute possibility and absolute actuality. Possibility and actuality fully coincide in God, whereas in finite beings actuality is always only a partial realization of possibility. Thus Cusanus can talk of God as the fullness of possibility in a way that does not impugn divine simplicity, but rather supports it, just as Aquinas's teaching that being and essence are one in God does. Cusanus aimed at nothing less than the creation of a new divine name, which would yield "the most pregnant and packed concept possible to express the image of God, and at the same time the relation to the world and the understanding of being in general" (Brüntrup, 15).

Stronger support for God as *posse* is found in the final treatise of Cusanus, *De Apice Theoriae* (1464), which abandons the word "being" and describes God as "the *posse* itself," "the *posse* of all *posse*." All actualized beings are now described as mere appearances of the *posse*, which is the supreme reality: "All beings (*entia*) are nothing but the various modes of appearance of the *posse* itself" (*De Apice*, 9). "Nothing can be added to the *posse* itself since it is the *posse* of all *posse*. Therefore the *posse* itself is not the *posse* of being or the *posse* of living or the *posse* of intellect, or any other *posse* with some addition. . . . A *posse* with some addition is an image of the *posse* itself" (*De Apice, Memoriale* I, 17; IV 20). Perhaps this version of Cusanus's thought is better cushioned against the charge of "mystical pantheism" that Kearney brings against the earlier account of God as already containing all that exists (*GMB*, 104–105). The absolute possible incommensurably transcends all finite possibles. Neoplatonic thinking on the One is now seen as foreshadowing this discovery of God as *posse*: "Those who affirmed that there is only One looked to the *posse* itself; those who said that there are One and Many looked to the *posse* itself and to the many modes of being of its appearance" (*De Apice*, 14). This *posse* beyond being replaces the *possest* as the supreme name of God (see Cranz). Cusanus reached this position by meditating on the nature of God that he initially determined as *possest*: "It is within his adumbrations of the notion of God themselves that there comes about the displacement of emphasis from *possest*, *by way of the posse facere* (*posse* as dynamic creativity, in *De Venatione Sapientiae*, 1462), to the *ipsum posse* (the *posse* of being, in the *Compendium*, 1463–1464), and finally to the *posse ipsum*" (Brüntrup, 113). *Posse* is the "absolute presupposition" of everything else: one does not walk unless one *can* walk, one is not unless one *can* be. Even radical Cartesian doubt would presuppose that one *can* doubt (Brüntrup, *Können und Sein*,

117). God is nothing other than the absolute "Can" that grounds every other "can" and that itself needs no ground.

Descartes revived the notion of *causa sui* in his first and fourth *Responsiones*, which Marion sees almost as the charter of modern rationalism. Marion's teacher, Ferdinand Alquié, comments: "The theory of Descartes amounts to subjecting God to causality. . . . The Spinozan conception of a self-caused God, modern conceptions of a God who makes himself, or even of a God who makes himself in the becoming of the world, have here their first source. With something like a presentiment of genius, Arnauld seems to perceive this" (Descartes, *Oeuvres philosophiques II*, 646). That is a somewhat livelier picture of the *causa sui* than Heidegger presents in *Identität und Differenz*, where it becomes a death's head that chills religious sentiment and imprisons the thinking of being. Some of Kearney's statements, read metaphysically, are close to this modern theory of "a God who makes himself in the becoming of the world"; "there is a free space gaping at the very core of the divinity: the space of the possible. . . . Transfiguring the possible into the actual . . . is not just something God does for us but also something we do for God. . . . God depends on us to be" (*GMB*, 4). Read phenomenologically, that might mean only that human beings can cooperate with God in making God more fully present in the creation. But references to Schelling and to Whitehead's idea of God's consequent nature, "a reservoir of possibilities to be creatively realized as world" (*GMB*, 123), invite a metaphysical reading.

The following statement is reminiscent of process philosophy: "God may henceforth be recognized as someone who *becomes with us*, someone as dependent on us as we are on Him" (*GMB*, 29–30). Process philosophers have revived the Greek idea, shunned in the orthodox tradition, of a developing God. We recall Plato's words in the *Timaeus* to the effect that "the Creator, in creating the world, creates himself; he is working out his own being. Considered as not creating, he has neither existence nor concrete meaning." Whitehead could say in his *Process and Reality*, "It is as true to say that God creates the World, as that the World creates God" (1978 ed., 348). Kearney calls for a "radical rethink *sub specie historiae*" (and, one might add, *sub specie evolutionis*) of "the orthodox onto-theological categories of omnipotence, omniscience, and self-causality" (*GMB*, 30). But such a rethink might go in the opposite direction to the one that process thinkers feel obliged to take. That is, the adventure of evolution and of historical human freedom, possibilized and teleologized by the attraction of the transcendent ultimate we call God, might be left much more to its own devices, with God acting generally as the *dunamis pantôn* without regulating and foreknowing in total detail the course of the creative adventure. Rather than "giving away his power" (*GMB*, 108), God may operate in the only way consistent with the nature of a universe in evolution, as Teilhard suggested. At each moment, God remains what God always is, infinitely gracious power, in no way dependent on what comes into being in response to it and in radical dependence on it. One reflection that may make us uneasy with this conception of God is that it seems to belong to an older world in which the changeless stars imaged the divine. Today's dynamic universe, in which even the stars are in a state of ebullition and flux, is very different from the one in which a supreme immutable could be imaged as "the love that moves the sun and the other stars" (Dante), and it has become a pressing task to rethink God *sub specie cosmologiae actualis*.

Where Kearney tends to favor a remythologization of philosophical God language by drawing on biblical sources, I would advocate the equal importance of demythologizing the Bible's highly charged anthropological language. A cooler philosophical vision of God as a transcendent principle of justice can retain the substance of the biblical vision and allow an enlightened redeployment of biblical rhetoric. The historical struggle for justice would still be a divine matter, and those involved in it would have to be in accord with divine truth and power, a sufficient basis for the biblical notions of the covenant, the chosen people, and the jealous, vulnerable God. As for the New Covenant, one can see it as human attunement to a special depth of the divine justice, manifest as the forgiveness of sins. "God was in Christ reconciling the world to himself" (2 Corinthians 5:19) would be less a matter of an anthropomorphically conceived divine initiative than of a threshold in the evolution of religious consciousness, centered on the figure of Jesus, who thus emerges as the divine Word spoken into history not merely as the law of justice but as the fullness of grace and truth (John 1:17). The ups and downs of a few thousand years of humankind's graced efforts to attune to the ineffable ultimate certainly provide precious testimony to the presence and action of the divine, and even what can be called revealed knowledge of God. But the abuse of the divine name by crusaders, inquisitors, and warmongers has made us suspicious of any immediate harmony between the divine and historical forces, even religious ones. Instead, the text of history offers us a chiaroscuro flickering with suggestions of divine meaning, a meaning we affirm in trust without being able to read it off. The God who thus hovers and flickers, a gentle breeze blowing where it will, indeed invites a name that is "beyond Being"—the name of the Possible. But perhaps the divine eludes that name too, at least as much as it eludes the name of Being.

Any contemporary discourse about God is bound to be afflicted with a certain unsteadiness. To navigate our way skillfully, we need to cleave to the spirit of biblical language while purging it of what has borne evil fruit, and we need to respect the labors of philosophical and theological minds who have sought to draw from that language of faith its full yield of rational intelligibility. These disciplines, however, cannot substitute for a creative renaming of the living God as encountered in a new way in present circumstances. Here the philosopher and theologian must cede to the prophet, and to the community of engaged believers. God does not depend on them in order to be God, but God is named, known, and glorified in them, if they have the tact and courage to "let God be God." Whatever the strictly philosophical merits of relational and incarnational thinking, it is surely right to think that God is best known when believers create an agapeic culture, enfleshed in the works of love. Such a God need not worry about stealing the limelight or being properly defined. He is "borne in upon our minds with power" by the radiance of the "divine milieu" that the loving and hoping community brings into being or, rather, that makes such a community possible.

a God who hovers & flickers

Mystic Maybes

KEVIN HART

I.

Matthew Arnold "objected to our carrying on a flirtation with mystic maybe's and calling it Religion."[1] Why should Augustine Birrill's words, occasioned by the death of Arnold, come to mind when I read Richard Kearney's *The God Who May Be?* Perhaps because Arnold and Kearney share a common purpose: dissociating metaphysics and the Bible. In *Literature and Dogma* (1873), Arnold seeks to show us that "when we come to put the right construction on the Bible, we give to the Bible a real experimental basis, and keep on this basis throughout."[2] In so doing, he thinks, we distance ourselves from metaphysics: we do not have to base our faith on an "unverifiable assumption to start with, followed by a string of other unverifiable assumptions of the like kind, such as the received theology necessitates" (*LD*, 151). Over a century later, and responding to different pressures, Kearney tells us that he proposes to explore and evaluate "two rival ways of interpreting the divine—the *eschatological* and the *onto-theological*" (*GMB*, 1). The latter yields the God of metaphysics, while the former, which Kearney warmly endorses, "privileges a God who possibilizes our world from out of the future, from the hoped-for *eschaton* which several religious traditions have promised will one day come." Where is this eschatological deity to be found? In the Bible, Kearney assures us, and he analyzes four biblical passages—

Moses and the burning bush, the transfiguration of Jesus on Mount Tabor, the Shulamite's Song, and God's pledge in Matthew 10 — to justify his claim. Like Arnold, Kearney has no doubt that the language of the Bible is literary, not scientific. Or, more precisely, he holds that the Bible is best approached by way of narrative theology rather than metaphysical theology.

For Arnold, what remains of the Bible once we submit it to the higher criticism is a canon of literary texts that are capable of improving us morally. Religion is mostly about our behavior in the world. Christianity is not essentially a matter of believing in the coming of the Son of Man, miracles such as the Incarnation and the Resurrection, and the triumph of the saints. That is just so much *Aberglaube*, "extra belief," and, quite frankly, no modern person can possibly credit it, Arnold argues. He agrees with Goethe: *der Aberglaube ist die Poesie des Lebens*, "extra belief is the poetry of life" (*LD*, 212). Those fairy tales are beautiful, and so long as we do not mistake their metaphors for literal truths, they can aid belief. Yet "it is impossible even to conceive Jesus himself uttering the introduction to the Fourth Gospel; because *theory* Jesus never touches, but bases himself invariably on experience" (*LD*, 297). Arnold's speculations about religion are loosely grounded in critical philosophy and, accordingly, they tell us next to nothing about God. We intuit something "not ourselves," he readily admits, for which insight we must thank the Jews, but this revelation is only "needed to breathe emotion into the laws of morality" (*LD*, 215). Arnold is far more interested in Jesus than Kant ever shows himself to be, for Christ transforms "the idea of righteousness," and "to do this, he brought a *method*, and he brought a *secret*" (*LD*, 286). Christ's method is repentance, and his secret is dying to the world and affirming the Kingdom of God.

Like Arnold, Kearney is also interested in the Kingdom that is to come, regarding the Bible as fundamentally orienting us to ethics, and he, too, is less than easy with the dogmas of the Church. Listen as he answers the question *D'où parlez-vous?*: "Religiously, I would say that if I hail from a Catholic tradition, it is with this proviso: where Catholicism offends love and justice, I prefer to call myself a Judeo-Christian theist; and where this tradition so offends, I prefer to call myself religious in the sense of seeking God in a way that neither excludes other religions nor purports to possess the final truth. And where the religion so offends, I would call myself a seeker of love and justice *tout court*" (*GMB*, 5–6). An unfriendly critic might quip, "Here I stand, but I can do other," or cite William of St. Thierry on those who equivocate about the faith: "They do not say: *yes, yes, no, no,* but whisper: *maybe, maybe*! Maybe it is so, they say; maybe it is not! Maybe it is otherwise; maybe it is otherwise than written—on account of something that was not written down."[3] I prefer to note how fully Kearney has digested the nonreligious interpretation of Christianity that started with Kant and has been inherited and variously inflected by Bonhoeffer, Levinas, and Derrida. Kearney, like Arnold, affirms experience over metaphysics and prizes the Bible for its exemplary narratives, its surplus of metaphoricity, and its prophetic cries for justice.

In contrast to Arnold, however, Kearney has the makings of a doctrine of God in his work. Where the Victorian dismisses eschatology as so much *Aberglaube*—the disciples put "their eschatology into the mouth of Jesus," he thinks—the postmodern makes it central to his faith (*LD*, 260). Kearney's doctrine of God begins to come into focus when we regard the deity as between ontotheology and negative theology or, as he also says, between being and non-being. I should say in passing that I do not think that a negative theology is ever a theology in itself; it is always braided with a positive theology. And I should also say that negative theologies do not construe God as non-being: in their different ways they indicate how the deity exceeds metaphysical determinations of being. That said, Kearney's doctrine of God is what he calls "metaxology," the study of what lies between extremes. This new *via tertia* is also a "dynamatology," a study of fresh possibilities, as well as a metaphorology: it develops not through speculation, but by attending to the surplus of metaphor in biblical stories. Most important, it is an onto-eschatology: "God, who is traditionally thought of as act or actuality, might better be rethought as possibility" (*GMB*, 1).

On the face of it, this claim is an odd way of introducing us to a nonmetaphysical understanding of God. After all, talk of possibility has been an enduring theme of metaphysics since Aristotle; and since the twelfth century philosophers have devoted considerable attention to it, Duns Scotus being not the least of them. How does Kearney rethink God as possibility? Not by urging us to conceive God by way of objective possibility, that is, by pointing out that there are no conditions, such as Sartre believed there to be, that prohibit the existence of the Judaic-Christian God. Not by pondering subjective possibility, that is, by proposing the deity will act in some ways rather than others. Kearney is also not especially interested in making it clear whether he is talking about contingency or possibility as such, an ambiguity in Aristotle's sense of "possibility" that John of Salisbury exposed in his *Metalogicon*.[4] Indeed, Kearney does not even discuss God in terms of a distinction between possibility and reality, building upon the labors of Suárez, Leibniz, and several modern logicians, not to mention a handful of contemporary theologians.

Kearney's *The God Who May Be* is a series of suggestive papers, not a treatise, and that must be realized before deciding the appropriate level of detail and rigor that one can properly ask of the author. And so I leave aside those moments when Kearney's understanding of the history of philosophy and theology seems somewhat imaginative. Kearney writes in order to intervene in debates about God rather than to establish a systematic account of the deity, and he uses the tradition solely to that end. As such, when he considers the concept of the possible, he briefly recalls the classical and medieval discussions with a view to developing a nonmetaphysical understanding of possibility in dialogue with the European thinkers to whom he is closest: Husserl, Heidegger, Ricoeur, Levinas, Derrida, and Marion. This nonmetaphysical sense of the possible has been on his mind since he was a graduate student working with Paul Ricoeur, as the published version of his dissertation, *Poétique du Possible* (1984), reminds us. However, when drawn to the Middle Ages, he responds to Nicholas of Cusa rather than John of Salisbury, to mysticism rather than logic, and when he reads the Bible, he finds eschatology before he finds conduct. Perhaps this is why Augustine Birrill's expression "mystic maybe's" comes to mind when I am reading *The God Who May Be*. If so, Kearney is at least as much unlike Arnold as he is like him.

I will return to that theme a little later, since it is important to stress and assess the experiential dimension of Kearney's hermeneutics of religion. For now, though, I would simply like to understand the teasing expression "the God who may be." The expression is a free translation of Nicholas of Cusa's *possest*—a word he creates by fusing *posse* and *est*—and Kearney aligns himself with Cusanus largely to distance himself from Aquinas. It is Thomas who, developing Aristotle, construes the deity as pure act without possibility (*Summa Theologiae*, 1, 3, 1c). The position is familiar—a little too familiar, perhaps—since a close reading of the *Summa Theologiae* will reveal a wrinkle in the text: Thomas admits that there is an "active potentiality" in God that is grounded in the pure act (*ST* 1, 25, 1c).[5]

Having distinguished Cusanus from Aquinas, perhaps a little too quickly, Kearney also distances himself from the mystic of possibility. The cardinal's preferred name for God, he thinks, is complicit with "a theodicy not altogether different from that later espoused by Hegel or Leibniz" (*GMB*, 105). Consequently, the question "of human freedom and creativity as a way of participating in the transfiguring play of creation" is foreclosed. Only an eschatological understanding of God will keep that question alive, Kearney thinks. Prophetic eschatology? Realized eschatology? Historical eschatology? Divine eschatology? The theologian used to thinking in these terms will have to extend the principle of charity across the board when reading *The God Who May Be* because Kearney does not attend to these distinctions.

I can best clarify the eschatology folded in the expression "the God who may be" by distinguishing it from the doctrine of Wolfhart Pannenberg. Kearney offers himself to us as a phenomenologist who has taken the turn toward hermeneutics (much like Ricoeur) and mildly protests incompetence in exegesis and theology. Yet by arguing that the metaphysical notion of God is mistaken and urging people to accept an eschatological account of the deity, he has already started doing theology. I would like him to continue. As such, I will walk a few steps with him in a field he claims not to know: contemporary European theology.

II.

Pannenberg, like Kearney, tries to disentangle the God of the Bible from the categories of Greek metaphysics. To say that God is immutable is to say too little, "since God not only immovably establishes and maintains present reality in its lawful course, but has within himself an infinite plenitude of ever new possibilities in the realization of which he manifests the freedom of his invisible essence."[6] While God is "unoriginate and indestructible," he is nevertheless "not immobile, but rather, in this inner plenitude, the living God" (*BQ*, 161). God is characterized by freedom, and this freedom is manifested in his particular acts of lordship in history: his decisions regarding *this* people, *this* woman, and *this* man do not fall outside his eternal essence, but rather constitute it. There is no opposition in God between historically contingent acts and his eternal essence, and it follows from this that we cannot abstract the deity from the historical acts that make up his lordship. His eternity is not to be understood as timelessness. We cannot unreservedly affirm that God *is* until we reach the end of history: "Only in the future of his Kingdom come will the statement 'God exists' prove to be definitively true," he writes. "But then it will be clear that it was always true.'"[7] To be sure, Pannenberg believes that the advent of Jesus provides us indirect knowledge of the Kingdom, but all direct knowledge of the deity is kept from us until the consummation of time.

This stripped-down Hegelianism offers a profoundly eschatological understanding of the deity, one that is close to the Kearney who asserts that God "is passionately involved in human affairs and history" and that "God will be God at the eschaton" (*GMB*, 2, 4). In Pannenberg's writings, we find a deity who "may be" in the sense that his existence can legitimately be debated, now and throughout all history. Yet Pannenberg also provides a realist account of God. He does not deny that the deity has acted in the past or the present, or that he will continue to do so in the future; and at no time does he deny that there is a truth to be discerned at the end of time. The truth is not absolute, however: we cannot absolve the truth claim "God exists" from the contingent acts that constitute God's lordship of history. Nor will the truth ever be absolute in the sense that Plato and Aristotle imagined it to be. Pannenberg is too deeply influenced by the Hebrew conception of truth, *emeth*, for that to be so. As he says, "The unity of truth is possible only if it includes the contingency of events and the openness of the future" (*BQ*, 27). The divine essence will be constituted partly by the acts of love and forgiveness, wrath and reconciliation that have characterized his lordship of history.

Is Kearney still close to Pannenberg? He is within shouting distance at least, for he subscribes to a realist account of the deity, albeit with just one quick flourish: "if God's future being is indeed conditional on our actions in history, God's infinite love is not" (*GMB*, 37). The loving God is with us, has always been with us, and his being and his lordship are inextricably linked. "If the play of eschatological possibility may indeed 'save us,' it is only to the extent that we choose to respond to it by acting to bring the coming Kingdom closer, making it more possible, as it were, by each of our actions, while acknowledging that its ultimate realization is impossible to us alone. That's what we mean when we say 'God may be'" (*GMB*, 110). In broad outline, these two sentences could have been uttered by Pannenberg, but the details would have been different. No theologian would place "save us" in quotation marks without a long explanation, one that in all likelihood would attend closely to the acts and preaching, the suffering and resurrection of Jesus as eschatological and soteriological. And no theologian would talk of our choosing to cooperate with the Father's bringing of the Kingdom without embedding the remarks in a discussion of prevenient grace.

Of course, Kearney has a rather different agenda from Pannenberg, though he does draw deeply from Pannenberg's *Doktorvater*. It was Ricoeur who reminded us a quarter of a century ago that the "tradition has interpreted the *Ehyeh asher ehyeh* in the sense of a positive, ontological assertion," and that the Septuagint translation ("I am who I am") hardly protected the secret given to Moses and instead "opened up an affirmative noetics of God's absolute being that could subsequently be transcribed into Neoplatonic and Augustinian ontology and then into Aristotelian and Thomistic metaphysics."[8] Ricoeur goes on to observe that "the theology of the name could pass over into an onto-theology capable of taking up and bracketing the theology of history" (*THR*, 94); Kearney follows suit in proposing an alternate theology of the name, one that brackets metaphysics in the name of history and in which *Ehyeh asher ehyeh* becomes "I Am Who May Be" (*GMB*, 20). Pannenberg would be in warm agreement. "In the Bible," he writes, "the divine name is not a formula for the essence of deity but a pointer to experience of his working (Exodus 3:14). . . . The question of the essence thus becomes that of the attributes that characterize God's working."[9] Kearney, however, is less interested in developing a doctrine of God than in intervening in contemporary debates in the philosophy of religion. If we see God anew, in terms of possibility rather than actuality, we might be able to avoid the two extremes that fascinate many today: "ecclesiastical mysticism" (Marion) and "apocalyptic postmodernism" (Zizek) (*GMB*, 34). There is a way of avoiding these extremes, Kearney tells us; one must embrace the God who may be. This requires us to work for the Kingdom. However, it needs to be underlined that the Kingdom has been eschatologically announced by and through Jesus. It is certainly feasible to rethink God by way of the Kingdom—it has been a powerful current of theology since the nineteenth century—but that thought becomes abstract if not developed in Christological and Trinitarian terms.[10]

While Pannenberg rejects the God of Greek philosophy, he does not wish to disengage metaphysics from theology, as Kearney does. Albrecht Ritchl's and Adolph von Harnack's attempts to theologize without metaphysics failed, Pannenberg maintains, because theology, like any intellectual enterprise, must refer its truth claims to metaphysics in order for them to be asserted and evaluated.[11] In this way, Pannenberg might well ask, "How does Kearney know that his propositions are true?"

III.

There are two approaches in contemporary theology by which the attempt is being made to learn to think God again. The one way, pursued by Wolfhart Pannenberg with impressive consequentiality, is to think God as "God having been removed" (*remoto deo*) in order to arrive at the disclosure of the thought of God which then functions as the framework for the Christian faith's own understanding of God. The studies in this book will take the opposite approach.[12] I introduce part of Eberhard Jüngel's foreword to *God as the Mystery of the World* (1983) because he offers opportunities for comparison, as well as for contrast, with respect to Pannenberg's work. Jüngel also affirms in a forceful manner the theological significance of possibility. Thoroughly hermeneutical, this theology rejects the necessary God of metaphysics in no uncertain terms, and this should be of interest to the author of *The God Who May Be*. At the same time, Jüngel does not suggest that we jettison metaphysics altogether. We need to make critical use of it, distinguishing the importance of the questions it poses from the answers that it gives (*GMW*, 48–49).

One metaphysical question that is supremely important for theology, Jüngel believes, is the relationship between actuality and possibility. The answer given by Aristotle has been received as authoritative. It is that actuality (*energeia*) precedes possibility (*dynamis*). The possible is that which can be actualized, Aristotle maintains, from which it follows that the possible has no part in being. Arguing against this view in an early essay, "The World as Possibility and Actuality" (1969), Jüngel maintains that the possible is prior to the actual:

In essence, the consequence of what has been proposed is the dismantling of the claim that actuality is prior to possibility, since the distinction between the possible and the impossible—and thus the distinction between God and the world—is more necessary than that between the actual and the not-yet-actual. In actuality, that which is already actual is at work as an act, which as such always proceeds from the past. To put the point more sharply, in actuality, that which is passing into the past is active. As such it has a certain value and its own necessity. But in the distinction between the possible and the impossible, being is distinguished from nothingness. Such a distinction comes out of the future. For nothingness has as little past as does the creative distinction of being from nothingness. When the possible is distinguished from the impossible in such a way that the possible becomes possible and the impossible becomes impossible, then there occurs something like an origin—whether it be an origin in the beginning or at the end: in both cases it is God's freedom as *love* which makes the possible be possible. In the very concept of creation it is essential to set God's love over against his omnipotence. God's omnipotence concerns actuality; God's love concerns possibility. God's love concerns the being which is in becoming.[13]

I would like to disentangle three threads that run through it and, indeed, through all of Jüngel's writings. As I do so, I will briefly relate them to Kearney's thinking of the God who may be.

First, a clarification of vocabulary: Kearney maintains that God can make the impossible possible, while Jüngel affirms that God allows the possible to be possible and deems the impossible to be impossible. For Jüngel, God gives us the possibility of possibility—not by way of a transcendental structure of being human, as Karl Rahner taught, but in the eschatological awakening of Jesus' parables of the Kingdom. Second, possibility is neither the shadowy partner of actuality nor is it consigned to non-being. Rather, the category of being is expanded such that it includes both actuality and possibility. It is in this divided medium that we live our days, and to the extent that we respond to the possibilities that God makes available to us, we can be changed for the better. These transformations cannot be figured outside mortality, but they are nonetheless to be regarded affirmatively: possibility is set decisively against impossibility or annihilation. In this way, the impossible for Jüngel is what destroys or erodes the possible, and it is God's wish eternally to separate the two. It is in thinking of possibility along these lines that Jüngel intersects with all that Kearney considers under the sign of *persona*, "the capacity to be transfigured . . . and to transfigure God in turn" (*GMB*, 2). Third, the deity is both actual and possible: he *is*, and (because the incarnate son is divine) his being is in becoming. Only a God whose reality encompasses possibilities, the "may be's," can freely offer himself in love to human beings. Between Kearney and Jüngel, only the latter places Christ at the center of the relation between actuality and possibility.

The free offering of God to human beings is revelation in Jüngel's system; in accepting that statement it is important to realize that he construes revelation by way of the coming of faith. It is revelation, then, that enables us to have "an experience with experience [*eine Erfahrung mit der Erfahrung*]," that is, to revaluate experience in the eerie light of non-being or impossibility (*GMW*, 32). This meditation can result in anxiety, as German philosophers from Schelling to Heidegger have indicated, but it can also yield to gratitude: we are preserved from nothingness by God's grace. To be thankful for life itself is to have been touched by the revelation of God; it is to have been turned toward new possibilities that come from the eschatological event of the incarnation and all that follows from it; these possibilities were never encoded in the future conceived as unfolding from the present and the past. There is a future of actuality and a future of possibility, Jüngel maintains, and, in exposing us to the latter, revelation gives us new senses of freedom and love. We are not so much transformed, which implies that we have nothing more than what we had in the past, as re-created.

Revelation occurs in time and reorients us to time. How does it occur? Jüngel insists that God comes to language in the form of metaphor or parable, which is metaphor cast as narrative. The thinking that wants to understand God will always be led back to narrative. The thought of God can be thought only as the telling of a story, whereby the concepts are to be carefully controlled. Jüngel concludes this thought with a sentence that will surely appeal to the author of *On Stories*: "If thinking wants to think God, then it must endeavor to tell stories" (*GMW*, 303). Stories open up new possibilities. As Jüngel puts it:

> Narrative fluctuates in the middle space between the arbitrary possibility of "this way and also another" on the one hand and the rigid necessity of "this way and no other" on the other. As the telling of history, it participates in the mode of being of history itself, which as reality incorporates within itself both the past possibility out of which it emerges and the future possibilities which it contains, and thus it is what it is only within the realm of its own possibilities. . . . To narrate history means to delve into its unique and irrevocable reality by returning to its *past* possibility from which it came, with regards as well to its *future* possibilities, and thus to grant to the past reality a future. (305)

Jüngel's general point is that narratives such as Jesus' parables have a twofold response to the actual. They do not deny the actual but expand it by introducing the possible into its realm. Metaphors and parables are true not because they effect a correspondence between themselves and reality, but because they speak of more reality than has been available; they involve the possible as well as the actual and, in doing so, account for more being than literal speech could ever do (*TE*, 57). If these basic moves sound familiar, it is because they are—at least if, like Kearney, you have read Ricoeur's *The Rule of Metaphor* (1978).[14] To know this book and, more generally, this philosopher, is also to sense how Kearney would reply to Pannenberg's question, "How do you know your propositions are true?" His answer would turn, I presume, on a Heideggerian understanding of truth as event and on a Ricoeurian account of second-order reference.

What Jüngel adds to Ricoeur's theory is a specific application of the philosopher's understanding of metaphor to Jesus' parables, which had been of interest to him as early as *Paulus und Jesus* (1962). What Jüngel takes away from Ricoeur's theory is its scope. For Jüngel, metaphor's "most proper function is realized in language about God"; indeed, metaphor constitutes the entire "language of faith," even its most prosaic parts, because in Christ "an eschatologically new context is given," requiring all words to carry a metaphorical charge (*TE*, 65, 24, 23). If we take Jüngel at his words, it follows that all secular poetry is somehow less bold and less impressive in its adventures with metaphor than religious language is. Yet any student of English literature will testify that Milton's *Paradise Lost* is metaphorically richer than the passages in Genesis on which it broods, and that Shakespeare's *Macbeth* is metaphorically thicker than the Gospel of Matthew. However, we should not quite take Jüngel at his words. In point of fact, he argues that secular poetry is doing all that it can do with metaphor; no matter how bold Shakespeare's or Donne's or Blake's or Hopkins's metaphors, they depend on the prior catachreses of the Old and New Testaments. A catachresis is an abuse of language or, as Jüngel might put it, an interruption of an actual linguistic order. The fundamental biblical "metaphors," as he calls them, are in fact catachreses. The poetry that responds to them can respond only to those primal abuses of language.

On Jüngel's understanding of metaphor, Jesus' parables will not be stories among other stories. They will call forth untold possibilities, and thereby transform the actual world in which they are told and in which they are heard. When one hears any of the parables, one does not remain in the same reality; the world has expanded and become more intense. For Jüngel, the parable performs what it evokes: it changes us, orienting us toward the Kingdom. The parables call Christ into presence, on this account, and do so in and through the poetic character of the parable. It was Arnold who taught, in *Literature and Dogma,* that the language of the Bible is "fluid, passing, and literary, not rigid, fixed, and scientific," and who used this to dismiss *Aberglaube* (*LD*, 162). We have come quite a way to hear Jüngel reverse the argument and maintain that the radical poetry of the Bible is what bespeaks its life as revelation.

IV.

"The God of Metaphysics," "The God of Experience": these are well-known essays by Matthew Arnold that may be found in *God and the Bible* (1875), the sequel to *Literature and Dogma.* Neither essay and neither book has been very well received: F. H. Bradley, T. S. Eliot, and F. R. Leavis were all scathing about Arnold's speculations on the Bible and doctrine, and since then he has fared little better at the hands of literary critics, philosophers, and theologians. When Kearney comes close to Arnold, it is to the man who affirms the God of experience, the man who values freedom and creativity. "We see that Jesus Christ never dreamed of assailing the Jewish Church," we read in *Literature and Dogma,* "all he cared for was to transform it, by transforming as many as were transformable of the individuals composing it" (*LD*, 154). Over a century later, we hear an echo: "the God-who-may-be offers us the possibility of realizing a promised kingdom by opening ourselves to the transfiguring power of transcendence," Kearney writes, dubbing this capacity to be transformed *"persona"* (*GMB*, 2). Transcendental theology has been born, raised, and criticized between Arnold and Kearney, and its influence can be discerned in *The God Who May Be.* Levinas has also written in the interval between the Victorian and the postmodern. Thus Kearney several pages later: "At a purely phenomenological level, *persona* is all that in others exceeds my searching gaze, safeguarding their inimitable and unique singularity. It is what escapes me toward another past that I cannot recover and another future I cannot predict" (*GMB*, 10). "This *persona* is what Levinas names *la trace d'autrui,*" we are told, but there is no equivalence: Levinas's thought is based on a fundamental asymmetry in which the Other is elevated above the Self, while Kearney maintains that both Self and Other have *personae* and that we can open ourselves to divine transformation.

We saw earlier that, for Arnold, the transformative power of Jesus turns on his method and his secret. To this "method" belongs his use of that important word which in the Greek is *"metanoia."* We translate it *repentance*, a groaning and lamenting over one's sins; we translate it wrong. Why do we make this mistake?

> Of *"metanoia,"* according to the meaning of Jesus, the bewailing one's sins was a small part. The main part was something far more active and fruitful—the setting up an immense *new inward movement* for obtaining one's rule of life. And *"metanoia,"* accordingly, is: *A change of the inner man.* (*LD*, 288–289)

A little later Arnold brings together Jesus' method with his secret:

> But for this world of busy inward movement created by the *method* of Jesus, a rule of action was wanted; and this rule was found in his *secret*. It was this of which the Apostle Paul afterwards possessed himself with such energy, and called it "the word of the cross," or *necrosis*, "dying." . . . *The word of the cross*, in short, turned out to be at the same time *the word of the kingdom.* (*LD*, 291, 293)

If Protestants tend to stress method, Catholics are disposed to prize the secret; the churches cry out for conversion, while the Church murmurs "peace, joy" (*LD*, 352). While method and secret cannot be separated, there is reason to link the latter to good conduct in the world. What Arnold determines to be "three-fourths of human life" turns out to be a consequence of dying to the world (*LD*, 173).

One does not find anything nearly as bleak as that in Kearney, even though he clings to a more solid deity than Arnold thought credible. Yet, for all his skepticism and sentimentalism, Arnold believed that our transformations in this life cost something. The charge for change is death: so Jesus teaches us, the Victorian sage declares. Kearney is strangely silent about such things in *The God Who May Be*, although he knows too much about the imagination and the Christian life not to recognize that nothing is had for nothing. What I find odd is that a Catholic can write a book that invites us to rethink God and yet say so little about the relations of Jesus and the Father. It is a wonderful thing to find Kearney, or anyone, evoking the *perichoresis*, the eternal dance of the divine *personae* in and around and through each other. Yet I am puzzled that the Trinity is regarded only as a perfect community, with no sense given to the divinity's dereliction at the torture and execution of the Son. Perhaps Kearney will tell us that he speaks only as a philosopher of religion or even a hermeneut of religion, and not as a theologian. Perhaps I am responding not so much to anything he has said or not said as to a general situation these days: the avoidance of theology in the name of the philosophy of religion. Perhaps, but it seems to me that if a Christian is talking about God, then he or she cannot suspend Christology and Trinitarian theology without severe loss at every level. A sound philosophy of religion requires an engagement with theology. That may well include a philosophy of theology and a theology of philosophy, but it should always avoid making a religion of philosophy.

The Maker Mind and Its Shade

JEAN GREISCH

I.

Richard Kearney and I have a common interest in Heidegger's existential and ontological understanding of the "possible," which moves far beyond the classical and modern logic of modalities and Nicolai Hartmann's modal ontology. Heidegger's statement that "the possible is more real than the real" (*Being and Time*, §31) could be augmented by Paul Celan's beautiful verse, "Alles ist weniger als es ist, alles ist mehr" (Everything is less than it is, everything is more). If I understand Kearney correctly, this statement must not be restricted to *Dasein*'s being-in-the-world and its finite self-understanding, but is also true of God's divinity.

In Hegel's understanding of philosophy, the owls of Minerva start their flight at dusk, when a historical world has come to its end and demands to be understood. In Kearney's work, we meet with a new breed of owls, which start their flight at dawn, looking ahead toward an as yet undiscovered future. His *The God Who May Be* is the last volume of a trilogy, which includes *On Stories* (2001) and *Strangers, Gods, and Monsters* (2002). I will focus on the last volume, which presents an exciting attempt at a new *itinerarium mentis in Deum*, which Kearney claims to be both "phenomenological" and "hermeneutical."[1]

Having just finished a trilogy in which I deal with the main expressions of hermeneutical phenomenology in contemporary thinking (*Heidegger: The Tree of Life and the Tree of Knowledge, The Wounded Cogito*, and *Ricoeur: The Wanderings of Meaning*), I have good reasons to be interested in Kearney's work in the field of contemporary hermeneutical phenomenology. These reasons have become even stronger since I am now engaged in working out a hermeneutical philosophy of religion, *The Burning Bush and the Enlightments of Reason*. My general aim is to show under which conditions the modern concept of critical reason, inherited from the Enlightment, helps us to understand what is at stake in the biblical episode of the burning bush, which Kearney discusses in the second chapter of his book.

Kearney's *The God Who May Be* begins with its main thesis: "God neither is nor is not but may be" (*GMB*, 1). Someone familiar with the classical features of philosophical theology will be taken aback by this statement, which abandons from the start the traditional paths of the questions regarding God's existence (*an sit?*), his attributes (*quid sit?*), the possibility of knowing and naming Him, and so on, without forgetting the frightful question of theodicy: Is God responsible for all the evil existing in the world? However important all these questions are, they leave out other possibilities, for instance, Nietzsche's question: "Wohin ist Gott?" (Where is God? or, rather, Where has he gone?). Kearney's "God who may be," as well as Marion's "God without Being" and Levinas's "God who is not contaminated by Being," must submit themselves to the test of Nietzsche's question. This is surely an unavoidable question in our present time, where nihilism, "the most disquieting of hosts," is knocking at our doors. To put it bluntly, does the "God Who May Be" put an end to Nietzsche's "*Requiem aeternam Deo*," which the madman, who proclaims the "Death of God" in the famous passage of the *Fröhliche Wissenschaft*, starts singing? Strangely enough, Nietzsche or, to quote the title of a recent book, Nietzsche's struggling with "the shade of God"[2] is never mentioned in Kearney's book.

At the same time, Kearney's "God of the possible" must confront the question "Who is God?"—the question of divine selfhood. This question is already at stake in the theophany of the burning bush, as Kearney shows in the second chapter of *The God Who May Be* through his reading of the *ehye asher ehye* as "I Am Who May Be." What, finally, of the "who"? (*GMB*, 36). This question is crucial in a time where the question "Who am I?" is no longer purely rhetorical.

II.

Before discussing further topics of the five chapters of the book, I will raise some questions regarding the introduction and the conclusion. In the introduction, Kearney claims to develop a "new hermeneutics of religion," which is also my own claim in the third volume of *The Burning Bush and the Lights of Reason*. Expecting the unavoidable critical question regarding his philosophical position, he qualifies it as a hermeneutics developed "from a phenomenological perspective" (*GMB*, 5). This is a qualification I have tried to assume through my phenomenological reading of Heidegger and Ricoeur. If there is a difficulty here, it has to do with Kearney's crossing of the threshold of phenomenology of religion by distinguishing "two rival ways of interpreting the divine—the *eschatological* and the *onto-theological*" (*GMB*, 1). Kearney's definition of "onto-theo-logy" is evidently the same as that of Heidegger: metaphysics is understood as "onto-theo-logy," from Plato and Aristotle up to Hegel and Nietzsche. In other words: All reflection upon Being as Being in its most universal sense leads back to a first being in which all other beings are grounded. Reflecting upon this primordial being implies the necessity of unfolding the question of Being as such. Within this "onto-theo-logical" structure, according to Heidegger, the proper philosophical name of God is "causa sui." In calling God "the one who may be," Kearney turns his back on the "causa sui," without pondering further other possibilities, especially the Neoplatonist "henological" understanding of the divine as the One beyond all determinations.

A second, very important point is Kearney's definition of the "eschatological," "which privileges a God who possibilizes our world from out of the future" (*GMB*, 1). There is no question that this is the God of the Bible. The real difficulty, stating the problem in Heidegger's language, is how this God "comes into philosophy as such" ("Wie kommt der Gott in die Philosophie?"), or, to put it in the language of Levinas, how this God "comes to our mind (*De Dieu qui à l'idée*)." Much more than the first formulation, the second requires precise phenomenological descriptions as found in Levinas's article "Dieu et la Philosophie." If one wishes to discuss Kearney's understanding of the "God who may be," one should meet him on his own philosophical ground, that is to say, one has to examine his phenomenological descriptions of what he calls the phenomenon of "*persona*" in the first chapter, the phenomenon of appearing and disappearing in the second, as well as "transfiguring," "desiring," and "possibilizing" God in the three last chapters.

Before having a look at these five phenomena, one should also pay attention to the three "methodological pseudonyms" of his "philosophy of *posse*," which he introduces at the end of the introduction in order to qualify his hermeneutics: *dynamatology, metaxology, metaphorology* (*GMB*, 6). The expression "dynamotology" speaks for itself, insofar as in Kearney's (and Heidegger's) world, the possible is more real than the factual. It is not a world where cats are on the mat, but a dynamic world where cats are expected to sit down on mats and leap up from them. The meaning of the second methodological pseudonym is more difficult. It alludes to the Greek *metaxy*, meaning a "middle way" between two extremes. In this respect, Kearney tries to work out a middle way between ontology and eschatology, as well as a middle way between radical negative theology (Levinas, Marion, Derrida) and the divine taken as the "Sublime" (in Lyotard's and not in Kant's or Hegel's sense), the "monstrous" (Campbell, Zizek), the "an-khorite" (Caputo), and so on. Clearly, the two first books of Kearney's trilogy lead to his "attempt to throw hermeneutic drawbridges" between both extremes (*GMB*, 7). Kearney would no longer be Kearney if he had no new stories, good or bad, to tell. A radical negative theology moves beyond the realm of narrative and fully respects Plato's prescription in the *Sophist*: "Do not tell stories, try to understand!" But Kearney would also not be Kearney if he no longer believed in the possibility of preparing a better future or expected the Kingdom to come. This is why the "monstrous" is for him not an answer but a challenge. This explains why he meets the postmodern thinkers in the same manner that Oedipus meets the Sphinx.

In order to appreciate the solidity of his drawbridges, one ought to remember what Aristotle says about the "middle way": it is not a lazy compromise between two extremes, which one meets halfway (in French, *couper la poire en deux*), but it must be radical in its own order. This is a good criterion to apply to Kearney's interpretation of the "God who may be."

At first sight, Kearney's third methodological pseudonym, "metaphorology," also speaks for itself; he claims it is directly borrowed from Ricoeur's inventive reading of religious texts. By inventing new metaphors, we become able to better understand the latent possibilities of the world in which we are dwelling and even to invent new manners of being in the world. Nevertheless, one should not wholly identify Ricoeur's analysis of "lively" metaphors with what he later calls a "poetics of reading." A poetics of reading has to deal with many tropes, with metonymies as well as with metaphors. Regarding

God talk, there are good reasons to ask, as does Michel de Certeau in his *Fable Mystique*, whether metonymy rather than metaphor is not the typical trope of mystical speech.

These three methodological qualifiers give us a first idea of the many tracks that Kearney's *The God Who May Be* opens, some of which he will surely explore further in future work. This is also the impression of his reader when he confronts the question "How do we describe the infinite May-be?" in his concluding remarks regarding a "Poetics of the Possible God" (*GMB*, 101). In this question, the verb "to describe" should not be overlooked, insofar as it requires not only a speculative but also a phenomenological treatment of the problem. Kearney does not really develop these descriptions in his book, and in this respect there is still hard phenomenological work ahead, struggling with "the matters themselves" (*Zu den Sachen selbst!*). Instead, he prepares the ground for such descriptions through his hermeneutical retrieval of the conceptions of possibility offered by Aristotle, Cusa, and Schelling. This leads him to introduce the "paradigm of God-play," which is also the real phenomenological playing ground for forthcoming descriptions.

His hermeneutical retrieval of the Aristotelian reading of *dynamis* and the doctrine of the *nous poetikos* is a daring one, but fully congruent with his poetics of the possible. It leads him to interpret the divine Creator "as transfiguring our being into a can-be," that is to say, "a being capable of creating and recreating new meanings in our world" (*GMB*, 102). In this respect, Kearney's understanding of the human being seems to agree fully with Ricoeur's phenomenology of human ability (*phénoménologie de l'homme capable*). But not all neo-Aristotelians will be ready to share Kearney's eschatological and theological interpretation of human ability.

Regarding this point, my problem is rather a "Heideggerian" one. By strongly stressing the eschatological horizon, is there not a danger of forgetting or shading out what Heidegger calls *Geworfenheit* and what I call *transpassibility*? In all his writings, Kearney is always looking out for undiscovered and not yet explored possibilities. Of course, opposing "possibility" and "passibility" makes no sense. Nevertheless, I wonder whether a hermeneutics of religion is not confronted with *passibility* as well as with possibility.

Asking "What kind of divinity comes after metaphysics?" (*GMB*, 2) understood as "onto-theo-logy" must not prevent us from pondering upon what I call, following Breton and Ricoeur, "la fonction meta." In my own interpretation of Heidegger's "metaphysics of *Da-*

sein," there are four fundamental ways of transcending oneself, which I call *trans-ascendence, trans-descendence, trans-possibility*, and *trans-passibility*. If I try to apply this personal *Geviert*, this metaphysical and phenomenological quadrangle, to the problem of a hermeneutics of religion, I wonder whether the "God who may be" is not only the God who possibilizes our world from out of the future but also the God who haunts our past and invades our present through the other. This is what I have in mind when I speak of the "shade of the Maker Mind."

Kearney's hermeneutic retrieval of Nicholas of Cusa's *Trialogus de Possest* is no less daring than his intepretation of Aristotle's "maker mind" insofar as he reinjects "eschatological radicality into the idea of a possibilizing God" (*GMB*, 105). I am not sure whether Nicholas of Cusa would have agreed with this interpretation, in which there is little space left for a negative theology. One should not forget that even if Nicholas claims that the *possest* is the best name we can find for God according to our human concept of him, in one other famous trialogue, he suggests that the proper name of God is "The Non-Other" (*Non Aliud*).[3] It would be interesting to know how Kearney sees the relation between these two equally Cusanian names of God.

Without looking further into Kearney's all-too-short treatment of Schelling's definition of the divine "can-be" (which includes the problem of God's "dark side," his "shade," so to speak), his most interesting suggestion from a phenomenological perspective is his interpretation of the "power of the possible" as "Godplay" (*GMB*, 106). He is well aware that this notion has no real *Sitz im Leben* in Heidegger's thinking. This does not mean that "the ontological notion of *Spiel* remains elusive in Heidegger's own work," as Kearney argues (*GMB*, 159, n. 20). Volume 27 of the *Gesamtausgabe* shows clearly that Kant's formula of the "great game of life" is crucial to Heidegger's understanding of transcendence at the time when he worked out his metaphysics of *Dasein*. After the *Kehre*, Heidegger's ontological interpretation of the phenomenon of play, as showing *Dasein*'s relation to the world, leads to the famous notion of the *Geviert*, which in Jean-François Mattéi's interpretation is the crucial feature of Heidegger's postmetaphysical thinking.[4]

In this respect, Kearney draws very interesting clues from Hugo Rahner's *Man at Play* (Rahner himself alludes to Huizinga's *Homo Ludens*). Here, too, despite the importance of these motifs, drawn from metaphysics and theology, as well as from the mystical tradition (for instance, Eckhart's idea that the "pure heart knows no bounds to its capabilities" [*GMB*, 108]), I would make a plea for a "phenomenology from below," including a close look at the anthropological and sociological phenomenon of play. (I have in mind Roger Caillois's book, *Les Jeux et les Hommes*.)[5] Caillois distinguishes four fundamental types of games: *agon* (combat), *mimesis* (imitation), *alea* (dice), and *illinx* (vertigo). A phenomenological description not only should focus on the act of playing, but also should deal with the different kinds of games. A philosophical interpretation of this fundamental human phenomenon—if we have no idea of a society in which storytelling makes no sense, we have no idea of a society in which nobody plays, either—has good reason to ask how these fundamental games actualize the notion of the possible. This again raises the question as to which notion of transcendence is brought into play in these four manifestations of playing. It is only after having worked out these questions on a phenomenological level that we are prepared to confront the final question in Kearney's book: "How, if at all, does the play of God relate to the play of Being?" (*GMB*, 110).

III.

Does the book present his readers with a new philosophical theology, or rather a "hermeneutics of religion," as claimed in the subtitle? Since Heraclitus argued that the "Absolute" may or may not be called God, philosophers have had to deal with the difficulty of distinguishing their understanding of the divine and the religious understanding deposited in specific religious traditions, without opposing them. "The God who may be" is a new philosophical name for the Absolute, which must be justified on its own grounds. At the same time, it must be confronted with the language of religious traditions. This is exactly what Kearney is aiming at in his reading of the epiphany of the burning bush, which he takes as an example of religious transfiguration.

Kearney's interpretation focuses on "the extraordinary phenomenon of a deity which appears and disappears in a fire that burns without burning out, that ignites without consuming, that names itself, paradoxically, as that which cannot be named, and that presents itself in the moment as that which is still to come" (*GMB*, 20). Two points in this description require close attention. The "God who may be" is a restless God, always "on the move," never reducible to a "constant presence" (*ständige Anwesenheit*) in Heidegger's sense. One thing that strikes me more and more in Heidegger's "last God" in the *Beiträge zur Philosophie* is that this God, whom Heidegger presents as "the totally other, especially over against the Christian God," can be encountered only through his "passing by" (*Vorübergang*). *Vorübergang* could well be Heidegger's postmetaphysical reading of "eternity." Should we describe Heidegger's "last God" as a "God who may be"? If so, how can one distinguish this last God from Kearney's God (the God of the Bible)?

Kearney alludes more than once to Meister Eckhart's interpretation of divine life as *bullitio* and *ebullitio*. The same motifs are stressed in Michel Henry's phenomenological interpretation of life as "self-affection." In this respect, one would have to compare Kearney's and Henry's interpretations of life. Is the notion of "absolute Life" compatible with the notion of possibility? This is a crucial question for current debates in French phenomenology. Maybe Kearney's "onto-eschatological" approach of the "God who may be" is closer to Levinas's understanding of "illeity" than to Henry's vision of eternal life.

The three fundamental tasks which Kearney confronts us with — "transfiguring God," "desiring God," and "possibilizing God" — call for a critical discussion of thinkers such as the late Scheler, who understands the "may be" as a "will be," meaning that humanity will give birth to a God who is becoming divine through history and who will be God only at the end of history. In the same critical perspective, one could also remember Rosenzweig's discussion of Vaihinger's "Philosophie des Als Ob" (philosophy of the "as if"), which would shed more light on Kearney's insistence upon the fact that the "may" must not be understood in a purely conditional or hypothetical sense.

In this respect, the first chapter, which presents us with a "phenomenology of the *persona*," is also the chapter where Kearney makes his most important hermeneutical decisions, placing the problem of personal identity in the eschatological aura of possibility of that which the self might become. Right from the start, he stresses the power of transfiguration, alluding to an image from the Book of Revelation, the stone on which is written a name that God alone knows.

Kearney establishes a strong link between the notion of the persona and that of the "trace of the other" (*la trace d'autrui*, in the sense of Levinas). Perhaps this link should be justified more explicitly. For what reason does he focus so strongly on the persona of the other, and not on that of the self? Kearney quotes Kristeva's book *Strangers to Ourselves*, in which she makes a point that a Levinasian interpretation of alterity tends to leave aside. Perhaps one should also recall that the notion of the "trace" plays an important role in philosophical theology, especially in the Neoplatonist tradition of henology and negative theology. I am interested in working out a phenomenology of the trace, which tries to compensate to some extent the exclusively "semiotic" orientation in hermeneutics, especially in Umberto Eco's work.

The second point that strikes me is that Kearney stresses more the power of transfiguration than that of disfiguration, which is also a possible meaning of *"persona." "Persona"* versus the "monsters" without and within us—is this battle already finished and won?

At the end of the first chapter, one comes across the notion of *prosopon*, which unfolds the idea of "prosopoieic substitution" (*GMB*, 116, n. 20). Because he calls himself "nobody" (*outis*), Ulysses escapes from the cavern of the Cyclops. Let us not forget that at the beginning of modern philosophy, we find Descartes's maxim *larvatus prodeo*, which in Marion's reading becomes *larvatus pro Deo*. Kearney deals with this possibility of disfiguration versus transfiguration in the second volume of his trilogy, *Strangers, Gods, and Monsters*.

At the end of *The God Who May Be*, which intends to open up a phenomenological and hermeneutical debate concerning "theological" issues of contemporary phenomenology, I wonder how we are to understand Kearney's paradoxical statement that "the phenomenon of the persona surpasses phenomenology altogether" (*GMB*, 16). In this context, Kearney claims to develop a new "quasi-phenomenology," which seems closer to ethics than to eidetics. Is this "quasi" to be understood in Vaihinger's sense of an "as if" phenomenology or, rather, as a "possible" phenomenology that "may be" and deserves to be? That would be my final question to Kearney.

Divine Metaxology

JAMES OLTHUIS

Richard Kearney is a possibility thinker, a philosopher, novelist, and poet fired by a passion for/of God. For Kearney, philosophy links imagination and affectivity with reason in a rhetoric of persuasion aiming for individual and societal transfiguration. In other words, as I read him, philosophy is not an abstract-theoretical exercise dedicated to getting things straight, finding solutions for particular theoretic problems. Rather, for Kearney, philosophy is a way of life, a spiritual exercise[1] working toward the incitement of passion for visionary transformation and cultural change rather than the elaboration of grand systems and the elimination of paradoxes. Indeed, it is ethics as "first philosophy,"[2] philosophy not as the love of wisdom but, as Levinas phrased it, "the wisdom of love at the service of love."[3]

This makes Richard my kind of person; his work, religious zeal, and philosophical drive flow together in a contagious vision of God as a May Be—whether as the possible impossiblity (a là Heidegger) or the impossible possibility (a là Derrida). Kearney seeks a middle way between the mystical authoritarianism of thinkers such as Jean-Luc Marion and certain negative theologians and the apocalyptic anarchism of postmodern prophets of the sublime such as Jean-François Lyotard and Slavoj Zizek.

The search for such a middle path is urgent because of Kearney's consuming conviction that seekers of love and justice can neither rest with the notion that God is immutable and impassive nor with the claim that it is impossible to distinguish God as love from God as monstrous. Paraphrasing Heidegger, how can we pray or sacrifice to gods of such ilk? Before God as immovable mover or as horrific, humans can neither play music nor dance. Kearney seeks to map a middle path in which the breaking open of a new order of existence is a promising possibility without dissolving into an abyssal void. He terms this new possibility a poetics of the possible, a hermeneutics of God as May-Be, a *deus adventurus*, a God both already here (incarnation) and always still to come (in-coming).

In his efforts at negotiating and reconnoitering a third way, Kearney has written a trilogy, *Philosophy at the Limit*, developing in Ricoeurian fashion a hermeneutics of critical discernment and narrative imagination dealing with limit situations "of death, deity, sublimity, trauma or terror" and addressing these experiences of extremity "beyond the strict frontiers of reason alone in efforts to imagine new possibilities of saying and being" (*SGM*, 229; *OS*, 157).

In anticipation of the discussion to follow, let me say, somewhat cryptically, that I will be suggesting that precisely at the limit situations that Kearney is addressing, his Ricouerian strategy of narrative imagination needs not so much supplementation (in either of Derrida's senses) as a radicalization in accord with, as I see it, its own internal dynamic. Kearney's Ricoeurian pulse beats palpably and audibly to the very end of the third book, where he summarizes his project: "my wager has been twofold: (a) that we are *beings at the limit* and (b) that we are *beings who narrate* (*SGM*, 230). I invite Kearney to supplement this second wager, modulating its beat ever so slightly: we are beings who, in undecidability, narrate in faith. This supplement nudges Kearney's "diacritical hermeneutics" in the direction of John D. Caputo's radical, more Derridean hermeneutics with its stronger emphasis on narratalogical undecidability, and the need to live in the unknowing of faith (*SGM*, 17).[4]

It is my modest wager that Kearney may not resist, and may even welcome, this little nudge. That is not only because in his book his emphasis on faith, testimony, and God as "the impossible" is already very Derridean, but also because, I hope to suggest, practicing radical hermeneutics, in the promise of the im/possible, need not be the overly cold and despairing performance that Caputo-cum-Derrida tend to make of it, an exercise that leaves Kearney (and me) shivering and somewhat disconsolate.

I want to begin with Kearney's "basic wager" that God as May Be "is much closer than the old deity of metaphysics and scholasticism to the God of desire and promise" of the "scriptural narratives" (*GMB*, 2). Does he, in fact, win this bet? I'm not sure. All I can say is Maybe![5]

I understand, applaud, and share Kearney's wish to open up conceptual space for reenvisioning a nonmetaphysical God. The question for me is whether Kearney's talk about God as possibility of being, possibility-to-be, is the most auspicious move in that direction. Or does it, at the same time, serve to confuse his project, perhaps even revealing a lurking presence of an ontotheological ghost? My basic query is whether the God Who May Be is to be read as a philosophical claim about God, which would make it distinctly and qualitatively different from an affirmation of faith, or does the philosophical avowal at the same time double as a testimony of faith (with the possible implication that the reason-faith distinction is being insufficiently honored or even blurred or effaced)?

In the philosophical reading, "May Be" would then be all one can judiciously (read: by reason alone) say within the confines of philosophy about God. Theoretically, then, God's possibility would be haunted by the possibility of God's impossibility. In which case, a Divine May Be would not be a sign of ambiguity or an indication of imprecision, but a marking of the limitation of the reach of reason.[6] In the second reading, the God Who May Be appears to double as both philosophical description and faith confession, in effect traversing the gulf between philosophy and testimony, between reason and faith. I would have no question if Kearney were simply proposing May Be along the lines of the first reading. My problem has to do with the way he employs texts of testimony in his philosophizing, in particular the jump I perceive him to make in reading the promissory I-shall-be of Exodus as the I-may-be of possibility. The fact that he appeals to scriptural texts is not the problem. The question is, rather, How are texts of confession and testimony to function in philosophical argumentation?

More precisely, is it legitimate for Kearney to translate the Exodic name of God as May Be as "*posse* (the possibility of being) rather than *esse* (the actuality of being as *fait accompli*)"? (*GMB*, 4). God is then "neither being, nor non-being, but as something before, between, and beyond the two: an eschatological may be" (*GMB*, 34). In so doing, Kearney seeks to reverse the order of actuality and possibility. However, in Exodus 3:14, the *'ehyeh* (I shall be) is in the promissory mode of covenantal faithfulness, which presupposes the actuality of the Promisor. To convert and rework this I-will-be promise into a quasi-metaphysical I-may-be statement about the priority of possibility over actuality seems to me to be a big—and, I suspect, an unwarranted—jump.

Nowhere does Kearney justify this particular leap. In fact, at points he would seem to call this jump into question. Thus, he describes Exodus 3:14 "as a pledge to remain constant to a promise" (*GMB*, 37). That is to say, possibility is grounded in actuality of the promisor. The I-will-be of a promise presupposes the actuality of the promisor and cannot, I would suggest, be read as turning God's actuality into possibility, in effect making God's existence conditional.

Kearney, at points, is seemingly aware of the problem. On the one hand, his text reiterates in various ways his contention that "God can be God only if we enable this to happen," that "God depends on us to be" (*GMB*, 2, 4). However, at one point he suddenly interjects: "Does this all amount to a *conditional* God?" His answer is clear: "No. For if God's future being is indeed conditional on our actions in history, God's infinite love is not. As a gift, God is unconditional giving" (*GMB*, 37).

I am wholly one with Kearney in his efforts to avoid ontotheology, on the one hand, with its "conceptual capture of God as a category of substance," and, on the other hand, a "mystical ontologism," which runs the danger of making it "impossible to distinguish [God] from monstrosity" (*GMB*, 24, 24, 34). My disquiet is that talking about God as "an eschatological may be" is that it does not so much negotiate a new and different way between extremes as it, chameleon-like, changes identity as it dialectically goes back and forth between these extremes (*GMB*, 34).

Thus, against any talk of *esse, ousia, substantia,* or *essentia* in reference to God, Kearney emphasizes the priority of possibility of being in respect to its actuality. But when this is read to imply the conditionality of God's existence, Kearney assures us that God's being is unconditional and that the may-be-ness has to do with understanding the being of God as dynamic, open-ended, and future-oriented. Well and good, but then, Kearney is not so much proposing an alternative to ontotheology as an alternative ontotheology, an "onto-eschatology," as he himself calls it (*GMB*, 34).

And then I wonder if talk in the mode of may-be—since may-be is still a modifier of being—is still not, even if grudgingly and by default, part of the metaphysical calculative-representational project of mastering reality in which God enters as centerpiece and keystone at the human bequest that Kearney wants to go beyond. Perhaps talk of God as May Be, intentions to the contrary, leaves us only with the God of the philosophers, thereby reinscribing Kearney into the very precincts of ontotheology that he sets out to overcome.

Thus, for example, Kearney's effort to use his eschatological understanding to forge a chiastic reconciliation between mysticism's *ek-stasis* and ontotheology's *hypostasis*, a nuptial chiasm of the play of God and the play of being, strikes me as still playing the ontotheological game of conceptual mastery of God, albeit in a censored version. I have the same reaction to his use of the doctrine of Trinitarian *perichoresis*, which I regard as a particularly speculative piece of ontotheology (*GMB*, 109).[7] Moreover, the fact that Greek Orthodox theologian John Zizioulas[8] is able to fully embrace Kearney's suggestions, provided that they are taken as descriptive of the economical and not the ontological Trinity, also strikes me as an indication of how Kearney can easily be read as working within the project of ontotheology.

But clearly Kearney wants more than the God of the philosophers. He even has a distinct preference for the God of Abraham and Sarah, Isaac and Rebekah. What is not so clear is how the two understandings of God relate and integrate. What does become clear is that, regardless of his critique of the "old deity of metaphysics and scholasticism," Kearney is loath to give up the category of being because "the danger of God without being is . . . that it becomes impossible to distinguish [God] from monstrosity—mystical or sublime" (*GMB*, 2, 34).

The implication or suggestion seems to be that talking of God as an in-between May Be provides the necessary criteria enabling us to distinguish God from monstrosity. What is less than clear is how this in fact works. For me, this still has the curious taste, at least aftertaste, of the very ontotheological gesture that Kearney resists, namely, subordinating God to the principles of reason.

Along similar lines, Kearney is afraid that Caputo (and with him Derrida) is "removing the very criteria whereby we distinguish . . . divine from human, good from evil, true from false" (*GMB*, 74). He searches for criteria "to identify divinity," afraid that otherwise we can be taken in by all comers. Without such criteria we "perhaps lose something of the God of Love" (*GMB*, 74). "In the last analysis, there seems no possibility of discerning between monsters and Messiahs" (*SGM*, 107). Again the idea seems to be that having such criteria will provide us with a clear, if sometimes fuzzy, line of demarcation that will empower reason to make the proper identifications, even if not always cleanly and surely.

Ironically enough, in searching for criteria, Kearney obscures his own emphasis that in the end, there is only testimony. In limit situations, he argues, we are beyond criteria, and live by faith and not by sight: "Testimony is the bottom line. . . . The rest is indeed silence" (*GMB*, 48). Indeed, what more can or need be said? At this point, Kearney is in very close proximity to Derrida and Caputo and their talk of the aporetics of the gift, justice, forgiveness, and the messianic. This is most evident when Kearney relates his poetics of the possible to Derrida's philosophical (non-concept) of the impossible.

Derrida's "the impossible" is not the simple logical opposite of the possible, but it is that absolute interruption which is unpredictable, always surprising, not programmable, and beyond the horizon of possibility. Kearney suggests—and I certainly agree—that Derrida's philosophical concept of the "perhaps," as the necessary condition of possibility for every experience that is truly an event, holds in particular for the experience of faith.

However, the concept of the impossible only brings us to the fissure between the declarations of reason and the affirmations of testimony. As a philosophical (nonobjectifying concept), a kind of Heideggerian formal indication, it can only point toward, or wave across, but never bridge the gap—a gap negotiated only in faith. Philosophical translation of faith's affirmations converts the discourse from a discourse *within* to a discourse *about*. While to think God is to risk thinking nothing, calling upon God is to confess the One to whom s/he has given his/her heart. Paying close heed to the distinctiveness of testimonial and philosophical accounts of God allows for the full-bodied excesses of faith and the minimalist constructions of philosophy not to infringe on one another, even as they can be mutually supportive. Thus, the Perhaps of philosophy can partner with the testimonies of the God of Surprise and Grace, the God of Promise with whom the "impossible"[9] is possible, both mutually supporting and mutually deconstructing one another. In other words, Kearney needs to keep more clearly in mind the important distinction between a philosophical declaration about the God Who May Be and a faith affirmation that God Will Be.

I am also interested by the possibility that Kearney's project could be enhanced by relating Derrida's philosophical concept of the "secret" to a believer's faith experience of God. For Derrida, the secret—let us say God—"is not phenomenalizable. Neither phenomenal nor noumenal." It cannot be accounted for, categorized, or defined by philosophy, theology, politics, or even religion. The secret is inviolable. That does not mean that we cannot speak of God or direct attention to God. God does not conceal the Godself. God "simply exceeds the play of veiling/unveiling, dissumulation/revelation,"[10] and I would add possibility/impossibility. God is the excess that exceeds any attempt to capture it. That is, although we can, do, and need to speak of God in many names. God remains "secret under all names, and it is its irreducibility to the very name which makes its secret." God is the unnameable to which all our names are responses; God is the unanswerable to which all questions, indeed all systems of thought, are rejoinders.

God is secret and not secret: secret in that in God, love remains inexhaustible, never runs out, with always more surprises to come. And yet, God is not secret. God does reveal the Godself by loving the world and its creatures into existence. To be alive is, thus, to speak from within the secret of this gifting love, and to respond to the call of that gifting.

Moreover, God is beyond and not-beyond. As the preoriginal opening that exceeds all systems, physical and metaphysical, and yet evokes such systems, God is beyond. As the Love revealed and incarnated in the world, God is not-beyond; the Godself is vulnerable, risks itself, opens itself to the possibility of being counterfeited.

In connecting God as the secret with Love, I am admittedly going further than Derrida. My emphasis on God as the beginning of loving (giving/calling), not the essence of being, parallels very closely at this point the thinking of Jean-Luc Marion. From Kearney's references to a loving God, I was hopeful that he, too, would move in this direction, replacing an ontology of being with a vision of love. However, Kearney seems hesitant to make a move of this kind. He is afraid that it may land him in what he calls Jean-Luc Marion's "celebration of blind mystical rapture" with its bracketing and minimizing of human hermeneutic responsibility to tell the difference between the divine and its opposites (*GMB*, 34). Although I share his concerns that Marion's emphasis on bedazzlement tends to downplay the role of interpretation, what interests me is the reappearance of Kearney's preoccupation with "identifiable" signs to help discriminate between good and evil specters. Ironically, Kearney is concerned that both Marion and Derrida-Caputo are poor guides in this limit situation. "Can we," he asks in reference to Derrida-Caputo, "desire God without *some* recourse to narrative imagination?" (*GMB*, 77). Later, Kearney laments that Derrida "prefers ghosts to gods," and parts company with him because Derrida leaves "matters open. He reserves judgment" (*GMB*, 99).

There are at least two related matters that deserve attention here. It seems to me that Kearney overreads Derrida's concept of undecidability as indecision, and underreads Derrida's deployment of narrative. For Derrida, the two concepts are intricately interwoven.

While convinced of the importance of recognizing and honoring alterity, Kearney is fearful that the experience of irreducible alterity will at bottom be indistinguishable from irreducible abjection, with the result that the other becomes alien and God becomes an abyss. At this point Kearney sees his diacritical hermeneutics as providing intercommunion, in contrast to romantic hermeneutics with its "congenial communion of fused horizons" (Schleiermacher, Dilthey, and Gadamer) and radical hermeneutics with its "apocalyptic rupture of non-communion" (Caputo, Derrida, Blanchot, and Lyotard) (*SGM*, 17, 18). For Kearney, the "basic undecidability . . . bequeathed by Levinas and the deconstructionists" is most inadequate and needs to be supplemented by a critical hermeneutics of the sort he is envisioning (*SGM*, 67).

However, Kearney misunderstands what these thinkers mean by undecidabilty. When Derrida and Caputo talk about absolute hospitality, they have in mind the norm of hospitality, which they very well recognize can never be totally put into practice. For them, undecidability does not "suspend all criteria of ethical discrimination," leaving us unable "to differentiate between good and evil" (*SGM*, 72). Indeed, undecidability calls for decision, decisions fraught with responsibility because, in spite of all criteria, there is no way to make infallibly a fail-safe decision. Decisions, in the end, are acts of faith, impossible necessities.

In *Given Time*, Derrida points us to the undecidability that haunts narrative, even as he fully recognizes that it is only by way of narrative that one starts. "The gift is the condition of the narrative, but simultaneously on the condition of possibility and impossibility of the narrative."[11] In other words, there is narratalogical undecidability at work that opens the way to the possibility of faith, even as faith opens up the possibility of undecidability. The aporia that Derrida and Caputo describe opens the space of testimony as both a response to being named (gifted and called) by God, and a denominating of God as the one who calls. To put it yet another way, paraphrasing Derrida, we cannot refer to this "real" [read: God] except in an interpretive experience.[12] God's giving calls for testimony in order to be received as God's giving.

As we have seen, Kearney is uneasy about undecidability. But if transcendence, God, and the gift are irreducible to my reception and consciousness of it, the maintenance of undecidability needs to be fully honored rather than eroded. Undecidability and the risk of refusal are the hallmarks of the gift. In other words, it is not because there is not a world of difference between God and the devil that we cannot have in our hands a guarantee of the difference. It is the nature of human experience as response—always mediated, always in the throes of undecidability.

In the experience of aporia, there is no surefire way of knowing. Nevertheless, the only way through the impasse is to give narrative testimonies witnessing from within the experience. God, that is, Love, is known not, in the first place, in words about, or as a matter of cognitive judgment about, but in the experience of being loved by God. It is in our experience that we tell the difference between God and the demonic, because in that experience God shows up as a God of justice, memory, and promise.

Speaking God from within the Event is always open to the possibility of perjury, of the counterfeit. Indeed, without the risk of contamination, there is no genuine response. I put my trust in my testimony and faith, not knowing whether I do so because I really know, or because I hope that I know it—that is the risk of my faith. I believe in the face of disbelief. I know that which I love in a different way than that which I do not love.

For Derrida, in fact, "responsibility and faith go together . . . and both should, in the same movement, exceed mastery and knowledge. The gift of death [or God] would be this marriage of responsibility and faith. History depends on such an excessive beginning."[13] Undecidability calls for an excessive beginning, that is, a beginning that cannot be programmed or computed, a step in faith. Working our way through undecidability, then, requires both calculation and faith, both the way of narrative and the way of faith. Narrative is both possible and impossible, and undecidability blurs them together. Two kinds of response are necessary: careful, responsible interpretation is called for because narrative is possible, and the response of faith is called for because narrative goes only so far. The site of impossibility is at the same time the site of the gift. Derrida's "marriage of responsibility and faith" puts him, it strikes me, on the same page as Kearney. Both Derrida and Caputo would join with Kearney in exhorting that "[w]e have to try to tell the difference, in sum, between narrative testimonies that transform or deform lives" (*GMB*, 48, 49).

How to read in the dark is Kearney's final and poignant question (*GMB*, 79). The answer is that we don't and, paradoxically, that we are always reading in the dark. Knock-down arguments, indisputable sightings, and crystal-clear readings are mirages, which is not to say that we are without guidance and lost; for there are other ways to knowledge than rational discernment. We taste, we touch, we smell, we feel, we listen, we cry, we rage, we reach out, we tell stories . . . and come to know, despite the mists of doubt, beyond the grasp and validation of rational knowing. And, as Kearney exclaims, "[w]hile God's lovers will always continue to seek and desire [God] whom their soul loves, they have always already been found, because already sought and desired by [God] whom their soul loves"(*GMB*, 79). In knowing, we are known. In other words, at the end, beyond criteria, in darkness, we read by faith and not by sight.

Theopoetics of the Possible

B. KEITH PUTT

> The knowledge of God is a mountain steep indeed, and difficult to climb.
>
> **Gregory of Nyssa**

> There are two things on which all interpretation of Scripture depends: the mode of ascertaining the proper meaning, and the mode of making known the meaning when it is ascertained . . . a great and arduous undertaking [*opus magnum et arduum*].
>
> **Augustine of Hippo**

Theology is a cartography (that is, an attempt to create maps, to mark out, to graph, or to plot a course or courses) that will lead to a place, a *topos*, where divine revelation may occur and knowledge of God may be discovered. At these various places (*topoi*) and through its various topics, theology concerns the "way," the right way, the proper way, *the* way, or one of many ways that can lead individuals to know something about God. Yet, as Gregory so honestly affirms, the journey to such knowledge, the progressing along various chosen ways to God, always occurs over rugged topography, an oftentimes "mountainous region" with steep grades. Even with a good map, one will find the journey difficult. Ironically, the trek is exacerbated by the fact that although one might have a map and, thereby, "know" the charted course, one can proceed up the way of ascent only by faith and not by sight; one searches for sites of divine manifestation in which new insights into God might be experienced, but the search takes place as if one were blind, unable to read the map clearly.

Yet, if theological maps are drawn and read in the dark, then the journey takes on an even more problematic character, given that reading and writing in the dark results in a dimming of hermeneutical lucidity. In other words, as Charles Winquist insists, if theology is writing, then it addresses the knowledge of God by engaging language about God, which in turn demands interpretation.[1] Even were one to possess *the* perfect map that leads up the face of the mountain to the very face of God, one would still have to interpret it, to read it, to decipher its semiotic and semantic implications. Consequently, theology is not only cartographical and topological, it is also tropological, concerned with the "ways" of language, with linguistic "tropes" (*tropoi*) that twist words and turn phrases. Theological language may strive to realize more specificity or rigor, but it always remains a second-order vocabulary dependent upon the first-order religious language of avowal, that is, the language of faith, testimony, and attestation.

Such first-order language for Christian theology derives from the texts of the Hebrew and Christian Scriptures, texts composed of a multiplicity of literary tropes, including figures of speech such as symbols, metaphors, and narratives that compose the plurality of biblical languages. Here, Augustine comes forth as the one to warn us how daunting a task it is to seek to interpret those languages, and in doing so, reprises Gregory's symbol of the difficulty in doing theology. Augustine insists that ascertaining and communicating the Bible's "proper meaning" requires a project both "great" and "arduous," a "*magnum opus et arduum.*" But *arduum* is Latin for "steep," so here again the way one might choose to arrive at proper biblical interpretation, the path one might walk in order to arrive at the hermeneutical destination of clear understanding, is, indeed, an upward journey, one fraught with danger and demanding hard work.

Imagination at the "Heart of the Theological Enterprise"

> As a form of imagination, faith is not an immediate knowledge. To apprehend the image of God in faith is not to have the unmediated vision of God; to be able to imagine God rightly is not to see God face to face. . . . Imagination belongs, therefore, in the language of traditional

Christian dogmatics, to the *regnum gratiae*, to the present
age between the times, in which believers look forward in
expectation because they can look back to the decisive
event of salvation.

Garrett Green

Can we desire God without *some* recourse to narrative
imagination? Without some appeal to tradition(s)? Without some guide for the perplex?

Richard Kearney

Richard Kearney certainly appreciates Gregory's and Augustine's
perspectives on the difficulty in making one's way toward understanding God. Although he humbly claims that the theological and
exegetical tasks necessary for scaling the steep slopes leading to
knowledge of the divine lie beyond his competence, he nonetheless
sets out on that journey and blazes an interesting and creative trail
leading to a postmetaphysical, perhaps even more biblical, linguistic
point of view (*GMB*, 9). Although his route follows along some of
tradition's well-marked trails, he is not reticent to step off those usual
paths and wander transgressively over different topographies. Ray
Hart claims that "tradition" is theology's technical term for the "linguistic debris" that accrues as each generation searches for the
"proper" method and language for doing theology.[2] He goes on to
state that when "theology recognizes that it cannot think the same
thing the tradition thought without thinking that thing in a *different*
way, the question of method has inserted itself into the heart of the
theological enterprise" (*UM*, 391; my emphasis). If Hart is correct,
then not all of theology's linguistic debris is incinerated or buried in
some methodological landfill, but is recycled into new conceptual
networks and new linguistic strategies through which the substance
of theology gets thought in a different way. In agreement with Hart,
Kearney insists that in the postmodern, postliberal, postcritical, and
postsecular cultural contexts, theology must think both with and
against the tradition, that it must adopt what Derrida calls a "filial
lack of piety" toward its linguistic detritus, and that it should salvage,
through the supplementation of a refiguration and a transfiguration,
the biblical language that imaginatively limns the revelation of God.[3]

Working with the dialectical attitudes of a hermeneutics of trust
and a hermeneutics of suspicion, Kearney prescribes an itinerary for
thinking God that includes a couple of steep segments, specifically

excursions up Mount Sinai with Moses in order to receive the Ineffable Name of God and up Mount Tabor with Jesus in order to do a projective phenomenology of the *eschaton*. He contends that at the summit of these mountains, one engages theophanies that call into question traditional interpretations of how one should envision and inscribe God. These manifestations of the deity actually reimage God and reimage images of God, and in doing so, necessitate a serious reappraisal of the creative language of Scripture, of those linguistic images, literary tropes, imaginative narratives, and fertile lacunae that signal transcendence, mystery, and divine sublimity. Such refiguring and transfiguring figures of speech lead him to reconfigure the theological methodology that best prosecutes the biblical theistic models.

In order to isolate Kearney's central theological methodology, one needs only to ascend the second of the above-named summits, Mount Tabor, the Mount of Transfiguration. As Kearney undertakes a "phenomenological-hermeneutic" of the transfiguration of Christ, he deciphers a specific moment of metamorphosis, the moment when the eschatologically glorified Christ is proleptically revealed, demonstrating Jesus' role as a mediation of God, as a passage or "way" to God. Yet, Jesus mediates God not in the sense of full presence or as a closure to the revelatory process, but as a "figure," or cipher, of the *eschaton* yet to be fulfilled (*GMB*, 39, 43). Consequently, the transfigured figure of Jesus bespeaks an openness that cannot be decisively deciphered, an "ontological incompleteness" and an eschatological infinity that demands constant re-interpretation (*UM*, 135). In other words, Jesus as the transfigured phenomenon of the "way" (*poros*) is a way that both reveals and conceals the way, discloses and closes the way; therefore, one might say that the transfiguration of Christ functions as an *aporia* (*a-poros*) that gets in the way of anyone who hopes to reach the final revelatory destination. Kearney asserts that this revelation with/out revelation means that the Christophanic event's ineffability becomes the motor of its *fability*—its translation into a variety of accounts, testimonies, fables, narratives, and doctrines ranging from the initial versions of John and extending down through the entire "effective-history" (*Wirkungsgeschichte*) of Christian theology (*GMB*, 47).

These resulting genres of translation, these mappings and remappings, inscriptions and reinscriptions, however, have either implicit or explicit ties to the imagination, the creative faculty through which order and novelty are discovered, produced, and/or synthesized in human existence. Kearney directly references the centrality of the imagination for construing the eschatological implications of this narrative by citing the Apostle Paul's refiguring of Jewish messianism and prefiguring of the Kingdom yet to come. Paul glosses these issues through an "iconic" Christology in which Jesus serves as an image of God, and Christ's followers reflect the divine glory as mirror images, awaiting the day when they shall repeat the *imago Dei* and be like God in an eschatological *imago Christi*. Paul's lexicon of symbols — "figuring," "imaging," and "reflecting" — derive implicitly from a context of imagination (*GMB*, 44–45). Consequently, one can postulate that the story of Christ's transfiguration inspires the imagination to witness the alterity of the event, the singular Otherness that breaks into the disciples' reality and offers to extend the transfiguring power of God through an existential metamorphosis of their *persona*, their "eschatological aura of 'possibility.'"[4] But the alterity of the human and divine *personae* demands that they be spoken figuratively, that language should deploy "imagination and interpretation to overreach their normal limits in efforts to grasp [alterity] — especially in the guise of metaphor and narrative" (*GMB*, 10). Kearney contends that the metaphorical, narrative imagination seeks "to interpret the images of the other and to transfigure one's own image of the world in response to this interpretation" (*PI*, 188). Yet considering that he esteems the narrative imagination as a sine qua non for expressing a "desire for God," one might contend that Kearney's legislating "way" (*hodos*) for following after (*meta*) God and for doing theology is the way of imagination (*GMB*, 77). The imagination, therefore, addresses both the methods (*meta-hodos*) for interpreting God and the aporia (*a-poros*) that ensure the asymptotic character of every theological endeavor.[5]

Although Kearney nowhere explicitly prosecutes the idea of an imaginative theological methodology, for two decades or more — at least since his published dissertation, *Poétique du Possible*, in 1984 — he has given significant attention to the central role of imagination as the creative power in a "poetics of the possible" and to how such a poetics relates to different narrative configurations of self and of God. As a result, one might say that his theological method does, indeed, rest upon the productive power of imagination; that is, for Kearney, theology is an imaginative construction, a creative mapping of theological topics as poetic expressions of the Inexpressible God. His method, then, correlates at significant points with Gordon Kaufman's thesis that theology is an imaginative endeavor to construct the concept of God. Actually, Kaufman contends that theologians imaginatively construct two primary ideas: the "world" as the unified context of experience and "God" as the limit to that unified context. In a somewhat Anselmian fashion, he considers God to be that imaginative construct than which nothing greater may be imagined.[6] The theological imagination operates at the interstices of the effable/ineffable, and of the imaginable/unimaginable, not only to construct (narrate, transfigure, poetize) the idea of God but also to analyze, criticize, and reconstruct traditional images of God (*ETM*, 43). As such, Kaufman posits that knowledge of God is mediated through imagination and is never intuited immediately within the context of some naïve theological realism.

Kearney would agree with Kaufman's basic reading of the theological imagination as productive and liminal. He makes it plain throughout his work—again in agreement with Kaufman—that the theological imagination must not be defined according to the colloquial understanding of imagination as a faculty for reproducing images of absent objects. He certainly criticizes any reductive explanation of imagination as limited only to perceptual remnants, such as Thomas Hobbes's theory that the imagination "is nothing but *decaying sense*."[7] Although Kearney admits that the imagination does have the reproductive function of evoking absent objects and constructing material forms in order to represent real things, his theological interest lies in the productive power of imagination, in its relationship to possibility, variation, and creative language. This understanding of the productive imagination betrays several key influences. The distinction between the reproductive and productive imagination indicates a Kantian influence (*PI*, 50–51), while the idea of imagination's intimate participation in the projection of possibility manifests Husserlian and Heideggerian phenomenological influences (*PI*, 16, 31).[8] Heidegger, in particular, fleshes out the phenomenology of imaginative possibility when he applies the Kantian model of the productive imagination to the grounds for *Dasein*'s "being-in-the-world" as "hermeneutically prefiguring one's world horizon as that towards which one projects one's possibilities" (*PI*, 53). In other words, Heidegger identifies *Dasein* as "a poetics of the possible" (PI, 54) and, in good Kierkegaardian fashion, states that "possibility stands higher than actuality" (*EPG*, 182).[9]

Yet of all the influences on Kearney's theological imagination, two take precedence: the Hebrew/Christian Scriptures and the phenomenological hermeneutics of Paul Ricoeur. Kearney's "biblical" interpretation of imagination centers on the Hebrew word *yetʃer*, a word that derives from a root meaning "to create." Although the Hebrew terms *tʃelem* and *∂emuth* mean "image" and "likeness," and would, therefore, appear to be the terms most associated with imagination, they actually do not function as the primary nomenclature for the productive power of imagination. Instead, the notion of *yetʃer* carries with it the connotation of mental purpose or impulse, that is, the passion to project the future and anticipate a different mode of being (*WI* 40). This passion is a product of the *imago Dei* in that God grants human beings the power to participate with God in creation—to be a "creative vicar of God" (*WI*, 65). But in granting humans this ability, God creates the risk that they will either misuse the power by seeking to usurp God's position as creator or fall into idolatry through vain attempts at creating imaginary replacements for God. Kearney contends that Adam's first sin results directly from a misuse of the imaginative passion, so that the first exercise of the gift of *yetʃer* was in the context of disobedience through which Adam and Eve gain ethical knowledge (the distinction between good and evil). This "fallen imagination," in turn, produces both the "knowledge of opposites" and the "birth of time," such that east of Eden, human beings confront the distinction between good and evil and the distinction between past and future. In other words, *yetʃer* "is the freedom to prospect a future of good and evil possibilities where [one] may choose to complete the Seventh Day of Creation . . . or choose . . . to lapse into idolatry of false images by locking [oneself] up in idle fantasies" (*PI*, 2). This duality comes to expression ethically as the *yetʃer hatov* and the *yetʃer hara*, the impulses toward good and evil, and comes to expression temporally as the narrative imagination, the ability to structure a story through memory and projection. Kearney determines that when taken together, these two expressions manifest the uniquely human capacity to project oneself into the "unreality" of the "different" and the "not yet," a capacity that he terms the "passion for the possible."[10]

It should be said that nowhere does Kearney explicitly tease out of his understanding of *yetʃer* the possibility that it might have something to do with divine revelation. There are, however, a few indications that he might embrace the idea that the imagination functions as a point of contact between God and humanity. For example, in questioning how to describe the indescribable God, he wonders what "metaphors or figures, what images or intimations . . . might we deploy to speak of [the] unspeakable enigma?" (*GMB*, 101). Again, when addressing the Talmudic understanding of *yetser hatov* as the dynamic propelling humans to participate in the ongoing task of divine creation, he writes that it "opens up history to an I-Thou dialogue between [humanity] and [its] Creator" (*WI*, 47). Using concepts such as "figures" and "images" in tandem with an interpretation of *yetser* as an "opening for dialogue" suggests strongly, if implicitly, that the imagination functions theologically as a medium and/or milieu for divine disclosure. At this point, Kearney's theology of imagination appears to track that of another theologian, Garrett Green, who contends explicitly that the imagination is the "point of contact" between God and human beings. Under the influences of Kant and Thomas Kuhn, Green develops a theory of the "paradigmatic imagination" as the formal principle for divine/human contact and correlates it with the material principle of the *imago Dei*.[11] Although he would agree with Kearney that the paradigmatic imagination has been marred through sin by becoming an unfaithful imagination falling into fantasy and idolatry, he argues from a Christian perspective that God seeks to redeem the imagination through the *imago Christi*, specifically, through the imaginative narratives of Christ's life, death, and resurrection. By divine appeals to the imagination and by revealing in Christ and Scripture a different "being-in-the-world," God offers individuals the possibility of faith, whereby they might "imagine God rightly." Green insists that by soliciting the imagination, God may summon individuals to redemption and obedience while simultaneously ensuring their freedom to respond (*IG*, 147). That is to say, God may effect a divine influence upon individuals through the imagination without that influence deteriorating into coercion or manipulation. When individuals respond by accepting God's call, their imaginations are redeemed and may then serve as the basis for analogical understanding, centered not on mimesis and what God *is*, but on the hermeneutical "as"—the "copula of imagination"—and what God is *like* (*IG*, 93, 140). From the perspective of a theological cartography, therefore, Green's method charts theology as principally hermeneutical and, therefore, as a way of articulating and comprehending "the grammar of Christian imagination."[12]

Kearney would certainly agree with Green on the point of correlating imagination, theology, and hermeneutics. This agreement results from the second significant influence on his theological imagination, the hermeneutical philosophy of Paul Ricoeur. For Ricoeur, theology develops out of the linguistic matrix of metaphor and limit expression, which, in turn, characterize the originary poetic language of faith.[13] This originary language purports to be a response to the creative word of God and attempts to name God through various textual genres that depend on the creative ability of figurative language to open new semantic fields.[14] The test case for this poetic dynamic is the metaphor, which Ricoeur centers in the imagination's ability to encounter the semantic impertinence of the metaphorical predication and to "see" new combinations of meaning and reference developing out of that impertinence through semantic innovation.[15] Of course, this means for Ricoeur that one cannot reduce the imagination to the traditional psychologistic or imagistic definitions, whereby imagination is nothing more than conjuring faint representations of absent or past objects. Instead, the imagination must be understood as linguistic, working in and through linguistic tropes and texts to create and discover new possibilities of meaning and existence. The semantic imagination exploits the polysemy of words and the plurivocity of texts in order to call into question the status quo and to project alternative worlds as possible ways of restructuring reality. By suspending literal descriptions of first-order references and replacing them with poetic redescriptions that mediate new meanings through second-order references, the imagination undertakes an "ontological exploration" that "sees" self, world, and even God in new and different ways (*TA*, 231). Through these "imaginative variations," the individual escapes the hegemony of the present and anticipates new possibilities in the future. Consequently, just as poetic texts in general present "models of" and "models for" reality and entice the reader to appropriate those models, so the poetic language of Christian theology offers models of and for self, world, Christ, and God.

The poetic energy of originary religious language and the play of the linguistic imagination specifically reference the theme of revelation. Through various creative genres of literature, such as wisdom, prophecy, hymn, parable, and eschatological sayings, one encounters a "call, into the heart of existence, of the imagination of the possible." This call of revelation manifests the "grace of imagination," the surging forth or exploding of new possibilities, resulting in the gifts of freedom, hope, and a redemption through imagination (*TA*, 237). Consequently, Ricoeur's "grace of the imagination" is a passion for the possible, or in Kearney's idiom, a "poetics of the possible." But precisely at this point, Ricoeur agrees with Garrett Green that the imagination offers the "point of contact" between God and humans in that it supplies the site of the confluence of divine revelation and human receptivity. Like Green, Ricoeur argues that revelatory language appeals first to the imagination in a nonviolent manner, and never coerces, but respects the individual's freedom to accept or reject God's self-disclosure.[16] God's revelation does not immediately demand a decision, an exercise of the will, but first gives to the imagination possibilities of a new reality, a new world, and a new self in the linguistic projections of God's new kingdom (FS, 44).

Given the importance of Ricoeur's philosophy for Kearney, one may again conclude that he, too, would accept that imagination forms the focus of revelation between God and humanity, that theology must, therefore, be an imaginative discipline, and that the "way" theology should be done must fix on the relationship between God and possibility. Kearney calls his theological way a *via tertia*, a third way, a way between ways, a metaxology or middle way, traversing a path down which one muddles through "with the help of a certain judicious mix of phronetic understanding, narrative imagination and hermeneutic judgement" (GMB, 34; SGM, 187). "Metaxology" is one of three "methodological pseudonyms" that Kearney employs, the others being (1) dynamatology, the preeminence of possibility; and (2) metaphorology, the necessity of poetic language (GMB, 6–8). Each of these "pseudonyms" references the imagination in one form or another. Consequently, Kearney's imaginative theological method works with and against various traditions, always within a context of suspicion, and extrapolates from them and against them certain new possibilities for imagining God, specifically for imagining God as *Peut-Être*, as the God Who May Be, a God of/as Possibility.

Possibility, *Kenosis*, and the Desire of God

> Suppose . . . that "God" is stationed not on the side of *arche* and the *principium*, or of timeless being and unchanging presence, of the true, the good, and the beautiful, but on the side of the an-archic and subversive, as the driving force—the *agens movens*—of a divine subversion?
>
> **John D. Caputo**

> This is a God who puns and tautologizes, flares up and withdraws, promising to return, to become again, to come to be what he is *not yet* for us. This God is the coming God who may-be.
>
> **Richard Kearney**

In order to examine how Kearney exercises his imaginative theological method, one need only make the journey up the steep slopes of Sinai along with Moses and experience the miraculous phenomenon of the burning bush. This mountaintop experience, as with the one on Mount Tabor, narrates a particularly enigmatic revelation of God, almost a *révélation sans révélation*, a disclosure that closes off any presumption on Moses' part of having attained direct and controlling knowledge of who God is. Of course, "who God is" is, indeed, the focus of the igneous interview between the God of Abraham and this son of Abraham. Moses experiences a "nominal" theophany, a manifestation of God that centers on the issue of naming. God knows Moses' name and summons him from out of the bush by repeating it, "Moses, Moses," and Moses responds with *"hinneni,"* "Here I am" or "Here I am *now.*" During the ensuing dialogue, however, Moses discovers that God has him at a disadvantage, for although God knows his name, he does not know God's name. He determines that he cannot go to Israel in the name of some Nameless deity; therefore, he requests that God "show" him some identification. God responds to Moses with *"ehyeh asher ehyeh"* — "I am who I am" — "tell them that I am has sent you." But that answer seems to be a "non-answer"; it sounds as if God gives Moses a name that is, indeed, no name. If *YHWH* is God's name, it is a nameless name that ensures that the unnameable deity remains unnameable. Consequently, calling God by this name will forever remind any who call upon this name that God's self-definition remains undefinable and that the God recognized by this name remains incognito.

How should one hear the cryptic name of God? How should one translate the surplus of meaning in the *"ehyeh asher ehyeh"*? What are the tense and the mood inherent in the divine voice as it speaks this Nameless Name? The plurivocity of this narrative text and its tradition of conflicting interpretations intrigue Kearney. He distills that tradition down to essentially two different readings that have legislated over the customary hermeneutical perspectives taken on this passage: (1) the ontological and (2) the eschatological. The first reading comes from philosophers who have removed their shoes, knelt before the burning bush, and confessed that in the voice of God, they hear the voice of Being itself. The God of Abraham, when speaking philosophical Greek, translates his name as *ego eimi, ho on*, "I am that am"; consequently, the Sinai theophany manifests a deity who identifies with the ontological structures of traditional metaphysics. To walk with Yahweh along the way enlightened by the burning bush, one must accompany Parmenides and his goddess on the way of truth, the way that leads to Being itself, which, as reason teaches, can only "be" and cannot "not be," can have no truck with motion, mutability, or multiplicity.[17] One must join Aristotle in his archaeology of motion as he sifts through the loose layers of causality until he reaches the bedrock *arche* of the Unmoved Mover, whose perfection demands the absence of any dynamism or any unactualized potentiality. As Being itself, God is "timeless, immutable, incorporeal, [and] understood as the subsisting act of all existing" (*TH*, 22). God must be Eternal in the sense of atemporal, must be pure act having no potentiality, must be impassible and unable to be affected by any other outside of God, and must be the cause of all that exists as the *causa sui*, the Self-Caused One.

Kearney demonstrates that Western theology with its interpretations of classical theism has accepted the conflation of God and Being and developed what has come to be known as ontotheology. Augustine, for example, reads the burning bush narrative as indicating a functional distinction between God *pro nobis* and God *in se. Pro nobis*, God manifests Godself as the God of Abraham and Isaac, a "more historico-anthropomorphic" deity; however, that is not what God is *in se*. God *in se* is the "I am," the *ipsum esse*, being itself as an immutable, atemporal *ousia*. St. Thomas continues this dual citizenship in Athens and Jerusalem when he writes, "Deus est actus purus non habens aliquid de potentialitate"— "God is pure act with no potentiality for potentiality" (*GMB*, 23–24). Of course, unless one mistakenly limits ontotheology to the Catholic tradition, one needs only to read a Protestant expression of the divine credentials in a document such as the Westminster Confession: "There is but one only, living, and true God, who is infinite in being and perfection, a most pure spirit, invisible, *without body, parts, or passions; immutable, immense, eternal, incomprehensible*."[18]

Kearney claims that the philosophical traits of Being and the biblical narratives of God significantly disconnect. The stories about God in the Hebrew and Christian Scriptures offer an alternative imaginative variation of the divine ego, a different figuration of who the God of Abraham is and how that God acts and interacts with creation. The second interpretation of the divine name, the eschatological reading of Exodus, strives to remain faithful to the biblical materials and to understand God's name as the name of one who promises a new future, who commissions individuals and communities to journey toward the future, and who commits the divine self to accompany them along the way. The God of Abraham, unlike the God of Aristotle, enters into covenants with human beings, obligates the divine self to remaining faithful to those covenants, opens the divine self to the conditional reciprocity inherent in such covenants, and limits divine action to responding to the response of the covenant partners.[19]

For Kearney, the relational aspects of the eschatological God come into distinct focus when one situates the divine naming in the context of God's encounter with Moses. Here again he depends on Ricoeur for guidance, since Ricoeur emphasizes the "vocation" motif of this narrative. God calls Moses to a mission, a mission that Moses reluctantly but finally accepts. In voicing the "Here I am," Moses vocalizes a promise, a commitment on his part to be faithful to God's charge. Moses commits himself in the present to a potential future, claims that he "is" now an individual who "will be" obedient to God's direction. Ironically, God enunciates something structurally similar to Moses's response. When asked for a name, God replies with a variation of the "Here I am"; "I am that I am" functions, then, not so much in a nominative and constative fashion as in a verbal and performative fashion. The "*ehyeh asher ehyeh*" may be translated as "I will be who I will be," and serves as an eschatological prolepsis through which God commits the divine self to a future fidelity. That is, the divine name expresses a divine promise (*pro-mittere*), gives God's "promissory note," a pledge to "be" with Moses and Israel wherever and whenever they need God (*GMB*, 58). God "is" in each moment the God who sends forth (*pro-mittere*) into the future a potential "being" that awaits an eschatological actualization.

The eschatological reading establishes ethical grounds now for the divine/human relationship. Moses and Israel have a responsibility to obey God's directions and follow God's leadership. Along the liberating journey of redemption, God will reveal to Israel the Torah, those principles of justice and mercy that should characterize all who "name the name" of God. Israel will have the obligation to exercise its *yetser hatov* and participate with God in realizing a Kingdom of love and righteousness. Yet, Kearney insists that God also immerses the divine self in this ethical context. God gives God's promises as gift, though not without conditions, conditions not only under which Israel operates but also under which God vows to operate. In other words, Kearney contends that God reveals Godself at Sinai as a God who has entered history in a genuine way through the divine promises of love and acceptance. God makes Godself vulnerable to the other, dependent on the other as to how the future will evolve, and in the vulnerability of divine obligation allows the other to affect who God may be in the future.

Kearney sums up in a fascinating and subversive translation of the Tetragrammaton the eschatological understanding of God as an engaged God, a God *of* and *in* history, a God of love, a God who calls and commits, and a God who promises and risks. In Kearney's lexicon, God does not name Godself as "Being itself" or as the "One Who Is in the Eternal Now," or as the immutable and impassible Greek deity; God names Godself as *"Posse,"* as the Divine "Perhaps," or better as *"Peut-Être,"* the "God Who May Be."[20] The biblical God is in actuality the God *of* possibility and God *as* possibility—the possibility-to-be—or *"Possest,"* a term Kearney co-opts from Nicholas of Cusa, who creates it by combining *posse* and *esse* and uses it to name God as absolute possibility. In doing so, Cusa offers a counterpoint to traditional metaphysical theology and emphasizes the necessity of imaginative language as a way to move from the nameable to the Unnameable.[21] Cusa recognizes that God as absolute possibility so transcends human actuality that only through the creative dynamic of figures of speech and literary tropes may one say something about the Unsayable. For Kearney, this means that the God Who May Be functions as a limit to reality, so that any encounter with this God will be a limit experience, for truly possibility limits actuality by calling into question its finality and completeness (*SGM*, 213). By offering the limitless possibility of an open future, God supplies the dynamic that moves history forward, that subverts any grounding principles, and that establishes a sacred discontent that anticipates what cannot be programmed or predicted—what eye has not seen nor ear heard, nor what has even entered into the *imagination*.

The naming of the God Who May Be in the book of Exodus complements the naming of the God Who Will Come in the book of Revelation: "I am the Alpha and the Omega," says the Lord God, "who is and who was and who *is to come*, the Almighty" (Revelation 1:8; emphasis added). Here God associates Godself with Being *and* with Coming, naming Godself once again with a verbal sign, a sign of the always "to come," the always "coming one." Kearney reads this eschatological "coming" of God according to Jürgen Moltmann's distinction between the *eschaton* as *futurus* and as *adventurus* (*PP*, 38). Moltmann contends that the French *avenir* and the German *Zukunft* do not translate the Latin *futurus*, meaning "what is going to *be*," but *adventurus*, "what is going to *come*."[22] For him, the eschatological

God-to-come is present in the word of promise, the divine vow that commits God to arrive always as the "ad-venturing" God, who both "is" (ontological) and "is not yet" (meontological).[23] Although essentially agreeing with Moltmann with regard to understanding the divine future as one of advent, Kearney will not express that future as a meontology, as a "non-being" in the sense of a "not-yet-being." He intends to move beyond being and non-being with his kinetic language of God's "coming." Yet, he functionally engages in a "May"-ontology when he describes God as *Peut-Être*, as the God Who *May Be.*

Yet, Kearney's *Peut-Être* need not necessarily be construed ontologically, at least according to Jacques Derrida, who translates it in a more "eventful" manner. One should not consider bringing Derrida into the discussion a non sequitur, given that he has emphasized for years that deconstruction concerns a passion for the impossible, for the advent of the future as the coming of an unprogrammable event, as a gift event—yes, even as a messianic event. Indeed, Derrida's interpolation of the concept of "perhaps" within the broader milieu of the coming of an impossible future has directly influenced Kearney's theology of God as possibility (*GMB*, 93–99). In the context of teasing out his deconstructive reading of "perhaps," Derrida broaches the issue of the singularity and uniqueness of "event." An "event" occurs only within the structure of the impossible, since a genuine event must have an aleatoric, essentially unpredictable, quality to it. It cannot be merely an actualization or fulfillment of something potential in reality, something programmable that evolves without novelty. Consequently, event as a messianic interruption is an impossible possibility or a possible impossibility.[24] One cannot predict the event; one can only remain open to receive it when it comes (*ad-venire*), not prevent it but affirm it as *l'invention de l'autre*, the inventing of the other when it breaks out (*e-venire*).[25] In the contest of these interpretations of event, Derrida defines *peut-être* as "it may *happen*," not as "it may *be*" (*AIP*, 344). Of course, Kearney contends that the God Who May Be reveals Godself as the God of/as "event," specifically "as a self-generating event," and as the in-coming (*in-venire*) of the Wholly Other who calls and promises.[26]

Now, given the complementarity of their views on event, Derrida's translation of "*Peut-Être*" contributes significantly to Kearney's theology. Perhaps one could read the Exodic naming, the "*ehyeh asher ehyeh*," as "I am who will happen," "I will be an event," or, better, "I will come as event." Such a reading further removes God from the conceptual network of ontological language and confirms God's transcendence as the coming one who cannot be reduced to possible forestructures of anticipation. Yet, from another perspective, Kearney is not so intent on avoiding ontological language completely. Although he does critique the traditional onto-theological reading of the divine name and does embrace the eschatological reading as a more valid and more biblical interpretation, he does not wish to remain solely on the side of the eschatological. His imaginative theological method as a *via tertia*, a third way, is the third way that synthesizes both the ontological and the eschatological expositions of the Exodic naming (*GMB*, 34). He refuses to separate God completely from the structures of being for two primary reasons. First, to do so would disallow any genuine historical and temporal interactions between God and humans. He disagrees, for example, with Jean-Luc Marion's contention in *God Without Being* that one must remove God completely from ontological categories in order to avoid the conceptual idolatry that reduces God to the metaphysical level of being (*GWB*, 31–33). Kearney certainly appreciates Marion's desire to free God from the claustrophobic categories of traditional metaphysics; however, he claims that a total separation of God and being would result in a divine alterity or transcendence that would lock God into the ineffability of the absolute and deny any genuine relationship with humanity. Although he claims early on that God does not interact with individuals as "another being," but as "otherwise than being" (*PP*, 231), Kearney insists that God's interaction has a reality to it, an empirical concreteness through which God reveals that God is not "so distant as to be defunct" (*GMB*, 79). Without some connection to being, God ceases to interact in history and in time, and to relate genuinely to humans in the reciprocity of promise and love.

Kearney's second reason for stipulating that God cannot be completely removed from ontology concerns the necessity for evaluating multiple instantiations of alterity. Kearney rejects any nondiscrimination policy with reference to experiences of alterity and difference on the basis that significant distinctions may obtain among various Others. He wants to establish functional categories that enable some sort of discernment by which one adjudicates the benevolence or malevolence of every Other who impinges upon an individual's experience; that is, whenever one entertains the Other, one may be welcoming an angel or a devil unawares (*SGM*, 67). Knowing the difference can be pivotal in determining the proper response. The need for such evaluative criteria escalates when the question of Otherness moves into theology. If one receives the Other *as* God when the Other *is not* God, then one might be receiving a monster and not a Messiah (*SGM,* 107).

Kearney addresses this fear specifically in response to the deconstructive philosophy of Jacques Derrida and the radical hermeneutics of John Caputo.[27] Based on his interpretation—and, one might add, misinterpretation—of their perspectives on the "theological" implications of desire, hospitality, undecidability, and *khora*, he concludes that they end with no benchmarks whatsoever for adjudicating among putative experiences with God. He laments that "the powers of human vision and imagination [may be] *so* mortified by the impossible God of deconstruction" that experiences with God will be both blind and empty (*DG,* 127). In lieu of the impossible God of deconstruction, that extreme *deus absconditus,* Kearney wants to posit the possibility of a God who passes through Being and gives some ontological signs or guidelines for adjudicating among various divine encounters.[28] He recognizes, of course, that Derrida and Caputo are correct in claiming that one will never reach absolute certainty, develop definite criteria, or achieve total transparency of vision; however, one needs some approximations of these before saying "yes," and "come," and "thy will be done" to some imaginary God (*GMB,* 76). He maintains that one must leave open the possibility of discerning between idols or demons and the God of love "who takes on very definite names, shapes, and actions at specific points in time . . . [and] who comes to bring life here and now and brings it more abundantly" (74). After all, Moses did see the burning bush and heard the nameless name; Jacob did grip the mysterious wrestler; and Jesus did offer his hands and side to Thomas (*DG,* 125). According to the texts that narrate these events, they occurred *existentially* and *phenomenologically* within the historical, temporal context of being, and enabled the individuals involved to recognize God.

For Kearney, recognizing God through the structures of being need not be construed in the sense of a premature closure, of a legislating metanarrative, or of a logocentric reductionism,[29] but may be understood as imaginative variations of the divine ego, as transfigurations of the creative dialogue between the God Who May Be and human individuals who respond to that God.[30] In agreement with Meister Eckhart and his contention that God reveals the divine being as iconoclastic and extravagant, Kearney wants to maintain that God's passage *beyond* being entails God's passage *through* it, and that by passing through being, God transfigures and redeems human beings. God, then, comes into being as the God who is not yet but always will be, as the God who comes as the one yet to come, as the God who may be other and different, while remaining the same as pure gift and real passage (*GMB*, 36–37). In this way, Kearney imagines a God Who May Be through the imaginatively theological third way of "onto-eschatological hermeneutics," which he declares to be a synonym for a *"poetics of the possible"* (*GMB*, 37). This poetics depends upon the possibilizing power of a God who is and who is not, who neither is nor is not, but who May Be, and may be as the God who involves humanity in creation, who awaits the creature's response, who does not predetermine the future Kingdom, but who beckons toward the Kingdom to come as a Kingdom of justice and love. This possibilizing God is the messianic God of resurrection and the dynamic God who gives the Holy Spirit in order to empower the church (*GMB*, 81; *PP*, 251–252). This God Who May Be comes after metaphysics as the God of Abraham, Isaac, Jacob, and Moses. This God as named in the poetic texts of Scripture reveals possible worlds of existence, imaginative variations of every status quo given—promised—unconditionally through a theopoetics of the possible.

The "onto-eschatological hermeneutics" of God is what Kearney expresses most recently through the nomenclature of the "fourth reduction," also known as the "Prosopic Reduction," an ad hominem, ad feminem, and ad rem return to the faces of other persons (*prosopon*) and to all of the factical milieux within which persons exist. This reduction to the vis-à-vis is a hermeneutical wager that the God Who May Be manifests Godself in the incarnate structures of created being, in the enfleshed Other who receives and returns one's gaze, especially the Other who is the "least of these" in need of clothing, or food, or love. Such a God of the theopoetics of the possible may be encountered through a "second naïveté," a humble belief that God is present in the actual as the absent God of the possible, the possible that lures reality ahead to an unfinished and imaginative reality.

Kearney insists that imagining God through the fourth reduction as the One Who May Be results in a more biblical theology. The God of ontotheology, the God of pure act, self-subsistent being, and immutability, impassibility, and omnipotence, does not cohere with the revelation of God in the texts of Scripture, where God is portrayed as wrestling with Godself, as lamenting, as regretting, and as being grieved in the heart (*GMB*, 30). The God of ontotheology certainly does not seem to be revealed in that most essential image of

God, Jesus Christ (*GMB*, 48). Kearney is particularly taken with St. Paul's explosive image of Jesus' incarnation as a process of *kenosis*, of divine emptying and disappropriation. Christ "empties" himself and transforms himself into the form of a servant, enfleshes himself, and enters into the temporal process of history precisely in order to reveal to humanity the very heart of God, in order to manifest the grace and forgiveness of the God who comes as one calling all people to receive the gift of redemption. The incarnation, God's passage through being and flesh, models the kenotic, self-giving love of a God who opens Godself to the sinful other, who accepts the risk of rejection and suffering, in order to possibilize the continual process of ushering in the Kingdom of justice and truth. *Kenosis* does not result from some external necessity being placed upon God, nor on some inherent lack or weakness within the divine being. Instead, it is a potentiality actualized freely by a God who loves so deeply, so infinitely, and so inexplicably that God is willing to sacrifice the divine self in order to actualize the potentiality that individuals might respond to the call of salvation with an obedient "yes."

Kearney affiliates God's kenotic love with *Posse* by utilizing Heidegger's ontological language of *Vermögen des Mögens*—"loving potency" or "possibilization of love." He claims that although Heidegger speaks of being and not God, this phrase captures something of the essential dynamic of God as a kenotic "May Be" by playing off of the similarity between "loving" (*mögen*) and "making possible" (*vermögen*) (*PP*, 226). This notion of "loving potency" not only overcomes the metaphysical prejudice of actuality over potentiality, but it also permits a renewed sensitivity to an eschatological interpretation of "the grace-giving *posse* of the Creator." Yet, following Heidegger, Kearney insists that eschatology should be conceived "topologically" or, better, "u-topologically," as the "no-place" (*u-topia*) that does not recapitulate the homogeneity of the actual but creates the unique event of the impossible possibility of an unforeseen future. God constantly creates the possibility of this "no-place" and comes to this impossible site "in hitherto unimagined ways" (*SGM*, 227–228). This divine possibilizing, however, always betrays the kinetics of a kenotic love of a God who always comes as the God Who May Be.[31]

Understanding God as this kenotic *Posse* helps to avoid three traditional antinomies associated with classical theism. First, it offers a way of explaining the contiguity of divine power and human freedom. If God's creative and redemptive power centers on the efficacy of possibilizing and not actualizing reality, and if in creating human beings as *imago Dei* God endows them with the gift of freedom in order to invite them to participate in the diachronic dynamism of creating the future Kingdom, then there is no inconsistency in holding both divine power and human freedom. Second, kenotic *Posse* addresses the problem of theodicy, for if God gives freedom to individuals such that they might participate with God in possibilizing the future, they also have the freedom to refuse to participate. God takes the divine risk that human beings will not receive the divine love, will not remain faithful to their promises, and, consequently, will not allow God's love and grace to be actualized in the structure of reality. Third, God as kenotic *Posse* offers a better image for comprehending and communicating a God who is intimately involved as an active power within history, as a God who truly loves the other and desires love from the other. In other words, God as the eschatological "May Be" avoids the tension between a doctrine of divine aseity and the ruling Christian metaphor "God is love." The traditional notion of aseity parallels an Aristotelian metaphysical explanation of God's engendering love as a human potential without actually loving human beings themselves. That is, God's perfection necessitates that God must be "Love-Loving-Itself" and not ever truly loving the other. On the contrary, however, the biblical God loves the other, not just God-self in the other. The God of Jesus is the loving Father, who through self-sacrifice risks vulnerability, allows the other to affect God, to wound God, to anger God, but also to love God and bring God joy (*PP*, 225–230). In other words, by doing his imaginative theology of the Christomorphic, kenotic God Who May Be, Kearney does a theopassionism, a postmodern theology of the suffering God.

Concluding Repetition

> The promise made to Abraham that his people would have a salvific relation with God is an inexhaustible promise . . . as such it opens a history in which this promise can be repeated and reinterpreted over and over again—with Moses, then David, and so on. So that the biblical narrative of this "not yet realized" promise creates a cumulative history of repetition.
>
> **Paul Ricoeur**

> I have the feeling there is loss when I know that things don't repeat and that the repetition I love is not possible;

> this is what I call loss of memory, the loss of repetition, not repetition in the mechanical sense of the term, but of resurrection, resuscitation, regeneration.
>
> **Jacques Derrida**

So what does Richard Kearney imagine when he imagines his God? He imagines an unimaginable God who should not be imagined according to the metaphysical categories of ontotheology with its semantically pertinent vocabulary of *actus purus, ipsum esse subsistens,* and *causa sui.* Such linguistic figures defigure God into either a stationary deity, lacking the kinesis of temporality and relationship, or some circulating deity whose only vector is the *curvatus in se* of thought thinking itself or love loving itself. Kearney prefers to imagine God according to a biblical poetics, those creative narratives and literary tropes that reveal through semantic *im*pertinence a living God, a lord of history, who acts and intervenes, who accompanies and leads forth, who calls and comes. These biblical twists and turns along the way lead him to transfigure God into kinetic images of playing and dancing. God reveals Godself in Scripture as a hyperactive creator who joins with human playmates in order to cavort in creation with delight and abandon (*GMB,* 268).[32] This playful God also reveals Godself as a triune deity who loves to dance. Traditionally, the Trinitarian relationship has been interpreted as *perichoresis* (to dance around) and *circumincession* (to give way or change position), terms that image the dancelike movements of the Father, Son, and Spirit as each gives way to the other, allowing the other to cut in and to change partners. This Trinitarian rondo takes on a unique quality through the image of incarnation, the movement into flesh, by which the Son transfigures himself into a servant, repositions himself in the world, and proclaims the good news that there are no Cinderellas, for everyone has been invited to the ball (*GMB,* 109; *SGM,* 207).[33] This Christocentric choreography is the motion of grace through the kinetics of *kenosis.*

Kinetics and *kenosis* are the two foci around which Kearney's refiguration of God elliptically revolves. God as playing, as dancing, as moving, as possibilizing, as coming, as incarnating, as passing through Being, as always escaping the claustrophobia of conceptual limitations— all of these are active images, images of a God who never remains still or absolutely immutable. No, his God cannot sit still, but always moves centrifugally, acts out of a passion to go forth toward the other, to empty the divine self, to dispossess the divine self in order to possess the other. Such *kenosis* actuates the ecstatic God of possibility and differentiates that God from the ontotheological, metaphysical God of stasis.

As one "listens" to Kearney's Irish theological brogue, one might well detect a certain Danish accent to it, for indeed one can argue that Kearney's theological cartography, his mapping out of a tropology along his imaginative itinerary toward understanding God, is quite reminiscent of Søren Kierkegaard. Kierkegaard discounts metaphysics because it centers on a love of immobility, an inability and/or refusal to take time and change seriously, to acknowledge or respect that life is movement, and to affirm that existence has horizons that constantly shift and beckon each individual to move forward toward possibility and impossibility. He proposes the movement of repetition as an existentially more potent alternative to metaphysics, one that not only celebrates motion but celebrates it in its passion for futurity. I contend that this Kierkegaardian concept offers an interesting translation of Kearney's theology of the God Who May Be, that one can apply that concept to God, mutatis mutandis, of course, and utilize it as something of a theologeme in order to develop prolegomena for any future imaginative systematics.

Kierkegaard develops his understanding of repetition in an eponymously titled work written under the pseudonym Constantin Constantius. In that text, Constantius discriminates between two perspectives on motion. He rightly interprets traditional metaphysics as always chafing against the friction of any genuine motion; therefore, metaphysics (1) denies motion in the Eleatic sense of the non-being of non-being, (2) subordinates motion to the Eternal in the Platonic sense of *anamnesis* (recollection), or (3) transmutes motion into commotion in the Hegelian sense of mediation (*Aufheben*).[34] The second perspective, that of repetition, counters with an appreciation for motion, a recognition that without motion, life becomes meaningless, and that for the existing individual, no possible attainment of a "self" may obtain without the particular type of motion offered by repetition (*R*, 149). For Constantius, repetition offers a significant counterpoint to the Platonic notion of recollection and the Hegelian idea of mediation. For the former, movement is a movement backward toward some previous manifestation of full presence, an archival passion to return to what has always been. For the latter, movement is synthesized in an immanent process that manifests full presence in the absolute knowledge of the system. In both cases, the teleological impact of the two movements is to terminate movement. Repetition, on the other hand, celebrates movement and directs it forward, not backward; keeps it active and not attenuated in an inertial process of mediation. It references genuine metamorphosis as resulting from transcendent dynamics, from eternity's breaking into temporality in the "Moment" (*Augenblick*), keeping time in motion toward a future of possibility. Repetition begins in actuality, proceeds through freedom, and realizes existence. The entire process establishes change within the milieu of continuity with the past and an openness toward the future through a passion for the possible. In other words, by means of inwardness, freedom, and transcendence, repetition activates the task of becoming a self through the resolute decisions based in a fidelity and commitment to the eternal.

Ironically, Constantius "abandons" his theory of repetition and does so specifically because it references transcendence, a movement that he simply cannot make. In a supplemental glossing of the text, Kierkegaard fleshes out Constantius's abandonment of repetition as his incapacity to take the step of religion, for repetition is, indeed, finally a religious gesture made "by virtue of the absurd" and ultimately manifested as the transformational dynamic of atonement (*R*, 324). Sin cannot be mediated but must be forgiven; the sinner cannot be renewed but must be re-created. The Christian religious notion of salvation as a new birth and of the redeemed individual as a new creature, therefore, best exemplifies repetition. By no longer holding to the past but pressing forward into the future, the redeemed individual passionately strives with fear and trembling toward the impossibility of the realization of self in relation to God.[35] Consequently, one may interpret repetition as a theological term, at least in the sense that religion and atonement eventually reference the idea of God and, for Kierkegaard, more accurately the personal God revealed through the Hebrew and Christian Scriptures.

Undoubtedly, Kierkegaard himself would not interpret repetition as a theological term or ever attribute it to God as an idiom for explaining God's interaction with existing individuals; however, given its religious and soteriological qualities, to use the concept as a theologically heuristic device, as a possible way of imagining how God affects existence, would not be completely inappropriate. John Caputo, for example, might be one who would approve of using repetition as a theological predicate. In one of his extended definitions of repetition, Constantius characterizes it as "the *interest* [*Interesse*] of metaphysics and also the interest upon which metaphysics comes to grief" (*R*, 149). *Inter-esse* etymologically means "being in the middle," or "in the middle of being"; therefore, "interest" as "involvement in" or "concern for" carries with it the idea of participation and solicitude. In other words, repetition references a genuine immersion in the kinetics of existence, a functional immanence within the flux of time and history, the place where real human beings live, suffer, laugh, cry, and die. In *Radical Hermeneutics*, Caputo interprets this "mediational" quality of repetition as "firmly placing oneself in and amidst the strife of temporal becoming" (*RH*, 33).[36] Recently, Caputo discusses a postmetaphysical reading of divine transcendence and concludes that one can no longer understand God's eminence as hyperousiological and homogeneous but as a "disturbing presence" that manifests a heterophilia, a love for the different and the other. He writes:

> in the religion of a deconstructionist, "God" stands not above being as a hyperpresence, but in the middle of being, by identifying with everything the world casts out and leaves out.[37]

Caputo qualifies God, then, as *inter-esse*, not "being" above being in some antiseptic sphere of the *epekeina tes ousias* nor as "being" beneath being in some sublime abyssal *Urgrund*, but as "being" in the midst of being in the gracious "interestedness" of a loving, kenotic presence. Caputo thus "speaks" of God with exactly the same nomenclature that Kierkegaard uses to "speak" of repetition. As a result, using repetition as a possible cipher for Kearney's kenotic God Who May Be might not be a category mistake after all.

Kearney's God Who May Be certainly reveals Godself as an "interested" deity, a God in the midst of time and history engaging real individuals within the very structures of their existence. Indeed, in his fourth reduction, Kearney explicitly notes that God leads back to the "little things" of factical existence, the "epiphanies of the everyday," by leading forward to the sacred possibilities yearning to be revealed. As repetition moves from actuality to existence, so God passes through being in order to repeat Godself in discrete moments of encounter, such as with Moses at the burning bush or in Christ with the disciples on Mount Tabor. When God relates to human beings, God does so as a God who desires to repeat those encounters, who waits for individuals to respond to his repeated calls for relationship. This divine interest in intimate relationships holds significant implications for God as creator. Kierkegaard claims that without repetition there would be no divine creation (*R*, 133). Likewise, Kearney insists that God desires humans to join him in the ongoing process of creation, to respond to God's repeated calls for relationship with the "Here I am" of commitment and obedience. Creation, then, is no punctilear occurrence, no aoristic singularity that winds the watch and walks away. Instead, for God as *Posse*, creation is always incomplete, with remainder, open to repeated engagements between a God who gives freedom and human beings who use it to join God in the creative process. One might say that the seventh day of creation is a day of repetition.

Divine repetition effects not only creation but redemption as well. God as *Posse* is not only the creating God but the coming God, the God who comes into the world as the one who is always to come. He repeats his coming again and again, for the sake of an "ad-venturous" repetition forward, seeking to realize an eschatological atonement. But God's reiterative coming remains a possibility within the context of undecidability, that is, God's coming disallows explicit predelineation but always occurs with the potential of surprise, as the unprogrammable, im/possible event. The incarnation manifests one such aleatoric repetition, since the divine presence comes into the world yet again, but in the unique and singular movement of kenotic enfleshment in Jesus of Nazareth. But this unique personal manifestation of God suffers and dies on the cross. Yet, he returns as the resurrected one, his life repeated by the quickening power of the same Holy Spirit who first conceived him in Mary's womb. This resurrected Christ offers atonement and redemption, the ultimate repetition of salvation that does not promise a recapitulation of a prior glory, no reiteration of Eden, but the promise of a new creation, a new heaven and new earth, a new eschatological reality that draws individuals forward toward a coming Kingdom. The same Christ who offers such a salvific movement forward promises to come again, to repeat his presence in the future. But who knows in what surprising ways this Christ might repeat his coming presence?

Kearney's creative and redemptive God of possibility is a God of promise, but promise itself is always a matter of repetition. To make a promise, to commit oneself to some future action, is to obligate oneself to repetition. For example, in a marriage ceremony, the couple "repeats" their vows after the minister and in the presence of the gathered witnesses; however, that formal repetition commits them to repeating their vows after themselves and often in the absence of each other until death makes repetition impossible. But fidelity demands that every vow be repeated in every context, that whenever one gives one's word, one must give it again and again. One keeps one's word only by giving it repeatedly. If one says "yes" to another, one cannot say it only once; therefore, it should come as no surprise that God restates his covenant constantly, at different times to different people. As Ricoeur states so beautifully, God establishes a history of repetition by dedicating the divine self to being/becoming faithful and repeating the "yes" of every divine promise. The manifestation of the unnameable divine name given to Moses at Sinai is itself a repetition. The God who names Godself "I am who I will be," who binds Godself to the other with the "(Here) I am," and who, thereby, promises the recurrence of divine grace and love, reminds Moses at the beginning of their conversation that God has been the God of Abraham, Isaac, and Jacob. God has already encountered others, revealed the divine self to others, and given the divine Word to others in order to establish covenant relationships of promise. Consequently, God is simply repeating Godself to Moses, saying "yes" again, and renewing God's obligation to say "yes" yet again, and again, and . . . again. For Caputo, individuals should respond to this divine promissory repetition with the complementary repetition of faith. He writes, "For faith means to live without keeping count, without taking account (*sine ratione*), and to say yes, a number of yeses, *oui, oui*, again and again, each day, day by day."[38]

Within the context of the kenotic movement of divine creation, redemption, and promise, the God Who May Be also pledges to forgive, which itself depends on the reiteration of gift and promise. Forgiving as for-*giving* must be a continual donation of freedom from vengeance and retribution, the gift of pardon that keeps on giving in two respects. First, forgiveness as promise falls under the repetitive nature of divine grace. As Derrida claims, "[i]n principle, there is no limit to forgiveness, no *measure*, no moderation, no 'to what point?' "[39] The book of Judges in the Hebrew Scriptures, for example, evidences God's unlimited commitment to release individuals and communities from the destructive implications of retribution. The narrative recounts episode after episode in which Israel breaks the divine commandments, suffers because of their infidelity, cries to God for mercy, and receives it. Time and time again, the repetition of rebellion is matched by the repetition of redemption. These narratives illustrate the Pauline principle that where sin abounds, grace abounds much more. Forgiveness always flows forth out of an extravagant abundance of grace, an abundance that reflects the infinite repetitive power of the God who comes to save and liberate.

That God considers the repetitive nature of forgiveness as quite significant may be witnessed in Jesus' encounter with the Apostle Peter when Peter inquires into the limits of forgiveness: "Lord, how often shall my brother sin against me and I forgive him? Up to seven times?" In other words, Peter asks Jesus how many times he should repeat the gift of forgiveness and, in asking, suggests that perhaps seven repetitions are more than generous. Jesus, however, rejects Peter's number and informs him that the limit is actually seventy times seven, an imaginary number for an eschatologically open process of forgiveness. Jesus tells Peter and all of his followers that in the Kingdom of God, one never ceases to repeat forgiveness, or, as Derrida would state it, that forgiveness has no limit. As Kearney claims, the desire of God as kenotic *Posse* comes not from deficiency, from a subtraction of divine sovereignty, but from "grace and gratuity, gift and surplus, less insufficiency than the bursting forth of the 'more' in the 'less'" (*DG*, 117).

Repetition and forgiveness correlate at a second point, one that has become a central theme in Caputo's postsecular philosophical theology. He contends that forgiveness must be a forgetting of the past and a "letting go" of vengeance. Forgiveness is gift and, consequently, must not be mistranslated into an economy of exchange, into the language of "debits and credits," into "treasuries of merit" against which one may borrow, or into a quid pro quo reciprocity whereby the injured party receives her "pound of flesh." Forgiveness should be interpreted according to the "mad economics" of the Kingdom of God, the noneconomic economy taught by Jesus when he instructs his followers to turn cheeks, love enemies, and, yes, forgive seventy times seven. Jesus even teaches such a mad economics of forgiveness when he instructs his disciples on how to pray: "Forgive us . . . as we forgive others." Is this not another instance of repetition, in that God's forgiveness of the disciple repeats the forgiveness given first by the disciple to the other? Caputo would concur, for in glossing this "prayerful" text, he claims that the "kingdom is the *repetition* beyond the resignation . . . the love beyond the obligation" (*PT*, 226). For Jesus, forgiveness cannot be "earned" or "deserved"; relational books cannot be balanced and the debt considered forgiven. To forgive a debt means to cancel it, not to have it paid back. It means that the loss is absorbed, that books are closed without a zero sum, and that the debtor is liberated from the burden of having to make up the difference. For Caputo, then, to forgive in the Christomorphic sense of the term leads one to say, "Forget it; it never happened."[40]

Yet, if the offense occurred, it did happen, and one cannot forget it. Caputo recognizes, therefore, that forgetting is impossible and, in certain situations, inappropriate. He accepts that the oppressed and violated victims of past malfeasance should be honored and in some sense "saved" through the "dangerous memory of suffering." The Holocaust must not be forgotten; Oklahoma City must not be forgotten; and 9/11 must not be forgotten. Still, in remembering those events, communities should not allow the past to fester into the vengeance and hatred that contaminate the present and the future. Nor should individuals allow such infestation of their temporality in contexts of personal offense and violation. Whenever forgiveness is granted, the one giving it actually pledges to repeat that gift in the future. Whenever the offense is remembered, the one who forgives must also remember the forgiveness. Throughout the future, then, one must constantly repeat the forgiveness, repeat the "letting go" of revenge and anger. Could one also imagine divine forgiveness as the amnesty of a recurring amnesia, as God's intent to remember to forget, to realize redemption by repeating the gift of pardon? Perhaps God provides just such an image in certain prophetic texts where God makes a new eschatological promise and obligates Godself to Israel through a new covenant written on their hearts, a covenant predicated upon divine forgiveness. Through the prophet Isaiah, God says, "I, even I, am the one who wipes out your transgressions for My own sake, And I will not *remember* your sins" (Isaiah 43:25; emphasis added). Then God repeats Godself in Jeremiah 31:34: "their sin I will *remember* no more" (emphasis added). The future tense of both "non-rememberings" indicates that through the divine imagination God projects a time to come in which God will respond to the repentance of Israel, a time when the God Who May Be may be a God of grace and compassion.

Kearney would undoubtedly accept much of Caputo's "radical" theory of forgiveness. Certainly he would accept the validity of forgiveness as repetition, for he states quite unequivocally that "amnesty is never amnesia: the past must be recollected, reimagined, rethought and worked-through so that we can identify, *grosso modo*, what it is that we are forgiving" (*SGM*, 105–106). He also explicitly agrees with Ricoeur that through the narrative imagination, communities and individuals forgive by remembering to relinquish vengeance and retribution, that is, remembering to repeat the "having let go" (*NER*, 27). Furthermore, extending forgiveness as repetition to God is quite consistent with Kearney's imaginative third way of transfiguring God as the One Who May Be as kenotic love. His God Who May Be is a God of grace and compassion, who gives the divine Word as a promise of redemption, obligates the divine self to actualize a possible eschatological renewal of the kingdom of righteousness, summons individuals to participate in possibilizing that Kingdom to come, and desires to hear the "yes" repeated by human beings whom God allows to affect who God will be. The prophet Isaiah joins Kearney in imagining such a God of unimaginable grace: "Therefore the Lord *longs* to be gracious to you, and therefore he *waits* on high to have compassion on you. For the Lord is a God of justice; how blessed are all those who *long* for Him" (30:18; emphasis added). Isaiah writes of the desire of God, a desire that is, indeed, God's desire for the desire of the human other who in freedom cultivates a desire of God. For Kearney, this desire of God, in both senses of the genitive, finds expression through the Christomorphic imagination of kenotic possibility.[41] In *Poétique du Possible*, when writing about the vulnerable God of the Bible and of the kenotic significance of the Exodic "I Am the One Who May Be," Kearney draws an interesting conclusion: "God will be, then, the loving [*aimant*] *Posse* who possibilizes humanity" (*PP*, 229). The linguistic sign *aimant* presents a fascinating semiotic iteration that Derrida would surely love and that summarizes with beautiful ambiguity Kearney's imaginative theology. As an adjective, *aimant* is French for "loving" and "affectionate"; however, as a noun, *aimant* is French for "magnet." This provocative surplus of meaning allows one to catch the imaginative dynamic of a God Who May Be as a loving God, a compassionate and affectionate God of possibility who also reveals Godself as a charismatic deity, one who is constantly attracting and luring human beings toward the impossibility of a future possibility of grace (*charis*). Kearney imagines the covenant-making God, the God of promise and obligation, to be a God "who persuades rather than coerces, invites rather than imposes, asks rather than impels" (*PP*, 30). The God Who May Be as the God of Advent comes as a "magnetic" event "breaking into" and "passing through" Being in order to draw individuals out of a static actuality toward the kinetics of possibility. The magnetic God of possibility entices and entreats individuals to repeat forward the "Here I am" of commitment and, thereby, to usher in God's Kingdom and, more important, under the influence of God's magnetic field, to participate in God's being the God that God desires to be. Now just imagine that!

Is God Diminished If We Abscond?

MARK PATRICK HEDERMAN

I.

Throughout his trilogy Philosophy at the Limit, Richard Kearney leads us "on the sinuous paths through postmodernity and beyond." Calling on the messenger god, Hermes, he pioneers a new way of interpreting three of the defining contours of our third-millennial profile: strangers, gods, and monsters, three different names for our experience of alterity and otherness. The three volumes, if you take them not in chronological order but in order of accessibility, could be said to follow a technique similar to that used by Kierkegaard. The latter's *Journal of a Seducer* was a best-selling page-turner available even in railway stations. It was meant to lead the unsuspecting reader from the sensational, through the ethical, to the religious.

Kearney's book *On Stories* is published in a new series called Thinking in Action, which "takes philosophy to its public." *Strangers, Gods and Monsters*, the second volume in the trilogy, provides an indelible object lesson in how "we often project onto others those unconscious fears which we recoil from in ourselves." In a phrase that typifies Kearney's capacity to synthesize pithily, he writes, "The adversary I so love to hate is often nothing less than myself in disguise" (*SGM*, 75). If, as Kearney holds, "the greatness of Kant was to recognize the need to pass from a purely 'theoretical' explanation of evil to a more 'practical' one," then the same can be said for Kearney in this book with regard to aliens and strangers (*SGM*, 87). He charts a much-needed third way between the somewhat masochistic metaphysics of Levinas and the almost autistic psychoanalysis of Freud. His proposal is "a hermeneutic pluralism of otherness," a sort of "polysemy of alterity." There can be no otherness so exterior (Levinas) or so unconscious (Freud) that it cannot be "minimally interpreted by a self" (*SGM*, 81). Kearney quotes Thich Nhat Hanh to the effect that "You won't regard anyone as an enemy when you have penetrated the reality of interbeing" (*SGM*, 45). His discerning and practical guidance here echoes Martin Buber's reply to the critique made by Levinas of his "I- Thou" relationship:[1]

> Levinas errs in a strange way when he supposes that I see in the *amitié toute spirituelle* the peak of the I-Thou relation. On the contrary, this relationship seems to me to win its true greatness and powerfulness precisely there where two men without a strong spiritual ground in common, even of very different kinds of spirit, yes of opposite dispositions, still stand over against each other so that each of the two knows and means, recognizes and acknowledges, accepts and confirms the other, even in the severest conflict, as this particular person. In the common situation, even in the common situation of fighting with each other, he holds present to himself the experience-side of the other, his living through this situation. This is no friendship, this is only the comradeship of the human creature, a comradeship that has reached fulfilment. No "ether," as Levinas thinks, but the hard human earth, the common in the uncommon.

This was Martin Buber months before his death, giving us the wisdom of a life spent in such dialogue with the "other." There is an experience of otherness, as commonality amid difference, a direct, almost unmediated, connection between persons as first principle acknowledging first principle, to which Buber gave living testimony through his life and his work. However, Kearney's purpose is more ambitious. Since he has lived for many years with postmodernism, the energy and aim of this trilogy would seem to be both phenomenological and proselytizing. He wants not only to pass through and beyond postmodernism himself, but he wants to take with him those with whom he has labored at the coal face: Ricoeur, Husserl, Derrida, Freud, Heidegger, Kristeva, and Levinas. However, to persuade such interlocutors that at the limits of our finitude, "at Land's End we require novel mappings of uncharted realms, lest we slip over the edge into the abyss of the unknowable," requires such depth and detail, such convolution of expression, such idiomatic exchange between the cognoscenti, that the public to whom this "thinking in action" was being targeted, at least in the first volume, could be left behind by the time they reach the third, *The God Who May Be*. Kearney chooses to remain within the orbit and the idiom of so-called postmodern philosophy while he expresses phenomenologically the relationship with the other as alien and/or stranger, and with God as the ultimate other.

II.

The God Who May Be opens with a provocative sentence: "God neither is nor is not but may be." The last two words are the enigmatic ones. Somehow permission for God to be, whether in conditional or subjunctive mood, depends upon us. "Without us no Word can be made flesh," the provocation continues (*GMB*, 4). So the first question is this: Will God be diminished if we abscond?

Apart from the style, which is, at times, unnecessarily arcane, there is the "surprising and creative answer to who or what God might be." This "penetrating and original" answer is built out of several pillars borrowed from other edifices and has a dome attributed to Nicholas of Cusa, but dismantled and reconstructed beyond recognition. "Possibility" as God's presence happens in our world and happens for us; indeed, it happens through us, and can't happen without us. This "possible" for Kearney is balanced somewhere between Husserl's, Bloch's, Heidegger's, and Derrida's attempts to articulate it.

Salvation for Bloch, for instance, becomes something like the trigonometry of navigation between the Scylla of hard reality and the Charybdis of "possibility," but at all times orchestrated and controlled by the mind and will of human endeavor. Derrida, a self-confessed atheist, provides the ultimate shield against any projection of humanist utopias and focuses the exact area of debate on the question of "genuine decision" (*GMB*, 94). Even Heidegger might be accused of identifying "the quiet power of the possible" with an essentially human property, until Kearney convinces us that in his later thought it is understood as "an unambiguous gift of Being itself" (*GMB*, 91).

But the question I would ask is whether it is possible for anyone to connect with the God Who May Be without paying the deepest and humblest attention to the tapping on the wall from the other side. Ultimately, it takes two to tango. If we restrict ourselves to the light of phenomenological and hermeneutic consciousness piercing outward to the dark or to the depths, there is no guarantee that the creatures whisking past our diving bell with its powerful artificial light from the upper world are not merely frantic caricatures of organic life: heteropods or skyphomedusas, compact monsters of slime.

On the other hand, genuine dialogue with the "Other," in whatever form that may take, must surely involve some address that will change the attitude and "consciousness" of the explorer. Such communication could even be as inarticulate as underwater sonar, bouncing pulsations off the other, and listening for an echo. There is an impression given at the end of *The God Who May Be* that the description given by Kearney of the connection with the "Possibilizing God" is somehow an extension of the trajectory outlined in the combined deliberations of the phenomenologists he quotes. I believe that this is as unfair to them as it is to another hidden source. The God of "perhaps" has surely been lurking in the hedgerows of this particular philosophical path. The English word "perhaps" might even be the nearest approximation to "the God Who May Be," given that "every experience is an event which registers that which comes from the unpredictable otherness of the future" (*GMB*, 94). "Perhaps" is not a direct translation of the French "*peut-être*." It percolates the future through (*per*) the plural of "hap," meaning "chance," suggesting that every crossroads presents a decisive happening for each of us as painters of the icon of the future. History becomes a hiding place where chance happenings can be undercover agents for an otherwise undetectable Other. "Coincidences," in Doris Lessing's formula, can be "God's way of remaining anonymous." These are not things we can prove; they are realities to which we must testify whenever we undertake to give an accurate account of what happened.

However, the postmodern and phenomenological debates can continue without prejudice if we limit ourselves to the precise mechanism of our human approach to the future. Here "decision" is the decisive term. This cannot be simply an activation of the will to power. Derrida prefers what he calls "*receptive* decision" or invention. Invention cannot be such unless it involves the impossible; anything less than this is a mere rehearsal of scenarios already contained within our own repertoire. God as possibility has to be totally implausible; otherwise he risks being déjà-vu. Kearney goes further. His God Who May Be involves "human freedom and creativity as a way of participating in the transfiguring play of creation" (*GMB*, 105). This is "the Kingdom of God." We are situated in the created world and involved in accomplishing a space that is cleared by the double *kenosis* of God and ourselves, "an alternative site from which to rebegin afresh" (*GMB*, 108). The chapter "God or *Khora*?" provides an interesting geography of such presence/absence in which the North Pole is *khora* (defended by Jacques Derrida and John Caputo) and the South Pole is God (of the metaphysical variety). "On the one side of the ring, Caputo lines up the idioms of paternal metaphysics . . . on the other . . . 'anarchic abandon'" (*SGM*, 207). The aim is to define or describe the amorphous space that precedes all that appears in our world. Is it being? Is it God? Both? Or before both? And which discipline is most adequate to address this elusive X? Cosmology? Ontology? Psychology? Theology? These are the questions that have been exercising a number of postmodern thinkers (*SGM*, 194). Kearney "wagers" that "*khora* is neither identical with God nor incompatible with God but marks an open site where the divine may dwell and heal."

I wonder to what extent his wager can be derived from any of the foregoing discussion. I would add two other sources which might support his conclusion. One of the original uses of *khora* in Greek theater is where the chorus acts as hyphen between the space of the stage and the space of the audience. In something of a similar juxtaposition, *khora* could be a hyphen between, a preposition, which both saves and situates God and ourselves. In a different context but with similar intent, the preposition used by St. Paul, *en* ["in Christ"], suggests that this no-man's land, zone, desert, or dividing line went right through the person of Christ as hybrid, as Siamese twins, joined by the *vinculum* of personhood. The word *perichoresis* is also a circumlocution around the empty *khora*, which forms the core of the word itself, a dance of persons around an uncontaminating center. The *kenosis* of divinity must ultimately imply the creation of such a Rubik's cube of possibility outside itself and from which the further possibility of free relationship becomes possible for us as equally free and infinite persons.

What allows this to happen in us is humility. Kearney describes it as "the renunciation of my will-to-power." By abandoning our egos, he suggests, we may allow "the infinite to beget itself in my persona." However, our experience of *khora* is dependent upon our capacity to listen to the silence, to feel the touch of otherness, to distinguish between darkness as vacant and darkness as velvet. Ultimately, it is to do with antennae beyond the orbit of vision or of mind as searchlight, allowing oneself to be touched. The question is whether one can adopt such an attitude without the trust and belief that penetration by the infinite is both possible and life-giving.

III.

If one takes Kant as originating grandfather of modernism, and Levinas and Derrida as paternal progenitors of postmodernism, and then join the plethora of artists and philosophers who are their progeny, and if one agrees to abide by the rules and not bring any extrinsic argument or influence to bear, then one is left to struggle within the prison walls of self-imposed autism with regard to contact with whatever might be beyond the orbit of comprehensibility. "All I know is a door into the dark." Beyond the reach of the omnidirectional human spotlight, whatever lurks in exterior darkness is the irrevocably other. This is unidentifiable alterity that remains uncategorizable and therefore is as likely to be an alien as an ally, a monster as a messenger, a stranger as a neighbor. Kearney is still confident that within the orbit of human interpretation and narrative imagination we can detect and discern the benevolence of such presence when it emanates from the divine.

Examining the category of the sublime in Kant (chapter 4 of *Strangers, Gods, and Monsters*), Kearney shows that this is not so much a description of something outside, an awe-inspiring object. Rather, is it an effect/affect on the inside, a revelation of the more in subjectivity, which is prised into exercise, surprised into self-identification by the shock of encounter with the unexpected. The event of alterity awakens the subliminal capacity in us, the otherwise dormant sensitivity to what is beyond us. Kearney goes further: the traces of "apparition" can be developed later into the transparencies of a slide show within the darkroom of the prison house.

The "story" that results from or is inspired by the shock of such encounter contains within itself the phosphorescence of the original insemination and becomes the way in which alterity can be examined within the dark confines of the "same," which is otherwise allergic to its unassimilable presence. The storyteller—Kearney quotes Arundhati Roy—"tells stories of the gods, but his yarn is spun from the ungodly, human heart" (quoted in *OS*, 9). Something from the outside touches us, and when we are touched, "the touch goes to our very nature and the will is shaken by the touch so that only now is the nature of willing made to appear and set in motion. Not until then do we will willingly."[2]

If we are to remain within the confines of postmodern philosophy to articulate such presence, then it seems to me that the later Heidegger phenomenologically excavated such unusual "decisiveness." As well as our conversion, our self-emptying, "turning implies that the Open itself must have turned toward us in a way that allows us to turn our unshieldedness towards it" (*PLT*, 122). Will is the motivating force and dominating energy in our lives. The will to power is perhaps the dominant mechanism of the universe as we find ourselves in it. But this is only because willing is the way we think we have to be, the way we crave to be, because it is the motor force that pushes us toward fulfillment. Conversion occurs because we are stopped in our tracks, the tracks laid down by our habitual way of perceiving our destiny. Something "touches" us, and this is the beginning of our "conversion," which is essentially a transformation of the nature and the movement of willing. All of which must occur in a place—although not a geographical one. Being "rooted," for Heidegger, is a metaphor; we are talking about the "inner domain of the heart" and "the conversion of consciousness and that inside the sphere of consciousness" (*PLT*, 127).

The mystery of the union of two wills is the kernel of the mystery that Kearney addresses in his trilogy. There is a space between, a difference between: "The inner domain of the heart is not only more inward than the interior that belongs to calculating representation, and therefore more invisible; it also extends further than does the realm of merely producible objects." This is "uncustomary consciousness," a new way of being mindful.[3]

The conversion of "turning" is the transformation of our inmost interior, which "gives space to the worldly whole of the Open" (*PLT*, 136). From our side of this duet, in terms of human nature, this transformation is often accounted for in terms of will. The "self-assertive" person is one who wills in the covetous fashion of the merchant, calculating from his perspective the vision of things, and the goal of all activity. Such willing is calculated toward productivity of the most useful and profitable kind. On the other hand, "the more venturesome" or "those who say in a greater degree, in the manner of the singer" are those "whose singing is turned away from all purposeful self-assertion. It is not willing in the sense of desire. Their song does not solicit anything to be produced" (*PLT*, 138). And yet, "the more venturesome will more strongly in that they will in a different way from the purposeful self-assertion of the objectifying of the world. Their willing wills nothing of this kind. If willing remains mere self-assertion, they will nothing" (*PLT*, 140).

If this is what Kearney means by story or narrative imagination, then it involves only a very rare kind of "poetry" and a subjectivity that might be described as porous. Dimensions of interiority have been unearthed that supersede the comparatively superficial dimension within which subjectivity is the beginning and end of its own meaning and activity. The "nothing" beyond the false self-sufficiency of humankind, which leads many theologians to the philosophical deduction of creation ex nihilo, leads Heidegger to a further dimension which is "the track into the dark of the world's night" (*PLT*, 141). This dimension can never be recuperated for humanity by the covetousness of subjectivity. It is as though the "heart" in our natural self-assertive order is concave, whereas in the "order of angels," it becomes convex. The convex attitude of "the heart" is a conversion of all the natural "covetous" shapes and gestures into an attitude that "accomplishes" rather than produces a song whose sound does not cling to something that is eventually attained, but which has "already shattered itself even in the sounding, so that there may occur only that which was sung itself" (*PLT*, 139). It is in this sense that "song is existence," because "song" is that "saying" between being and ourselves. "Story" could be another name for such a song.

The singer of such songs, if Kearney's and Heidegger's views on "poetics" are correct, is one who allows the breath of existence to find its way through. It is a "middle voice" whose reality is neither within nor without, "a step back from the thinking that merely represents—that is, explains—to the thinking that responds and recalls" (*PLT*, 181). The God Who May Be is, in this scenario, one who requires "sayers who more sayingly say . . . a saying other than the rest of human saying" (*PLT*, 140).

Putting this in the context of the "fourth reduction" and admitting unashamedly a belief in the presence of the Trinitarian God of Judeo-Christianity, it is possible to offer solutions to the ingenious crossword presented by Richard Kearney and John Manoussakis, as if one could see the reverse side of the tapestry or had a preview of the crossword answers in tomorrow's newspaper.

The fourth reduction can be interpreted theologically through four descents in the *kenosis* of God. The first, "transcendental," reduction is situating God as above and beyond anything which we experience subjectively as "us," God as beyond and above our epistemological radar screens. The second, "ontological," reduction could be interpreted as creation of the world: "The world is charged with the grandeur of God," in Hopkins's phrase. This involves more specifically the first person of the Trinity as Father, originator, and creator. The third, "dosological," reduction is the *kenosis* of the Son, the second person of the Trinity, who emptied Himself, taking the form of a slave. Incarnation is more properly viewed in terms of this third level of gift or "givenness" in terms of "hypostatic union between phenomenon and phenomenality," as Manoussakis puts it: Christ as gift and sacrifice of himself. The fourth, or "prosopic," reduction becomes most fittingly, then, the further *kenosis* of the Trinitarian God in and through the "impersonatisation" of the Holy Spirit. "The eschatological reduction retrieves and repeats the *possibilizing* of essence, being and gift which seemed impossible before the return to the gracious deep underlying and sustaining them" (Kearney). This is not incarnation as such, but the deeper impregnation of the personhood principle constitutive of an ecclesial world. "Prosopon, therefore, is not the face of the Other (a 'where') but rather the way (the 'how') of the relationship through which the Other gives himself or herself to me" (Manoussakis). Through the Spirit, with the Spirit, in the Spirit, the mystical body of the communion of saints is "prosoponised," allowing Christ to play "in ten thousand places,/lovely in limbs, and lovely in eyes not his/To the father through the features of men's faces" (Hopkins). The fourth reduction of God is the fourth person of the Trinity: ourselves as recapitulated into the body of Christ, through the pleromatic personhood of the Holy Spirit.

Prosopon and Icon: Two Premodern Ways of Thinking God

JOHN PANTELEIMON MANOUSSAKIS

I. Ontological Necessity: Freedom Toward Death and Toward Love

Aristotle, in distinguishing between actuality (ἐνέργεια) and possibility (δύναμις), undertook two crucial steps that have haunted the history of Western metaphysics ever since: he gave a qualitative priority to actuality over potency, and then he identified the former with pure essence. Possibility, for Aristotle, is a mode that denotes transition and corruption, and thus imperfection. However, the risk that he acknowledges and fears most is that potency is ambiguous and undecidable. In his words, "the possible could be both a being and a non-being . . . it could equally be both things and neither" (1050b10, 1051a1). It is this *coincidentia oppositorum* that prevails in possibility that forced Aristotle to exclude it from the categories that properly define God. For Aristotle, a "possible God" might not be a God at all, since "a possible being may not be" (1071b15). The risk that the God of the possible runs is that He might choose *not* to exist and, in this case, "there would be nothing" (1071b25). That is why Aristotle argues for the concept of a God that subsists as pure activity (ἐνέργεια), eternally (ἀϊδίως) and continuously (συνεχῶς), a *noesis* totally identified with its *noema* (1072b25–30).

As such, the Aristotelian God enthrones Himself in the summit of ontotheological assertions. Bound to the absolute necessity, that of ontology, He not only cannot be but His own being, but also He cannot cease to be. His very essence condemns Him to an unavoidable yet tautological existence. Enclosed in the monism of his ipseity, He autistically thinks Himself. Being is the prison of God. Of course, in front of such a God one "can neither pray nor sacrifice. . . . Before the *causa sui*, man can neither fall to his knees in awe nor can he play music and dance before this god."[1] Thus the fact of His existence, proven or not, remains our most indifferent reality.

Aristotelian philosophy was inherited, via the exegesis of Averroës, by Scholastic theology, and the identification of God's essence with pure actuality was carried on in Aquinas's system: "Deus est actus purus non habens aliquid de potentialitate." As Kearney has shown in the exemplary case of Exodus 3:14, a great dose of Greek metaphysics had been injected into Christian theology long before the Thomistic tradition and already with the translation of the Bible by the LXX. By translating the epiphanic name of God (*'ehyeh 'aser 'ehyeh*) as ἐγώ εἰμι ὁ ὤν and thus crystallizing God's identity as His own being, they "missed too much of the original dynamism of the Hebraic expression, and conceded too much to Hellenistic ontology" (*GMB*, 28). Since then, the highest understanding that we can have of God is that of a motionless and apathetic presencing of His being. In this way, however, "the God of Exodus secure[s] ontological tenure in the God of metaphysics . . . a tendency to reify God by reducing Him to a being—albeit the highest, first, and most indeterminate of all beings" (*GMB* 24).

Although metaphysicians had desperately tried to avoid the introduction of any kind of necessity into the concept of God, what they did accomplish was exactly that: the subjection of God to the absolute necessity of existence. "ἐξ ἀνάγκης ἄρα ἐστὶν ὄν," writes Aristotle of the "unmoved mover" in Book 12 of his *Metaphysics*, condemning God's existence to necessity. He exists, therefore, of necessity! The price that God is called to pay for His existence is something much more important than His being: His freedom.

II. Freedom Prior to Existence: The God-Who-May-Be

The aporia here is our inability to imagine freedom prior to existence. And reasonably so. How are we ever to imagine a choice *prior* to its agent? How can we possibly stretch freedom that far back, even *before* the moment when for the first time existence emerges?[2] For us humans, it is impossible. Our freedom is limited and conditioned by our existence, which is given. It is precisely this "givenness" of our existence—beyond our will—that constitutes our facticity. I exist, it is true, but it was not my decision. Our only possibility for freedom lies on the other edge of the existential phenomenon, namely, death. As Kirilov says in Dostoevsky's *Demons*: "Whoever wants the main freedom must dare to kill himself. There is no further freedom; here is everything and there is nothing further. He who dares to kill himself is God" (115–116). And later he adds: "If there is God, then the will is all his, and I cannot get out of his will. If not, the will is all mine, and it is my duty to proclaim self-will. . . . It is my duty to shoot myself because the fullest point of my self-will is for me to kill myself. . . . I kill myself to show my insubordination and my new fearsome freedom" (617–619). This is a kind of freedom that confirms Sartre's nothingness; it is a freedom for nihilism. Even through this handicapped freedom, however, we can discern our thirst to become God by imitating God's freedom; "he who dares to kill himself is God." The only difference is that we have to imagine not only (no matter how unthinkable it is) a God who is free in his existence, but also a God who is free *from* and *before* His existence.[3] God, in other words, *chooses to exist,* and it is this choice prior even to His own existence that is self-generating, like the burning bush from which it announces itself. This God-choosing-to-be-before-He-is, is *not*. If we wish to render His freedom back to Him, we have to imagine, following Kearney's proposition, a God who is *not* but who may be.

God "is" not. For such a statement would imply an idolatrous understanding of God not in terms of His divinity but only in terms of (our) limited ontology. God should be able to transcend the necessity of being by affirming His existence, not as the acceptance of a fact (a facticity) or a reality but as a result of freedom. It is the freedom of the *posse* of God that brings God into *esse*. If Heidegger's critique of ontotheology has caused theological thought to abandon the question "what is God" for the question "who is God," Kearney's poetics of the possible take us a step further: neither the what nor the who of God, but rather *how* and *when* God comes-to-be: "The *possest* contains the possibility of *esse* within itself . . . the realization of *possest's* divine *esse* if and when it occurs, if and when the kingdom comes, will be a new *esse*, refigured and transfigured in a mirror play where it recognizes its other and not just the image of itself returning to itself—in this way, *posse* brings being beyond being into new being, other-being!" (*GMB*, 111). This other way of being beyond being answers the *how* and *when* of God's being as being-for-the-other and being-with-the-other.

III. God as Trinity: A Personal God

If God were a *single* God, we would have to accept His ontological necessity. Thus, any attempt to imagine a God who may be would have found the door of theology long sealed. However, the Christian God, contrary to the God of the philosophers, is a triune God who exists as loving relation among the three Persons of the Trinity.[4] The Trinitarian God has revealed Himself as the God of Abraham and Isaac and Jacob, that is, a personal God who is Himself a person. What does it mean to say that He is a *personal* God instead of an *essential* one? Or, simply, that God is a person and not an essence? At the end of his study on the Exodic epiphany of God, Kearney proposes a new interpretation of God as neither being (ontotheology) nor non-being (postmodernism), but as something between the two: an eschatological promise that *may be*. According to the "eschatological reading" of the passage, this promise—that is, God—"is granted within an I-Thou relationship," and furthermore, it is "granted unconditionally, as pure gift." A gift that, à la Derrida, "neither is nor is not; it gives" (*GMB*, 29). To be requires no other; to give as well as to promise presupposes the existence of another. No one promises or gives gifts to oneself. A God who gives and promises is a God who relates, and is thus a personal God. By these characterizations we do not intend just to describe an attribute of God, but to point directly to the core of the mode of divine existence.[5]

Kearney writes, "Mount Thabor unfolds accordingly as a Gospel replay of Mount Sinai, with the transfigured Christ both re-figuring the Burning Bush and pre-figuring the coming of the messianic kingdom" (*GMB*, 42).[6] If so, can we, then, look at the narration of Christ's metamorphosis for another revelation of God's identity, similar to that made by God to Moses in Exodus? I believe yes. Reading the passage, as it is recorded by all three evangelists, we notice that God appears not as "He who is," neither as a single entity, nor as an eternal essence, but as Trinity. All three Persons become manifest at once in the moment of transfiguration: the Father in the voice that identifies Christ as His beloved Son; the Son in the shining face of Christ; and the Holy Spirit as the cloud that overshadows Christ and brings together both Moses and Elijah, while occasioning the event of transfiguration. A small and yet important detail does not go unnoticed by Kearney, who writes, "note that it is the *face* that registers the transfiguring event" (*GMB*, 40). Is it accidental that it is the face (*prosopon*, all the accounts say) that becomes the register of the Trinitarian theophany?

The personhood (*prosopon*) of God is the very mode of God's self-generation into being. The person of God is that instant where we can touch with the tips of our fingers, so to speak, the very mystery of the *passage* from *posse* to *esse*. Only in the event of personhood is God's "possible" hypostasized as an ecstasy out of Himself. He exists because He ek-sists. From as early as the third century, the Fathers had conceived a synthesis of tremendous importance, that of *hypostasis* with person (*prosopon*).[7] God as *prosopon* is neither an *ekstasis* without *hypostasis* (radical mysticism) nor a *hypostasis* without *ekstasis* (idolatry), but rather the chiasmic crossroad of the two.[8] The term that Kearney uses to express the grasping of the other as present in absence, as both incarnate in flesh (*hypostasis*) and transcendent in time (*ekstasis*) is that of *persona*. Although his understanding and analysis of *persona* is in perfect harmony with the Patristic *prosopon*, however, the term *persona* has the disadvantage of alluding to the superficiality of a mask, that is, to the realm of theater. Transferred into theological language, it brings the risk of Sabellianism—of interpreting, in other words, the Trinity as different roles that the *one* and the *same* God has performed throughout history.[9] There is yet another reason for which I prefer the term *prosopon* to *persona*: the etymology of *prosopon* eloquently illustrates and recapitulates, as if in a nutshell, all the dynamics of being as being-for-the-other and with-the-other.

IV. The Hermeneutics of Prosopon

Aesthetics

We usually translate *prosopon* as "face," and hence as "person." Indeed, *prosopon* is the face and the person, but it means much more than that. Let us say that the term is used exclusively with the verb "to be" and never with the verb "to have." It makes sense only if one states that someone *is* a *prosopon*. To say that someone *has* a *prosopon* diminishes the term into something that someone possesses, namely, a mask. What does it mean to be a *prosopon*? *Pros* means "toward, in front of," and "opos," the genitive of the noun ὤψ, means a face, and especially an eye (as in our word "optics"). As such, to be a *pros-opon* means nothing more than *to be-toward-a-face*, to stand *in front of someone's face*, to be present in her/his presence and in her/his vision.

We should not let go unnoticed the fact that in classical Greek literature the term *prosopon* only rarely occurs in the form that we are using here, that is, in its singular form. Homer, for example, seems to prefer the plural form, *prosopa*, even when he is referring to a single person (e.g., *Iliad*, VII, 211–212). The plural upsets the strict rules of grammar and the structure of syntax, since the single subject of a sentence is modified by a noun in the plural. This is only one example, but it has dramatic effects when we observe its various instances throughout the poetry of Homer (e.g., *Iliad*, XVIII, 414; *Odyssey*, 19.361) and Sophocles (*Electra*, 1277; *Oedipus at Colonus*, 314). The Greek language is too strict to allow such an anomaly to occur without good reason. Perhaps, since *prosopon*, by definition, cannot exist solely as one person, it always needs (and always refers to) at least one other person and to the relationship between them. Being-toward-a-face always presupposes the other, in front of whom we stand. This other, in turn, by standing in front of me, has to be a *prosopon* as well.

Both components of the term show some interesting characteristics. First, let us examine the preposition *"pros."* To be a *pros*-opon means to be on your way toward the Other. This also situates my being into a perpetual *ek-sistence* (i.e., existence as ecstasy), a stepping-out-of-myself and a being-toward-the-Other. *Prosopon*, as a term that indicates the reciprocal movement toward the Other, underscores the ecstatic character of the personal (*prosopic*) relationship. The gaze and the face of the Other, in front of whom I stand, invite me to this exodus to the unknown, unknowable, and yet promised land of the Other. The step toward this land, however, also amounts to a step away from everything familiar, from myself, a self that I am called to leave behind me. The abandonment of the Same for the sake of the Other locates my existence as this passage from what I once was, but am not any more, to what I am to become, but am not yet. Between these two poles I belong nowhere because I am to be found in none. *Prosopon* strongly implies the reciprocity of gaze through which the self is interpellated by the Other and, ultimately, "othered." The passage toward the Other leaves my existence vulnerable to the fear and trembling of the infinite possibilities that await me. In this sense, the dynamic (i.e., full of potential) character of the person makes "the possible" a personal (*prosopic*) category par excellence. Personhood, far from being a synonym for selfhood or identity, is never to be understood as a fait accompli or a once-and-for-all given that somehow we possess. Rather, to be a person suggests a process continuously occasioned by the unreserved exposure to the Other.

Perhaps we could better grasp the semantics of the *prosopon* by juxtaposing it with its opposite. The antonym of a *prosopon* is described in the Greek language by the term *atomon*. *Prosopon* and *atomon* seem to be the two diametrically opposite poles that exhaust the existential possibilities open to a human being. To be an *atomon* means to be in fragmentation (from the privative prefix "a-" and the verb *temno*, to cut; therefore, the a-tomic is that which cannot be cut any further). As in the English language, the in-dividual is one who has been "divided" so many times that he or she has reached this point where no further split is possible. The individual stands in sharp opposition to the *prosopon*. Where the latter gathers and unites, the former cuts off, separates, alienates, and negates. Where, then, does the individual belong? One could say that it belongs to Hades, the place of non-being, the underworld, the place where there is no *seeing*. Ἅιδης properly names the place where there is neither gaze nor face, where the possibility to see the Other, face-to-face, has disappeared, and along with it, the dynamics of being a *prosopon* and of being as such. Hades is surrounded by the river Lethe; *a-letheia*, therefore, has no place there. This is the reign of existential death. As Kearney, reversing Sartre, puts it, the only hell in this scenario is that of self condemned to self. The empty, choosing will. The idolatry of each-for-itself.[10]

Ethics

Kierkegaard calls the individualism of the *atomon* the demonic. In his discussion of anxiety about the good, he makes clear that the demonic is defined by the very rejection of relationship and communion. "The demonic is unfreedom that wants to close itself off"; solipsistic enclosedness (*det Indesluttede*) that "closes itself up within itself."[11] In contradistinction to the ecstatic movement of the *prosopon*, the demonic remains withdrawn in this lonely prison made up of the fragments of a mirror that reflect the selfsame images of itself. Condemned to this monotonous existence, we should not be surprised by Kierkegaard's apt observation that monologue and soliloquy are the modes of demonic expression and that the discontinuity of the sudden—always the same, without memory or expectation—becomes the form of its manifestation.[12] A last but telling point: the demonic does not "partake of communion" (*communicere*), which means that it does not communicate, but also (and it is Kierkegaard himself who invites us to think of this sense) that it does not receive communion.[13]

With regard to the ethical considerations of personhood, then, let us say that the *prosopon* resists being used as a tool or as the means toward an end. In the *prosopon* we are not allowed to see the Other as serving the fulfillment of our intentions or our desires. There are two types of desire that we need to differentiate with regard to the *prosopon*: the desire *of* the Other and the desire *for* the Other. A lover of pleasures, who sees in the Other a body given for his satisfaction, sees *only* that (and therefore, he misses the person because he reduces the otherness of the Other into his own desire). Similarly, the money lover, who sees in the Other the means of making a profit, reduces the person to a customer or a client, stripping him or her of any other personal characteristic. These descriptions formulate modes of seeing the Other as "this" or "that," in which the Other "is," or rather "becomes," what I desire him or her to be. Our desire prevents the Other as such from appearing or, according to Heidegger's expression, to "show itself in itself" (*Being and Time*, 28). Thus, our desire finds in others "only what we ourselves put into them" (*Critique of Pure Reason*, B xviii). And that means that, in my desire of the Other, the otherness of the Other is lost, the Other gradually ceases to be any other (different) than me. Insofar as the Other reflects my desire, he becomes the narcissistic idol of myself. I am freed from this desire only by the desire *for* the Other. (In opposition to the possessive genitive of the "of," the "for" here hits at the ecstatic movement of the *prosopon*: outside of oneself and toward the Other, so one can finally meet the Other, not in the "here" of my sameness but "there" where the Other resides.)

Poetically, the *prosopic* relationship has found its best expression yet in Paul Celan's saying *Ich bin du, wenn ich ich bin* (from the poem "Lob der Ferne"). This is a cry of almost erotic anguish that the *prosopon* addresses to its Other, recognizing in him or her the source of itself—"I am *you*, when I am myself," or as Paul writes to his Letter to the Galatians, "I no longer live, but Christ lives in me" (2:20). Contra Heidegger's analysis of authenticity, what constitutes the core of my authentic existence is not the "mineness" or the "own-ness" (*Eigentlichkeit*) of the being that concerns me, "which is always mine" (*Being and Time*, 42) but, rather, the Other and the paradoxical understanding that I *am* only insofar as the Other is. Or, put differently, I am mine only insofar I am his.[14] That is why, to the ecstatic/

erotic confession of the *prosopon*, the voice of the Other can respond with these strange words: *sis tu tuus et ego ero tuus*—"be yours, and I will be yours as well" (Nicholas of Cusa, *De Visione Dei*, vii, 25).

Religion

Already by the title of his work, Nicholas of Cusa lets the ambiguity of the double genitive to be heard—for this will become the very ambiguity of *the vision of God*, to be defined as a seeing (of God) and being seen (by God).

> What other, O Lord, is your seeing, when you look upon me with the eye of mercy, than your being seen by me? In seeing me you, who are the hidden God, give yourself to be seen by me. No one can see you except in the measure you grant to be seen. Nor is your being seen other than your seeing one who sees you. (V, 13)[15]

The principle behind this understanding of the vision of God is that of the inverted intentionality. I can see God only by means of being seen by Him. This principle, which has found its concrete application in icons, philosophy borrows from the artistic technique of inverted perspective.[16] It is far from being an accident, then, that Nicholas of Cusa takes an icon as the point of departure and, indeed, the center of his speech. A speech that does what it says and effects what it describes, for as soon as his speech turns to the subject of the vision of God, Cusanus delivers his entire essay no longer as a speech *about* the icon, but as a speech addressed *to* an icon. For Cusanus, the theology of God's vision cannot be separated from a theology of the icon.

Cusanus's text seems to allude to a passage in Genesis where Hagar, Abraham's maid and mother of Ishmael, encounters God. The passage reads as follows: "Then, she called the name of the Lord who spoke to her, You-Are-the-God-Who-Sees; for she said, Have I also here seen Him who sees me?" (16:13). The Greek text of the LXX has ἐνώπιον εἶδον for the name of God. And Hagar names the well by which God spoke to her "Beer-lahai-roi," which is also rendered into Greek as ἐνώπιον. The word *enopion* (ἐνώπιον) literally means "face-to-face" (according to Liddell-Scott), and it shares the same etymological root as *prosopon* (πρόσωπον). The God who speaks to Hagar and whom she calls The-God-Who-Sees is a personal God, namely, a God who allows His face to be seen by him or her who, called into being by this face-to-face relationship with Him, is given the status of a person (*prosopon*). To see His Face consists precisely in being seen by Him.

But who is this face?

> The Biblical experience of God in both the Old and the New Testaments is characterized as a whole by the fact that the essentially "invisible" and "unapproachable" God enters the sphere of creaturely visibleness, not by means of intermediary beings, but in himself. . . . This structure of Biblical revelation should neither be sold short nor overplayed. . . . It could be overplayed by the view that all that God has instituted for our salvation, culminating in his Incarnation, is in the end only something preliminary which must finally be transcended by either a mystical or an eschatologico-celestial immediacy that would surpass and make superfluous the form of salvation, or, put concretely, *the humanity* of Jesus Christ. This last danger is not so far removed from the Platonising currents of Christian spirituality as one would hope or want to believe: *the impulsive search for an immediate vision of God* that would no longer be mediated by the Son of Man, that is, by the whole of God's form in the world, is the conscious or unconscious basis for many eschatological speculations. . . . *The Incarnation is the eschaton and, as such, is unsurpassable.*[17]

We do recognize in this "impulsive search for an immediate vision of God" our own desire to see God and to see Him immediately. What Balthasar emphasizes in this passage is that there never is, and never will be, an *immediate* givenness of God, insofar as a mediator (i.e., Christ; see Timothy 3:5) is given to us. We can "see" God, so to speak, only in and through Christ (we recall here the saying "no one comes to the Father but through me"; John 14:5). And this seems to be the paradox. Because in Christ we *don't* see God. I think that the "folly of Incarnation" (the fact that God "appeared" in flesh, concealing, as it were, His appearance under flesh) plays with the double mode of any seeing of God: in seeing God, one can only see oneself. This can very well be the case with Christ: when I see Christ, one could argue, I only see someone *like* me, a mere human being. And this is indeed the case, but not the entire truth. In seeing God, I must come to recognize the other(ness) of other human beings. This last thought has far-reaching consequences. If, as von Balthasar strongly states, I can only see God in Christ and no other "vision" would ever be given to me, that could mean that I can see God only in the other human being ("in *the humanity* of Jesus Christ"). The entire Gospel seems to serve as a pointer toward such an understanding: phrases such as "as often as you did it for one of my least brothers [the hungry and thirsty, the stranger and sick, the ones in prison], you did it for me" (Matthew 25:40) ring now with a more literal sense. On the other hand, one would not want to trivialize the uniqueness of Christ's person by extending the same attributes (God's mediator, Word incarnate) to everybody, as if saying, "We are all Christ." And yet, if we can see Adam, the first man, in all of us, according to sameness, then we should learn to recognize Christ, the Second Adam and last man, in all of us, according to otherness. Isn't it this the principle of Incarnation, namely, "that God became a human so that we, humans, become gods"? Of course, such a statement should be taken as an open invitation, and not as a fact (a fait accompli) already effected by the Incarnation. If we pay attention to the "so that . . ." of the sentence above, we will understand the Incarnation as the opening of a *possibility*. We have been given our Adamic body by means of our birth in the World; we strive for our Christic body by means of our rebirth in the Church. Christ's humanity opens the way (and shows us the way) to man's divinity (the *theosis*, of which the mystical Fathers so often speak). "Each one of you is a son of God because of your faith in Christ Jesus. All of you who have been baptized into Christ have clothed yourselves with him" (Galatians 3:26–27). What is expressed by Paul, in this passage and throughout his Letters, is succinctly stated by the Fathers: *Christianus alter Christus* —the Christian is another Christ.

For von Balthasar, then, as well as for Cusanus, the face of God cannot be anything else but this one: Christ's. However, by entering into this face-to-face relationship with Christ, every face reflects His face.

> When, therefore, I consider how this face is the truth and the most adequate measure of all faces, I am numbed with astonishment. For this face, which is the truth of all faces, is not a face of quantity. . . . Thus, O Lord, I comprehend that your face precedes every formable face, that it is the exemplar and truth of all faces and that *all are images of your face*. . . . Every face, therefore, which can behold your face sees nothing that is other or different from itself, because it sees there its own truth (vi, 18).[18]

That we are the icons of the truth of this face, the true icon (*vera icona*) of His face, as the archetypal and *acheiropoietos* icon of Veronica, meditated by Dante in his *Paradiso*, prompts Jorge Luis Borges to say the following:

> Mankind has lost a face, an irretrievable face. At one time everyone wanted to be the pilgrim who was dreamed up in the Empyrean under the sign of the Rose, the one who sees the Veronica in Rome and fervently mutters: "Jesus Christ, my God, truly God: so this is what your face was like?" . . . These features have been lost to us the way a kaleidoscope design is lost forever, or a magic number composed of everyday figures. We can be looking at them and still not know them. The profile of a Jewish man in the subway may well be the same as Christ's; the hands that give us some change at the ticket window could be identical to the hands that soldiers one day nailed to the cross. Some features of the crucified face may lurk in every mirror. Maybe the face died and faded away so that God could become all (*Paradiso* XXXI, 108).[19]

V. Icon and Perichoresis

Artistically, it has been noted that the icon embodies this turn (about which Nicholas of Cusa so eloquently speaks)[20] from the point of *seeing* to that of *being seen* in a unique way. This turn is aptly expressed by a shift in perspective whose technical name, *umgekehrte Perspektive*, suggests that much: the inverse or inverted perspective.[21] The model that the iconic technique inverts is the one that the Renaissance had mastered: the background of the painting is delineated by a horizontal line into which every point vanishes—thus the false impression of depth takes effect. Anything close to the observer assumes its "real-life" dimensions but, to the extent that it distances itself from that privileged point of view, it is engulfed by the voracious distance that yawns between the viewer and that remote horizon.

The icon, on the other hand, projects this horizon outward, behind and beyond the viewer toward whom it always extends itself. There is nothing—no horizon—to be seen behind the person depicted in the icon, because the horizon is now on the other side, *our* side. But by relocating its perspective, by exteriorizing it, the icon demands *not* to be seen—if anything, it is the icon that sees. The icon, strictly speaking, then, refuses to be the *object* of our observation (it is not accidental that an icon invariably depicts a *subject*, that is, a *person*); it denies our claims to turn it into an object for our eyes—it is *we* who appear to the icon and not vice versa.

The icon—like its philosophical synonym, the *prosopon*—is intrinsically *relational*. One of the defenders of the icons during the second phase of the iconoclastic controversy, Patriarch Nicephorus, does not hesitate to use even Aristotelian terminology in order to define the icon as purely relational. He notes that an icon is always the image of something (πρός τι), and therefore it denotes relation (as defined by Aristotle in his *Categories*).[22] It is telling that the πρός by way of which we inquire into the proper status of the icon also happens to be the first element, the πρός, of the *prosopon*. The relational character of the icon, however, is not exhausted in such minor points of etymology. It is manifested primarily in its theology. For the icon makes apparent, literally at a glance, all the intricacies of Trinitarian and Christological dogma—better yet, as Cardinal Schönborn has shown, the icon is made possible by the very truths pronounced by Christian doctrine. For how else could we justify that paradox that every icon claims to be, namely, that it is the visible image of the invisible God? The answer to this crucial question is relevant for our discussion only insofar as it demonstrates the relational (and thus *prosopic*) character of the icon.

The depiction (or "circumscription," as the ancient texts have it) of God's form becomes possible with the incarnation of the Second Person of the Trinity in Jesus. It is Christ and only Him that an icon can depict by virtue of His incarnation (therefore, the Father and the Holy Spirit are never to be represented). The Christological foundation here is evident: in Christ two radically different natures are united without confusion but also without separation (as the Fourth Ecumenical Council at Chalcedon formulated it): the invisible and thus unrepresentable divine nature and the visible and thus depictable human one. Thanks to the union with the latter, the former, too, became circumscribed not only in the time of history but also in the space of artistic representation. On a first level, then, the icon shows us the *relation* of the two natures in Christ's person. [23]

The question that arises next makes things a bit more complicated. What is the particular characteristic (i.e., the *hypostasis*) of Christ's divine nature that allows it to become united with the human nature? This question brings us to the core of the Trinitarian mystery, for what we are asking for can be found only in the relationship of the three Persons with each other. Maximus the Confessor shows that what *distinguishes* the Father from the Son (the Son's begottenness) is also the very thing that *unites* Him with our flesh.[24] What distinguishes the Father from the Son is nothing else than His "sonship" (by being the Son of the Father, He is also said to be the consubstantial *icon* of the Father's *prosopon*). The "sonship" of the Son describes precisely His relation to the Father. It is this relation, then (that denotes at once the *perichoretic* identity of *ousia* and the difference of *hypostasis*), that unites Him, in Jesus' person, with our humanity. On a second level, then, the icon also shows us the *relation* of the Persons in the Trinity.

On a third and final level, the icon relates the historic moment of the Incarnation (which has happened in the past) with the eschatological promise of a future yet to come. It is easy to understand how the iconic depiction of Christ is based, as we have just seen, on the event of the Incarnation: in this sense, the icon shows us Christ as He was. To the extent, however, that we give some credibility to the testimony of the angels on the day of the Ascension (Acts 1:11; "Men of Galilee, what stand ye beholding into heaven? This Jesus, who is taken up from you into heaven, shall come *in the same way* . . .), the icon also shows us Christ as He will be. For the Incarnation, as Balthasar so aptly put it in the passage cited above, *is* the *eschaton*.

The icon, therefore, is essentially relational; in each of the three cases discussed above, the icon always "relates" to a point beyond itself: Christ's human nature points toward His divinity, the Son refers to the Father, the Incarnation promises the *eschaton*. Like the *prosopon*, the icon expresses a relation that remains beyond the scope of representation, for it is always inexhaustible. In "Transfiguring God" (as well as in its earlier version, "La Transfiguration de la Personne" from the *Poétique du Possible*), Kearney articulates the scheme of a never-fully-exhausted icon as the alternative to a totalizing idol. Thus, the icon becomes the terminological double of the *persona*. "It is easier to mistake the other's *persona* for an idol than accept it as an icon of transcendence. . . . There is a thin line, of course, between seeking to capture the other as divine (*qua* idol) and receiving the divine through the other (*qua* icon)" (*GMB*, 11). His linkage of the *persona* to the *icon* finds theological and historical confirmation, besides the points that we have already seen, in the axiomatic sentence πρόσωπον γάρ ἐστι καὶ εἰκών ὁ Υἱός τοῦ Πατρός,"[25] where the Son is said to be the *prosopon* and the *eikon* of the Father, coining the two terms as synonymous. The resistance of the icon to confinement within the territory of the Same ("the eyes of the icon that look through us from beyond us" and "the other as an icon for the passage of the infinite") finds its theological expression in the image of *perichoresis*. *Perichoresis* in Greek, or *circumincessio* in Latin, "referred to a circular movement where Father, Son and Spirit gave place to each other in a gesture of reciprocal dispossession, rather than fusing into a single substance or identical presence" (*GMB*, 109). Neither substance nor presence counts as a way according to which the *how* and *when* of God's come-to-be happens. Instead, God's existence is revealed in "the sacred dance-play" of *perichoresis*, where the principle of Divine existence is conceived as "an image of three distinct persons moving *towards* each other in a gesture of immanence and *away from* each other in a gesture of transcendence . . . an interplay of loving and letting go" (*GMB*, 109).

John Damascene (c. 749) speaks of the Trinitarian *perichoresis* using a language loaded with dance metaphors: the three persons "hold each other," as in a cyclical dance: "the Son with the Father and Spirit, the Spirit with the Father and Son, the Father with the Son and Spirit in one and the same movement, in one leap, in one movement of the three hypostases" (*De Fide Orthodoxa*, 1000B). An earlier source, a fragment by Amphilochios of Iconium (c. 394), affirms and reinforces that all we can speak and know about God is not His *whatness* but rather His *howness*, and this is as "Father, Son and Spirit," which reveals the way that God exists (τρόπον ὑπάρξεως) but not what He is (οὐσίας). In another text, we read that God exists only by virtue of this loving interplay with the other Persons (the Father begetting the Son and processing the Spirit). That is why His existence is not subject to any causality but it is, finally, "of any necessity free."[26]

VI. Synergy: Eschatology and the Kingdom

At another level, "this Trinitarian play includes humanity . . . to the extent that the second person becomes incarnate and enters history" (*GMB*, 109). How could we possibly imagine the momentous implications of this "entering" where the a-chronic came to be measured in time and the u-topian to be confined in space? Incarnation is the event where transcendence intersects history without being swallowed up by historicity. It grafts radical otherness onto the body of self-sameness in a way that is precisely described in the Chalcedonian formula: "without division and without confusion." It produces a surplus. To argue in Levinasian terminology, "a *surplus always exterior to the totality*," that is, infinity, and yet to be "reflected *within* the totality and history, *within* experience" (*Totality and Infinity*, 22–23). It is from this surplus that eschatology arises as the rupture of totality (eschatology as the beyond of history). The eschatological paradox of "always here and yet still to come" can only and always be understood as "transcendence in the face of the Other — [*le visage d'autrui*]" (*Totality and Infinity*, 24), in this case, the face of the incarnate Son, the face of Christ. This surplus is produced each time the Divine crosses paths with humanity: in the Exodic revelation of God to Moses, where the "surplus saves God from being reduced to a mere signified transcendental or otherwise" (*GMB*, 28), and in the episode of Christ's transfiguration, which "signals a surplus or incommensurability between *persona* and person even as it inscribes the one in and through the other," and it "invites a history of plural readings" (*GMB*, 28).

With these remarks, we reach the most crucial and perhaps the most revolutionary moment in the thought of Kearney: *synergy*. A double-edged synergy, where God gives but He also waits to be given, as the one who "persuades rather than coerces; invites rather than imposes; asks rather than impels. This God . . . cannot be God without relating to his other — humanity" (*GMB*, 30). God's alleged omnipotence is thus dramatically limited, if not totally given up, by his loving potency to relate as a personal God. "By choosing to be a player rather than an emperor of the creation, God chooses powerlessness" (*GMB*, 108). It is the Kingdom of this God that unfolds less as a power of immanent potency laboring toward fulfillment than as a power of the powerless, a vision that also invokes Christ's antinomy when, speaking to Paul, he said, "my power reaches perfection in weakness" (2 Corinthians 12:9). God's power of powerlessness implies, however, neither an ontological nor a metaphysical, but rather an ethical, imperative for humanity: to help God *be* God. Here lies the radicality of such a double-edged synergy. For it is not only God who helps us by His grace to become "gods," it is also we who help Him, by our actions, to become fully God.[27] "God may henceforth be recognized as someone who *becomes with* us, someone as dependent on us as we are on Him" (*GMB*, 29–30). God's *pleroma* will be attained with the coming of His Kingdom, he *will* be when he becomes his Kingdom and his Kingdom comes on earth. During the vigilant advent of His Kingdom, it is crucial to remember that the Kingdom "always comes through the face of the most vulnerable, the cry of 'the smallest of these,' the widow, the orphaned, the hungry who asks 'where are you?' the defenseless ones who forbid murder." Therefore, if we desire to see God "face-to-face" eschatologically, we need first to recognize His face in the face of the powerless historically, and, in doing so, we are called to assume both a synergetic *and* an energetic awareness. If we respond to this call, we will have transformed the world without deforming it. "If God has created the world for us, we recreated the world for God" (*GMB*, 110). And in this way, by returning to God the gift of love *with* love (the double genitive in Derrida's "the desire of God"), we become forerunners of His be-coming. "God cannot become fully God, nor the Word fully flesh, until creation becomes a "new heaven and a new earth'"" (*GMB*, 110). Neither God by Himself nor humanity alone can achieve the eschatological vision, to the extent that the Kingdom will signal the end of all the monisms; what is needed here is "a mutual answerability and co-creation" (*GMB*, 30). "The eschatological dance cannot be danced without two partners" (*GMB*, 110).

But we may choose *not* to dance at all. To God's invitation we may choose *not* to respond. And the fact that we have this choice confirms God's dependency on us, regardless of how offensive such a thought may be to some. The Kingdom in absolutely no way should repeat the Garden of Eden. The *eschaton* cannot simply repeat the *arche*— this would be catastrophic—but it should constitute the way out, the *hyperbaton* of our facticity. This was the *felix culpa* that took place in the fall from the Edenesque state, when man chose *not* to accept God's invitation to an existence of blind obedience and servile subordination by making his choice, that is, by choosing his freedom even at the price of death. Since then, we have been paying for our freedom with a freedom toward death. By means of this freedom, however, man became like God: "then the Lord God said: 'See! The man has become like one of us, knowing what is good and what is bad!'" (Genesis 3:21). When the moment for God to become a man came, there again human freedom was at stake. For could the incarnation have ever taken place if the Virgin Mary had *not* accepted God's invitation? In the moment of the Annunciation we can see again how crucial this double synergy can be. God offers the plan of salvation as *possible* (it is the possibility that the angel announces to her; note how many times the term δύναμις is repeated in the passage), but it is up to humans to say the final "yes": "Let it be done to me as you say" (Luke 1:38). It is also up to us to choose if we will lose or regain God's paradise. In this way, we should also imagine the angel returning to God and bringing to Him, too, the Good News of (His) salvation. And still, man could not eradicate his death until God assumed it as well. The Garden of Eden is "undone" only in the Garden of Gethsemane. There the agonizing Christ, although asking "if it is *possible* [δυνατόν], let this cup pass me by," had to say "yes" to His awaiting passion: "let it be as you would have it, not as I" (Matthew 26:39).[28]

This double-edged synergy, thus understood, not only will put God's omnipotence under question but, far more dramatically, will bring doubt to God's claim to omniscience as well. In Book XI of the *Confessions,* Augustine, discussing the concept of time in general, understands God as standing outside of time. If God knows no time, then God, by necessity, knows everything. Whatever constitutes for us a tripartite structure of future-present-past (or expectation, sight, and memory, as Augustine argues), for God is only "a today which does not yield place to any tomorrow or follow upon any yesterday"; this motionless, unchangeable moment is precisely God's eternity. By virtue of His eternity, God knows everything because the triptych of our history (past, present, future) lies in front of Him as an open book. Augustine employs the example of a well-known canticle that one is reciting: "for to such a mind nothing would be hidden of ages past or ages still to come, any more than when I am singing my canticle anything is unknown to me of what I have sung from the beginning, of what remains to me to sing to the end." Thus, God already knows the "end of the story" and always knew it. It is as if God is watching the same movie over and over again, a movie that he himself wrote and directed and now, ex officio, is condemned to be its only and eternal viewer. Such knowledge will sentence him to an equally eternal boredom. This boredom is the essential meaning of the theological predestination. If God knows everything with a necessary knowledge, then every single effort we make to change both ourselves and the world will always already be in vain, no less than every effort God makes to do things otherwise will be prescribed as impossible. Neither a miracle nor prayer can appeal to a bored, albeit omniscient, God.

The God who may be (but is not yet), the insufficient and inadequate God who always lacks and depends on His other, cannot be accused of theodicy. Such a God, neither omnipotent nor omniscient, fails every time that one of us falls short in her or his life, in her or his hopes. He fails in each moment of my despair, in my distress, and in my solitude. He fails, for my witness of suffering and misery takes away from Him the chance to be. He fails with me; my failure doesn't escape Him, and He can't escape my agony. In each of these moments, God fails to be God. My betrayed hopes and my abandoned dreams, my tears and my fears, send God down to the Hades of my incapacity. Broken lives and wounded bodies put together the pieces of the cross on which God is "lifted up." The same cross, nonetheless, constitutes God's only glory (John 3:14, 8:28, 12:32). For it is only in His ultimate humiliation and suffering that God, contrary to all human understanding and beyond human comprehension, reveals His unfathomable glory. That is why depictions of the crucifixion that did not sacrifice theological signification to historical accuracy present Christ on the cross under the inscription not of *Rex Judaeorum* but rather of *Rex Gloriae*. The antinomy between image and text is an evident one: on the one hand, the image of a body naked, harassed, wounded, dirty with blood and dust, lifeless; on the other hand, the solemn inscription that proclaims this very miserable spectacle as nothing less than "the King of Glory." It is this "folly of the cross" that ultimately reveals another meaning in my failure: failure's very opposite. God's wounds transform my solitude and my suffering into a triumphant song of doxology. Handicapped and outcast, sick and wounded, lost and distressed, we are all becoming voices in God's magnificat. "To God's 'I may be' each one of us is invited to reply 'I can.' Just as to each 'I can,' God replies 'I may be'" (*GMB*, 108). "Jesus Christ," says Paul, "whom I preached to you as Son of God, was not alternately 'yes' and 'no,' *he was never anything but 'yes'*" (2 Corinthians 1:19). It is through this endless exchange of "yeses" that little by little, "by acting each moment," we bring the *posse* of God to the *esse* of history, we "make the impossible that bit more possible" (*GMB*, 111).

PART III

Recapitulations

Desire of God: An Exchange

JACQUES DERRIDA,
JOHN D. CAPUTO,
AND RICHARD KEARNEY

KEARNEY: Derrida's own response to the postmodern dilemma of undecidability would seem to be twofold—*believe* and *read*! In spite of our inability to know for sure "who speaks" behind the many voices and visages that float before us—now present, now absent; now here, now elsewhere—Derrida tells us that we must continue to trust and have faith. "Je ne sais pas, il faut croire," as the refrain of *Memoirs of the Blind* goes. But if our belief is blind, and each moment of faithful decision terrifying, Derrida suggests that we can always be helped by the vigilant practice of meticulous, rabbinical reading. We must never abandon our responsibility to read between the lines:

In order to overcome hallucination, we have to listen to and closely read the other. Reading, in the broad sense which I attribute to this word, is an ethical and political responsibility. In attempting to overcome hallucinations, we must decipher and interpret the other by reading. We cannot be sure that we are not hallucinating by saying simply "I see." "I see" is, after all, just what the hallucinating person says. No, in order to check that you are not hallucinating, you have to read in a certain way.

In what way? we might ask. How can we tell the difference between true and false prophets? Between gods and ghosts? Between messiahs and madmen? "I have no rule for that," Derrida humbly concedes. "Who can decide what counts as the end of hallucination? It is difficult. I, too, have difficulties with my own work."

But in spite of these avowed difficulties, Derrida has done more than most other living philosophers—theist or atheist—to make us sensitive to issues of messianicity and messianism and to the three calls of God: *donne, pardonne, abandonne*. The problem is that these calls are, for deconstruction, always made in the dark, where the need to discern seems so impossible. So my final question is: How do we read in the dark?

CAPUTO: The distinction between the messianic and the messianisms is a tension that we inhabit, and it would never be a question of choosing one or the other. With that in mind, let me briefly make three points:

(1) The notion of justice as *à-venir* refers structurally to the vulnerable; to the victim, not the producer of the victim. It would never be the case that the "other" one to come would be Charles Manson, or some plunderer or rapist. The very notion of the to-come refers to the one who is not being heard, who is silenced, victimized by the existing structures. It will always be the case that someone is being injured by the present order, so that the worst injustice would be to say that present order represents perfect justice.

(2) We are always situated within concrete historical traditions and structures. The point of a distinction like that between justice and law, or the messianic and the concrete messianisms, is to prevent the existing traditions, which are all we have, from closing in upon themselves, from becoming monoliths. There is no such a thing as the one tradition. Tradition is always rife with conflicts, silenced voices, and the prestige of the "tradition" is implicated in the dead bodies it produced in order to establish itself. Still, all we have is traditions, languages, cultures, social and institutional structures, our legacies, and we must both mourn everything that has been erased in those traditions and pray for the justice that these traditions promise. Deconstruction seeks to inhabit the tension between mourning and the promise, between recognizing that this is the only world I have and appreciating its finitude, keeping it open to what it cannot foresee. I can inhabit any tradition justly only if I appreciate that it is blind and that it tends structurally to close itself off from its other.

(3) I am worried about your desire for criteria. I think we have situated decisions in contexts and traditions, about which we need to know as much as possible. But there comes a moment when all our

knowing, all our study of norms and standards, fails us. Then there comes the moment that I understand deconstruction to be describing, that moment of singularity in which we need to choose. This is not decisionism, because it does not have to do with an autonomous ego making a wild leap, but a profound responsibility to everything in that situation which has hold of me. I am at that moment, in that *Augenblick,* on my own. I don't think that mixes me up with Charles Manson, but demands an act of radical responsibility in a singular situation in which I cannot excuse myself by saying that I am just doing what the rides require.

KEARNEY: I agree, Jack. I agree with your reading in *The Prayers and Tears of Jacques Derrida.* We are fellow travelers. But I still think there are difficulties. There is a certain madness of decision, a holy madness, which you invoke, which is so difficult and so terrifying and so risky that it needs the counterbalancing gesture of prudence, of law, of reading. Deconstruction is open to the victim, because deconstruction is justice. That is true. But there are moments in the deconstructive enterprise when it is not as simple as Mother Teresa going out into the streets of Calcutta and embracing suffering victims. There is a real sense of risk in deconstruction that the other who comes may destroy your house. Hospitality, to quote Derrida, may turn into "wild war and aggression." Pure hospitality, pure openness to the in-coming of the other, is dangerous unless it invokes certain criteria, unless it is dependent, as Kant insisted (Derrida discusses this in *Cosmopolites*), on certain *conditions* of hospitality, for example, that the visit of strangers be temporary, nonviolent, and law-abiding. Now that is already not very hospitable, because you are laying down certain criteria. But it is a recognition that if we were to actually practice absolute hospitality toward the absolute other, *sans vision, sans verité, sans révélation* — we might be opening the door to the monster who destroys our house, to wild war and aggression. I think that there is that difficult moment of absolute terror, of fear and trembling, in deconstruction, which in a way is somewhat sanitized by simply saying, in the heel of the hunt, "It is not any other, it is only the other as *victim.*" I think that makes it too quick and too easy. There is something utterly radical in deconstruction that calls, in my opinion, for the countervailing and the counterbalancing gesture of hermeneutic interpretation and prudence.

DERRIDA: As you can imagine, it is really impossible to address such difficult questions by improvising. I wanted to thank you especially, Richard, because I was overwhelmed by the lucidity with which you pointed to the difficulties, my own difficulties, and you were fair enough to mention also the fact that I was trying to face the difficulties without really hiding or dissimulating them. So just a few words, which will not be proportionate to what you said. Your last question was "How do we read in the dark?," referring to what I said in Dublin. How could we read, properly speaking, if not in the dark? If we read, if reading were simply seeing, we would not read. When I say we read in the dark, I do not mean that we have to read without seeing anything, but that the essential feature of reading implies some darkness. That is what distinguishes reading from seeing, from perception. You can transfer this law to the relationship between knowledge and faith, and to the question of criteria that you were addressing. If I were simply perceiving a text, I would not read it. No doubt, I read it while looking at it, seeing something in it. Even if I close my eyes, I see something visible in it. This visibility is indispensable. Even if I read in my memory, if I were blind, this visibility is indispensable, but it is not constitutive of the act of reading. I read to the extent that I exceed visibility. So we always read in the dark, and write in the dark, not only, as I sometimes do, when I try to write down a dream and I wake up and it is totally illegible. We have to read in the dark, and this is a general law which accounts for all the questions that you raise.

To go back to the problem of hospitality that Jack Caputo mentioned a moment ago: as you know, I am aware that you cannot found the politics of hospitality on the principle of unconditional hospitality, of opening the borders to any newcomer. I am aware of those problems. What I mean is that when we control a border, when we try to discriminate, when we try to find criteria to discriminate between the enemy and the friend, or between the monster and the god, then the indispensable act of knowing, discriminating, adjusting the politics, is indispensable, no doubt, but it is a way of limiting hospitality. We have to be aware that, to the extent that we are looking for criteria, for conditions, for passports, borders, and so on, we are limiting hospitality, hospitality as such, if there is such a thing. I'm not sure there is pure hospitality. But if we want to understand what hospitality means, we have to think of unconditional hospitality, that is, openness to whomever, to any newcomer. And of course, if I want to know in advance who is the good one, who is the bad one—in advance!—if I want to have an available criterion to distinguish between the good immigrant and the bad immigrant, then I would have no relation to the other as such. So to welcome the other as such, you have to suspend the use of criteria. I would not recommend giving up all criteria, all knowledge and politics. I would simply say that if I want to improve hospitality—and I think we would agree about that—if I want to improve the conditions of hospitality, the politics of hospitality, I have to refer to pure hospitality, if only to have a criterion to distinguish between the more limited hospitality and the less limited hospitality. So I need what Kant would call the regulating idea of pure hospitality, if only to control the distance between inhospitality, less hospitality, and more hospitality. This could also lead us beyond Kant's own concept of hospitality as a Regulative Idea.

So at some point I have to take into account the need for criteria but without really believing that this need for criteria has an essential link to hospitality, or to the relation to the other as such, or to the singular other. And I would like to follow this thread in order to go back to what was finally the center of your concern, Richard, which, as you know, I share. I'm going to read in the dark. At one point you ask, "Where do we draw a line in the sand between deconstruction as desertification of God and as desertion of God?" There is no line. As soon as you look for a line, a clear line between desertification and desertion, between an authentic God and a false God or false prophet, as soon as you look for this—and you cannot help looking for this—but as soon as you rely on this desire, or as soon as you think you have gotten this criterion, that is the end of faith. You can be sure that God has left. When you are sure it is the real one, and that you have a criterion to identify Him, you can be sure that in that case you have the bad one. I am not here pleading for faith or religion, I'm just analyzing a structure. As soon as you have or think you have this line that you want to draw in the sand between desertification of God and desertion of God, as soon as you have it or think you have it, you've lost it. You've lost what you're looking for. So you have to resist this resistance to this openness to a possible monstrosity and to this evil. What is difficult—and I confess this difficulty and I experience it as you do—occurs when, taking what I just said into account, you nevertheless have to make decisions, for instance, political decisions, ethical decisions. Then you have not only to discover but to produce criteria, to invent politics, for instance, and you have to negotiate between this absolute non-knowledge or indeterminacy, which is a necessary openness to the singularity of others, and the necessity of criteria, politics, ethics, and so on. So you have to negotiate between what is nonnegotiable and what has to be negotiated.

And this is a terrible moment. You said this better than I can. But this is the moment of decision. You have to make a decision not simply to open your house—that's not the decision, you open your house to anyone, this is pure hospitality, it requires no decision. It's impossible, but it requires no decision. Now if you close the border and the house, there is no decision either, no hospitality. The decision occurs when you want to reach an agreement between your desire for pure, unconditional hospitality and the necessity of discrimination. It is filtering. I don't want to host anyone who would destroy not only me but my wife and children. For this decision, I have no criteria. That's what makes a decision a decision. If I had criteria, a set of norms, that I would simply apply or enforce, there would be no decision. There is a decision to the extent that even if I have criteria, the criteria are not determining; that I make a decision beyond the criteria, even if I know what the best criteria are; even if I apply them, the decision occurs to the extent that I do more than apply them. Otherwise it would be a mechanical development, a mechanical explicitation, not a decision.

So there must be a decision, not in the sense of decisionism, as Jack said. But what is the difference? Here I go back to the point of departure in your book, *The God Who May Be*, and in particular that chapter titled "Desiring God," with the ambiguity that "desiring" conveys. Whose decision is it? If it is my decision, my own decision, meaning by that a possibility which lies in myself, a potentiality—"I am able to make such a decision"—this would mean the decision would be mine because it would simply follow my own habitus, my own substance, my own subjectivity. It would look like a predicate of myself. The decision follows from what I am. If I give because I am generous, the gift is a predicate of my generosity, of my nature, so it would be my decision because it would follow what I am myself, my own subjectivity. For this very reason, the decision wouldn't be a decision. So here we reach the most difficult point, where a responsible decision, to be responsible, must not be mine. My own decision, my own responsible decision, must in myself be the other's; if it's simply mine, it's not a decision. When I say that a decision must be the other's in myself, I do not mean that I am irresponsible, that I am simply passive or simply obeying the other. I must deal with this paradox. That is, my decision is the other's. Otherwise we will fall into Schmitt's decisionism, in which the notions of subject, of will, of the sovereignty of the subject are again revalidated or confirmed. No, we have not to account for, but to experience, the fact that the freest decision in myself is a decision of the other in myself. The other is in me; the other is my freedom, so to speak. You can transfer what I'm saying about decision to desire. The desire of my desire is not mine. That's where desire stops. If my desire for the other, for the *tout autre,* were simply *my* desire, I would be enclosed in my desire. If my desire is so powerful in myself, it is because it is not mine. That does not mean that I'm simply passively registering or welcoming another's desire. It simply means that I experience my own desire as the other's desire. Of course, God, what may be called God's desire, is part of this scenario. When I say in French *tout autre est tout autre,* which is difficult to translate, this does not mean, as you say, inclusiveness. It means simply that every other, without and before any determination, any specification, man or woman, man or God, man or animal, any other whatever is infinitely other, is absolutely other. That is the only condition for the experience of otherness. This sentence is virtually an objection to Levinas, of course, for whom *le tout autre* is first of all God. Every other is infinitely other. That is not a logic of inclusion but, on the contrary, a logic of alterity.

I would add just one last point, because this *tout autre est tout autre* is also the axiom of what I call messianicity. I am not sure I would say, as perhaps Jack Caputo has said, that messianism is on the side of war and messianicity is on the side of peace. I do not know if he said that literally. Of course, there is always a risk of war with messianicity; messianicity is not peace. I would not identify messianism in the classical sense as the experience of wars. But again, according to the same logic of contamination, if I make reference to the Messiah, to the tradition of messianisms in our culture, in order to name messianicity, it is in order to keep this memory. Even if messianicity is totally heterogeneous to messianism, there is this belonging to a tradition, which is mine as well as yours. I do not refer to it the way you do here, but it is our language, our tradition, and I would try to translate one into the other without erasing the heterogeneity of the two.

KEARNEY: I want to thank you for your responses. I am grateful. In closing, I want to say something about the necessity of the work you are doing—these micrological worryings about the need for decision and the appreciation of how difficult is the question of discernment, and whether it is possible or impossible. What is punctually so important about this work, and why it intrigues me, is that at the level of our contemporary social imaginary, there is, I believe, a need for discernment and discrimination which the academies and universities are not taking on. When I referred, at the end, to *mondialiena-tion*, I had in mind a tendency to see the other as alien, to demonize the other. I think that this has a lot to do with political constellations, with the end of the Soviet Union and other traditional enemies. I think that the whole problem of the immigrant and the victim, which is at the center of Jacques Derrida's recent reflections on hospitality, on cosmopolitanism, on Kant, and of course of Jack's book *The Prayers and Tears of Jacques Derrida*, is absolutely essential—lest the other become invariably the scapegoated monster. That is certainly becoming a very real problem for us in Europe today, where there is a growing problem of closure to the other. I am sure, if it has not already become a problem here in the United States, it will become one—the problem of how one can relate openly and hospitably and justly to the other, without demonization. When I look at the films and the videos today that are capturing the popular unconscious and expressing our social imaginary, what I see is a culture of paranoia, of fear of the other, and an inability to be able to tell the difference between the victim and the aggressor. That sort of radical confusion requires the close, micrological, quasi-rabbinical reading of deconstruction as a close attention to detail and singularity, without rushing to premature verdicts. That is the great virtue, I believe, of your most recent work.

Richard Kearney's Enthusiasm

JOHN D. CAPUTO

Richard Kearney is a genuine "enthusiast," in the genuine sense of
the word. His writings are contagiously enthusiastic, charged and exciting, moving and inciting, full of prayers and tears. His beautiful
and powerful prose is a perfect testimony to what his friend Seamus
Heaney meant when Heaney said that the Irish are a people who
took over their invader's tongue and improved it for them. His
thoughts dance; his erudition dazzles us. His imagination, his favorite
theme, races ahead of the rest of us who are left in his dust. An in-
sightful reader of Levinas, Kearney has a glorious and productive
case of insomnia, which keeps him up at night reading everything
and writing about it until the cock crows.

But Kearney is an enthusiast in the ancient and literal sense of *en-
theos*, a man filled with God, driven by a passion for God, and that is
the Kearney who interests me here. His passion is not simply one for
the God who is, or for the God who is and was and will be—that
would never be enough. His passion is for the God who *may be*, who
may be more than we imagine, more than our imagination can contain; the God who may be more than God, who is yet to be what God
can be; the God who, as one might say in American English, hasn't
shown us anything yet. Such a God is a self-surpassing, self-tran-
scending possibility whose *posse* exceeds his *esse*, who has passed
right through and gone beyond being, who leaves being in the dust.
If Thomas Aquinas said that God is the act of all acts, the *actus om-*

nium actuum, Kearney will go the Angelic Doctor one better and up the ante. In keeping with a line from Heidegger that he cites, that "possibility is higher than actuality"[1] (one of the many lines that Heidegger lifted from Kierkegaard without citation), Kearney has pursued this thought down to its most radical conclusion. For Kearney, God is the possibility of all possibilities, the possibility *beyond* all possibilities, and, as Kearney says in a recent writing that gives me great joy, in which he joins hands with the eminent quasi-Augustinian, quasi-Jewish, slightly atheistic quasi-theologian Jacques Derrida, God is even the possibility of the impossible.[2] Kearney, who chiefly draws upon the resources of Levinas and Ricoeur, has been known to give Derrida a hard time in the past. Regarding this new alliance, I myself, off in the distance, try to observe this ring dance of Kearney, Derrida, Levinas, and Ricoeur through my clouded binoculars and can only say *oui, oui*, Amen, yes, yes, I said, yes, I will, yes.

First, I would like to sketch the possibility of Kearney's God of possibility, of God as the *posse* beyond *esse*. Then I will add a second word about Kearney's enthusiasm, aimed not at tempering or moderating it, because enthusiasm properly understood is the love of God, and the only measure of love is love without measure. A moderate, temperate love is the love of a mediocre fellow. No, I will add a word aimed at complicating Kearney's enthusiasm, bedeviling it, making it all the more ambiguous and aporetic. I have always stood for giving the devil his due, in particular the devil of undecidability. I have always thought we get the best results by facing up to all the difficulties that beset us in the wake of what I like to call a "devilish" hermeneutics. Aporias and undecidability are not all bad news for me, for such devilish aporetics only serve to intensify the passion of faith and to heighten the intensity and to raise the pitch of genuine enthusiasm — Kearney's, mine, Derrida's — the enthusiasm of all those who, like St. Augustine, keep disturbing their tranquillity with the question, *quid ergo amo cum deum meum amo*?

The God Who May Be More Than God

Richard Kearney's philosophical theology turns on a distinction between what he calls the "eschatological" and the "ontotheological" concepts of possibility. In its most classical metaphysical terms, possibility is subordinated to actuality as the imperfect to the perfect, for possibility is taken to mean potency, latency, and unactualized or unrealized potential, every trace of which must be removed from an all-perfect God conceived as pure act, as the perfection of *ousia, hyperousia, substantia, esse subsistens.* In its modern form, possibility refers to the ideal limit of the Idea in the Kantian sense, God as a regulative ideal. This is at bottom a profoundly Greek way to think about God, Athenian and ontotheological, a God spun out by an *Aufklärer,* or by leisured aristocrats speculating on the nature of a being they called *theos,* endlessly cutting lazy circles in the heavens, utterly unmindful of us suffering mortals here below. Despite the enormous prestige it has accumulated in the official theologies of the several churches, it is very questionable what this *theos* has to do with the biblical God, with the passionately involved God of the prophets, or with the intimate one whom Jesus dared call *abba.*

In questioning the God of pure act, Kearney thus joins hands with what I would call the fundamental theological project of contemporary Continental philosophy, which lies in overcoming the God of metaphysics and asking the question "What, or who, comes after the God of metaphysics?" From the time of his doctoral dissertation, written under Paul Ricoeur and Stanislas Breton, Kearney has focused this question on the notion of possibility. Thus, to the detached pure act of Greco-onto-theo-logic, devoid of all potency, Kearney opposes the biblical God, the "eschatological" God, where possibility is taken not ontotheologically, but eschatologically, not as potency or latency, but as the *dynamis* up ahead, the possibility to come, *à venir,* the futural event that draws the present beyond itself. This yields the God who is to come, who is here but still coming, who must be thought in terms of the future and the promise, which the theologians call the "Lord of History." The famous text of Exodus 3:14 is not to be understood, according to Kearney, onto-theo-logically as "I am who am," or "I am pure and subsistent being," as it was read in the Middle Ages, but eschatologically: "I am the one who will always be faithful, and by my faithfulness all future generations will know me and call me; I am the promise to remain with my people, and they can all count on me in the future." "I am the God not only of their memories and of their fathers and mothers, but also of their hopes and aspirations, of their sons and daughters." God will be God, Kearney says, at the *eschaton.*

Kearney argues that it is wiser to interpret the God of Exodus neither as pure being in the manner of ontotheology, nor as pure non-being in the manner of negative theology, which is his criticism of Marion, but as an eschatological "may-be," *peut-être.* Kearney postulates a chiasmus in which Yahweh, the Lord of History, meets *einai,*

blessedly clear

in which, as he says, God puts being into question and being gives flesh to God, albeit a flesh that remains untouchable, in a narrative with no end in sight. He cites Meister Eckhart, for whom the *ego sum qui sum* meant *ebullutio*, overflowing being, light within light, penetrating everything, the way light fills the air. God penetrates and passes through being. God takes his leave of being, but only after a transit through it, not into the pure ether of non-being, but into the future, so that God is the excess of *posse* beyond *esse*, the God that may be, the God that may be God, the God yet to come.

At this point, Kearney says, eschatological theology can join hands with Derrida and speak of God as the possibility or becoming possible of "*the* impossible," as the still, small voice that cries "perhaps," as the prophetic promise of a justice or a democracy to come. Kearney's argument reaches a point that is most interesting to me when, following a recent piece of Derrida's titled "Comme si c'Était Possible," Kearney posits a point of contact between his own conception of "a poetics of the possible," which turns on a postmetaphysical eschatological concept of possibility, and Derrida's notion of "*the* impossible."[3] Derrida has always stressed that by "*the* impossible" he does not mean the simple logical opposite of the possible, and he does not mean a simple logical or ontological impossibility, such as *p* and *not-p*. On the contrary, he has in mind a nonmetaphysical idea of the impossible, a quasi-phenomenological one, as that which is unforeseeable, unprogrammable, as the *tout autre* that shatters the horizon of possibility. Of this Derridean idea of *the* impossible, Kearney says that it marks "an invaluable opening to a new eschatological understanding of God as *posse*." What Kearney and I agree about (and we both have recourse to Derrida's work at this point) is that the category of "the impossible" is a central religious category. We are told throughout the Scriptures that with God nothing is impossible (Luke 1:37), that the impossible is God's business, part of his job description, as it were. The impossible, Kearney argues, delimits the autonomy or autarchy, the *Seinskönnen* of the subject vis-à-vis the power of something that eclipses subjectivity. We find ourselves pushed to our limits, driven to a point described by Derrida as *sans voir, sans avoir, sans savoir*, where faith must make up for our lack of *voir*, hope must compensate for our lack of *avoir*, and charity must supplement our lack of *savoir*. In "Comme si c'Était Possible," Derrida argues that the "perhaps" is the necessary condition of possibility of every experience that is truly an "experience," that something arising from the unpredictable otherness of the future, which is what he means by the possibility of the impossible. This "perhaps" hovers over every decision in order to give it "responsibility," since there would be no decision or responsibility without the undecidable perhaps. Beyond our own possibilities, the impossible is still possible, and indeed it is, as Kearney says, using a phrase from his early *Poétique du Possible*, which Derrida cites in "Comme si c'Était Possible," "more than impossible" (*plus qu'impossible*) (*CSP*, 505, n. 5). For the "im-" of "im-possible," Derrida says, does not mean a denial or negation of possibility, but something that propels us into the most radical of all possibilities, the possibility of *the* impossible, which is a matter of *faith*. If, for Derrida, the "perhaps" of the impossible is a condition of experience in general, Kearney would say, and I would fully agree with him, it is also a condition of religious experience in particular, which also implies that experience in general, experience in its sharpest sense, has a certain religious quality.[4]

Complicating Enthusiasm

Throughout his work, Kearney voices a constant and legitimate concern about nihilism, the fall into what some might call the "abyss," of being overwhelmed by what Levinas calls the *il y a*, of being stranded in what Derrida calls the desert of *khora*.[5] Kearney does not want to be consumed by these monsters. He wants to oppose these anonymous forces with all the force of the personal, and he invokes the name of God, or the name of what Levinas calls the *illéité* beyond *il y a*, to keep us safe. Now, for all the positive things he has lately said about Derrida, he still thinks that Derrida, and I along with Derrida, have failed to provide such safety, that we leave everything dangling in undecidability, and that we lack the steel to make a decision that would steer us out of this chaos.

The abyss, *il y a*, and *khora* are not necessarily synonymous descriptions of limit states that delimit the sphere of meaning, sense, direction, on the one hand, and hope, joy, aspiration, on the other hand. They point to an underlying stratum of anonymity that inhabits and disturbs our world from within. They cover a wide and disparate range of phenomena that, I think, neither Kearney nor I have been careful enough to discriminate in sufficient detail. If time permitted, we would have to sort them out. Kearney tends to single out the most extreme states of madness, misery, terror, torture, depression, and desolation, the nightmare of a prisoner trapped in the ground or a child crushed by rubble. Such phenomena must be distinguished from the mystical abyss, which for Meister Eckhart is a font of love, not terror. Both of these extreme states in turn would need to be differentiated from *différance*, in virtue of which we make any distinctions or differentiations at all. *Différance*, while maddening enough at times, does not constitute a state of literal madness, of insanity and terror, let alone of torture or imprisonment, but rather of the inescapable "spacing," the play of traces, within which we constitute or "forge" our beliefs and practices. *Différance* is that condition in virtue of which whatever meaning we constitute is made possible and also impossible, that is, the quasi-transcendental that sees to it that a meaning is a temporary unity forged from the flux of signifiers or traces and that lasts just as long as the purpose it serves and the contexts in which it can function endure. It is in virtue of *différance* that whatever we can do with words can also come undone. That is useful enough, and it is at times also annoying enough, but it is not exactly the terror of the abyss, madness, torture, or desolation. Whatever it is, it is not God unless one has an exceedingly odd idea of God, which is always possible.

Khora, Derrida says, is a surname for *différance*,[6] that is, it is a figure found in the history of philosophy, in Plato's *Timaeus*, where the brute "out of which" quality that simulates *différance*, which inhabits all our beliefs and structures, shows through the seams of metaphysics and, here, of that most classical of classical metaphysicians, Plato himself. The *khora* thus constitutes a kind of counterpart to the *agathon*, a counterimage not beyond *ousia* but below it, a structure that falls below the level of sense and sensibility, of meaning and being, rather than exceeding them. Thus it is used by Derrida to show how *différance* insinuates itself into everything. Whatever we say or pray, think or believe, dream or desire, is inscribed in the shifting sands of *différance*, that is, inscribed in *khora*.

Derrida is interested in the mirror-image effect of the Platonic *agathon* and *khora*, in the way that the beyond being and below being mirror one another; neither is a "thing" that yields to a simple intelligible or sensible presence, that has a simple being or truth. Now put that beside Levinas's observation that *illéité* (which is his way of appropriating the *agathon*) is so far beyond the other one (*autrui*), so other than the other one (*autre qu'autrui*) that it begins to fall into a "possible confusion" with *il y a*.[7] If we put these two mirror effects side by side, we see that there is a certain ambiguity or undecidability between the two. While we can for all practical purposes keep them apart, upon closer consideration we find that they do share common characteristics, that is, neither belongs to the medium-sized phenomena of daily life, neither has the determinacy, the form, the structure of a definite thing or being. That is why, in the Middle Ages, David of Dinant made the argument that God is prime matter because God does not have and cannot be restricted by "form." Thomas Aquinas thought that this was a particularly stupid thing to say, and that David should have distinguished the way *ipsum esse subsistens* is beyond form from the way prime matter is below form. While Thomas was right to say that we can keep these concepts apart, I would say that David had hit upon a phenomenological point, that our *experiences* of the two are not necessarily so widely divided, for in both cases we experience a certain confusion (Levinas), a kind of bedazzlement (Marion), or what Derrida and I would call an "undecidability," which I think can be resolved only by *faith*, and on this point Marion has become rather more forthright lately.

However, Kearney, and this is my main complaint with his work, has muddied the waters of this debate. To begin with, I do not think he has carefully discriminated the chiefly semiotic and quasi-transcendental function of *différance* as "spacing" from terror, torture, and desolation. Trading on that ambiguity, he says that Derrida and I have consigned us all to live in an unlivable desert called *khora*, without hope or faith, wallowing without decision in the waters of undecidability. Kearney argues that Caputo and Derrida, still infected with a residual nihilism as they are, think that *khora*, conceived especially as terror, is what is really real, what is really there; that everything else, every sense or meaning, is a forgery, a fake, a simulacrum, an impostor—in short, the anonymous rustling of the there is, which is eventually going to gobble us up or turn us to ash. *Il y a là cendre.* He thinks that Caputo and Derrida have not been able to reassure us that *khora* is "temporary," that we can "get beyond it," and that they have not shown us how we can be saved or redeemed. They would be, rather, one of those hearty chevaliers, those knights not of faith but of nocturnal *khora*, who go chin to chin with the abyss and try to stare it down. For the true anchorites (an-*khora*-ites), on the other hand, the desert was a medium through which they must pass on the way to redemption. You must first lose yourself if you would save yourself, according to the ancient economy. Caputo and Derrida are knights of infinite resignation, whereas it is only the knight of faith that gets Isaac back.

But, I would say, Kearney's argument falls wide of the mark on two counts.

First, he has confused undecidability with indecision, whereas undecidability is not indecision, but the condition of possibility of a decision. The opposite of undecidability is not a decision or decisiveness, but rather "programmability." That is, if a situation were *not* inhabited by undecidability, then the decision could be made by a decision procedure, by a program or an algorithm that would process the components of the problem and render the decision in a formal, rule-governed process. That would be a programmed result, not truly a "decision" in the genuine sense of any exercise of "judgment" and "responsibility." Undecidability means that a human decision is required, which means entering into an idiosyncratic situation that is not covered by the rules. Undecidability was first recognized by Aristotle in the *Nicomachean Ethics*, where *phronesis* was precisely the acquired skill of figuring out what to do in situations that are unique enough to fall below the radar of rules and universals. The emphasis on singularity in Kierkegaard and Heidegger, and in Derrida and Levinas, is a radicalization of Aristotle's point, which is why I am willing to describe deconstruction as a form of "radical hermeneutics."[8]

Hence, when I say that as we approach the God who comes after metaphysics, we enter a region where we do not know whether it is "God or *khora*," I am not leaving us twisting slowly in the winds of indecision. Rather, I am describing the sphere, the desert sphere, in which any genuine decision or movement of faith is to be made, where God and *khora* bleed into one another and create an element of ambiguity and undecidability *within which the movement of faith is made*. Without *khora*, we would programmed to God, divine automatons hardwired to the divine being, devoid of freedom, responsibility, decision, judgment, and faith.

Second, because Kearney has misconstrued undecidability as indecision, he thinks that the movement of decision, here faith in God, would somehow or another extinguish *khora*, get us past it, put it behind us. That view goes along with a "linear" interpretation of Levinas that I reject, namely, that we can so decisively surpass *il y a* that it goes away, that we can get on top of it or beyond it, dominate it and drive it off, and then, resting from a hard day's work, get a good night's sleep safe from its insomnia. I, on the other hand, think the ghost of *il y a* is inextinguishable and irrepressible, that it disturbs our days and haunts our nights, that it is never driven out, and that, as such, it is precisely the condition of possibility for any ethical decision. In other words, in rigorously Derridean fashion, *il y a* is the very thing that makes ethical transcendence possible and impossible. That is, it makes ethics possible, by confronting it with something to be overcome, and impossible, by delimiting ethics as the ever-haunting possibility of the anonymous that never goes away, that refuses to be banished, that returns night after night. That is why ethics is ethics, why ethics is a *beau risque*.[9]

Without *il y a* there is no *risque*, just the *beau*.

Without *khora*, there is no *faith*, because then God plainly and unambiguously would have revealed Himself, without any possible confusion.

Without *khora*, there is triumphalism, dogmatism, and the illusion that we have been granted a secret access to the Secret. That is the illusion that makes religion so consummately dangerous and fires the fundamental religious hallucination. That is why religious people think that they have been hardwired to the Almighty, that they know in some privileged way the Secret that has been communicated to *them*, because God prefers *them* to *others*, Jews to Egyptians, or Christians to Jews, or Protestants to Catholics, or Unionists to Republicans, or xenophobic, homophobic gun-toting redneck Southern Baptists to effete, Northeastern liberals! Without *khora*, there is no "impossible," no poetics of the possible, no poetics of the possibility of the impossible, because there would be nothing to drive us to the impossible. Without *khora*, we would know everything that we need to know, and we would not be pushed to the point of keeping *faith* alive just when faith seems incredible and impossible. After all, believing only what is highly credible is the mark of a mediocre fellow; rather than a *beau risque*, it always bets on the favorite. Without *khora*, we would have every reason to think that we will succeed and not be forced into the impossible situation of hoping against hope, hoping when hope is impossible. Without *khora*, we would see the sense of playing ball with others, of trading tit for tat, and we would not face the madness of expenditure without return, of loving those who do not deserve it, of loving our enemies, which is impossible.

Without *khora*, the situation that evokes the impossible, that demands the impossible of us, that elicits faith, hope, and charity would not obtain. *Khora* is the *felix culpa* of a phenomenology of the impossible, the happy fault of a poetics of the possible, the heartless heart of an ethical and religious eschatology. *Khora* is the devil that justice demands we give his due.

Hermeneutics of Revelation

JEAN-LUC MARION AND RICHARD KEARNEY

I. Boston College, October 2, 2001

KEARNEY: There are many similarities between your work, Jean-Luc, and mine: we both owe a great deal of our philosophical formation to the phenomenologies of Husserl and Heidegger; we have both engaged ourselves in close dialogue with Levinas, Ricoeur, and Derrida. Given these evident similarities, it would be more fruitful and interesting, it seems to me, if we take a look here into some of the *differences* in our respective positions in regard to the phenomenology of God. One question that I would like to put to you, Jean Luc, and which, in fact, I have put in a more elaborate form on page 33 of *The God Who May Be,* is the question of the hermeneutical status of the "saturated phenomenon." It seems to me that if there is a difference between us, given all our common readings and assumptions, it is this: I would pass from phenomenology to hermeneutics more rapidly than you would. It strikes me that your approach is more strictly phenomenological, since for you the "saturated phenomenon" is fundamentally *irrégardable*, a pure event without horizon or context, without "I" or agent. As such, it appears to *defy* interpretation. You do, of, course make some concessions to hermeneutics, as when you say—on the very last page of your essay "The Saturated Phenomenon"—that this phenomenon is communal and communicable and historic. Here you do seem to acknowledge the possibility of a hermeneutic response, but my suspicion, and please correct me if I'm mistaken, is that the example you privilege—Revelation—requires a *pure phenomenology of the pure event.* Whereas I would argue that there is no pure phenomenon as such, that appearing—no matter how iconic or saturated it may be—always already involves an interpretation of some kind. Phenomenological description and intuition, in my account, always imply some degree of hermeneutic reading, albeit that of a prereflective preunderstanding or preconscious affection for the most part. My question, then, would be: How do we interpret— and by extension, how do we judge—the saturated phenomenon without betraying it?

MARION: This is an old question. The first version of *The Saturated Phenomenon* was written as a paper just after *Reduction and Givenness*; then a more elaborate version followed as it is now found in *Étant Donné*. The first to raise this question was Jean Grondin, a specialist in Gadamer at the University of Montreal; after him, Jean Greisch asked me the same question, and although I am stubborn and narrow-minded, I am not completely closed to critical remarks! Let us put aside for a moment the question of Christian revelation, which is not directly related to the saturated phenomenon. The saturated phenomenon is a kind of phenomenon that is characterized by a deficit in *concept* vis-à-vis *intuition*: such phenomena include the *event*, the *idol*, the *flesh*, and the *other*. In all these cases, there is a surplus of intuition over intention. It is precisely because of this surplus of intuition, I have argued, that we need hermeneutics. Why? Because hermeneutics is always an inquiry for further concepts: hermeneutics is generated when we witness an excess of information rather than lack. In *Étant Donné*, where I discuss the four types of saturated phenomena, I say that the icon is "the icon of endless hermeneutics." Why an endless hermeneutics? Precisely because there is there a conceptual deficit. I have learned my hermeneutics with Ricoeur, and Ricoeur is very clear on this: if we are to have hermeneutics, it has to be an endless hermeneutics. There, where the need of hermeneutics arises, it is completely impossible to imagine that we may get at any moment an adequate, final concept. Subjectivity, history, and the question of God—the question of history is very important for our discussion here, for the historical event is the most simple kind of saturated phenomenon—in all these cases, the question of hermeneutics is totally unavoidable. Hermeneutical investigation never completes its mission. It is never finished and should never be finished, and that is why there cannot be a hermeneutics of what I call the *common range* phenomenon. It is why, for example, the history of mathematics is not a part of mathematics, why the history of science in general is not *science*. Because, in the case of pure mathematics or pure science there is no deficit of phenomenality, there is no saturated phenomenon, and thus, no need of hermeneutics.

KEARNEY: In two of your texts, the *De Surcroît* and *Étant Donné*, you delineated the four types of saturated phenomena, all of them characterized by a superabundance of intuition over intention. As you say, they do not necessarily point toward a "theological turn"—actually, they could be quite a-theological—but you have also written of the saturated phenomenon as a theological event. Since we are focusing our discussion here on the phenomenology and hermeneutics of God, let me come back to this theme and ask: Can we have a hermeneutics of God qua saturated phenomenon? For example, in some texts, you speak of the saturated phenomenon in terms of a superabundance that surpasses all narration and predication, and fills us with a certain stupor and terror whose very "incomprehensibility imposes on us." Regarding this notion of incomprehensibility, you would seem to suggest an *absence of hermeneutics* and point to a theology of absence where the role of narratives and images and even conceptual interpretations appears to be a betrayal, in some sense, of the very unconditional absoluteness of the religious event. In *God Without Being* you actually speak of a "eucharistic hermeneutics"; but here again, we are faced with what you call the "unspeakable word," which seems to mean that we find the Word already given, gained, and available. In addition to that, there is the question of the theologian who, by definition, ultimately has the *last word* of interpretation. Such a view seems to me to delimit the notion of an endless hermeneutics. Moreover, those that do not participate in the praxis of the Eucharistic phenomenon seem to be excluded not only from its experience but also from its interpretation.

MARION: Let us go back, then, to the theological character of the saturated phenomenon. My final position on that is that the four types of saturated phenomena mentioned above could all be recapitulated in the field of a phenomenology of revelation. Nevertheless, if we are allowed to take revelation—a theological concept—as a phenomenological question, then, I think, it should be done to the degree that revelation can be described as the combination of the four types of saturated phenomena. I refer here to the Judeo-Christian Revelation; to describe it, you would need to employ the type of (1) the *event,* since it always occurs as an event; (2) the *idol,* since it bedazzles us with its appearance, when it appears; (3) the *flesh,* since it is always an appearance that has to appeal to our senses; and, finally, (4) the *other,* that is, the otherness of the other. Revelation combines and recapitulates in itself all of the four types; it is, we might say, a phenomenon saturated to the square. The kind of hermeneutics that we would need to employ vis-à-vis Revelation is already at work on each of these kinds of saturated phenomena. I would say that revelation is a rather good paradigmatic case of what I call the saturated phenomenon. What is given in revelation is precisely what surpasses any expectation. The fact that we face something beyond any expectation and any final conception solicits an endless hermeneutics. That is why the field of hermeneutics is absolutely and widely open to any possible direction and to any level of interpretation. Take, for example, the Creed, the Apostolic *credo.* Strictly speaking, it is a document that reveals a set of doctrines shared in common by all the churches and all the theologians; on the other hand, however, it is open to different interpretations which are not always consistent with each other, even within the same church or the same tradition. I see these differences of interpretation as many different hermeneutic possibilities. I would also say that the Jesuit spirituality, for example, is another example of a possible interpretation, of another type of hermeneutics within the tradition of Catholic spirituality.

KEARNEY: Would you, then, admit to a comparative phenomenology of the religious along the lines of someone like Mircea Eliade? Do you think that the phenomenon of God can be experienced outside a specifically monotheistic context? Is there something in the notion of Revelation as an absolute saturated phenomenon that requires a Judeo-Christian theology? It is not just *any* God that appears in Revelation, is it? And how can we tell the difference?

MARION: I think that the "game," so to speak, is completely open to anyone who has to do what he can do and as much as his abilities allow. What happens at the moment of the revelation is like a tremendous explosion: it affects everyone, from those at "ground zero" to those at the remotest periphery, but no matter where we stand, or how much or how little intuition we receive, each one of us has to take that much and make out if it whatever we can. And this is an ongoing process; it is a story that never reaches its end.

KEARNEY: So one could have a Buddhist or Hindu hermeneutics of the phenomenon of God?

MARION: I do think that the question of God is so great that, to some extent, we have to admit that all the different traditions, including those that are apparently foreign to the biblical heritage, are needed in order to say something about God. Buddhism is a way of living the experience of the infinite prior to or beside the phenomenon of revelation; Buddhism concerns itself with what we would call "natural revelation." And this, too, is needed. It is like putting the question of revelation in a different way: What would have happened if no Revelation had happened?

KEARNEY: You say "different" as negative to positive or as different to same?

MARION: It cannot be completely different because what is at stake here, the human being, is the same, in the sense that it is *us* who raise the question of revelation. It can be raised differently, but it is always raised within the common structures of human experience. The experience of the infinite, with or without Revelation, does not compel us to choose this or that tradition.

KEARNEY: Why do you say "without revelation"? Are there not kinds of revelations and epiphanies—as well as all kinds of saturated phenomena—that do *not* presuppose any theological or monotheistic given . . .

MARION: Yes. . . .

KEARNEY: . . . and which are surely available to nonmonotheistic traditions . . .

MARION: There could be . . .

KEARNEY: . . . whether it is a work of art or an icon or a sacred moment in some Eastern religion or simply an act of love or justice, giving a cup of cold water to a thirsty person.

MARION: Yes . . . I have no authority to decide whether the Buddhist, for example, would or should use this or that interpretation of his experience of the infinite. . . . My point regarding the relation of the saturated phenomenon to Revelation is an old issue between theology and metaphysics.

KEARNEY: To clarify: when you say "revelation," do you mean "Revelation"—with a capital R—that is, a monotheistic Revelation, or you mean "revelation" in the phenomenological sense, which is obviously more inclusive?

MARION: My answer will have to be a long one. An old question that concerned me for some time was why metaphysics since the sixteenth century became so interested in explaining the very notion of natural revelation—not a terribly consistent concept anyway. When, in modern times, philosophy was understood as the doctrine of the a priori, it became immediately apparent that if there are a priori, then any possible experience must be limited and admitted by them. Within this context, very roughly sketched here, the question of revelation needed to be addressed because, in the mode of revelation, the limitations of our experience are supposed to be given by revelation itself, or by the One revealed through revelation, and not controlled by the modalities of the transcendental apparatuses. The conflict between these two horizons was an unavoidable one, and the final conclusion reached, in different ways by both Fichte and Kant, was the limitation of religion "within the limits of reason alone." Let us recall here Fichte's criticism of any possible concept of revelation, Christian and non-Christian alike, and the answer that Hegel gave, where the Concept allows revelation to happen but, at the end, it is the Concept itself that *is* the truth of revelation. The moral of this story was that philosophy *alone* is responsible for deciding what is acceptable as "revelation" and what is not. With the advent of the crisis in metaphysics, however, what we know today as "the end of metaphysics," the picture changes. The question that led metaphysics into crisis was precisely the one that questioned the role of metaphysics as the ultimate authority that decides which kinds of phenomena are admissible to philosophical discourse and which are not, which questions the legitimacy of metaphysics and, along with all this, the question of the possibility of revelation. Together with the crisis in metaphysics, or as a consequence of this very crisis, the question of revelation per se was reopened. Under this light, the experience of a Buddhist, for example, faces the same problem and the same critique as the question of experience of (Judeo-Christian) revelation. Neither can be taken as "rational" by the standards of philosophical and scientific rationality. On the other hand, Buddhists as well as Christians think that they have the right to be taken as reasonable and capable of performing sound reasoning and philosophical questioning, regardless of their faith. Obviously, a broader and less rigid concept of rationality is in order here. If you want to focus on the interreligious discourse (understood not in the sense of ecumenism but as the question of what constitutes, or not, revelation), such a matter can be addressed only when you assume that revelation nullifies any natural experience. But to assume that you must already know what revelation is or does is the same as saying that the hermeneutics of revelation is now over, that revelation has nothing to reveal, and thus, by definition, that there is no revelation. If we speak of revelation, then, we have to accept that hermeneutics is still going on, that revelation is open since history is still in the making. There is no contradiction in saying that everything was fully revealed and achieved but that, even today, we don't know, we can't know, how far it reaches.

KEARNEY: Would you at this point in your work revise your position in the *God Without Being* regarding the hermeneutics of the text as being conditioned by the community itself? How do you feel now, for example, about the passage that you wrote: "Hermeneutics of the text by the community, thanks to the service of the theologian, but on the condition that the community itself be interpreted by the Word and assimilated to the place where theological interpretation can be exercised, thanks to the liturgical service of the theologian par excellence, the bishop . . . ," for it is "only the bishop that merits in its full sense the title of theologian"? (152–53). The *God Without Being* is undoubtedly inscribed within a monotheistic tradition. Is this theological position one which you would still defend? Or do you think that the brackets have to be reopened again to a more "interfaith" phenomenon of revelation?

MARION: I would like to say this. When I said that "only the bishop merits the title of theologian," I was not, of course, taking sides in the present-day differences between, say, bishops and theologians; I was referring back to the tradition where most of our great theologians were, at the same time, bishops in their communities. I am thinking here of examples such as the two Gregorys, Basil the Great, or John the Chrysostom. For a long time in the common tradition of the Church, the *place* to teach theology was the pulpit from which the bishop, during the liturgy, had to explain the Gospel. All of our great Patristic books were, in fact, connected to these homiletic practices.

KEARNEY: But some of these books were burned by the bishops. Master Eckhart was on the Index, and John Scotus Eriugena. Even Aquinas at one point! These were great teachers and hermeneuts. But none of theme were bishops!

MARION: But this very situation was the symptom of a corruption of what I am trying to explain here. It is difficult for us to think today about how theology was originally not supposed to be the outcome of intellectual curiosity, logical dexterity, or academic career. Theology grew out of the task of commenting on the Scriptures. Not because you chose to be a professional exegete of the Scriptures, but because that was an essential part of the liturgy, of the Eucharistic gathering of the faithful. In this sense, theology was a communal event. It was the theology of a community and not the solitary research task of a theologian. The great theologians of the tradition were not writing books because they wished to get published, but because they needed to address specific questions that were of importance in their communities. Their theology was built in direct relation to their pastoral service. With the advent of the universities, we are in a new, terrible situation where you have on the one side the bishop, who has administrative power (and often a rather low level of scholarship), and on the other side, the university professor, who has a high level of scholarship but who is removed from the believing community and its act of celebration. The result is that each one uses his old weapons to get rid of the other in the struggle over the monopoly of truth. The academic claims that the bishop is deeply involved in politics, and thus unable to do serious theology, while the bishop says that we should not take seriously all these uncommitted professors and researchers. Things have changed radically.

II. Rome, the Feast of the Epiphany, 2002

MANOUSSAKIS: We meet here, in Rome, in order to continue the conversation that you held with Richard Kearney a few months ago in Boston. I would like to start, then, by asking: how can we think of God today and what language should we employ to address the phenomenon of God?

MARION: For a long time, one could actually say since the times of Plato, philosophy has been thinking of God in terms of "being-ness," of the *ouſia* that grounds or is grounded by the highest being. And for a good reason, being is *our* ultimate concern: the being we have or the being we lack. But when translated and projected as God, being becomes an idol and perhaps the most resistant idol of God. That is why I have been trying to speak of God *without* Being or in terms that are *otherwise* than Being, such as the event, the icon, the other. I was happy to see that I am not alone in this effort. Richard Kearney's recent book, *The God Who May Be*, signals a new way of thinking of God or, better still, as a call that provokes us to think of the phenomenon of God in new ways. First, a remark on the title *The God Who May Be*. This title may be to some extent, or to some people, upsetting because it seems as if the actual being of God may be discussed and questioned. This is true. We have to remind ourselves that "the God who may be" is a way to translate or express the very classical name of God as it is found in the Bible, that is, the name of God in Exodus 3:14. The God of the Exodus is not the God who "is," but rather the God "who may be." This formula is not the actual future tense, but rather an incomplete tense which indicates that God's way of being is to come. This is a very strong feature of the Judeo-Christian God that sees divine existence as a process of opening and revealing His glory. God does not stay what He is, but He is insofar as He will come. In the New Testament one of the technical titles of Christ that points to His divinity is that of the one "who comes," *ho erchomenos*. The time of Christ is "the hour to come and behold it is now." Christ is the one who "comes into the world and the world receives Him not," and the one who is "to come again," and so on. This is the name of the God who may be.

My second point is that the title chosen by Richard Kearney, regardless of its biblical connections, is also provocative insofar it may suggest that "to be" or "being" itself is not enough to give us access to God. The crux of philosophy is always the question of the validity of being in general, and in particular the validity of being as an attribute of God. There is, however, the possibility of a deeper way for God to reveal the richness and the glory of His divinity, and this way, following Kearney's breakthrough, might be none other than the experience of "possibility" itself. I completely agree with Richard Kearney in embracing the axiom that possibility stands higher than actuality. This, as you know, is a statement that Heidegger makes about being in paragraph 7 of *Being and Time*, but it might be truer about God. In any case, we should remind ourselves of another fact, closely connected to Richard's own intellectual history; Richard started his philosophical work by writing his thesis, *La Poétique du Possible*, under the direction of Ricoeur, in Paris. To a large extent, then, I read *The God Who May Be* as a fuller realization of his first intuition on the significance of possibility. His thought is reaching its maturity as he is returning . . .

MANOUSSAKIS: . . . full circle, one could say, to the very beginnings of his philosophical insights . . .

MARION: . . . to possibility as the best way to think of God. Now I would like to consider a last point with regard to *The God Who May Be*. When we think and speak about God, we risk a great deal of danger, but it seems to me that the real threat is not that we may go astray in formulating unorthodox positions about God. There is yet another danger, hidden but no less threatening, namely, to narrow our approach to God, treating God as if He were part of our objective reality, part of our language, part of our experience of the world. The surprising connection that Richard Kearney attempts between God and history makes clear that if we believe that God has created our world, then, by definition, God stands beyond creation; hence the need to direct back to God every experience of the world, without exception. In that context, the use of a deconstructive critique of the limitations of metaphysical patterns, and the attempt to use either literary expressions or apophatic phrases in reference to God, are all perfectly acceptable because everything available to us should be directed back to God, who is beyond creation and by whom creation was made possible. God, then, should be seen as overcoming and trespassing all the conditions of our understanding. Apophatic language, deconstruction, and the critique of metaphysics are precisely to the point here, since the transcendence of God cannot be expressed insofar as we remain within the limitations of our metaphysical view of the word. In all these respects, Richard Kearney's work is not only very useful, it is also very "fair" to God.

MANOUSSAKIS: It seems to me that both you and Kearney see in the possible, in the thinking of God as one who is not yet but who may be, an element that *safeguards* God's otherness. If being became an idol after all, that was because being was too static and immutable. If the difference between God and us is understood only in terms of being, then it is a difference of degree and not of kind. The inexhaustible possibilities of the possible, on the other hand, open our thinking to an *otherwise* and to an *elsewhere*.

MARION: The question of the otherness of the other is a very important one for both Kearney and me. Could I ever, though, perceive the otherness of the other if first I am not myself different from my-self? Here there is something very well known in modern philoso-phy: the lack of a strict identity of the self. For everything else but me, "to be" is to stay and to endure in the same condition that it is. In my case, however (and before anything else, I am aware of my-self), to remain what I am and stay always the same—if this were ever possible, which I doubt—would amount to the definition of someone who is dead. Unfortunately, we know many people who are exactly what they are with no change, no improvement, not even decay, for years after years; what we all know about them is that they are dead, although they are still living. To be alive as a human being does not always mean to live in a better way, or in a more exciting way, and so on; what to be means is, rather, the process of becoming not what you are but what you are *not*. That is why our existence is historical; the historical is made possible because our being is first of all in its deepest root possibility rather than actuality. Only when we die for the first time are we what we are, equal to ourselves, without change . . .

MANOUSSAKIS: . . . but for those people who are dead before they die, those people who remain unchanged because they grasp what they are without letting it go . . .

MARION: . . . for them this is an anticipation of physical death . . .

MANOUSSAKIS: . . . maybe for them, a God-without-being or a God-who-may-be could signal a very uncomfortable imperative for change. . . .

MARION: Yes, indeed. I'm saying that if you imagine God remain-ing exactly what He is supposed to be forever, then there is some-thing idolatrous about this imagination; and what makes it idolatrous is the mirroring, the duplication of our own apprehension of our-selves, because that is *our* dream to be without limit or end. That is the desire that we project onto God, as so-called eternity. But that which hides behind it is nothing less than what we really hope for *ourselves*.

MANOUSSAKIS: It is a kind of conceptual anthropomorphism, then: the projection of our desire onto God. . . .

MARION: Yes, our lack of desire . . .

MANOUSSAKIS: . . . or desire's lack.

III. Dublin, January 11, 2003

MARION: I take the opportunity of this seminar to answer a comment made by Richard Kearney, which is very fruitful, and which is a very good example of how far the concept of the saturated phenomenon can be applied.

If we consider Kearney's hermeneutic reading of Exodus 3:14 in chapter 2 of *The God Who May Be*, it is very fascinating, because there are three possible interpretations. The first interpretation is the *kataphatic*: we take "I am who I am" as "I am," "I am an *ousia*," and, more than that, "I am Being itself," and so on. Then you have the negative or *apophatic* interpretation: "I am who I am, and you will never know who I am"—which is a very old and traditional interpretation, too. And there is a third one, which is beyond both affirmation and negation, namely, the *hyperbolical* one, where the two previous readings are both surpassed and assumed—"I am the one who shall be. Forever." Shall be what? He who can say "Here I am," because "Here I am" is the name under which the encounter between God and man is made, throughout all Revelation. Thus, "I will be the one always able to answer or to call." And so, with the same words of Exodus 3:14, the same intuition, to some extent, we have three possible significations, and we need at least those three. This is mystical theology. It is also a saturated phenomenon. And this is, finally, the possibility of an endless hermeneutic. The Exodic revelation may be repeated for other *logia*. I think Richard and I agree on this issue.

KEARNEY: Yes we are in agreement here. But I would like to expand a little further. In the *God Who May Be*, I tried to explore how Meister Eckhart revisits certain metaphysical terms—*sum, ego, qui est*, and so on—and reinterprets them in a way that opens them up to a postmetaphysical, eschatological interpretation. And I think we could apply this move more generally to a variety of postmetaphysical movements in contemporary philosophy and theology. Maybe this is a slight difference of emphasis I have with Jean-Luc Marion, Heidegger, and Derrida. Rather than affirming "the metaphysics of presence," or ontotheology, which from Aristotle to Husserl is caught up in a metaphysics of "conceptual idolatry," what I try to advance with my notion of "diacritical hermeneutics" is the suggestion that, in spite of the language of cause, substance, ground, *essentia, esse*, which can lend itself to conceptual idolatry, there is also within metaphysics a metaphysical desire to understand, to conceptualize, to reason with, to reckon with, to make sense of, to debate with questions of the ultimate. That metaphysical desire, it seems to me, is utterly respectable; and it can be recognized in most of the great metaphysicians. There are two ways of approaching Plato, for example. On the one hand, there is Plato as ontotheology and the metaphysics of presence. But on the other hand there is Plato—as Levinas revisits him—as the exponent of a metaphysics of eros, of desire. In that sense, when Levinas speaks of metaphysical desire in *Totality and Infinity*, he is not saying we should return to Aristotelian or Scholastic metaphysics qua speculative system. He is saying that there is some drive within all metaphysical attempts to name the unnameable, which is retrievable and which can be reread eschatologically. That's not just true of Plato: it's true of Augustine, where there is this restless desire for God; and it is true of Descartes, too. As Levinas and you, Jean-Luc, have both pointed out, Descartes's "idea of the Infinite" is something that comes through metaphysics, but it can't be contained *within metaphysics*. . . .

So, I would make that differentiation. Does this bring us close to something like process theology? As a metaphysical desire for God, yes. But not as a need to form a system, with grounds and causes and reasons and concepts that, in process theology as I read it, tend toward a "pantheism," where there's a beginning, middle, and end, and a Master Narrative which reduces God to an immanent, historical process. I do not have any quarrel with the description of God as an immanent, historical process up to a point; but I think it is only half of the story. It's the story of us responding to the call of God and trying to work toward the Kingdom. But there is another side to the story, which I do not really see recognized in Hartshorne or Whitehead, and that recounts how historical becoming is a *response* to a divine call that comes from *beyond* history. So the question is: Is there a notion in process theology of God as radical transcendence, ulteriority, exteriority, alterity? Does process theology sufficiently acknowledge the *difference* between immanence and transcendence? . . .

MARION: There is no contradiction between Eckhart's saying *Gott wirt und Gott entwirt* and the saturated phenomenon. The very experience of the *excess* of intuition over signification makes clear that the excess may be felt and expressed as a disappointment. The experience of disappointment means that I make an experience which I cannot understand, because I have no concept for it. So the excess and the disappointment can come together. The saturated phenomenon doesn't mean that we never have the experience of being in the desert. The reverse is the case: the desertification is an excess, in some way. The experience of something that is unconditional is, for me, something occasioned by the fact that I am disappointed, that I am in the situation of encountering something without having the possibility to understand it. This is not nothing. This is a very important figure of phenomenality.

And so back to desire now. I would not be so optimistic about desire as some are. Indeed, in philosophy, from the beginning, there is something that is not purely conceptual, working "behind," being the secret energy of the system, the desire of knowing things. Desire of knowing. There are two possibilities opened up here. First, desire is quite different from knowledge itself—"All men desire to know," as Aristotle says. Second, desire is finally incorporated into the knowledge itself. To some extent this is done with Hegel, where knowledge—rooted in the dialectic—includes in itself the desire to know. And so at that moment desire is recalled and recollected, confirmed within metaphysics. Or you may argue—and I think it was part of Levinas's reading of Plato—that the desire is prior to the philosophical intention to know and has to be taken seriously as such. So you may try to focus your attention on desire "as such." This can explain an aspect of Neoplatonism, for instance, regarding desire "as such." But the question is whether desire does not claim far more than mere philosophy understood as a theory of knowledge. Perhaps the question of desire is too serious to be explained within the same horizons as the question of knowledge. Perhaps the question of desire not only cannot be answered but cannot even be asked in the horizon of Being. This is a reason why I think desire is the "backstage" of metaphysics, something never enlightened by metaphysics (which is unable to do so). And so now we perhaps have to open a new horizon where the question of desire may be taken seriously. And it is not taken seriously, for instance, in psychoanalysis—because psychoanalysis can consider and describe desire, but it takes desire as simply a drive, an unconscious drive; it is nothing more than a drive, largely and maybe for ever. But there is perhaps a deep rationality and consciousness of desire which is other than and goes far beyond mere unconsciousness. To open this new horizon, we have to get rid of the horizon of Being, which is, at the end of metaphysics, quite unable, because not broad enough, to do justice to desire.

KEARNEY: Perhaps we could link the notions of "desert" and "desire." Take Eckhart's notion of *Abgescheidenheit* as the abandonment of desire, the experience of releasement and dispossession. This is not incompatible with the experience of the saturated phenomenon, and may actually be concomitant with it. I think there are two ways of approaching the divine, saturated, phenomenon. One is ecstasy—the traditional beatific vision of the fusion with God, mystical *jouissance*. But there is also *Abgeschiedenheit*, the sense of being disinherited, disinvested—John of the Cross's dark night of the soul. Sometimes the saturated phenomenon seems closer to Augustine's or Dante's beatific vision; sometimes it approximates more to the experience of the desert, devastation, the void. Other times again, it can be both together.

In the transfiguration of Christ, for example, if we can take that as a divine saturated phenomenon, we witness an extraordinary fascination with the *whiteness* of the event, but also an experience of fear, such that the voice from the clouds on Mount Tabor has to say, "Do not be afraid." There is fascination but also recoil. Jesus cautions his disciples to keep a distance from the event, not to say anything to anyone about it, not to construct a monument or memorial. All these are ways, it seems to me, of acknowledging the importance of *Abgeschiedenheit*. We are very close to something that could burn us up. We need a distance, and to be faithful to it, we need to be cautious, discreet, and diffident. So I think it's a complex double move of ecstasy *and Abgeschiedenheit*, of attraction *and* disappropriation.

Relating this back to desire, I think it's important to distinguish between two different kinds—ontological and eschatological. Ontological desire comes from lack, which is, I think, the Hegelian and Lacanian definition of desire—*manque à être*—but it also goes back, in fact, to Plato. One interpretation of Plato in *The Symposium* is that *eros* is the offspring of Poros and Penia, of fullness and lack, and therefore is a lack striving to be fulfilled. This *ontological* notion of desire strives for possession, fusion, appropriation. I would oppose this to *eschatological* desire, which doesn't issue from lack, but from superabundance, excess, and surplus. This latter is also operative in Plato. But it's most emphatically evident, I think, in a biblical text like the Song of Songs, where there's a sort of theo-erotic drama between the divine and the human.

MARION: If I may comment about that. You know the formulation in the commentary on the Song of Songs by Gregory of Nyssa: What is eternity in paradise? It is the fulfillment of pleasure, where each fulfillment is a new *arche*, without end. That is exactly the reverse of

our experience of biological desire, which cannot survive its fulfillment. And in that nonbiological, nonontical desire, which is not
based on lack, the reverse is true: the more it is fulfilled, the more
there is a rebirth of desire, without end. This kind of desire—which
is nourished by excess, not destroyed by it—is quite different. When
we feel that kind of desire, it's very clear that the original Platonic
model, which is, I think, ruling all of metaphysics up to Lacan, is
quite insufficient and cannot match the requirement of what is beyond even the way of knowledge. This is true for the question of will
also. Because will, according to metaphysics, as will to will, will to
knowledge, will to power, is quite different from the will involved in
the question of meeting the other person, the question of love. So
there is a real equivocity about concepts like will, desire, and so on.
And that equivocity is further evidence that there is really some limitation to metaphysics.

KEARNEY: Taking up Gregory of Nyssa's point, we might also
mention here his notion of *perichoresis* to describe the love between
the Three Persons of the Trinity. This is a telling analogy because
what you've got here in the Three Persons is a love, a desire, a loving
desire, that cedes the place to the other (*cedere*), that gives room. But
it is also a movement of attraction *toward* the other (*sedere*), a movement of immanence. Father to Son, Son to Spirit, and so on in an
endless circle. Hence the ambivalence of the double Latin translation
as both *circum-in-Cessio* and *circum-in-Sessio*. But what is this movement that both yields and attracts? What does the *peri* or *circum* refer
to? Around what? *Khora*, an empty space, a space of detachment, and
distance, and disappropriation. The immanent movement in the free
play of each Person toward the other is accompanied by a movement
of desire which is also a granting or ceding of a place to the other.
And it's that double move of ecstasy-*Abgeschiedenheit* that you find
within the very play of divine desire, which then translates into
human-divine desire.

And if I may be permitted, a further comment on Hegel. Where I
would have a fundamental problem with Hegel is on the question of
the "Ruse of Reason." Whether Hegel's desire is an ontological drive
or an eschatological one is open to interpretation. But certainly in the
Phenomenology of the Spirit it seems to me that it is still caught in a kind
of metaphysical totality. The movement is there, and the energy and
dynamism are there, within the dialectic. But in the final analysis,
there's a Cunning of Reason that has rigged the game. All the stakes

are already set. Where I have a big issue with Hegel is not just with the definition of God as Absolute Consciousness—a God who has really decided everything before the play has even begun—but also with his notion of evil. It is the old question of theodicy, where everything is ultimately justified within the System. In contrast to Hegel, I propose a diacritical hermeneutics which approaches the problem of evil in a less extreme, more tolerant way, a way that allows for greater understanding. This is a very undogmatic claim, a hypothesis, a wager. It is a suggestion that this is a better way of doing things, as a description and as an interpretation. But the only way it can be shown to be better (or worse), because I'm just part of a dialogue that others have begun long before me and will continue long after me—the only evidence is actually the intersubjective community of dialogue. In other words, it works if people are persuaded by this as an accurate description. As Merleau-Ponty says about the evidence of phenomenology, you read Husserl, you read Heidegger, and either you're persuaded by their descriptions or you're not. There are no extraphenomenological or extrahermeneutical criteria that you can appeal to, as a metaphysical foundation, or ground, or cause, that proves you right and others wrong. So in that sense it is always tentative. Indeed, it seems to me that the virtue of philosophy is this tentativeness—which doesn't mean being relativist or uncommitted. We all operate from beliefs, faiths, and commitments; all our philosophizing is preceded and followed by conviction. Before we enter the realm of philosophy, we are already hermeneutically engaged. We come out the other end—no one being able to live by philosophy alone—we recommit to our convictions, our beliefs, and so on. We move from action to text and back to action. But the important point, it seems to me, is that one *acknowledges* when one goes into the philosophical debate that these are one's hermeneutical presuppositions, prejudices, and prejudgments—momentarily and methodologically suspended for the sake of the conversation. Maybe when you come back to your commitments again, you do so with a greater sensitivity to a plurality of interpretations. This is not relativism; it is a democracy of thought.

MARION: Yes. May I repeat that point in another way? There is no other argument to choose between different interpretations of the same data than the power of one interpretation in front of the other. This is a very fair battle, where the winner, posited at the end, is the one able to produce more rationality than the other, and you are convinced simply by the *idea vera index sui et fallacia*. The hypothesis that produces more rationality than the other is the superior. And it is why it is a weakness in philosophy always to stick to a narrow interpretation of a situation, which is unable to make sense out of large parts of experience and to say, "Well, you have no right to go beyond that limit." For me, it is the defeat of reason, of philosophy, when a philosopher says, "You have no right to make sense of that part of experience; this is meaningless, and should remain meaningless." It is an improvement in philosophy when a new field, which was taken to be meaningless, suddenly makes sense. . . . For instance, you begin with a situation where everyone has an even chance. Everyone can say, "This sunset is a question of biology," or of aesthetics, or of religion. Everyone has his possible interpretation, his constitution of the phenomenon. And everyone tries to go as far as they can. The result and the conviction which are gained, or not, are the result only of the power of that interpretation. Let us take the example of Levinas. The question of the Other remained a puzzling issue until the move made by Levinas, considering that in the case of the phenomenon of the Other, we cannot understand it unless we *reverse the intention*. In that case, we no longer have an intention coming from me to the Other as the objective, the object, but there is a reverse intentionality, and we have to reconstruct all of the phenomenon that way. By saying that, suddenly a large range of phenomena were available, I would say, for the first time in the history of philosophy. There is no other demonstration than the simple visibility of the phenomenon of the Other.

KEARNEY: I agree. I don't think that the different hermeneutics have to be seen as incompatible. If that were the case, then you'd have to say, "My hermeneutics is right, the saturated phenomenon is God, and Heideggerians are wrong to call it *Ereignis* and deconstructionists are wrong to call it *khora*." That is not, in my view, what it is about. I would rather use the term *equi-primordial* here. For example, say you are depressed. You go to a Heideggerian philosopher and s/he will tell you this is *Angst*, it is an existential experience of your being-toward-death. You go to a psychopharmaceutical therapist, and s/he will give you Prozac. The thing is, it is not a question of saying one is right and one is wrong. Here, I think, Julia Kristeva is correct. If you are to be more fully responsive to the pain of the sufferer, it is not a debate as to whether this is a biochemical crisis *or* an existential one. It can be both. And you can be helped at both levels.

But it is not a matter of saying they're the same thing either. They are operating at *different* levels. I think that is important, to recognize the different claims, interests, and levels of interpretation. . . .

MARION: The question of love is also very crucial. For instance, to fall in love implies a very special type of reduction, a self-reduction, but at the level of an erotic reduction, and it is very true that the experience of the Other in love is the experience of the saturated phenomenon par excellence. It's absolutely clear that you will "see" the other before knowing him or her. . . . On the other hand, "blessed are those who believe without seeing." What does that mean, exactly? It may be to some extent the distinction between philosophy and theology, simply that. Because in philosophy we have to "see" to believe. What does that mean, to believe? For us, because we start from a philosophical point of view, we spontaneously think that to believe is to take for true, to assume something as if it were true, without any proof. This is our interpretation of belief. In that case, it is either belief or seeing. But is this the real meaning of belief? In fact, belief is also to commit yourself, and in that case, it is also, perhaps, a theoretical attitude. Because, by committing yourself to somebody else, you open a field of experience. And so it's not only a substitute for not knowing, it is an act which makes a new kind of experience possible. It is because I believe that I will see, and not as a compensation. It's the very fact that you believe which makes you see new things, which would not be seen if you did not believe. It's the *credo ut intelligam.* So, all this makes clear that what is at stake with the end of metaphysics, and with phenomenology, is that the distinction between the theoretical attitude and the practical attitude should be questioned. At the end of metaphysics, both theory and practical situations are quite different. But I think there are practical or ethical requirements even in a theoretical point of view. There is no pure theoretical point of view. You assume a complete attitude toward the world. And this has to be questioned. It is why questions about what is given, and what you believe, of love, are perhaps the unavoidable issues now.

KEARNEY: On this question of seeing, I think it's important to recognize hermeneutically that there is a plurality of seeing. We can see in different ways. The empiricist sees the burning bush as a fact. (John Locke would probably describe it in terms of impressions, and John Searle would probably start cooking sausages.) That is a certain approach: a positivist, materialist, pragmatist approach. By contrast, Husserl or Heidegger, for example, might see it as a manifestation, a *Lichtung*, or disclosure of Being. For Husserl, it would be a kind of categorial seeing: we're not just looking at the fire as it burns us, as it lights up, we're also looking at the *being* of the fire. Heidegger would deepen this ontological seeing. But then we could add another mode of seeing, a further reduction, which would be an eschatological seeing, where you hear the voice and you see the fire as a manifestation of the divine. Either you see it or you don't. And it doesn't mean, philosophically, that one is right and one is wrong. John Locke and the empiricists would come to Mount Horeb to describe the impression of a fire. Unlike Moses, who came with a burning question: How do I liberate my people from bondage in Egypt? Moses is lost, he is disoriented, his people are enslaved; he's looking for liberty, for hope. He comes with the desire for a promise, the desire for revelation. And so Moses sees something that the empiricist is not going to see. There are different modes of seeing. They are not incompatible: maybe Moses initially saw the fire empirically (you have to, even to approach it); but then he hears the voice. And that hearing and seeing *otherwise* is what trips the hermeneutic switch. Belief and desire are indispensable to interpretation.

As you know yourselves, when you're talking to someone about a difficult concept—love, beauty, the sublime, Being, God—you tend, even colloquially, to say "Do you see what I mean?" Now it's that "seeing-as," that "Do you see it *as* I see it?" that signals a different mode of seeing. In all modes of seeing, there is a "seeing-as," and therefore a belief, a presupposition, a reading (no matter how spontaneous or prereflective). In the case of Moses, there is what we might call a theological-eschatological "seeing-as": he sees the burning bush *as* a manifestation of God. For Moses and for subsequent believers, that is what it is, that is how it strikes them. But for someone who doesn't come with that faith, they're not going to see it that way.

MARION: Is that "seeing-as" simply the application of the same phenomenological "as-structure" in Heidegger, in *Sein und Zeit*?

KEARNEY: Yes, although not at exactly the same level. It would be confessional rather than purely existential.

MARION: You suggest that the case of seeing-as according to faith is a variation of *die Als-Struktur*?

KEARNEY: Yes, but you will interpret the seeing eschatalogically, as a seeing of something that precedes you and overwhelms you and exceeds you. . . .

MARION: What is very important to make clear against Barth's or Bultmann's way of thinking is that there is some continuity between the general structure of hermeneutics and the case of faith, which is not irrational. This is my point. There is a deep rationality in the operations of faith, understanding, interpretation, which cannot be reduced to the usual rules of hermeneutics and phenomenology. But there is a connection. I think we are no longer in a situation where you have "reason or faith." Reason is a construct. It is not optional, it is done. I would say that the difficulty for Christian theology now is perhaps that Christian theology assumes too much of the former figure of metaphysics and philosophy, which is already deconstructed. And this opens, I think, new fields for creative theology. But many theologians, if I may say so, have not taken quite seriously the end of metaphysics, and deconstruction, and so they miss these open opportunities. It is perhaps surprising that philosophers are maybe more aware of new possibilities for theology than theologians (or at least some them).

KEARNEY: An afterthought on the question of the hermeneutic "as." I would say that the everyday way of seeing the world is always inscribed by an "as." We see everything "as." Wittgenstein, of course, makes the same point. Seeing is always seeing as. But when we go to practice philosophical hermeneutics, we bring the everyday "as" of prereflective lived experience (what Heidegger calls our pre-understanding/*Vor-verstandnis*) to a level of conscious clarification and critical reflection. I think we then switch the hermeneutic "as" into an "as if." There we enter into a position where we pretend we don't have our belief structures, we act "as if" we were free of convictions or presuppositions. It is a version of methodological bracketing or suspension. We put our everyday lived beliefs into parentheses. Not to renounce them, not to disown them, but to see them all the better. We go into a methodological laboratory of possibilities where our faith commitments and convictions—and it doesn't have to be religious faith, it can be political or cultural faith—become certain ones among others. The so-called "neutrality" of philosophical hermeneutics is therefore strategic, artificial, contrived—but very helpful as a pull toward common understanding or consensus. I acknowledge the *seeing as* of my everyday preunderstanding, I put that on the table, and then I act *as if* I did not have it, and so I am now more open to empathizing with and listening to these other perspectives. The provisional bracketing of my "prejudices" prompts a more open mind. Then, finally, of course, one returns after the thought experiment of the hermeneutic "as if" to the former convictions of one's lived world. After the detour of methodological suspension one returns to one's primordial *seeing as* —but hopefully with a more enlarged, amplified, and attentive attitude. An attitude more sensitive and alert to other points of view. . . .

MARION: We should emphasize, before concluding, that there is also a *temporality* in the experience of the saturated phenomenon. We may be in quite different situations in front of the saturated phenomenon. Some saturated phenomena will, after a certain time, perhaps be reduced to average objects. Perhaps after more information, other concepts, we shall be able to constitute them as objects. So there are some states—like admiration, according to Descartes—which change. Some admiration should disappear after a time: when there is no surprise anymore, complete understanding, no admiration left. We have that possibility. But there is the other possibility with saturated phenomena that the more we understand them, the more they keep appearing *as* saturated phenomena. For example, the saturated phenomena of the ur-impression of time: it is always renewed. Or the experience of living and knowing the Other, when it is successful: the more you know the Other, the more it remains a saturated phenomenon. And you may perhaps assume the same about the historical event: the more you study the historical event, the more it appears again and again as a nonobjective phenomenon, a saturated phenomenon. So I think there are a lot of different epistemological situations. The saturated phenomenon does not stop epistemological inquiry, it makes it quite different.

God: The Possible/Impossible

DAVID TRACY
Interviewed by Christian Sheppard

SHEPPARD: Before discussing this new book, *The God Who May Be: A Hermeneutics of Religion* (Indiana University Press, 2001), please comment on Richard Kearney's work up until this point.

TRACY: He's a remarkable philosopher. He reminds me of Blanchot and Sartre in that he has written on narrative and metaphor (and hermeneutics), and he has also written some very fine novels. He is also a remarkable interviewer. He asks questions in order to really understand what someone is thinking, and thus is able to draw them out and get them to say things that perhaps they wouldn't otherwise. As a result, his interviews are very important, for example, the ones with Levinas, Derrida, and Ricoeur, among others.

Having said that, in general, I remember I read what it turns out was his thesis, I believe, *Poétique du Possible*. A version of it appears in his different books, including the one we are discussing. I remember being quite struck that it was a very original taking of Ricoeur, who was his director, and Levinas, who was his examiner, I believe, and taking their work forward into what all along has been a major philosophical and, I would say, theological category, on the possible. He developed the category of the possible in ways that even they had not done, that no one had quite done.

One of the most important things, I think, to watch in contemporary thinkers is what fragments of the past they appeal to. For Levinas, famously, it is the fragment on being in Plato; and perhaps even more famously, ignoring the rest of Descartes's meditations, only to take that one extraordinary moment when the very idea of the infinite breaks the categories, something Kant never would have allowed, something no one had quite noticed because we were all reading along in the argument about God. And I see Richard Kearney recovering important fragments, certain biblical passages—for example, the Transfiguration—and from Nicholas of Cusa, a figure who for a long time I have thought ought to be part of the present discussion but rarely is.

Moreover, starting from this *Poétique du Possible*, his books have been very generous to others and, as his own critical mind is at always work, always fruitful: *The Wake of the Imagination*, *The Poetics of Modernity*, and edited books, such as the one on the Irish mind, a really great book, and now this new trilogy.

I admit that *On Stories* didn't surprise me. On metaphor and narrative, I had already learned from Ricoeur, as did he, and from Kearney's own hermeneutical work as well as from his own actual narratives. I was more taken by his last book, *Strangers, Gods, and Monsters*, where he insists, in the context of current debates on the Other, "But it might be a monster!" and that not to face this possibility could be . . . deadly. He shows us the need for some kind of criteria, especially ethical criteria, for assessing what shows up, what shows itself. . . .

SHEPPARD: Kearney approaches the question of the Other with perhaps more caution than other postmodern thinkers. . . .

TRACY: Yes, he is more cautious, but *he* uses the word, correctly, "prudent." I have tried to do something similar, as you may know, by revising William James's very general criteria for the same purpose. So I am with Kearney in this. After the initial moment of encounter, there is a need for a hermeneutical moment (even if you agree with that initial moment), and therefore a focus on genres, symbols, narrative, metaphor, and so on. We need this more than Derrida, Marion, or Levinas admits. And then there is the need for some criteria, the need for what I prefer to call, with Gadamer, *phronesis*, rather than "prudence" with Thomas and Kearney (but it is the same virtue), and the same call for some general criteria of judgment, especially but not solely ethical judgment of what shows itself as Other.

Now the first hermeneutical moment, I already agreed to be important, so *On Stories* wasn't so surprising to me. But in terms of the second critical moment, with his notion of the monster in *Strangers, Gods, and Monsters*, especially as so sensitively and persuasively applied to contemporary culture, to science fiction and film, I think he is breaking new ground, that even Levinas, who has influenced so many on the ethics of the Other, had not. But the real breakthrough philosophically and, in my opinion, theologically is where you see Kearney going back to his early work on the possible and taking advantage of all that he has done since — on the imagination, on modernity, on the Bible, on writing novels — in this amazing book, *The God Who May Be.*

SHEPPARD: You refer to Kearney repeatedly as both a philosopher and a theologian. In that light, he becomes conspicuous to me, in contrast to other participants in this contemporary conversation (Derrida, Marion, Levinas), who all take great pains to differentiate theology from philosophy. Kearney is often doing both theology and philosophy at the same time. What do you think are the dangers and rewards of this tack?

TRACY: The danger first is very clear. It is Rosenzweig's danger, the danger that the philosophers won't read you. When Rosenzweig, who was a philosopher, was driven by his philosophy to theology in *The Star of Redemption*, the philosophers stopped reading him. I have always thought that Levinas was aware of this, and so made a sharp division between his philosophy and his Talmudic commentary. I noticed at the Levinas conference I attended that this was the issue, with many Jewish thinkers saying that he's Jewish and many philosophers saying that he's purely a philosopher. But I must say that Levinas is both. I would say the same of Marion; he's both. Philosophy and theology feed one another. Eventually, as this philosophical move toward theology becomes more familiar, acknowledged by the wider intellectual public, people will become less nervous about it. Although even recently in France, there were still attacks, for example, by Deleuze. And in American culture it is worse. So the debate is not over, certainly. One must acknowledge the prudential character of those, such as Levinas and Marion, who want to make the distinction. Derrida, of course, is not a theologian and does not want to be, though he, too, uses recognizably Jewish resources in his messianic ethics. Since I am a theologian, I am not troubled, and am very happy to see that Richard Kearney is much less troubled. Moreover,

I admire his daring to interpret central biblical passages. What's more central than Exodus 3:14 for Western philosophy and theology, and he gives a great reading of it. I admire such daring. Maybe it's because he's Irish. . . .

SHEPPARD: What do you see as the present state of the conversation on the category of the Impossible, and where do you and Richard Kearney enter it?

TRACY: First of all, as far as I am aware, there are two predecessors of the present debate on the category of the Impossible for speaking of God: Angelus Silesius and Kierkegaard writing under the pseudonym Johannes de Silentio. And it is Derrida who has most fruitfully reread for us the crucial fragments from their texts. The Impossible is not a major category for Levinas, although he may appeal to it once or twice. We must thank Derrida for this category, even if we disagree with him on other issues, because modern thinkers were all confined by the Kantian notion of the limits of the possible, and the best we could do, if we wanted to think about God, was to realize that God was a limit idea or a limit concept that could be thought but never known, which Derrida himself shows, in his reading of the Second Critique especially, and yet there is an amazing desire for more than this. Kierkegaard saw, in his own reading of Kant, that the Impossible could be a quite positive category that we desire. Angelus Silesius saw this even before Kierkegaard and on his own, but he was a mystic. What freed many of us—not everyone, not Ricoeur, not Levinas, and certainly not Deleuze—was to be able to appreciate, particularly after Derrida, the positive character of the category of the Impossible, not only as a positive limit concept, but as a category that is desired and as what comes into the possible.

After Angelus Silesius and Kierkegaard, the crucial moment is, of course, Heidegger's, in his famous statement at the beginning of *Being and Time*, that the possible is more important than the actual. Husserl at the end, Kearney reminds us in the *God Who May Be*, was also working on this category in his work on crisis. And in a different, but very influential way in political theology, Metz and Moltmann, for example, work on the Impossible after it had already become a political category, through Bloch, of the possible above the actual, the utopian possible. However, I believe it is Derrida who has shown us that the category of the Impossible can and should be rethought.

To do this, one has to have made a couple of steps. One has to have already agreed phenomenologically with Heidegger on the possible over the actual, which is a very difficult step. And most philosophers don't agree with Heidegger. Unless you already agree with that, this discussion does not seem to be able to get off the ground. But if you can, and I think there are very good reasons philosophically why you can agree with the Heidegger position, then you can develop something that Heidegger may have hinted at in his own struggles with the issue, but never fully developed: namely, the fully positive category of the Impossible, the Impossible as what is desired and the Impossible that may, in some odd way, desire. It's the desire of the Impossible, and the "of" is both the subjective and objective genitive, and it comes upon us from the future. Thinkers like Levinas would be more inclined here to use the category of the Infinite, which is, of course, very valuable to break totality and has a family resemblance to the Impossible. The Impossible is initially, I would say, an epistemological, and then with Heidegger a phenomenological, category that then becomes, I would put it, an intellectually, ethically, and religiously empowering category for rethinking where we are.

Richard Kearney in *The God Who May Be* enters this conversation by rereading fragments from Cusa on *posse*. Before Kearney I had always read Cusa on *posse* as, at best, only a premonition of what Heidegger was to say, the possible as above the actual. But for thinking about God, Kearney shows how the possible can be a post-onto-theological category for thinking the *posse* above *esse* rather than the *esse* above *posse*. It's a wonderful move.

SHEPPARD: Angelus Silesius, Kierkegaard, and even Heidegger, for that matter, seem to develop the category of the Impossible in relation to either spirituality or poetics. It's not simply epistemology. For example, Nicholas of Cusa develops his thought on the possible in relation to a spiritual practice of Dionysian prayer, just as one might say Richard Kearney develops his thinking in relation to a poetics and a poetic practice.

TRACY: I agree, and would add that Kearney is also clearly not hesitant about spirituality. I see this in his present and earliest philosophical work on the possible, in his novels, and in that collection I like so much on the Irish mind.

SHEPPARD: In *The God Who May Be*, if Kearney develops a spirituality, on the one hand, then it is in a prophetic mode. It is a spirituality of action aimed at making the world more just.

TRACY: Yes, on the one hand. . . .

SHEPPARD: On the other hand, his more contemplative side seems funneled into his strong appreciation of literature, art, and film. What he doesn't develop, in contrast to Nicholas of Cusa or Jean-Luc Marion, is a classic Christian sense of contemplative prayer in terms of liturgy or spiritual practice.

TRACY: I believe that Kearney affirms such things, but does not develop them, and perhaps on such things one would be better reading Marion. But because of the ethical, and via Levinas's critique of Heidegger, and because of Kearney's own prophetic emphasis, he is even, in my judgment, properly hesitant simply to follow his natural poetic leanings into mysticism. He is an artist who has written on the imagination. But like many of us, who have those sympathies but have also learned so much on the ethical and its import, even as first philosophy, from Levinas, we have become hesitant about Heidegger's, for want of a better word, *pagan* god as well as his sole appeal to a poetics.

I would agree that Marion has more to say on the mystical. But on the poetic, Kearney has a great deal to say. This book even ends, I was rather surprised but not altogether happy to see, with the appeal to play. That is not a prophetic moment, but a poetic moment. His thought, like all thinking, I would say, tends to move back and forth. And there are those of us who are naturally inclined to the poetic, who love literature and art, and therefore the later Heidegger is a wonderful resource to open our thinking toward the mystical. (See Marion on painting.) But that is not what we all who have this natural sympathy need; what we, Kearney and I, have seen through Ricoeur and Levinas is the ethical, an ethics of the Other, and thereby the prophetic. It is even right to call this back-and-forth movement of thinking a dialectic, as Ricoeur calls it a dialectic of manifestation and proclamation; or, as I try to do in other ways, of the mystic and the prophetic; or more radically, of the apophatic and the apocalyptic. I resist, as much as I understand Kearney to resist, anyone who doesn't have both the poetic and the ethical in their reading of philosophy, culture, and religion. I resist, for example, Levinas's dismissal of mysticism, of the Hasidic movement—he doesn't want dancing! Those are the Hasids he didn't like from the beginning. He ignores Scholem's work and those aspects of Rosenzweig. I think Levinas is too nervous about this Other, and quite wrong, frankly. On the other hand, those who tend to be good at recovering aspects of the mystical, such as Lacan, for example, often make one ask, Where's the ethics? Kearney has both. Ricoeur, more than anyone, has strived to work out both, from the beginning has been trying to have a poetics and in these last years an ethics. Derrida also tries to have both.

I think in Western ethics there are three great options: Aristotle, Kant, and Levinas. Most now see the great possibilities, but also the limits, of Aristotle. We can't do that. It depends on a world we don't live in and don't wish to live in, a world of slavery. But there are great resources in Aristotle still. And we can't do Kant. There is the universalizability principle of the categorical imperative, admirable as it is, but the only thing that interests me is its second formulation: you can treat the Other only as an end, never as a means. There is also Kant's own desire, showing up in his thoughts on immortality, not for the ego but in order to give you more time to work out your moral problems. Then there is Levinas, a genuine third option that had not been thought of.

To return to Kearney, I think *The God Who May Be* ends too abruptly with the play metaphor, and does not relate play—he juxtaposes them, but does not work them out—to what is more dominant in the book, the prophetic.

SHEPPARD: Kearney, in *The God Who May Be,* is in conversation with Aristotle, Kant, and Levinas, and out of this conversation on ethics does develop the notion of the Persona.

TRACY: Along with his rethinking of Nicholas of Cusa and the category of the possible, to me the philosophically and theologically most important intellectual moment in the book is on the Persona. Kearney appeals to all sorts of thinkers, but to my knowledge, he develops it quite originally. He develops, from the Greek notion of *prosopon*, the Latin Persona so that it turns out to mean, initially, the Levinasian Other with all the surplus of the Other. Not the individual, as he says so nicely. The individual is the atom. That's where hell is. Sartre's quite wrong. Hell is not other people. Hell is the self trapped without the Other. Kearney then appeals to John Manoussakis, whose work I'm not acquainted with, but who tells us that in the original Greek, and especially as used in the Greek Patristic tradition, which Kearney appeals to as much as Marion but with different results, *prosopon* also meant toward the I, toward the face, toward the Other, ("From Exodus to Eschaton," *Modern Theology* 18, no. 1, [2002]). Most interesting. So Persona is not simply, as most of us had thought it in the Western tradition (though it is also this, he admits), the mask of the actor. By reading together a lot of Greek scholarship and biblical scholarship, Kearney has really developed this very fruitful notion of the *prosopon* and the Persona as in the very notion "Toward the Other," and not toward the individual, and not toward what it became in the Scholastic tradition, from Boethius through Aquinas: namely, the *subsistens distinctum in natura intellecturali*, a distinct subsistence in intellectual nature, with the emphasis on "intellectual." After reading Nietzsche, one can become very interested in the mask in Greek tragedy in relation to Persona. Kearney is less interested, I don't know why, in the voice and the face of the mask; but others and I have tried to work on a phenomenology of the face and the voice. You must always remember that there's a hole in the mask for the voice to come through. This is in Greek drama, but also in the Old Testament: although you can't see the face of God—you cannot see the face, or you die—there is God's voice. In Job, there is the voice in the whirlwind. There is the still, small voice. In terms of the mask, the voice comes through the face as the Persona in the Latin. As well as being a tragic mask or a comic mask or the mask of Oedipus with the bloody eyes, the actor with his voice is also individuating.

Now Kearney's notion of Persona is really fruitful here, because it's not just the voice that individuates through the mouth of the mask, or in the biblical case, it's not just the face that can't be seen, but the voice that must be heard and, as Levinas says, "seen" with your ears (both of which are true), but it is also this fascinating notion which he has developed from *prosopon* as already related to, as already toward, the Other. Already! What he calls the *prosopon* or Persona, as distinct from the empirical, biological individual, is that surplus, that excess, that mystery, even if you love that someone, that you can never exhaust and that you can never possess; and if you try to possess it, you destroy yourself and them.

And, finally, what he does not develop but he could—and I hope eventually will—perhaps the most difficult issue, is to clear the brush away as we are all trying to do, in anti-ontotheology, what we are all united in, since Heidegger. After you make the move to Persona, what do you do with all of the debates on personal language for God? You can say they are ontotheology, which they are, but they are doing something else, too. To appreciate this, one must read Paul Mendes-Flohr's brilliant essay defending Buber's use of personal language against the Spinozaist critique, or Tillich's argument with

Einstein (Einstein was a Spinozaist). I at one time began to think, like Schleiermacher, for example, like Eckhart in another way, that perhaps we need to deny personal language for God: it's too immediately anthropomorphizing, it's bowdlerizing, it's trivializing, it's part of the problem. Well, it is, if it means what "person" usually means. But impersonal language has grave difficulties, and personal language saturates the Bible and the tradition, so you need a new notion of person.

If Kearney's notion of the *prosopon* could be developed into a notion of God, via the category of the Impossible and the possible, you then could reintroduce Persona via what is in fact the original Greek and the original biblical notion of person, and have personal language of a sort that is more faithful to the Bible and apparently to the Greeks, it turns out, at least in the Greek Patristic tradition. Who are most interesting, I have always thought, because they didn't seem to have this same kind of problem with personal language. I thought, don't they see it's a problem? Well, if they had this notion of *prosopon*, they didn't have to have the same kind of problem that the West from Boethius forward has had.

SHEPPARD: Is that just deferring the problem of ontotheology onto a problem of onto-Christology? Here someone who was sympathetic to my earlier question about the separation of philosophy and theology might say, isn't it interesting that two Christians, Richard Kearney and David Tracy, are both wondering how can we get the Greeks and the Hebrew Bible to come together and find the answer: Matthew, Mark, Luke, John. . . .

TRACY: That is what's wonderful about Christianity. I don't think it is a problem, but why it is a resource not only to Christians, but also to Western culture and people thinking with it, because it does bring the two together. Christians, after all, seek God by seeing the face of this unsubstitutable Jesus of Nazareth who is the Christ. I think Jews see it in the people Israel. And then both have learned to see it in any Other, which was always part of the tradition of naming God. But in the philosophical tradition (I'll put aside theology for the moment) since Spinoza, who is the most crucial figure for the modern rethinking of God, for all sorts of good and unhappy reasons, it's he who says you can't have this personal language, it's anthropomorphic, it's not God. He's sort of saying, let God be God, don't use this cheap personal language, or even this highly intellectualized Boethius/Thomist language, on person, or this Trinitarian language on person, which even as early as Augustine goes too quickly to this "distinct individual in intellectual nature." Now that's not a foolish tradition, but it is ontotheological, and part of the ontotheological problem is this notion of person, which is pure logos, is intellectual nature.

It is, of course, true that Christians instinctively want the two together. Even Derrida does, you know, by quoting Joyce, "Jewgreek, Greekjew." That's who we are. It's not a bad thing. But here the Eastern theological tradition was wiser than the West, on *prosopon*. They kept *prosopon* without allowing it to be individualized or purely intellectualized, and they, particularly Gregory of Nyssa and Maximus the Confessor, as Kearney cites them, can give us this impressive notion of *prosopon* that means, first of all, surplus, excess, enigma, the mystery of the Other, which we have had ways to think about in the West, but that now also means (*pros*) "toward the other" and "toward the face" (*opos*) of the Other. *That*, until now, we in the West did not have.

SHEPPARD: So suddenly with the Eastern Christian notion of *prosopon*, specifically as developed by Kearney as Persona, the mystical may open up to a real prophetic sense, a call for ethics. Where Levinas allowed us an ethics of the Other but without the mystical, here we have the possibility of the balance you call for.

TRACY: Yes. Here is where I remain very Western. To my knowledge, the Eastern Christian tradition and contemporary thinkers, whether psychological, such as Lacan, or philosophical-theological, such as Marion, as brilliant as they are in recovering the mystical — and love and icon — they don't seem able to develop an ethics of justice. And without that we are lost. Martin Luther King was right; anyone who thinks we can solve societal problems or even our own personal problems with "reason alone," as secular liberals say, or with "love alone," as say some liberal Christians . . . it's just not possible. Our human situation calls for, and the biblical prophetic tradition, and Jesus in the New Testament, especially in Luke, call for justice.

SHEPPARD: And Kearney never forgets that.

TRACY: Never, and none of us should. Ricoeur is right: the only thing that makes sense is a dialectic between manifestation and proclamation, or, as I would say, between the mystical and the prophetic. I was in the Buddhist/Christian discussion for many years, and after three years we were supposed to say what we had learned. And I said, and most of the Christians said something like I said, that the Buddhists had taught me, even though to me they were originally the most Other of the other world religions in the sense that they hold that there really is no God—I mean, what is emptiness—but, among many other things, they helped me to read Meister Eckhart, whom I had always had such trouble reading. A Japanese Zen Buddhist said that what he had taken from the conversation was that while he had always tried to be compassionate (the great Buddhist virtue, just as the great Christian virtue is love) toward the minorities of Japan, the Koreans and the indigenous peoples of Japan, Christians made him realize that maybe that is not enough, maybe you ought to try to change society's structures so they may be more just for all people in Japan. He appreciated the Christian and Jewish obsession with trying to understand, in each particular situation, the relationship between love and justice, and never settling for one without the other.

SHEPPARD: Earlier you praised Richard Kearney's "Irish" appreciation of the poetic, but do you think that his particular Irish historical situation, of living in Ireland during the Troubles, what some might describe as finding oneself at the wrong place at the wrong time, perhaps has been the right place and the right time for the right person for philosophy and theology, a person who has allowed his natural poetic sensibility to be tempered by a real felt need for justice?

TRACY: Yes, I agree. And do you know, and Kearney's book on the Irish mind brings this out, that Ireland was one of the few European countries to be colonized? You can and should reread Joyce and all of Irish history as postcolonial, so as to better understand this Irish call for justice. You can't miss it, unless you're not alive.

One of the things that Kearney's collection on the Irish mind taught me was the distinctively Irish love of very complex figuration. Notice Kearney's own work on figuration and narrative. Joyce (I learned from that book) carried the Book of Kells with him. He claimed it represented the Irish genius. He was right. Just think of the difference between Eriugena's Neoplatonism and Nicholas of Cusa or even Pseudo-Dionysius. There is something peculiarly Irish about seeking, and seeking to render truth's disclosure through a highly complex set of figures and subtle orders, as one sees in the Book of Kells. I've said the same thing about Iris Murdoch. Some critics complain that her Gifford lectures were not structured clearly enough. She's Irish. What do they want her to be, Locke? And Richard Kearney, who writes novels and works on the imagination, what he most opposes in Derrida, in Levinas, in Marion, in Caputo—all people whom he obviously respects—is that they don't bring all of this back in, they don't bring back the metaphors, the narrative, the figuration. He'll do a brilliant reading, for example of the Transfiguration in the Bible, precisely by bringing all of this in.

I don't romanticize Irish culture. I no longer say I am Irish-American, but that I am an American of Irish heritage. But I am attracted to Irish culture. And another thing, it's either chance, fate, or providence, as Simone Weil says, that the Irish intellectual life is extraordinarily rich and creative, and it's not just Richard Kearney, it's a number of them, and it's because of these two factors. They were a colonized European people where the sense of injustice was so strong. They were treated so outrageously. I, and Richard Kearney, am against romantic nationalist versions of Ireland. That is not the point. The point is that these are people that did suffer injustice. It's in their bones. And at the same time, they are Celts. They have the Celtic imagination. It's not surprising that Richard Kearney, a philosopher, also writes novels, that he sees both the radical point being made about the anti-ontotheological and the need for a new beginning, and yet isn't happy when the new beginning (with Levinas, Derrida, Marion, Caputo, although not with Ricoeur) doesn't involve figuration, metaphor, narrative. Among other things—it's, for example, philosophically and hermeneutically more correct—it's also peculiarly Irish.

SHEPPARD: If you are more American than Irish, where does your great affinity with Kearney's work begin to depart?

TRACY: I am American. All you have to do is go elsewhere to see how American you are, just as Europeans learn about themselves by coming here. Unlike Europeans, I am much more likely, after William James, to want to allow great variety and to celebrate plurality. How can you be American and not be for plurality? This is what we are all about. William James also shows that by allowing plurality, you require some set of at least general criteria for dealing with Others in all their variety. James has that, and I redid them.

SHEPPARD: So you find James more useful than the Neo-Aristotelian criteria that Kearney and Ricoeur develop?

TRACY: Yes. James starts with an empirical attitude, an attitude fostered by the American experience, of let us appreciate as much as possible of the various possibilities, but let's also admit that some of them can be sick, or evil, or, in Kearney's language, monstrous. You don't have to go back to Aristotle. In fact, he is not the most helpful. Aristotle is always helpful, but he is not much of a pluralist. In *Varieties of Religious Experience*, what does James do? He starts sorting things out fruitfully. Sick souls and healthy minds, mysticism as a problem of some people claiming to know things that we don't and the chance to give even the nonmystics among us a sense of "there's something more." Saints are most interesting even for the non-saints among us because they seem to be able to do easily what the rest of us can do only as duty and with great struggle. And best of all, in James, is what he calls "immediate luminosity." I think it's his characterization of what we would call today the Impossible. And that's the key, if you can think it. James was trying to think it. He didn't get too far thinking about it, but he knew that this was what religion was about. He wouldn't have had trouble with the Impossible, but he would have developed criteria. He would have asked, How does this relate to what you otherwise know or believe to be the case? If it's totally against what you've learned from science, then you have an intellectual problem. Creation is nuts as a reading of Genesis, not only as a reading of evolution. But most important—James could not work the second out but he saw the need, as do Kearney and I, after Levinas and Ricoeur—there is the need for an ethics of the Other and the Other as facing one with surplus, excess, the Impossible, and splitting the self, not in the usual way but for the good.

SHEPPARD: What we are getting from Levinas, a sense of the demand that the Other makes on us, you are somehow coordinating with James's American empirical interest: let's see what's out there, and what's out there has needs; the variety of Others we find out there demands that we seek, to quote James, "the moral equivalent of war."

TRACY: That's why American pragmatism, so called, although I have never particularly liked the phrase, with James is ethically serious, unlike the versions of Rorty and others. You can't just stop with James's formulation, but it is a good place to start.

SHEPPARD: That's the cultural difference between the two of you. What's the difference between your God and the God Who May Be?

TRACY: First of all, let me say what I have learned from *The God Who May Be*, which is the best book I have read in the last ten years on how to think about God today, for thinking post-ontotheologically about God, with the kinds of qualifications that few see (only he and Ricoeur see) that we need to make. What I learned most from Kearney is thanks to his recovery of Cusa on the possible. That is Kearney's fragment. Just as Levinas and Marion take their fragments from Descartes, the infinite that we finite minds could not think up, but *is* and crashes into our categories. I appeal to other fragments of Cusa, because I am interested in the very notion of the fragment. The fragmentation Cusa describes (see especially in *De Visione Dei*) as our crashing against the walls of Paradise, causing sparks—it's almost like Schlegel is writing at certain moments in Cusa—sparks that suddenly disclose this one door through the walls of Paradise, and that door is Christ. This is the mystical Dionysian Cusa. But what I have learned from Kearney's reading of Cusa on *posse* is that *posse* can be more than a premonition of what Heidegger has to say on the possible as above the actual. For thinking about God particularly, which really Heidegger doesn't but which Kearney does, the possible is a post-ontotheological category for thinking the *posse* above *esse* rather than the *esse* above *posse*. It's a wonderful move, which I hope he will develop further, along with *prosopon*.

The main difference between us, I think, is that I don't understand why he doesn't have—although he does have a sense of justice—a stronger focus on suffering. He has a sense of suffering but doesn't develop it enough or reflect upon it. So that when he does the Christian symbol system and the Christian story or the Hebrew Bible, he will characteristically do Transfiguration and Song of Songs but not Job; John, but less Mark. And I'm the opposite. If you do the symbols, and I'm not just saying let's have a full version—who cares about that?—you can't do any one of them and have the right complexity; you need the entire story, all of the metaphors. Similarly, you can't have just Incarnation and Resurrection—he's very good on Resurrection, as was Cusa. He's less good, in my opinion, on Cross and on Second Coming, and its apocalyptic character. The result is, he even says at one point in the book, that the *deus adventurus*, the God Who May Be, that version of eschatology, is more important than the *deus absconditus*. I do not agree. It's of course important, both in Cusa's Dionysian sense of the radical incomprehensibility and the overflow of love, but it does not give us the sense of love as desire, as lack, and the sense in Luther, Calvin, Pascal, Simone Weil, the Book of Job, Lamentations, and the Gospel of Mark of the Cross, and how that changes everything, in terms of what is this face of the

Christ, and what is suffering, or, to use Derridean language (although neither Derrida nor Caputo develops it as such), what is this passivity beyond passivity understood there, and what is the terror of God that we experience in relation to God? That's why I don't like the book ending with play. Although unlike Cusa, Kearney develops an eschatology, his eschatology does not seem to include Cross or Apocalypse. For example, he reads liberation and political theology as saying the same thing, but they are not. He reads Metz and Moltmann as saying the same thing as Bloch, but they are not. Metz really changed the notion of apocalypse in significant ways in relation to the issue of suffering. Unless you take more seriously the *deus absconditus* in the sense of terror and fear, you'll never be able to work out the eschatology. Your *deus absconditus* won't be what the Book of Revelation means, what Mark means; it won't be enough. One must take sufficient heed of Levinas's comment that any philosophy that cannot speak to—not answer; theoretically, there is no answer, none—innocent suffering is inadequate. The ultimate horror of ontotheology is theodicy. Kearney's rejection of theodicy does not become an occasion to reflect upon innocent suffering, the Cross, Apocalypse, but there is no reason why his thought cannot be developed in this way.

SHEPPARD: Let's end on this appropriate note of advent and apocalypse. Thank you.

Casimir Pulaski Day, March 1, 2004
Chicago

Kearney's Endless Morning

CATHERINE KELLER

In at least two registers—one of genre and one of doctrine—Richard Kearney's philosophical theology appears suddenly and luminously at the forefront of theology itself. In other words, it invokes a "possible God," and thus a possible theology. Theology has wanted the fully actual, active God, however, not a possible one—and so has generated an impossible one. The possible God suggests a third space, indeed a certain kind of *posse* of theology itself, a "paradox of future anteriority" (Kearney's Levinas) for a freshly Christian sense of eschatological possibility. Responding to his work mainly by way of his Villanova lecture, "Enabling God," I'll sound these two registers, then ask, soliciting the metaphor that ends the lecture—how endless is Kearney's "morning that never ends"?

First, in terms of genre of possible speech about "God," Kearney is exploring what may be called a theopoetics. For this work he does not seek to define the proper style for God talk so much as perform it by example, as in the intensive citation of poetry of his "literary circle." He finds here "explicitly poetic epiphanies of the possible," enabling him to "transcend the confessional limits of theism or atheism" ("Enabling God," 12). He does not thereby attenuate the (possible) content of God talk so much as gently shift its potency from the propositional to the imaginal. This hermeneutical motion supports the sense of those who believe that theology must risk a return *in style* to the heteroglossia of Scripture and the multimedia of liturgy, to the affective and aesthetic genres of the spiritual imaginations—if it is to stand a chance of postmodern rebirth. And if, therefore, it is to address anyone besides "believers."

Kearney's appeal (via G. M. Hopkins) to a deity "of transfiguration rather than coercion, of *posse* rather than power, of little rather than large things" (12), pertains to rhetorical genre as well as to dogmatic content. For a God of coercive power requires a theology of coercive arguments. As Kearney I think implies, a poetic discourse already forfeits a certain univocal *force* of reference, and therefore does not properly signify an omnipotent God. What we may call a transfigural discourse does not control, but "enables," its significance. So also a deity of transfiguration does not control, but enables, its creatures. In other words, a theopoetics in genre *disables* divine omnipotence in dogma. In so doing, it enables Kearney's "enabling God," as a God who enables the creatures in their own creativity.

Second, only such a deity can be "good" in the sense that Kearney derives from Plato, Jesus, and Cusa: "not able to be non-good," and thus "not responsible for evil." This means that God cannot be classically omnipotent—whether in the sense of a Scholastic primary cause, which "permits" but does not "cause" evil, or in the less squeamish sense of Calvin, who decries permission and affirms the admittedly "horrible doctrine" of double predestination (the eternal damnation of unbaptized infants is for God's glory). Either way, nothing happens apart from the will of God. In the switch from a discourse of divine controlling power to that of enabling love, Kearney offers a beautiful gift to theology. Besides process theology and much feminist or ecological theology, few Christian thinkers have risked giving—or is it accepting?—this gift.

Some will find Kearney's God too sweet 'n' low, indeed "powerless." From the vantage point of a self-deifying masculinity, God is either omnipotent or impotent. This would be a familiar objection to process theologians, whose God, operating by "divine lure" rather than "controlling power," controls no outcomes in history. For each event is a concrescence of divine desire and creaturely freedom—a freedom free to thwart a Good that is, as for Kearney, inseparable from God. As one able to be a theologian only by way of a certain transfigural feminism, I applaud Kearney's contribution to the deconstruction of omnipotence. Kearney is helping to unfold—indeed, to "explicate" in Cusa's sense—the third way of an (en)abling power. Among his metaphors, I prefer "enabling God" to "power of the powerless." The divine is better conceived as the alternative, enabling power rather than as an external force who might rescue the inherently powerless, suggestive of victims properly lacking agency. Though without the benefit of Kearney's reading of Cusa, I had in *Face of the Deep* explored the *explicatio/implicatio/complicatio* triad in terms of divine "capacities." That is, instead of the moribund anthropomorphism of "persons," these capacities *capacitate* (enable!) creaturely unfolding—and fold back into the divine becoming. I imagine a rhythmic interchange in which any fixed division between transcendence and immanence can be exposed as arbitrary, as *forced*. In acts of doctrinal force, human authorities build themselves up in the image of omnipotence. It is no surprise that they require a coercive God, with a coercive dogma, to establish and fix the zone of transcendence—from which the force then flows.

Process theology, in the Whiteheadian form that I find persuasive, unfolds something very like Kearney's "microtheology." Process theology analyzes each event as microcosm. Yet it displays more interest than Kearney in spatial *macrocosms*—in the widest possible undulations of the universe. To his own limit question of what God will do if we destroy ourselves, Kearney replies that God can start again (as after the suicide of a spouse)—as though God would not at this moment be wed to a multitude of complex life-forms throughout the billions of galaxies we now know to exist. In the interest of recognizing our own limitations, had we not best weaken our limitation of God to an interest in merely human history? I'm not sure this would render God polygamous (heaven forbid)—just "wed" to the whole universe, rather than merely to our bit of it. Kearney, on the other hand, cares more than process theology about the *temporal* macrocosm. He imagines, as do most Christians and Jews, some quite definite end point of history, at or as which the Messiah "comes" (again).

Third, here comes my question. Is Kearney anticipating a final consummation—a generous, indeed all-saving, but conclusive one? He proposes—or, to be fair, invokes—a "morning that never ends," an endless feast, understood, I think, as a biblical "new earth" rather than a supernatural or disembodied heaven. What could be more inviting! Indeed it's all about invitation—rather than coercion or exclusion. Invitation capacitates projects of just love in history. Yet if I am not misreading him, this *parousia* will be singular, final, and total. Indeed, however poetic his images remain, I wonder if here they adorn a quite literal sense of the end of human history, at least of history read as the dynamism of temporal, ambiguous, and open-ended finitude. In Kearney's inviting vision, does the evanescence of life evaporate? For finally there is "no door unopened, no creature, however small or inconsequential, left out in the cold, hungry, thirsty, uncared for, unloved, unredeemed." This is an ideal worth enabling.

Yet does the ideal then threaten to *disable* the entire project of historical ethics—a project and a passion key to Kearney's turn to theology? Social and ecological justice emanate from a humanity enabled and enabling in its responsible agency. By rendering the poetics of *eschaton* as a literally final (rather than normative, transcendental, figural, or just *possible*) new creation, in which only the redeemed remain, do we violate the freedom, the spontaneity, and the agency of the creature? (These are the sorts of questions that one asks of Jürgen Moltmann and of Wolfhart Pannenberg—theologians of a hope that in the interest of historical liberation threatens to liberate us *from* history.) Would the "endless morning" in fact once again—as in all classical eschatology—mean in fact the end of history—and so of all terrestrial mornings? If so, then to achieve this final end, in which presumably there can be "no more tears," "no more death," and of course no more sun—for God will have panoptically replaced the motion of the material star—does one not in fact require an act of final intervention? Must this intervention not be that of the omnipotent One, whose power may have been withheld in a historical *zim-zum*, but is now released to be all-in-all?

Would this omnipotence close down not only evil, but history itself, with its threatening, open-ended uncertainties? This danger of closure characterizes some of the most generous-spirited of Christian eschatologies, those who emphasize, with Origen, Barth, and Moltmann, and against orthodoxy, the final salvation of all. For they seem not to worry that the latter requires an omnipotence that precludes "the free character of her 'yes'" (2). Let me with perhaps Protestant perplexity postpone the question of Mary's consent—and the wide spectrum of feminist Mariologies from, recently, Elizabeth Johnson's *Truly Our Sister* to Marcella Althaus Reid's "indecent virgin." One can certainly make a strong case for the biblical privilege of human responsible agency over God-dependent passivity. Does Kearney's loving messianism suffer from the danger of an omnipotence lurking in the eschatological closet? Can his "retrieval forward of the past as future"(22) read as "the closure of the future as a past retrieved?" The question seems to me open. His eschatological imaginary remains, if aloof from process theology, very much in process.

There is an open-endedness even in his formulation of his fulfilling closure.

Fourth, my final question, or phase two of the same question: Can the closure be pried open, for the sake of Kearney's own "endless morning"? Is there a less terminal approach to the messianic hope for an all-inclusive feast of salvation? I think so, and in Kearney's own terms. Can we not intensify our theopoetics precisely in the register of the possible, the *posse?* For the future as *kairos*, not *chronos*, is precisely the not-yet-actual, the not-to-be-predicted-from-the-actual. We may hope *because we do not know*; we may have faith *because we lack certainty*. As Kearney rightly insists against Heidegger, we do not only "wait for God"—we act, *because we are enabled.*

The possibilities of Kearney's divine *posse* ripen into nonlinear and yet irreversible actualizations. Kearney's final invocation (thanks to his daughter) of the Rilkean image of God as the "ultimate fruit of a tree whose leaves we are" might pose a helpful resistance to his own messianic finalism. Rilke describes a divine energy flowing altogether within history: "your life as a painful and lovely day in the history of a great pregnancy." This hope for the birth of God leads one to ask about the place, the space of the pregnancy. What is this womb? One infinitely greater than that of Mary—that of Job 38:8: "Who shut in the sea with doors when it burst out from the womb?"

Here I would refer to Kearney's wonderfully staged encounter between "God" and "*khora*" (and between Caputo's mystics and Caputo's Derrida). He spots a surprising dichotomy, in which the chaotic emptiness of *khora* is privileged over the "desire of God." He gracefully resists a forced choice between God and *khora*—and challenges the deconstructive preference for *khora*. While recognizing that we must honestly face up to our abysms, he heartily prefers the God, the Good. Yet he seems to suggest that the only alternative to privileging the desert abyss is to "rise up from the *khora* dust so that (with a few more prayers and tears) . . . we may soon find our Shepherd again and be guided toward the Kingdom"(*PG*, 205). Do I misread him here as accepting the very dichotomy he had problematized, only in reverse? Does he succumb to the sort of "alternativism" for which he (with kindly charm) scolds the deconstructors?

Kearney catches Caputo's fleeting association of *khora* with the biblical *tohuvabohu*. I have elsewhere analyzed this biblical chaos—the *tehom* of Genesis 1:2—relating it both to the Derridean *khora* and to the apophatic divinity. Few have engaged this configuration of primal metonyms. When I diagnosed an ancient and very present syndrome I called tehomophobia, which either demonizes or vaporizes the waters of the bottomless, I began to sound out the Patristic linkage between the dogmas of *creatio ex nihilo* and of omnipotence. Indeed, it is the eschatological desire for a final consummation that motivates Athanasius to look back and demand of God an all-powerful creation from nothing—else He would not have the power to guarantee us a full bodily resurrection from the nothingness of death! A terminal eschatology requires an absolute origin.

I hope that as Kearney develops his eschatological theopoetics, he remains mindful of the force by which, precisely at the messianic moment, an uninvited omnipotence may arrive to disfigure the most generous possibilities. Indeed, he himself warns us astutely that it does just this in the Mariological case of J.-L. Marion's "ravishing love." Kearney's contribution to the deconstruction of omnipotence and the reconstruction of a "possible God" bursts in all brilliance from the deep. So let it not inadvertently "enable" some gentler, kinder version of the dominative transcendence.

The "endless morning" at the end of "Enabling God" arises at the horizon, where hope generates for Kearney a post-*khoric* festival of vision. Not the unbearable desert sun but the lightness of morning—that "great gettin' up morning" of the slave song. I worry still: Does Kearney's rising-sun God preclude all future resistance to its own goodness? Would this be a form of what I call light *supremacism*—a cultural passion to annihilate the darkness, whether evil, mystical, epidermal—or uteral? What about the darkness over the face of *tehom*? Never more? In my work on the doctrine of creation, I found an ancient series of hints as to the *tehomic* maternity. What if we read the *tehom/khora* as the womb in which the "great pregnancy" is unfolding? Will a spirited ambivalence rather than mere transcendence best guide our relation to the primal chaos? Such a move would be, I think, all the more compatible with Kearney's own insistence on "many degrees of latitude" between the poles of *khora* and God. He would "liberate a space of chiasmic play between *khora* and *hyperousia*," the very space of the "possible God." That chiasmus, when freed of any absolute origin and final closure of the struggling, evolving, failing, and beginning-again beauties of creation, suggests the poetic logic of the Joycean chaosmos.

Here we do not anticipate endless morning, as though night itself were inferior or evil, to be forever left behind—but rather an awakening to that light which Cusa has said includes the dark: "This whom it worships as inaccessible light is not light whose opposite is darkness, but is light, in which darkness is infinite light" (Cusa, cited in *FD*, 202). This nondualistic moment in negative theology suggests the negation of every bright and blazing certainty, including that of a happy ending. Instead, there dawns an infinite luminosity whose brightness is not overcome by dark — *nor overcomes the dark*. The shadows are not erased, but drawn into relation to the light. But Kearney is imagining a party continuing into the wee hours of the morning — and forever. So perhaps after all he has in mind not a final, flat, fluorescent glare, an endless morning-after; but the mobile spectrum of light, dark, and color that thrills through the dawn. Worth staying up for.

reading in the dark

Reflecting God

SALLIE McFAGUE

Kearney's hermeneutics of religion might be called a "covenantal process view without the metaphysics" or, perhaps more accurately, with only intimations of metaphysics. The ontological claim is *there*—God is coming, will come, can come—but only if we help God come, only if we do our part by witnessing to love and justice in the world. The relations between God and human beings are built on invitation and response, on the possibilities the divine offers us and our acceptance of these possibilities as our life vocation. "If we are waiting for God, God is waiting for us" ("Re-Imagining God," 9). Not waiting for us to become something, but to do something: what Kearney calls the small things, things like giving a cup of cold water to a thirsty person. He says this is "micro-eschatology."

There are several things I like about Kearney's vision. First, his God is not beyond being, but emptied into being, on the side of being. "There is more to God than being. Granted. But to pass beyond being you have to pass through it" ("The God Who May Be," in *Questioning God*, ed. Caputo et al., 169). By "being" he includes the least of beings to whom we owe justice and love. The incarnate God appears to need us in order to become fully embodied. Kearney has a healthy Catholic sacramental sensibility that sees God everywhere and especially in the despised, the small, the particular, the details. This kenotic Christology is nontriumphalist; it is also a paradigm for us to follow as we answer, when called, "Here we are." Needless to say, this understanding of God puts a large burden on us. Are we up to it? In Kearney's view, God's power appears to be entirely in powerlessness. What of the immanence of divine love as the source of the world's empowerment? Is his covenantal process view too slight in its ontological claim? Can we answer if we are not already empowered to do so or, as the tradition would say, already "in grace"? For Kearney, God is in the details (the small and the least), and rightly so, but do we also "live and move and have our being in God"?

Another feature of Kearney's work that I like is his ease in moving among different disciplines and genres. As a theologian whose ancillary field has been literature and literary theory rather than philosophy, I have sometimes felt second-class. One of the healthy deconstructive moves of the last few decades has been the blurring of disciplinary boundaries and the realization that concepts are not more "true" than are images. I believe Kearney would agree that metaphorical language—language that makes connections by novel associations—is more appropriate for the God who never stays still than is conceptual language which pretends to finality and certainty. The Scriptures, after all, are poetic texts, and any reliance on them as a source or resource for theology needs to take that fact seriously. Kearney's use of Scripture, testimony, and literature builds a strong argument, not by logic or reason but by the piling up of wonderful, powerful images, testimonies, poems, and stories that *create* the meaning toward which he is groping. He leads the reader through signs, signals, images, and suggestions in the hope that an intimation of the God of possibility will appear. It did for me. His method of polymorphous suggestion enriches and builds with the hope that insight will occur at one or another level—scriptural, testimonial, literary.

Finally, I find Kearney's brand of deconstructive theology deeply satisfying as a Christian. He balances the two sides of Christianity: the Catholic, sacramental, incarnational side with the Protestant prophetic, iconoclastic side. Most deconstructionists work happily within the "Protestant" side; in fact, one could say that deconstruction is another version of Karl Barth's *Nein!* to all ideologies or Paul Tillich's Protestant Principle that denies absoluteness to any finite symbol. The "No" is easier to say than the "Yes," especially the appropriate, minimal, humble, small, kenotic "Yes." Christian faith, I believe, says *both*. What deconstruction reminds us is that our "Yes" must be small and honest. Kearney adheres to this admonition, but he *does* say "Yes": we are invited to the feast, to the banquet, by the

One who becomes embodied as we feed and clothe the least. It happens, says, Kearney; a movable feast takes place as we help God to be God.

It is difficult for me to criticize this covenantal process theology because I like it so much: I find it personally relevant, scripturally sound, and a powerful motivator for acts of justice and love. If I have a problem with it, it is what I mentioned earlier: Are we up to it? What will cause us to answer "Here I am" when we hear the call "Where are you?" A traditional Christian theology will say that grace enables us to answer; a metaphysical process view will say that God lures us with the possibilities that will fulfill us. Kearney seems to be saying that God knocks and knocks and knocks, hoping we will answer. Perhaps it is enough that, as Kearney says, quoting Mark 10, for us it is impossible, but all things are made possible by God. We can agree with that answer but still realize that *we* have to open ourselves to the knocking. Some light is shone on this dilemma in Kearney's essay "Desire of God," where he suggests that desire and responsibility are the traces of God, the urgings, if you will, that allow us to *hear* God knocking. He ends this essay with the question: "How do we read in the dark"? (*God, the Gift, and Postmodernism*, ed. Caputo et al., 130). How indeed? We need the traces—the stories, promises, covenants, and good works—which are the intimations of transcendence making it possible for our weak wills to open the door.

I would like to close on the note with which I opened these comments. Kearney's God is one before whom we can dance and sing and pray ("Desire for God," 128). This God is not the One who *never* comes but the One who is *always* coming, inviting us to "A morning that never ends" ("Re-Imagining God," 23).

In Place of a Response

RICHARD KEARNEY
Interviewed by Mark Manolopoulos

MANOLOPOULOS: In your debate with Derrida and Marion, "On the Gift" (Villanova, 1997), you ask the question "Is there a Christian philosophy of the gift?"[1] Do you think either Derrida or Marion provides handy directions? Could you summarize or interpret their insights? And whose argument do you personally find more persuasive?

KEARNEY: They did avoid the question. In Derrida's case that is logical because he will always—reasonably, for a deconstructionist—try to avoid tying the messianicity of the gift to any specific messianism as such, be it Christian, Jewish, Islamic, or any other kind. So it makes sense for him not to engage in that debate per se because he would say something like "That's beyond my competence. I'm not a Christian. 'I rightly pass for an atheist.'[2] I respect Christianity. I'm fascinated by their theological and philosophical expressions of the notion of the gift—I learn from it—but it's not my thing." Marion I find a little bit more perplexing in this regard because he *is* a Christian philosopher. He has talked about "Eucharistic hermeneutics" in *God Without Being*.[3] Christ is a "saturated phenomenon" for Marion.[4] But Marion is going through a phase—and this was evident at both Villanova conferences (1997 and 2003)—where he doesn't want to be labeled as a "Christian philosopher"—and certainly not as a Christian *theologian*. He wants to be a phenomenologist. So, being true—at least to some extent—to Husserl's phenomenology as a universal science, he wants to be independent of presuppositions regarding this or that particular theological revelation: Christian, Jewish, or otherwise. I think that's why in his essays on "the saturated phenomenon," Marion goes back to Kant. The Kantian sublime offers a way into the saturated phenomenon, as does the notion of the gift or donation, which—like Husserlian phenomenology—ostensibly *precedes* the question of theological confession and denomination. And I think Marion wants to retreat to that position so that he won't be labeled a Christian apologist—which I think he is. I think he's a Christian thinker who's trying not to be one. Personally, my own response here would be to say that there are two ways of doing philosophy—and both are equally valid. One is to begin with certain theological and religious presuppositions, with the life of faith and conviction. The other is to operate a phenomenological reduction, where you say, "We're not going to raise theological issues here." The latter follows the basic Husserlian and Heideggerian line. In his *Introduction to Metaphysics* Heidegger says something like "The answer to the question 'Why is there something rather than nothing?'—if you fail to bracket out theology—is 'because God created the world.'"[5] But if you bracket it out, you *don't* begin with theological presuppositions—and that bracketing is what Husserl does, what Heidegger does, and what Derrida does. I think Marion mixes the two, although in *Being Given* and the Villanova exchange with Derrida I suspect he is trying to get back to a kind of *pure* phenomenology. He keeps saying: "I'm a phenomenologist! I'm doing phenomenology, not theology!" But the lady doth protest too much.

Then there is the other way of doing phenomenology *in dialogue with* theology, which doesn't bracket it out but *half-*suspends it. We might call this a quasi-theological phenomenology or a quasi-phenomenological theology. In other words, one acknowledges that there's a certain hybridity, but one doesn't want to presuppose straight off which comes *first*: the giving of the gift as a phenomenological event or the divine creation of the world as source of all gifts. This allows for a certain ambiguous intermeshing, intermixing, crossweaving. What Merleau-Ponty described as a chiasmic interlacing. And it seems to me that that's perfectly legitimate. Even though it is methodologically more complex and more ambivalent than the Husserlian move of saying "Bracket out all political, theological, ideological, cultural presuppositions," it is actually truer to life because life *is* the natural attitude. And the natural attitude *is* infused with presuppositions. And it includes *both* (a) experiences of the gift as pure gift and (b) experiences of the gift for believers as coming from Yahweh or Christ or Allah or the Sun God/dess. And it seems to me that the phenomenology of unbracketed experience, the phenomenology of the natural attitude—which I think Merleau-Ponty gets pretty close to—is what I am practicing in *The God Who May Be*.[6] I'm not writing as a theologian because I don't have the theological competence and I don't presuppose the truth claims and doctrines of Revelation. I'm writing as a philosopher, but one who, as a philosopher, feels quite entitled to draw from religious scriptures as sources, and to draw from phenomenology as a method. I'll draw from anything that will help me clarify the question. And I think drawing ambidextrously from both can open a "middle path" into some interesting questions, even though the Husserlians and the Heideggerians can shout, "Foul! You're bringing religion into this!" And the theologians can say, "Oh, well, you're not a theologian! Did you pass your doctoral exam in dogmatic theology?!" And I respond, "No. I'm just doing a hermeneutic reading of texts—some phenomenological, some religious—and I'm going to mix them. If there be interference, let it be a creative interference. If there be contamination, let it be a fruitful contamination."

MANOLOPOULOS: If you provided a theology of the gift, what would be some characteristics or axioms?

KEARNEY: Well, I repeat, what I'm doing in *The God Who May Be* is not theology as such, but a "hermeneutics of religion." It is, I hope, a contribution to the phenomenology of the gift. I usually call "the gift" by other names: (1) the "transfiguring" God; (2) the "desiring" God; (3) the "possibilizing" God; (4) the "poeticizing" God, that is, the creating God (qua *poiesis*). They would be my four categories of gifting. *Poiesis* or the poeticizing God engages in a cocreation with us. God can't create the Kingdom unless we create the space for the Kingdom to come. God created the world in six days and left the seventh day free for us to complete it.

MANOLOPOULOS: That's interesting in light of Catherine Keller's thesis that creation *ex nihilo* is too one-way.[7]

KEARNEY: I agree with Catherine on this. But one thing I like about the *creatio ex nihilo*—though I can see that it's nonreciprocal—is that it's an unconditional giving. It's not a giving because there's some problem to be solved that precedes the giving. To use Derrida's language, it comes before economy, although it cannot continue without economy. As soon as there's history and finitude and humanity, there's economy, there's negotiation. And there is, to my mind, reciprocity. Here I disagree with Caputo, Derrida, and Lyotard and the postmodern deconstructionists who repudiate the notion of reciprocity or reconciliation. They see it as going back to Hegel or conceding to some kind of economy. I don't think it is as simple as that. I am wary of the polarity between the absolutely-unconditional-gift versus the gift-as-compromised-by-the-economy (which gets rid of the gift as pure gift). I just think that's an unhelpful dichotomy, as I think messianicity versus messianism is an unhelpful dichotomy. It's an interesting idea; it's good for an argument. But I think it's ultimately unworkable because I don't think you can investigate messianicity without messianism; and I don't think you can have genuine messianism without messianicity. Now maybe Derrida would agree with that. But there's still a difference of emphasis. I don't see anything wrong with the mix. Whereas Derrida and Caputo seem to think it is all that is *possible* for us humans, mortal beings; but what they are really interested in is the *impossible*. I leave the impossible to God and get on with the possible. Because that's where I find myself: I'm in the economic order. I look to something called "God"—what Derrida calls "the impossible"—to guarantee that the economy doesn't close in on itself. But I don't hold out God as something that we should even entertain as an option for us because God is not an option for us. God is an option for God. Humanity is an option for us. If we can be more human, that's our business. Our business is not to become God. It's God's vocation to become more fully God; ours, to become more fully human. We answer to the Other without ever *fusing* in some kind of metaphysical unity or identity. When I say "I'm for reciprocity, equity, and reconciliation," I'm not for premature Hegelian synthesis. I'm not for metaphysical appropriation or some ineluctable evolving "process" of integration. I'm not for reducing the otherness of God to being as such. But, on the other hand, and this may sound paradoxical, I'm all for *traversings* of one by the other—anything that muddies the waters and makes the borders between God and us porous. I don't believe in an omnipotent God out there and then a completely compromised humanity here. I think there are constant to-ings and fro-ings. So the phenomenology of the gift that I'm trying to articulate in terms of poeticizing is a cocreation of history by humanity and God, leading to the Kingdom. A new heaven and a new earth. We don't know what that will be because we haven't reached it. We can imagine but we can't pronounce. It goes beyond the sphere of the phenomenology of history because it involves a posthistorical situation. It's an *eschaton*. We can prefigure it as eschatology, but it's really something that God knows more about than we do. But the God who interests me is not a God who *knows* so much as a God who loves, gives, and desires.

MANOLOPOULOS: What do you mean when you say "giving is desiring"?

KEARNEY: I argue that giving is desiring because desire is not just the movement from lack to fulfillment, or from potency to act, or from the insufficient to the sufficient—these are ontological notions of desire. I'm taking the idea of desire as coming from "more" to "less," from a fullness toward an absence as much as coming from an absence to a fullness. For example, *kenosis* is a form of desire. And it doesn't come from God being empty and wanting to become full. It comes from God being full and wanting to empty His divinity in order to be more fully in dialogue with the human because, as Levinas says, *on s'amuse mieux à deux.* "It's better to be two than one."[8] And it's "better" in the sense of being *more* good, *more* just, *more* loving. It's Eckhart's idea of *ebullitio*, this "bubbling over," this excess or surplus of desire. Not a surplus of being but of desire. Desire is always the desire of more desire. And also the desire for an answer: What's the point in God desiring and having nobody to answer the divine desire? That's why Song of Songs says it all: the desire of the Shulamite woman—representing humanity—for the Lord (Solomon the lover) is a desire that actually expresses itself not just as frustration, emptiness, lack, looking for her lover, but also as a desire that sings its encounter with the lover, that celebrates its *being found*. In the Song of Songs, the lover *finds* the Shulamite woman, and that is the inaugural moment, as it were, of the song of desire. It's a desire based not on *fine amor* and romantic passion—which is frustration, prohibition, or absence. It's a desire of plenitude—not of presence, because that's fusional. It's a desire of excess, not of deficiency. A desire that stems from being taken by God. A response to the desire of the absolute. So that's another form of giving. In other words, the desire of the Shulamite woman is a gift. It's not a subjective hankering. It's a gift; it's a response to a gift. And what's the gift? The gift is desire. So you've got two desires at work. The traditional view has been to consider the human as desiring the fullness of God because the human is full of lack, insufficiency, and finitude. But what I'm trying to do is to see it as much more complex than that. It's a question of both lack *and* fullness in God and humanity. There's a lack in

God and there's a lack in humanity. What's the lack in humanity? It's that humanity is not divine. What's the lack in God? That God is *not* human. So, in a way, the Kingdom as a second coming or second Incarnation is what we're looking for. But as soon as you have that meeting of the finite and the infinite, you've left history behind—not to return to some kind of fusion or "oceanic oneness" à la Freud. Let's imagine it hermeneutically, poetically: What would the Kingdom be if the desire of the Shulamite woman and the desire of the Lover Lord were to meet and mesh in a posthistorical fashion? The first answer is: we don't know. But if we were to imagine it—as various religions have done—it would be a dance; it would be a *perichoresis*. It would be the dance-around of the three persons, for where there are two gathered, there is always a third. So the *perichoresis* is the refusal—even in *parousia* and *pleroma*, in the eschatology of the Kingdom—to compromise in terms of a closed economy. It never closes. The economy is still bubbling, is still flowering, is still bursting into life and being by virtue of this dance-around which, as *perichoresis*, is something I explore in *The God Who May Be*. The *perichoresis* is the dance around the *khora*. *Peri-chora*. The dance-around is each person of the Trinity—whether you interpret that as Father-Son-Holy Ghost, or God-humanity-Kingdom (one doesn't have to be patriarchal and gender-exclusive on this)—is a trialogue with the others. We're just fantasizing here, of course—something most theologians aren't allowed to do. They would say, "Well, now, is that according to Saint Thomas or Saint Augustine, etc.?" At certain points in history you could be burned for thinking too freely about such things (remember Bruno or Marguerite Porete). But let's assume we're not going to be burned in this day and age for imagining what might go on in the Kingdom.

Now, in terms of this desiring relationship among the three persons, there's a double movement that I'm arguing will or *could* continue—let's imagine—in the Kingdom when history as we know it has ended and when the Shulamite woman who desires God has come face-to-face with her lover. The double movement is this: it's a movement of approach and of distance. The term *perichoresis* is translated into Latin as *circum-in-cessio*, which is taken from two phonetically similar verbs (a) *cedo*, "to leave place," "to absent yourself," and (b) *sedo*, meaning "to sit," "to assume or take up a position." So there is a double movement of immanence and transcendence; of distantiation and approximation. Of moving *toward* each other and then moving *away* from each other—as in a dance. A dance-around where each person cedes his/her place to the other, and then that other to its other, and so on. So it's not just two persons. There's a third person in this divine dance whom you're always acknowledging and invoking. This third person is very important in Levinas, and I think it's very important in most Christian notions of the Trinity. Because the danger of two is that two can become one; face-to-face can become a candlelit dinner where romantic lovers look into one another's eyes and see themselves reflected in the other. Whereas the third introduces a little bit of "symbolic castration" that safeguards a distance and therefore allows for desire. If desire were to reach its end, it would end. And a God who is not desiring is a God who's not giving. And a God who is not giving is not God.

MM: What about the "transfiguring God"?

RK: The transfiguring God is the God who transfigures us as we transfigure God. Basically, God transfigures us through creation, through interventions in history—whether it's the burning bush or Christ or the saints or the epiphanies that Joyce and Proust talk about: *that*, to me, is divinity transfiguring the everyday. So presumably if God is giving, God is giving as a constant process and practice of transfiguring. We may not see it. We may not know that it's there. And we may refuse to acknowledge it, in which case it doesn't affect our lives. In a way, that's God's loss, too, because if God's transfiguring goes unheeded and unheard, we're going to have wars, evil, and so on. I'm Augustinian in that regard: evil is a *privatio boni*, the *absence* of God as transfiguring, desiring, poeticizing, and possibilizing—I'll come back to this fourth category in a moment. But transfiguring is not just something God does to us: it's also something that we do to God. And we transfigure God to the extent that we create art, we create justice, we create love. We bring into being, through our actions—poetical and ethical—a transfiguration of the world. It's a human task as much as a divine gift. God gives to us a transfiguring promise; we give back to God a transfigured world—and we can transfigure it in ways that God can't. We can author a poem like a Shakespearean sonnet. God can't do that. But we can coauthor with God a poem called *poiesis*, creation, the "real" world as well as the imaginary world. That's a different kind of poem, where God and the human meet one another, complement one another. But either can withdraw from the dance, in which case the other just falls on his or her face. That's the end of it. We can destroy God. That's why I speak of a God who *may be*, which is an interpretation of the Hebrew

"I am the God who will be, who may be."[9] If God were to declare that He is who he simply *is*, that is already accomplished, already completely there, then God would sacrifice his role as promise. But God is the infinity of possibility, as Cusanus rightly says. And that means that at any point we can pull the plug on God. As one of the victims of the Holocaust, Etty Hillesum, says: "We must help God to be God."[10] And that's where we can make a link with people like Eckhart and Cusanus and some of the other Church Fathers and biblical prophets.

MANOLOPOULOS: At first glance the notion that "We must help God to be God" sounds arrogant.

KEARNEY: Maybe, but what it's actually saying is that *God is not arrogant,* that God does not presume to be able to stop evil. God *can't* stop evil. Why? Because evil is the absence of God. God has no power over what God is not—namely, evil. God can only be good—unconditionally good in gifting, loving, creating. That is where the Gnostics and theodicists were wrong: God is not *both* good *and* evil. Even Hegel and Jung made that mistake. God is *not* omnipotent when it comes to evil. God is utterly powerless. And that's terribly important. You find that in the Christian story: Jesus before Pilate, the crucifixion: he couldn't do anything. It's "the power of the powerless," as Vaclav Havel calls it—and he is right. God helps us to be more fully human; we help God to be more fully God—or we don't. If we don't, we can blow up the world and that's the end of humanity, and that's the end of God qua Kingdom on earth because there's nobody here anymore to fulfill the promise. There is no one home to receive God's call. In that instance, God remains as pure *desiring,* of course, as pure *poeticizing*—except God's world has just been broken up by God's own creatures—us. And to revisit the terms of *The God Who May Be,* God remains *transfiguring*; but there's nothing left to transfigure because we've destroyed it.

MANOLOPOULOS: You also mention the "possibilizing God."

KEARNEY: Basically, that means that divinity is a constant offer of the possibility of the Kingdom which can be interpreted in two ways (and you find this in the Scriptures). One is the Kingdom as eschatological promise after history, at the *end* of history. The other is the Kingdom *now*: in the mustard seed, in the little, everyday, fragile, most insignificant of acts. The Kingdom is present in the "least of these" (*elachistoi*). Just as Christ is present in the giving of a cup of cold water. That means that in every moment there is the possibility of good and there is the possibility of non-good. There's the possibility of love; there's the possibility of hate, violence, aggression. We're choosing constantly. And every moment we are actualizing the Kingdom or not-actualizing the Kingdom. As Walter Benjamin says so beautifully: "Every moment is a portal through which the Messiah might come." Now what we've got to get away from is thinking that the Messiah comes and then it's all over. If you're a Christian—and I am, up to a point: I am a Christian up to the point where the love of "Christians" respects justice, and after that I'm not "Christian" anymore—you draw from the Christian story and testimony the notion that *each little act* makes a difference. For example, the woman with the hemorrhage: you help her—you don't want to, but you help her.[11] There's no wine: okay, Jesus reluctantly changes the water.[12] And so on and so forth. One does all of these little things—most of them almost imperceptible—and one doesn't make a big fuss about it. And when the Messiah comes—even if this happens to be a pretty extraordinary, exemplary instance of the divine in the human—as I believe Christ is—you don't say, "Now it's all over." You *can* say, "Now it's all over for me." But history isn't over. The coming of Christ *wasn't* the end of the world: the Messiah always comes again in history. And the Messiah is always—including the Christian Messiah—a God who is *still* to come (even when the Messiah has already come). The Messiah is one who has already come and is always still to come. And that's why I see the Christian story as exemplary. (But it's not the only story in town. And, in my view, it has no absolute prerogative vis-à-vis other world religions. God speaks in many voices and in many traditions.) But to return to the Bible, I could take the Mosaic story as well: in the burning bush God came. With Elijah in the cave the Messiah came. But that wasn't the end of it. The Messiah came to John the Baptist, too, the voice crying in the wilderness. God always comes *and* goes. And that's the nature of the Messiah: it's already here—the Kingdom is already here—but it is also not yet fully here. And it's this double moment that's terribly important because the possible does not mean The End: the telos of universal history coming to an end at the end of time—that's Hegel. That's triumphalism. That's the kind of monotheistic tyranny that leads to religious wars. "We own The Promised Land." "*This* and only *this* is the Absolute." All or nothing. In contrast to such triumphalist teleologies and ideologies of power, the divine possible I am speaking of comes in tiny, almost imperceptible acts of love and poetic justice. It is in "the music of what happens," as Seamus Heaney says. Or in what Joyce called "epiphanies"; Baudelaire, "correspondences"; Proust, "reminiscences." These are all poetic testimonies to the possible that becomes incarnate in all these little moments of eschatological enfleshment.

MANOLOPOULOS: What does "eschatology" mean for you?

KEARNEY: If and when the Kingdom comes, I believe it will be a great kind of "recollection," "retrieval," or "recapitulation" (*anakephalaiosis* is the term used by Paul) of all those special moments of love. But you can't even see it in terms of past, present, and future because the eternal is outside time, even though it comes *into* time all the time. Christ is just an exemplary figure of it. What does Christ say at the end? He says, "Time for me to go. Don't touch me. *Noli me tangere.* Don't possess me. I cannot be an idol that you possess." Messianicity always defers itself. And here I often draw great sustenance from Blanchot's tale of the beggar waiting for the Messiah at the gates of Rome. The Messiah comes, and the beggar goes up to him and says, "Are you the Messiah?" And the Messiah responds, "Yes." And the beggar asks, "When will you come?" And that is the perfect follow-up question because the Messiah is always still to come. The Messiah is *still to come* even as the Messiah is *there*. Because we're temporal, we're confronted with this unsolvable paradox or aporia—namely, that the Kingdom has already come and yet is not here. And that's the way it is for our finite phenomenological minds. And no metaphysics and no theology or philosophy can resolve that one. So, to the extent that deconstruction is a reminder of the *impossibility* of ever having the total take on God as absolute, then I'm for deconstruction. But as an endless kind of "soft-shoe shuffle" of infinite qualifications and refinements, forever declining any kind of incarnation, I find deconstruction too deserted, too *désertique*, too desertlike, too hard. Derrida's deconstruction is too inconsolable for me. It's overly uncompromising. Too puritanical—in a way, strangely. It's all about the impossible. But for me, God is the possibilizing of the impossible. "What is impossible to us is possible to God."[13] We actualize what God possibilizes and God possibilizes what remains impossible for us. To sum up: God as gift means God is *poeticizing, possibilizing, transfiguring,* and *desiring.* That's my religious phenomenology of the gift. Incidentally, I also did a prereligious phenomenology of the gift in the first part of *Poétique du Possible,* published in 1984.[14] And if I were to do that again, I would certainly include readings of Proustian and

Joycean epiphanies or just everyday testimonies to people's kindness, the small ways in which love and creativity work in the world—irrespective of whether people are religious or not. You can go either way.

MANOLOPOULOS: You've answered the question of a "theology of gift" in terms of thinking God as gift. To think creation as gift: briefly, what would that entail for you?

KEARNEY: If we're talking about divine creation—because I think there's two creations going on: divine and human—I would probably go back to the idea of *poiesis*: God as *poiesis*, the *nous poetikos* as Aristotle calls it, and the *possest* as Cusanus says. Poeticizing is the act of constantly opening horizons of possibility, gifts of possibility, for human beings to realize. The divine gift as creation is powerless to impose that gift on somebody who doesn't want it, because that would not be good: that would be evil. If you say to somebody, "I love you," and they say, "I don't want your love," and you say, "Sorry, I love you, and whether you like it or not, you are going to be transfigured by my love"—that's coercion, violence, tyranny. That's what so-called benevolent dictators do. That's the imposition of the good on somebody who doesn't want it. Sadism in the name of God. How many times has religion done that? The Taliban were doing it. The Inquisition was doing it. The New England Puritans were doing it to the "witches" down in Salem. "For your good, we are going to impose the good!" "But thank you very much, I don't want your good." That's why God loves rebels: God loves the Steven Daedaluses of this world who say, "I will not serve that in which I no longer believe," whether it calls itself religion, language, or homeland. (It's in Joyce's *Portrait of the Artist*.) I suspect that God would prefer people not to serve that in which they do not believe. God prefers honest people who rebel rather than the lackeys, the "creeping Jesuses who would do anything to please us" (Blake). I don't want to get into a cult of the rebel here. But God admires people like Job and David—who argue with God. God admires Jesus on the cross, who says: "Why have you forsaken me? Come on, give me an answer to this." God likes that.

MANOLOPOULOS: In "Desiring God" (1999) you mention, quite prophetically: "There is a growing problem of closure to the other. I am sure, if it has not already become a problem here in the United States, it will become one—the problem of how one can relate openly and hospitably and justly to the other, without demonization."[15] These words obviously resonate in light of the current wave of terrorism. However, let's ask this question from an ecocentric perspective: Do you have any thoughts on how one can or should relate openly and hospitably and justly to the nonhuman other—animate and inanimate? We also demonize the nonhuman—

KEARNEY: We demonize all the time. When people want to show what the devil is, they usually take an animal. Just look at medieval and Renaissance portraits of demons. In *Strangers, Gods, and Monsters*, I try to show that the iconography of the Last Judgment is full of this—goats, bats, snakes, dragons, griffins, dogs, gargoyles. I think that's a real question. I think it's something we in Western philosophy and in our excessive anthropocentrism have sometimes ignored, that is, the *alterity* of nature: of trees and of animals, and so on. One thing I've taken great courage and guidance from is my own children's sensitivity in this regard. They are vegetarians and very opposed to wearing fur coats or buying factory-produced food. I think there's a growing awareness in the new generation which is very important, as long as it's kept in balance, of being good to your neighbor who's starving down the street (and perhaps can afford only factory food). I find there are many young people in Boston or New York who go down to protest against Bush or the death penalty as often as they will concern themselves with cruelty to animals and the pollution of nature. That's good. The balance is important. There's no point ignoring social and human issues out of some kind of obsession with eating "natural" food. That's just taking food as a surrogate symbol that can be "purified" as the world disintegrates before the ravages of global poverty and capitalism. There can sometimes be— for example, the New England obsession with health and the natural— a demonization of smoke, a demonization of alcohol, a demonization of sex (although it often goes hand-in-hand with fantasy sex or subworld sex in Las Vegas and Hollywood, so it can be very ambiguous). There is a residual *puritanism* in American culture, I think, and a certain demonization of the pagan earthiness of things. That may include prohibitions against eating fish or "killing" tomatoes, as well as the stringent laws against smoking, drinking, or sexual language. But that's only *half* the story—the official version, as it were. The other half is very different, and leads to all kinds of perversion, doublethink and double-talk. It's a messy world, full of double messages. I'm not saying, therefore, that you should tolerate cruelty to animals and indiscriminately chop down trees. I'm saying you do your best, wherever possible and within the limits of the possible, to remain human while doing the *least* amount of harm to nature or to animals or to your fellow human beings. But to pretend that you can enter into some realm of pure consumption where everything is as "organic," as in Bread and Circus food markets, is to ignore the fact that Bread and Circus can exist only for the wealthy, who pay twice as much for their fish and vegetables while the poor have to go to bottom-end supermarket chains and buy factory-produced food. I approve of going to Bread and Circus—I just wish it were available to everybody. Somewhere along the line, the refusal of smoking, sex, alcohol, and meat in an *absolutist* fashion can, to my mind, smack of puritanism. It can slip into demonization even with the very best of intentions—and I'm always wary of that. So I would say: "Be vegetarian. Fine. But when you find yourself in another country and there's only meat on the table, have some meat." If I go to a tribe in Africa and they give me goats' eyeballs, I may not particularly like it, but I'm not going to offend my host by saying "I don't eat goats' eyeballs!" I'll eat it—raw or cooked. That's the kind thing to do. That's accepting the hospitality of the other as other. Or, as the Dalai Lama advised his monks, "Eat whatever is dropped into your begging bowl."

MANOLOPOULOS: In *The God Who May Be* and *Strangers, Gods, and Monsters* you open up the question of discernment, whether we're facing saturation or the desert. You claim that "For the theist Marion, no less than for the atheist Derrida, we are left with the dilemma of 'holy madness,' how to judge between true and false prophets, between good and evil ghosts, between holy and unholy messiahs."[16] Even though Caputo and Derrida are suspicious of criteria—I guess we all are a little suspicious—how should we nevertheless judge between the true and the false, the good and the evil? After Derrida, how do you treat criteria?

KEARNEY: You do so by trying to discern and judge more carefully, more cautiously, more critically. And, I would say, more hermeneutically. You don't have to get rid of criteria altogether. Derrida would say, "Well, of course we have to make decisions all the time. We judge and we use criteria. We have to do that: we couldn't not do it." Strictly speaking, that's already a compromise. That's already entering into the economy of things. And I just find the gap deconstruction insists on between our decisions and undecidability too polar. That's my problem: it's too antithetical, too aporetical, too impossible. Decisions are "too difficult" in the deconstructive scenario. They are all made in "fear and trembling" because we're "in the dark"! At the 1999 Villanova exchange I asked Derrida, "How can you read in the dark?" He said: "We can *only* read in the dark." But I want to turn the light on! Even if it's only a flashlight—that will remove a little of the darkness and confusion. I don't believe in absolute light or total enlightenment for us ordinary mortals. It doesn't have to be either absolute light or total darkness. It doesn't have to be that hard. We're not all desperate Desert Fathers waiting for Godot as the apocalyptic dusk descends! It need not be that angst-ridden or melodramatic. The world is a place of light and dark: we always have a bit of both.

MANOLOPOULOS: Derrida might say that the world is in such a mess because we assume we can read in the light, and that all decisions are easy.

KEARNEY: I can understand what he's saying in terms of an excessive hubris and arrogance on behalf of a certain enlightenment, on behalf of excessive rationalism, on behalf of the hegemony of science and technology. There I agree with him. But I'm not sure that's the way most people in the world today actually think or live. Most people are confused and bewildered. They're not cocksure *cogitos* in need of deconstruction, but wounded, insecure, fragile subjects in search of meaning.

MANOLOPOULOS: What about religious dogmatism?

KEARNEY: Oh, before the Enlightenment it was worse. That's for sure. What I'm saying is: to think you possess the light and everybody else is in darkness is a recipe for imperialism, colonization, injustice, holy war, jihad, "Good versus Evil." We're witnessing it again today. Nobody has a monopoly on light or the good. But that doesn't mean we're all condemned to total darkness, *khora*, undecidability. I think everything should be deconstructed, but the question for me is What's it like *after* deconstruction? That's why I still believe in hermeneutics. Derrida doesn't. I believe in reminiscences, resurrections, reconciliations. They're all temporary, they're all provisional, they're all muddling through. Granted—but they do happen. I believe in paths. Not massive metaphysical viaducts or Golden Gate Bridges between the contingent and the absolute, but I do believe in little footbridges—the kind you get in Harrison Ford movies. Hermeneutic bridges, connections, ladders. I find that deconstruction follows the template of the Lazarus parable: the implacable metaphor

"/: the people going up and down ladders"

of the gulf that separates (a) paradise, the Absolute, the impossible from (b) the land of the living—our finite, everyday, contingent, mortal world. The deconstructive gulf radically segregates the two. There's an unbridgeable gap between the divine and the human, the impossible and the possible. The deconstructionist Abraham won't allow Lazarus to send a message back to his brothers to warn and instruct them. It is too late. The kind of hermeneutics of religion that I'm talking about in my recent trilogy, by contrast, would be much more guided by the paradigm of Jacob's ladder, where there's to-ing and fro-ing, lots of people going up and down, in both directions. No absolute descent or absolute ascent. It's little people going up and down ladders. And that, to me, is how you work toward the Kingdom. "Every step you take . . ." (as the song goes). Each step counts. Messianic incursion, incarnation, epiphany is a possibility for every moment of our lives. Because we are finite and temporal, the infinite can pass through time, but it can never remain or take up residence in some triumphant or permanent present. That's the difference between the eternal and time. They can crisscross back and forth, up and down, like the angels on Jacob's ladder. But they are never identical, never the same. That's what a hermeneutic affirmation of *differ-ence* is all about. As opposed to deconstructive *différance*, which, in my view, gives up hope in the *real possibility* of mediation and transition.

MANOLOPOULOS: One more question about your idea of a "Desiring God." Whereas someone like Marion may turn to mystical theology and a phenomenology of saturation, I concur with you in your affirmation of "hermeneutical retrievals and reimaginings of biblical narratives and stories."[17] Could you briefly comment on the possible nature or direction of these retrievals and reimaginings? And could you perhaps suggest how such retrievals could inform—and be informed by—a philosophical theology of gift/ing? For Kevin Hart and Jean-Luc Marion and others draw from mystical theology, but they seem to be turning away from biblical resources.

KEARNEY: That's why I'm into the hermeneutics of narrative imagination, whereas they're into a more deconstructionist position (yes, even Marion, in my view)—and there *is* a difference in that regard. So while I learn from deconstruction, I really am closer to hermeneutics—I try to negotiate between the two, but I'm closer to hermeneutics—what I call a "diacritical hermeneutics" in *Strangers, Gods, and Monsters*. It's not the romantic hermeneutics of Gadamer and Heidegger and Schleiermacher: getting back to the original event and reappropriating the inaugural moment. I don't believe in that kind of hermeneutic retrieval of the original and the originary—some primal unity. Nor would I uncritically endorse what Jack Caputo calls "radical hermeneutics"—which is really another word for deconstruction—because it doesn't sufficiently allow, in my view, for valid retrievals, recognitions, or reconciliations. In *Strangers, Gods, and Monsters* I propose a diacritical hermeneutics which is a third way.[18] I propose mediations, connections, interlinks, and passages back and forth. So it's neither reappropriation and fusion of horizons à la Gadamer, nor is it a complete gulf, separation, or rupture à la Caputo, Lyotard, and Derrida. Diacritical hermeneutics holds that faith is helped by narratives. Now I don't privilege in any exclusivist sense the Christian narratives over the Jewish or the Islamic or indeed the nonmonotheistic. I just say, "They're the ones I know best." If I was a Muslim, I'd work with Muslim narratives. If I was Jewish, I'd work with Jewish texts. (Indeed, as a Christian, I generally work with both Christian *and* Jewish narratives.) My niece has become a Buddhist: I learn from Buddhist stories and I try to include them in my work. I still do it from a Christian perspective because that's what I'm most familiar with. But if I'd grown up in Kyoto, I would invoke the Buddhist texts first. I don't believe that any religion has an absolute right to the Absolute. There is no one Royal Route. There should be no proprietal prerogatives here. They're all narrative paths toward the Absolute. And if you happen to be born on this particular road or highway rather than another one, and you've walked it for twenty or thirty years, then you know it better, and you can help other people walk it. And from your knowledge of it, when you come to a crossroads, you may have more interesting and intelligent dialogue with the person who has come along the other highway. You know where you've come from and you can talk to them about it. They can learn from you and you can learn from them. Whereas if you say immediately, "Oh, well, to hell with my highway! I'm only interested in yours," they might well respond, "Well, I'll tell you about mine, but do you have anything to add to the conversation?" And you'll say, "No, no! I hate everything about my road! I've learned nothing. That's only a load of baloney!" I'm always a bit suspicious of zealous converts who repudiate everything in their own tradition and look to some New Age, trendy alternative for a solution—and that can be, for example, a Buddhist becoming a Christian as much as a Christian becoming a Buddhist. I'm all for dialogue between the two. Some people have to change their religion to shake off the tyranny of their tradition. Their experience may be *so* negative that they *need* to do that. And here you can have a kind of religious or cultural transvestism that is very helpful: you wear the clothes of another religion, and through it you can see the spiritual in a way which you couldn't have done previously. I'm not against conversion as such, unless it's from one absolutist disposition to another absolutist disposition. I don't think any religion should be absolutist. I think it should be *searching for* the Absolute, but the *search itself* should not be absolutist, because that's to presume we can own the Absolute. Where I am wary of a certain mystical New Ageism or deconstructionism is their tendency to repudiate historical narratives and memories as invariably compromising and totalizing. I see narratives and memories as necessary mediations. If you don't go down the route of hermeneutic reinterpretation—which is a long route, as Ricoeur says, an arduous labor of reading and rereading—then you must go toward the desert like Derrida and Caputo and their *ana-khorites*. Which is hard. Or else you go toward the opposite, mystical extreme—not toward *khora* this time (with Derrida and Caputo) but toward the "saturated phenomenon" or hyperessential divinity (with Marion or Michel Henry). But then it's another kind of "holy terror," because you're completely *blinded* by it. You embrace another kind of "dark" (from overexposure to the Absolute). Here, too, it seems to me, there is no interpretation possible. It's immediate, non-mediated presence. In both cases—whether you're going into the emptiness and undecidability of the *khora* or whether you're going into the blinding, overexposed splendor of divine saturation—you are subjected to an experience of "holy madness." Now, I'm not against that *as a moment*. But you can't live like that: you've got to interpret it after the event. Otherwise, what's the difference between Moses before the burning bush and Peter Sutcliffe in his pickup truck claiming he heard a so-called divine voice that says: "Go and kill prostitutes, do my will and clear the world of this evil scourge"?[19] What's the difference? There *must* be a difference. And we must try to discern as best we can between (a) psychopaths like Charlie Manson or Peter Sutcliffe, who think they're on a divine mission to kill in the name of God and (b) prophets like Moses or Isaiah, who go out to liberate and comfort their enslaved people. You have to be able to even vaguely and approximately tell the difference. No?

MANOLOPOULOS: So we return to the problem of Abraham sacrificing his son?

KEARNEY: Yes, but my reading of this episode is very different from Kierkegaard's and closer to Levinas's. The way to read that, I suggest, involves a critical hermeneutic retrieval. For me the story illustrates how monotheistic revelation is anti-sacrifice; it marks a move away from human sacrifice. This may be read, accordingly, as a story about the transition from a prerevelation to revelation mono-theism. The first voice that Abraham hears—"Kill your son"—is, by this account, his *own voice*. It's the voice of his ancestral, tribal, sacri-ficial religion. But the second voice, that says "Do *not* kill your son," is the voice of the Kingdom. That's how I read it. I think we should read every story in the Gospel according to the principle "Where is justice being served here and where injustice?" Where there's evil, you have to say no to it. You can find passages in the Bible that say "Go out and kill all Canaanites." If you take that literally, you're into the Palestinian/Israeli situation. You are into holy war. Ditto for the Christian invocation of a "blood libel" against Jews. We should read such texts hermeneutically, critically, and say, "No! That was an in-terpolation by certain zealous scribes during a certain century. . . ." We need historical research on this. We need to demythologize it and say, "They were trying to justify the occupation of their neighbors' lands." So ignore that *misrepresentation* of divine revelation and look rather to the Psalms, where God calls for the protection of the widow, the stranger, and the orphan. The stranger is your neigh-bor—*that's* God speaking. "Go out and kill Canaanites" is *not* God speaking—that's *us* speaking. Knowing the difference is a matter of hermeneutic discernment. And it's a matter which concerns every be-liever, every reader of Scripture.

MANOLOPOULOS: Nietzsche asks, "Can there be a God beyond good and evil?"[20] Maybe we're just projecting our idea that God is "simply good"; that God can only do "purely good things."

KEARNEY: Everyone makes their choice, but the God of love and justice is the only God I'm interested in. I'm not interested in the God of evil, torture, and sadism. I'm just not interested in those Gnostic (or neo-Gnostic) notions that see the dark side of God—destruction and holocaust—as an indispensable counterpart to the good side. Such theories or theodicies can justify anything.

MANOLOPOULOS: But there is that possibility?

KEARNEY: There *isn't* that possibility for me, or at least it is one I refuse. It's how you interpret it. You can, of course, interpret divinity in terms of a narrowly moralizing God where you say, "Oh, homo-sexuality, masturbation, divorce, sex outside of marriage, etc., is evil." That's the Christian Coalition, Jerry Falwell, Ian Paisley—they seem to know what's good for all of us! I'm against such a *moralizing* God, but I'm not against an *ethical* God. There's a big difference. I *don't know* what the absolutely good is. How could anyone know? But I do *believe*—precisely because I can't know—the good exists; and I will do everything to try to differentiate and discern (according to what Ignatius calls "the discernment of spirits") as best I can between the God of love and the pseudo God of hate. I do believe that the divine is the good. In fact, for me "God" is another name for "the good" rather than "the good" being another name for God. We don't know what the good is. We don't know what God is either. But they *must* be the same, because if they're not, there's no way to avoid theodicy and its ruinous logic: "This war was necessary. It's all part of the will of God. It's the necessary dark side of God." Jung's answer to Job. Pangloss's answer to the Lisbon earthquake. Hegel's answer to the Terror. The divine "Ruse of Reason" run amok. As humans, I agree, we have to confront the *thanatos*, the shadow in ourselves, the sadistic instincts, the perversions, the hate, the evil, the aggression. *We* have to confront the shadow in ourselves. But divinity doesn't have to confront the shadow in itself—because if it has evil in itself, it is not God. If you say "The shadow in God—the sacrifice of innocent children, the torture of victims—is part of God's will," well, frankly I'd prefer to burn in hell than believe in a God who justifies the torture of innocent children. And I'm not ambiguous about that. That said, I take a very dramatic example here that very few people would say is good because on many occasions it's very hard to tell what's absolutely good or evil. It is very hard for people to justify the torture of an innocent child. Should the Americans have dropped the atomic bomb on Hiroshima? I would say "No," but I'm not going to be too moralistic about that because I know there's a strong argument for it. You can negotiate that. Should a woman have an abortion? I would say "Ideally not, but it's her right, and if she believes she is doing what is right, on balance, it may be the right thing for her to do." So I think a law that says "You can never have an abortion" is wrong. Abortion is very complex. It can be right in some respects, and wrong in others—*at the same time*. It may be right *and* wrong. Morality is often gray on gray; it's not black and white. Let's just say it is morally difficult. And everyone—for or against—has a right to discuss it. That's what human morality is. It's not about absolutes. But when it comes to God, who is absolute, either God is good or I'm not interested in God. The mixing of evil with God is worrying.

I wrote my second novel, *Walking at Sea Level*, as an argument against that.

MANOLOPOULOS: There are all these other metaphysical characteristics ascribed to God: God is one, God is pure, and so on, and to say, "God is purely good"—

KEARNEY: Well, I'm not sure I would use the word "purely" here, because then you're back into puritanism. But I do insist on the claim that God is unconditionally and absolutely good, or God is not God. I would not claim that I know exactly what the good is. I would simply *try* to discern better between what is good and what is evil, or what is better and what is worse, what is more or less just, in a *given* situation. I can recognize many instances of good acts where people put others before themselves and give up their life or give up their wealth—that, to me, is a good thing to do. I want to reserve the right to say that. Whereas when somebody chops a child's head off, I want to be able to say, "That's *not* a good thing." I think most people would agree. That's not an absolutist disposition; it is common sense, practical wisdom, what the Greeks called *phronesis;* the Romans, *prudentia.* Whenever someone does a good act—gives a cup of cold water to a parched neighbor—he or she is making God that little bit *more* real and actual and incarnate in the world. When someone does evil—torturing innocent children or simply stealing the cup of cold water from the parched neighbor who needs it more—he or she is refusing the possibilizing, desiring, transfiguring promise of God. In that sense evil is the refusal to let God exist.

MANOLOPOULOS: In your legendary 1982 interview with Derrida, he explains that there have always been "heterogeneous elements" in Christianity.[21] Was he referring to scriptural motifs or mystical theology? Or both?

KEARNEY: I don't know. You'd have to ask him. But I suspect that what he means by that is probably similar to what I've just been saying. There's no one pure religion. Christianity is heterogeneous. It draws from pagan elements, Jewish elements, Greek elements, etc.

MANOLOPOULOS: The context was Greek philosophy or metaphysics, mainstream Christianity, and you referred to the official dogmas of the dominant churches, and then Derrida said: "Oh, no, I can see that there are heterogeneous elements." But I didn't know if he meant biblical theology and some of the mystical texts.

KEARNEY: Generally speaking, when Derrida says "There are heterogeneous elements," that's good news from his point of view. So I think he just wants to say, "Look, as I would interpret it, Christianity isn't just this triumphalist, totalizing, dogmatic, absolutist, intolerant body of beliefs. It's actually quite porous and permeable to dialogue with its others." And I would agree wholeheartedly with him here.

MANOLOPOULOS: And there are marginal voices.

KEARNEY: Exactly.

MANOLOPOULOS: Having cited that line, do you think Derrida prefers the biblical over the mystical?

KEARNEY: It depends how you define "the biblical" and "the mystical." There are elements of the mystical in Derrida. He is very taken, for example, by Pseudo-Dionysius, Eckhart, Silesius, Cusanus. But I think there are other forms of mysticism that Derrida would not have much time for, particularly the fusional and somewhat hysterical claim to be "one with God."

MANOLOPOULOS: Several of the essays in this volume compare or contrast your recent philosophy of religion with certain aspects of mystical thought. Mystical theologians say we can't speak about God, and then—

KEARNEY: They go and speak about God.

MANOLOPOULOS: Yes, and affirm all the dogmas and say "God is definitely Trinitarian," "God is this," and "God is that," and they just seem to slide back into this totalizing discourse.

KEARNEY: Then they're not really good mystics, I would say. A really profound mystical thinker like Nicholas of Cusa—whose notion of *possest* has greatly influenced my whole hermeneutics of the possible God—tried to combine a sensitivity to mystery and enigma with a respect for practical wisdom and understanding. "The love of God made firm by understanding intoxicates the mind" (*amor Dei cum intelligentia conditus inebriat mentem*). So while Cusanus goes beyond the *rationes necessariae* of Anselm and the Thomist *ratio* of proportional analogy, he still holds to a notion of *intellectus* as a way of thinking through contradictions and beyond opposites. *Videre aenigmatice et symbolice*, as Cusanus says. A poetics of interpreting the ineffable and unnamable. This kind of hermeneutic wisdom is close, I believe, to the idea of diacritical understanding which I am trying to explore in my trilogy *Philosophy at the Limit*. It is about trying to discern between the extremes of what can be said and thought and what cannot. This is what I would call a responsible mysticism.

MANOLOPOULOS: Wouldn't mystical theology—taken to its logical or a/logical conclusion—have to say, "I'm going to suspend my beliefs on, say, the creeds of the churches, because the creeds are as positive as you can get?" I was just wondering how the mystics can balance their mysticism with their denominational affirmations. Dionysius wasn't considered a heretic.

KEARNEY: Many of them were. Eckhart was. John Scotus Eriugena was. Marguerite Porete and Bruno were. The last two were burned alive by the Inquisition. They were in favor one moment, out the next. These thinkers were trying to make sense to their fellow believers. They had had these deep, spiritual experiences and were profoundly touched, and were trying to reconcile these experiences with the doctrine of the Virgin Birth or the Filioque or something like that. They were mucking along. They were trying to be loved and accepted by their brethren in the monastery. Otherwise, they were out in the rain with no food. We compromise and we muddle through. I would say here, again, that Derrida often discriminates: he picks and chooses—and rightly so. He's an à la carte rabbinical interpreter. Just think of his reflections on biblical passages in *Schibboleth* or "Circumfession," for example.[22] Or again in *Donner la Mort* (*The Gift of Death*), where Derrida goes back to the Abraham story.[23] He takes what inspires him and rejects the kind of Zionist triumphalism which says "Death to all Arabs." So he discriminates. One might say, and I do in the Villanova exchange in this volume, "Well, *how* do you discriminate, Mr. Derrida, since there are no criteria and we can only read in the dark?" But that's another day's work. Maybe it's a performative contradiction but, happily, Derrida does exercise it. He discriminates. He differentiates. He discerns. Deconstructive thinkers like Derrida, Caputo, and Hart are on the side of the good. Deconstruction is not a justification for evil. It's not an apologia for an "anything goes" relativism—as some of its critics unconditionally suggest.

MANOLOPOULOS: In the end, deconstruction is just trying to affirm whatever is going on in the world—

KEARNEY: No, that's Heidegger. Derrida and Caputo, as I understand them, are saying, "We are for justice. We are for the gift. We are for the good. We are for the democracy to come." They are not saying, "It doesn't matter whether it's democracy or totalitarianism. It doesn't matter whether it's justice or injustice. It doesn't matter whether it's gift or selfishness." They are not saying that at all. All their thinking, politically and ethically, is emancipatory. The differences I have with deconstruction are not in terms of values—but how one gets there. That's a practical question, a pragmatic question. I think hermeneutics—informed by a certain deconstructive caution, vigilance, and scrupulosity—is a better way of getting there than deconstruction on its own (without hermeneutics). That's where I part company with Caputo, Derrida, and Lyotard. But they're all on the side of the good as I see it. I'm not saying "We're all morally pure." I'm saying that the good is something we aspire to, something that is "impossible," to be sure, in its *absolute* sense, but possible in all kinds of different tiny practical ways. The messianic is potentially present in *every* moment, here and now, even though we can never be sure whether it comes or goes.

great ess]

Notes

Introduction
John Panteleimon Manoussakis

1. Most notably "How to Avoid Speaking" (1987), *"Khôra"* (1987), *Circumfession* (1990), *The Gift of Death* (1992), and "Faith and Reason" (1992).

2. Among these we might mention the following: the American Academy of Religion (Toronto), the Society for Phenomenology and Existential Philosophy (Chicago), the Inter-American Congress in Philosophy (Lima, Peru), the American Catholic Philosophical Association (Cincinnati), the Canadian Society of Hermeneutics (Halifax), the International Symposium of the American College of Greece (Athens), the European University Institute Intervarsity Seminar (Florence, Italy), the Erasmus Exchange Seminar of the Institut Catholique de Paris, and the European Society for the Study of Religion (Louvain). Several of the contributions to these international symposia are featured in this volume.

3. Recent bibliography also testifies to the timely and pressing character of the questions addressed in this volume. In the last few years we have seen a growing number of articles and monographs on the importance of Continental philosophy (phenomenology, hermeneutics, and deconstruction in particular) to questions of divine alterity, ultimacy, and transcendence. Three series in particular carry on their shoulders the weight of such a project in North America: John D. Caputo's Perspectives in Continental Philosophy by Fordham University Press, Merold Westphal's Series in the Philosophy of Religion by Indiana, and Mieke Bal and Hent de Vries's Cultural Memory in the Present by Stanford University Press. I believe that this volume contributes in a significant way to this important debate.

Epiphanies of the Everyday

Richard Kearney

1. Two of the most powerful literary evocations of "epiphany" (a term explicitly used by James Joyce) in modern literature are to be found in Joyce's *Ulysses* and Proust's *Remembrance of Things Past*, both of which are invoked in the above paragraph. In his early work *Stephen Hero*, Joyce describes "epiphany" thus: "Its soul, its whatness, leaps to us from the vestment of its appearance. The soul of the commonest object, the structure of which is so adjusted, seems to us radiant. The object achieves its epiphany" (chapter 23). See my essay "Epiphanies in Joyce and Proust," in *Traversing the Imaginary: Richard Kearney's Postmodern Challenge*, edited by John Manoussakis and Peter Gratton (Evanston, Ill.: Northwestern University Press, 2006). One lesson to be learned from a poetics of epiphany would be that divinity is manifest in the most mundane of things, events, and persons, just as the sacred is revealed through embodied human figures in the great Wisdom traditions: Christ in Jesus, Visnu in Krishna, Buddha in Siddartha, Elohim in the widow–orphan–stranger, and so on. I consider the present essay to be a companion piece to "Traversing the Imaginary." Both were written during the summer–fall of 2004, as two preliminary sketches of a micro-eschatology of epiphany.

2. G. M. Hopkins, "That Nature Is a Heraclitean Fire. . . ." For an illuminating account of the influence of Duns Scotus on Hopkins, especially as it relates to the notions of "inscape," "instress," "incarnationalism," and Creation as *ensarkosis*, see Philip Ballinger, *The Poem as Sacrament: The Theological Aesthetic of Gerard Manley Hopkins* (Louvain: Peters Press, 2000), 103–50. See also the Appendix on "Scotus and Hopkins" in *The Sermons and Devotional Writings of Gerard Manley Hopkins*, edited by Christopher Devlin (Oxford University Press, 1959), 338–52 and the section "Scot et Hopkins—l'individuation" in *Jean Duns-Scot ou la Révolution Subtile*, edited by Christine Goémé (Paris: FAC, 1982).

3. See, in particular, Jean-Luc Marion, *Being Given: Towards a Phenomenology of Givenness* (Stanford, Calif.: Stanford University Press, 2002); Jacques Derrida, *The Gift of Death* (Chicago: University of Chicago Press, 1995); and the contributions by Marion, Derrida, John Caputo, et al. in *God, the Gift, and Postmodernism*, edited by John Caputo and Michael Scanlon (Bloomington: Indiana University Press, 1999), in particular, "On the Gift: A Discussion Between Jacques Derrida and Jean-Luc Marion, Moderated by Richard Kearney," 54–78. See also Jean-Louis Chrétien, *The Call and the Response* (New York: Fordham University Press, 2004). Marion was the first to speak of the first three phenomenological reductions: (1) to essence (Husserl); (2) to Being (Heidegger); and (3) to givenness (Marion himself). I am indebted to him for this helpful if somewhat schematic formula. No necessary, dialectical, or supercessionist claim is intended in our presentation. Hegelian synthesis and periodization is a temptation I hope

(like Ricoeur in *Time and Narrative*, vol. 3) to avoid. It might be noted here that the four reductions differ less in kind than in degree and emphasis. We are really concerned here with four different *aspects* of the same process of bracketing and redirecting—each reduction focusing more on one angle than another but not necessarily to the exclusion of the others. In other words, I do not want to claim that the eschatological reduction is completely absent from the other three, only that the eschaton is sidelined or passed over for the most part in the interest of other foci, namely, *essence, being,* or *gift.*

4. The term *prosopon* here is taken in the sense outlined in my earlier volume *The God Who May Be* (Bloomington: Indiana University Press, 2002), namely, as a face-to-face that brings the singularity of one self into liaison with the singularity of another. There is, as we tried to show in that work, always something uniquely irreplaceable and yet inextricably inter-subjective about the *prosopon*. The normal translation into English is "person," via the French *personne* and the Latin *persona*. With each etymological reduction we find the term accruing further layers of meaning—for instance, as we move from our somewhat overused English "person" to the French *personne* with its double sense of "someone" and a quasi-universal "no one," and then move further back to the theatrical sense of both "actor" and "agent" in the Latin *persona*, before arriving back finally at the Greek *prosopon* with all its rich connotations of both (a) an aesthetic dramatization/personification and (b) an ethical vis-à-vis of self and other. The purpose of this semantic and philological reduction from "person" to *prosopon* is not, of course, to endorse nostalgic regression to some pristine Greek root accessible only to the pre-Socratics or a coterie of visionary poets (à la Heidegger). Its aim is, rather, to revisit *prosopon* as "person" and vice versa: a sort of double revision that attempts to get behind the contemporary clichés of personhood to neglected layers of meaning contained in the genealogical sources and resources of this term.

This implies, moreover, that the history of metaphysics is not something that has condemned us to forgetfulness, but serves as a palimpsest of texts and terms that call out for reduction and retrieval. There is, I suspect, a micrometaphysics of epiphany operative in the genesis glance of all great metaphysical thinkers. It can be witnessed in the moment when Socrates "goes down" (*katabasis*), when Augustine undergoes his existential-mystical "conversion" in *The Confessions*, when Thomas realizes that his grand *summa theologica* is constructed as "straw," when Duns Scotus sees that the most ultimate reality (*realitas ultima entis*) is in the most basic "thisness" of things, when Descartes glimpses the accident of the "infinite" traversing his me-thodically doubting cogitation, like lightning across the sky, and so on. The fourth reduction becomes, then, a way of recalling these often forgotten in-stants—inaugural, medial, terminal—that serve as seed (and deconstructive aporia) for all complex systems of thought.

bewilderment ↗

As such, we might say that epiphanies of the absolute recognize the need for a certain a-theistic detour in order to recover lost divinities. As though the absolute needed to absolve itself provisionally into a moment of nothing—*nihil, nemo, me onta, personne, apophasis, katargein*—in order to return to itself again in the simplest of things. In that sense, we would say that a-theism, as *à-dieu*, as interlude or prelude to theism, is not just a noncommittal realm of disinterested spectatorship, but its own kind of faith. The belief that there is only finitude—opposing and contesting the infinite—is still a mode of belief, and one that is no more verifiable than its opposite. That is why we keep insisting that the fourth reduction opens a free space where the conflicting beliefs of atheism and theism can communicate and converse. On the question of *prosopon* and the prosopic reduction, I am greatly indebted to my friend and colleague at Boston College, John Manoussakis, and his work *God After Metaphysics* (Bloomington: Indiana University Press, 2006).

Wm. James

5. See Stanislas Breton, *Unicité et Monothéisme* (Paris: Cerf, 1981), and his essay in this volume, "On the God of the Possible," especially the second section. On the question of religious pluralism and interreligious dialogue, I am much indebted to my Boston College colleagues Francis Clooney, John Makransky, and Catherine Cornille. See also my "Thinking After Terror: An Interreligious Challenge," in *Religion and Violence*, edited by Clayton Crocked (Charlottesville: University Press of Virginia, 2005). See also Raymond Panikkar, *The Interreligious Dialogue* (New York: Paulist Press, 1978).

oops ···

Here Panikkar speaks of the relationship between Christ and Krishna neither as one of "flat identity" nor as one of incommensurable, mutually exclusive difference, but rather as two manifestations of the "mysterious presence of the Lord in a multitude of epiphanies" (15). Describing his peregrination through interreligous dialogue, Panikkar writes: "I 'left' as a Christian, I 'found' myself a Hindu and I 'return' a Buddhist, without having ceased to be a Christian" (2). This return to his initial position, enlarged in faith and amplified in understanding, epitomizes a possible trajectory of what we are calling the fourth reduction.

6. See my development of this theme—in dialogue with Derrida and Caputo—in "God or Khora?" in *Strangers, Gods, and Monsters* (New York: Routledge, 2003), 191–212. See J. Caputo, *The Weakness of God: A Theology of the Event* (Bloomington: Indiana University Press, 2005).

7. See Paul Ricoeur, "Experience and Language in Religious Discourse," in *Phenomenology and the "Theological Turn,"* edited by Dominique Janicaud et al. (New York: Fordham University Press, 2000), 131–32. Here we witness radical phenomenology returning to radical hermeneutics. See also John Caputo, *More Radical Hermeneutics* (Bloomington: Indiana University Press, 2000); David Tracey, *God* (Chicago: University of Chicago Press, 2005); and Jean Greisch, *Le Buisson Ardent*, 3 vols. (Paris: Cerf, 2001–4).

8. Lao Tzu, *Tao Te-Ching*, translated by W. Chan (Princeton, N.J.: Princeton University Press, 1998), 8, 4.

9. As Henri Le Saux (Abhishiktananda), Bede Griffiths's Benedictine confrere, put it, in such a space one exists "deeply, with all the infinite capacity for being which comes from the love of God." *Ascent to the Depth of the Heart* (Delhi: ISPCK, 1998), 241. Le Saux was mentor to Bede Griffiths at the Shantivanam ashram in southern India. See Bede Griffiths, *River of Compassion* (New York: Continuum, 1995). One also thinks here of the aquatic idiom of overflowing abundance in the Upanishads invoked by Anne Sexton in her verse: "Then the well spoke to me / It said, Abundance is / scooped from Abundance. Yet abundance remains." I am grateful to Peggy McLoughlin for this and several other references in this paper, and to my colleagues Frank Clooney and John Makransky for showing me how movement of repetition and return between emptiness and fullness is to be found, in different ways, in both Hindu and Buddhist teachings.

10. Nicholas of Cusa, "On the Summit of Contemplation," in *Nicholas of Cusa: Selected Spiritual Writings* (New York: Paulist Press, 1997), especially 291–303. See also "Trialogus de Possest" ("On Actualized Possibility"), in *A Concise Introduction to the Philosophy of Nicholas of Cusa,* edited by J. Hopkins (Minneapolis: University of Minnesota Press, 1980).

11. See my earlier efforts to elaborate an eschatological poetics of the possible in *Poétique du Possible* (Paris: Beauchesne, 1984) and in *The God Who May Be* (Bloomington: Indiana University Press, 2001), especially "Possibilising God" and "Conclusion: Poetics of the Possible God." Such an eschatological poetics of the everyday is not confined to biblical, mystical, or religious texts. It is also available, I believe, in some of the oldest texts of Greek philosophy. See, for example, Aristotle when he writes: "Every realm of nature is marvelous: and as Heraclitus, when the strangers who came to visit him found him warming himself at the furnace in the kitchen and hesitated to go in, is reported to have bidden them not to be afraid to enter, as even in that kitchen divinities were present, so we should venture on the study of every kind of (lower thing/animal) without distaste: for each and all will reveal to us something natural and something beautiful" (*On the Parts of Animals*, 645a15–23).

12. Maurice Merleau-Ponty, *Phenomenology of Perception* (London: Routledge, 2002), xxi.

13. See my detailed analysis of these transitional "return" scenes in Proust and Joyce in "Epiphanies in Joyce and Proust," in *Traversing the Imaginary,* edited by John Manoussakis (Evanston, Ill.: Northwestern University Press, 2006). See also "Epiphanies in Joyce" in *Global Ireland*, edited by Ondrej Pliny and Clare Wallace (Prague: Litteraria Pragensia Press, 2006).

14. Paul Ricoeur, *Oneself as Another* (Chicago: University of Chicago Press, 1992).

15. Martha Nussbaum, *Love's Knowledge* (New York: Oxford University Press, 1990), 283.

Toward a Fourth Reduction?
John Panteleimon Manoussakis

1. The number 3 is a simplification for the sake of our analysis. A more in-depth inquiry would have identified more kinds of phenomenological reductions—indeed, in Husserl alone one could count at least three different ways: the Cartesian, the psychological, and the ontological. See Dan Zahavi, *Husserl's Phenomenology* (Stanford, Calif.: Stanford University Press, 2003), 47.

2. A term we coined from *δόσις* (Greek for "givenness) to name the return to the event of the gift chiefly proposed in Jean-Luc Marion's work.

3. We borrow the term from Alfred North Whitehead's *Process and Reality* (1960), wishing to acknowledge, at the same time, the original work advanced by the studies of Harold H. Oliver, such as *A Relational Metaphysic* (1981) and *Relatedness* (1984).

4. David Bohm, *Quantum Theory* (London: Constable and Company, 1954), 161; emphasis added. For a philosophical appropriation of quantum theory, see H. H. Oliver, *A Relational Metaphysic* (The Hague: Martinus Nijhoff, 1981). I am greatly indebted to Prof. Oliver's analysis.

5. Pavel Florensky, *The Pillar and Ground of the Truth*, translated by Boris Jakim (Princeton, N.J.: Princeton University Press, 1997), 35. One can provide further evidence for the centrality of relation: for instance, Dionysius the Aeropagite's captivating remark that ἡ δὲ σχέσις σώζει καὶ εἶναι ποιεῖ ("it is relation that saves and creates Being"; *DN*, IV, 23:21).

6. W. Norris Clarke, *Explorations in Metaphysics: Being, God, Person* (Notre Dame, Ind.: University of Notre Dame Press, 1994), 216.

7. For example, the revelation of Christ (the phenomenon) and Christ the revealer (the phenomenality) are indistinguishable; in the words of Jean-Luc Nancy: ". . .l'idée de la révélation chrétien est qu'au bout de compte *rien n'est révélé*, rien sinon la fin de la révélation elle-même, sinon ceci que la révélation veut dire le sens de dévoile purement comme sens, en personne, mais en une personne telle que tout le sens de cette personne consiste à se révéler . . . ce qui est révélé est le révélable" (La Déconstruction du Christianisme," *Les Études Philosophiques* 4 [1998]: 511).

8. "The best formulation of the reduction is probably that given by Eugene Fink, Husserl's assistant, when he spoke of " 'wonder' in the face of the world." Merleau-Ponty, *Phenomenology of Perception* (London: Routledge, 2002), xv.

9. The case in point here could be the Greek as well as the Eastern attitudes of personhood. Because Plato and Buddha (to mention two names representative of two different systems of thought) lack the solid ground for an incarnational understanding of the human person, they are forced to

come up with its substitute: an endless series of reincarnations. What is lost, however, in the process of reincarnation is the specificity of the person, who by being many is really none. Reincarnation, in fact, is really a process of *de-fleshment*. No wonder, then, that for both systems flesh is a prison, the worthless shell of the soul, from which one has to flee toward a faceless and depersonalized Nothing.

10. An interesting observation about the character of the early Church is the Christian community's choice of (a) a name for themselves and (b) the architectural style according to which they built their meeting places (i.e., their churches). The word *ecclesia* predates Christianity. It was used by ancient Greek polis for the assembly of its citizens (*ekklesia* means "call together"), a body with a purely civic function. The architectonic rhythm after which the first Christians chose to build their churches was neither, as one might expect, the style of the *naos*, the Greco–Roman religious center, nor that of the Judaic temple, but something altogether different. The early Christian community made a conscious choice of the basilica, a civic forum with no religious connotations whatsoever.

It is interesting to note here that the Greco–Roman cultic temple housed only the cultic statue of the god or goddess; the worshiping people were required to stay outside the temple. The Christian Church inverted this model: the church was built to house the "assembly of the faithful," the *ecclesia*, who, gathered in His name, are the manifestation of God. See Fred S. Kleiner and Christian J. Mamiya, *Gardner's Art Through the Ages*, vol. I (Belmont, Calif.: Wadsworth, 2005), 310. It is perhaps in light of such evidence that political theorists such as Marcel Gauchet speak of Christianity as "a religion for departing from religion" or the "religious" after religion. See M. Gauchet, *The Disenchantment of the World: A Political History of Religion*, translated by Oscar Burge (Princeton, N.J.: Princeton University Press, 1997).

11. And the community that the *prosopon* creates, i.e., the ecclesial event (not to be confused with the merely ecclesiastical).

12. In one of his earlier phenomenological studies, *Existence and Existents*, Levinas does not hesitate to go so far as to identify the sacred with the nocturnal *il y a*: "The impersonality of the sacred in primitive religions, which for Durkheim is the 'still' impersonal God from which will issue one day the God of advanced religions, on the contrary describes a world where nothing prepares for the apparition of a God. Rather than to a God, the notion of the *there is* leads us to the absence of God, the absence of any being" (translated by Alphonso Lingis [The Hague: Martinus Nijhoff, 1978], 61). What allows the identification of the *il y a* with the religious category of the sacred is their common denial of the face of the Other (note how Levinas speaks of the "*impersonality* of the sacred"). To fully understand what is at stake here, one needs to be aware of the linguistic as well as the semantic nuances behind the distinction of the "sacred" and the "saintly" (cf. E. Benveniste's *Le Vocabulaire des Institutions Indoeuropéennes* [Paris, 1969], 2:180), two terms

that unfortunately are used interchangeably, although they name two dia-metrically different worldviews. Freud utilized this distinction in his study of Judaism, *Moses and Monotheism*, and Levinas has dedicated an entire vol-ume to the subject (*Du Sacré au Saint* [Paris: Éditions de Minuit, 1977]). I wish to acknowledge Prof. Thanos Lipowatz, whose erudition on this mat-ter helped me understand better the conceptual difference between these two terms.

Enabling God
Richard Kearney

1. Walter Benjamin, "Theologico-Political Fragment" (1921), in *One Way Street* (London: NLB, 1979), 155f.

2. Rashi, *The Torah: With Rashi's Commentary* (New York: Mesorah Pub-lications, 1997). It would be interesting to relate Rashi's rabbinical interpre-tation to Isaac Luria's Kabbalist reading of God in terms of a generous withholding or "withdrawal" (*zimzum*) which invites human creatures to subsequently retrieve and reanimate the fragments of the "broken vessels" of divine love that lie scattered like tiny seeds throughout the created uni-verse. This reading, which exerted a deep influence on Hasidic thinkers as well as on philosophers such as Simone Weil, seems to confirm our own account of God's refusal to impose himself on creation—as some kind of omnipotent fulfilled being (*ipsum esse subsistens*), Sufficient Reason, or Su-preme Cause (*ens causa sui*)—preferring to relate to humans in the realm of the "possible" rather than the purely "actual" or "necessary." I am grateful to my Boston College colleague Marty Cohen for bringing the insights of the Lurianic Kabbala to my attention. See in particular his article "Sarach's Harp," *Parabola* 22, no. 3 (Fall 1997).

3. Etty Hillesum, *An Interrupted Life* (New York: Owl Books, 1996), 176.

4. Nicholas of Cusa, *Trialogus de Possest*, in *A Concise Introduction to the Philosophy of Nicholas of Cusa* (Minneapolis: University of Minnesota Press, 1980), 69. The original Latin reads "Deus est omne id quod esse potest."

5. Pseudo-Dionysius the Areopagite, *The Divine Names and Mystical The-ology*, translated by J. D. Jones (Milwaukee, Wis.: Marquette University Press, 1980), 182.

6. Ibid., 188. For a further exploration of the link between negative the-ology and my micro-eschatology, see Stanislas Breton, *The Word and the Cross* (New York: Fordham University Press, 2002), 8–11, 49–50, 60–70, 80–91, 112–114. See in particular Breton's radical claim that we must give to God the being he has not, qua thirsting, kenotic, crucified stranger (121–22). The *dunamis* of God is here identified with the *germen nihili* or "power of nothing" that reveals itself as a "'double nothingness'" and powerless-ness, which liberates those oppressed by the power of *ta onta*, sowing the

seed of non-being epitomized by the Beatitudes so that the eschatological tree of love and justice may flower and flourish (80–84, xxiv–xxvi). For it is in and as a "seed of non-being" that, in Eckhart's resonant phrase, "God becomes verdant in all the honor of his being" (80). See also here Hildegard of Bingen's notion of divine "greening" or "viriditas" (note 10 below). A more postmodern take on this notion of a micro-eschatology is hinted at by Slavoj Zizek in *The Fragile Absolute* (London: Verso, 2000), when he writes: ". . . the ultimate mystery of love is that incompleteness is a way *higher than completion*. . . . Perhaps the true achievement of Christianity is to elevate a loving (imperfect) Being to the place of God—that is, of ultimate perfection" (146–47).

7. See the illuminating reading of Hopkins in Mark Patrick Hederman, *Anchoring the Altar: Christianity and the Work of Art* (Dublin: Veritas, 2002), 131f. It is important to note that this microtheological emphasis on God as less rather than more is not confined to the Judeo–Christian tradition. It is also to be found in much of the Buddhist and Hindu wisdom literature. See, for instance, the following passage from Krishnamurti: "The silence which is not the silence of the ending of noise is only a small beginning. It is like going through a small hole to an enormous, wide, expansive ocean, to an immeasurable, timeless state" (*Freedom from the Known* [San Francisco: Harper, 1969], 109). Interestingly, one of the "siddhis," the powers that a yogi/yogini may acquire, is to become as small as an atom. The Taoist master, Lao-tse, spoke from a similar perspective in *Tao Te Ching* when he wrote: "Know the high / But keep to the low / Become a valley / To all under heaven. / As a valley provides in abundance, / Give in constant Virtue; / Return to natural simplicity" (chapter 28); or again in chapter 34, when he writes: 'The Great Way flows everywhere / . . . It clothes and feeds all things, / Yet does not claim / To be their lord. / It asks for nothing in return. / It may be called the Small. . . . So too the wise may become great, / By becoming small." Even Rabbit in *Winnie the Pooh* knows this, as in the following passage: "'It is hard to be brave,' said Piglet, sniffing slightly, 'when you're only a Very Small Animal.' Rabbit, who had begun to write very busily, looked up and said: 'It is because you are a very small animal that you will be Useful in the adventure before us'" (commented by Benjamin Hoff, *The Te of Piglet* [London: Egmont, 1992]).

8. Robert Musil, *A Man Without Qualities*, cited in my *Poétique du Possible* (Paris: Beauchesne, 1984), 4.

9. Rainer Maria Rilke, *Letters to a Young Poet*, translated by Stephen Mitchel (New York: Vintage Books, 1986), 61–63. The emphasis here on the earth as correspondent for divine eros highlights, once again, the incarnational tendency of theoeroticism. The earth is full of the seeds of the divine (what Augustine, borrowing from the Stoics, called *logoi spermaticoi*), incubating within the finite historical world like latent potencies waiting to

be animated and actualized by the infinitely incoming grace of God as transcendent *posse*. If one removes transcendent *posse* from this equation, one relapses into a purely immanentist dialectic (evolutionary materialism or, at best, process theology). On the other hand, if one ignores the immanence of terrestrial and human potencies, one is left with an inordinately inaccessible and abstract deity—a sort of acosmic alterity without face or voice (e.g., deism or deconstruction). A hermeneutical poetics of divine *posse* tries to preserve a delicate balance between these opposite extremes.

10. I am grateful to my wise friend and teacher, Peggy McLoughlin, for this reference and the quotes below. Here is one verse in which the term *viriditas* appears:

> O most noble greening power (*O nobilissima viriditas*)
> Rooted in the sun,
> Who shines in dazzling serenity
> In a sphere
> That no earthly excellence
> Can comprehend.
> You are enclosed
> In the embrace of divine mysteries,
> You blush like the dawn and burn like a flame of the sun.

"For her, the energy that drives the universe—which she calls VIRIDITAS, or the greening force—is also the power of the Living Light, which is Love-caritas. The expression of this in the creation is music. The original creation was a miracle of equilibrium, of perfect harmony, which the Fall disturbed; the incarnation restores a new harmony—indeed the Word of God is music itself, and the soul of mankind is symphonic: *symphonialis est anima*. . . . Here she finds the dynamic expression of the love of God and his promise to bring mankind back to him, the expression in the body of the green-growing grace of *viriditas*" (*Great Spirits 1000–2000: The Fifty-two Christians Who Most Influenced Their Millennium*, edited by Selina O'Grady and John Wilkins [New York: Paulist Press, 2002]).

11. Joachim Jeremias, *The Eucharistic Words of Jesus* (Philadelphia: Fortress Press, 1977), 249. I am indebted to two of my colleagues at Boston College, Gary Gurtler and John Manoussakis, for bringing these comments and references by Dionysius and Jeremias to my attention.

12. Ibid., 252.

13. *The Passover Haggadah* (New York: Schocken Books, 1953), 63.

14. Jeremias, 252. One might see a repetition of the eschatological forgetting and remembering from the finite human perspective in Dante's *Divine Comedy* ("Purgatory," canto 28), where the Pilgrim encounters the two inexhaustible streams of the garden, Lethe and Eunoe, of which the former washes away all memory of sin while the latter retrieves the memory of good deeds and life-giving moments.

15. Ibid., 253.

Maybe, Maybe Not: Richard Kearney and God
William Desmond

1. *On Stories*, Thinking in Action (New York: Routledge, 2001); *Strangers, Gods, and Monsters: Ideas of Otherness* (New York: Routledge, 2003); *The God Who May Be: A Hermeneutics of Religion* (Bloomington: Indiana University Press, 2001).

2. In a work in progress, *God and the Between*, I speak of the hyperboles of being: overdeterminacies of being in finitude that exceed finite determination and that yet communicate something of the ultimate. Among the hyperboles: the idiocy of being (the "that it is"); the aesthetics of happening; the erotics of selving; the agapeics of community.

3. *Poétique du Possible: Phénoménologie Herméneutique de la Figuration* (Paris: Beauchesne, 1984). The notion of the May Be is broached on page 235. The whole of chapter 12 deals with *Le Dieu du Possible*, including discussions of Heidegger and the critique of ontotheology, then the possible as kenotic, as eschatological, and as ethical. The analogy of the possible is also discussed (219–222). I offered some thoughts in a review article in which *Poétique du Possible* was discussed in *The Irish Theological Quarterly* 3 (1988): 237–42.

4. On this more extensively, see my *Art, Origins, Otherness: Between Philosophy and Art* (Albany: State University of New York Press, 2003), chapter 7; see also *Is There a Sabbath for Thought? Between Religion and Philosophy* (New York: Fordham University Press, 2005), chapter 10.

5. Similarly below with respect to creation and coming to be: though here we seem to be in the space communicated by the origin, and hence more on *this* side of the reserve of the origin, we *are*, as in the communication of creation; and as *being*, we can know something of the possible/actual, though of what is *above* the possible, we must be reserved.

6. See my "Hyperbolic Thoughts: On Creation and Nothing," in *Framing a Vision of the World: Essays in Philosophy, Science, and Religion*, edited by Santiago Sia and Andre Cloots (Leuven: Universitaire Pers Leuven, 1999), 23–43; also chapters 6 and 7, on origin and creation, in *Being and the Between* (Albany: State University of New York Press, 1995).

7. See my *Is There a Sabbath for Thought?* chapter 3.

8. *Hegel's God—A Counterfeit Double?* (Aldershot, U.K.: Ashgate, 2003).

9. In Charles Dickens's *David Copperfield*, chapter 49: "'Gentlemen!' said Mr Micawber, after the first salutations, 'you are friends in need, and friends indeed. Allow me to offer my inquiries with reference to the physical welfare of Mrs. Copperfield *in esse* and Mrs. Traddles *in posse*,—presuming, that is to say, that my friend Mr. Traddles is not yet united to the object of his affections, for weal and for woe.'"

Hermeneutics and the God of Promise
Merold Westphal

1. By "metafuture," I mean eternity understood as that which lies not only ahead of us but ahead of all we now know as time and history.

2. In Ephesians 2:12, Paul puts "having no hope" in apposition to "without God in the world." The Hebrew Scriptures are filled with admonitions to hope in the Lord or in God's word, and Jeremiah identifies God as the "hope of Israel" (17:13; cf. Acts 28:20). Unless otherwise indicated, biblical quotations are from the New Revised Standard Version (NRSV).

3. See my *Overcoming Onto-Theology* (New York: Fordham University Press, 2001) and *Transcendence and Self-Transcendence* (Bloomington: Indiana University Press, 2005).

4. Kearney's intention is interfaith, and he appeals to "the *eschaton* which several religious traditions have promised will one day come," but the texts to which he turns are biblical (*GMB*, 1). He writes, "I would like to think that the kind of reflections advanced in this book are vigorously ecumenical in terms of interfaith dialogue. . . . If I do not make reference to non-Western religious thought in the chapters below, it is not, therefore, out of any Eurocentric presumption but because my limited competence confines me to the Judeo-Christian and Greco-Roman traditions" (6).

5. Martin Heidegger, "The Onto-theo-logical Constitution of Metaphysics," in *Identity and Difference*, translated by Joan Stambaugh (New York: Harper and Row, 1969), 57, 60. Henceforth cited as *ID*.

6. See especially *The Principle of Reason*, translated by Reginald Lilly (Bloomington: Indiana University Press, 1991), and my Heidegger chapter in *Transcendence and Self-Transcendence*.

7. For Heidegger, it is the inextricable combination of presence and absence, unconcealment and concealment, that precludes any possibility of absolute knowledge (*ID*, 64–67).

8. From the 1949 introduction to "What Is Metaphysics?," titled "The Way Back into the Ground of Metaphysics," in *Pathways*, edited by William McNeill (New York: Cambridge University Press, 1998), 287–88.

9. See Jean-Luc Marion, *God Without Being*, translated by Thomas A. Carlson (Chicago: University of Chicago Press, 1991), 73–83.

10. The Levinasian character of this account is evident, but Kearney is also drawing on John Manoussakis, "Prosopon and Icon," in this volume.

11. The natural law tradition has tried to claim Aristotle by virtue of his appeal to reason, but a close look will show that reason is defined in terms of what society's "best and brightest" think and do. Nurture defines nature, and the *phronimos* is the measure of reason, not vice versa. Aristotle is a Hegelian, for whom ethics is a matter of *Sittlichkeit*, the laws and customs of one's people.

12. This notion, explicitly in Spinoza and implicitly in Hegel, is the ground of their versions of the ontological argument, which give us not the God to whom Anselm speaks in prayer, but an *ultima ratio* to whom no one would be tempted to pray.

13. F. H. Bradley, *The Principles of Logic*, 2nd ed., rev. (London: Oxford University Press, 1922), 2:591. Compare Bradley's "bloodless" with Kear-

ney's "disembodied," cited above. I am not suggesting that Bradley shares Kearney's concerns or that their projects are even in the same ball park.

14. According to George Hunsinger, personalism is one of the six fundamental motifs of *Church Dogmatics*. See *How to Read Karl Barth: The Shape of His Theology* (New York: Oxford University Press, 1991), chapters 1 and 6.

15. *Church Dogmatics*, vol. 1, part 1, *The Doctrine of the Word of God*, translated by G. T. Thomson (Edinburgh: T. and T. Clark, 1936), xiv.

16. See Bruce L. McCormack, *Karl Barth's Critically Realistic Dialectical Theology* (Oxford: Clarendon Press, 1995). Hunsinger speaks of Barth's "objectivism," meaning the same thing: that theology is not about us, but about a reality quite independent of us.

17. "Fate and Idea in Theology," in *The Way of Theology in Karl Barth: Essays and Comments*, edited by H. Martin Rumscheidt (Allison Park, Pa.: Pickwick Publications, 1986), 36–37.

18. Aquinas writes that "matter is said to *comprehend* form when nothing remains in the matter which has not been perfected by the form. It is in this latter manner that a knowing power is said to comprehend its object, namely, insofar as what is known lies perfectly under its cognition." This is the ontotheological project. But Aquinas continues, "When the thing known exceeds its grasp, then the knowing power falls short of comprehension. . . . Consequently, it is impossible for any created intellect to comprehend the divine essence, not because it does not know some part of the essence, but because it cannot attain the perfect manner of knowing it." *Truth [De Veritate]*, 3 vols., translated by Robert W. Mulligan et al. (Indianapolis, Ind.: Hackett, 1994), vol. 1, 8.2, 318–19. This notion is prominent in Eastern Christianity. See, for example, Gregory of Nyssa, *The Life of Moses*, translated by Abraham J. Malherbe and Everett Ferguson (New York: Paulist Press, 1978), 111–20 and 146 n. 61.

19. I owe this insight to my colleague Gerry McCool, S.J., now retired, who was quite startled to hear his reading of Aquinas described as "Hegelian."

20. In opposition to foundationalism, Hegel finds the ground at the end of the journey. Thus *Aufhebung*, he likes to point out punningly, is the *zu Grunde gehen* of what is *aufgehoben*, at once its going under or perishing and its finding its foundation and its proper place.

21. *New Seeds of Contemplation* (New York: New Directions, 1962), 36.

22. See the 1958 preface to the second edition of *Anselm: Fides Quaerens Intellectum*, translated by Ian W. Robertson (New York: World Publishing, 1962), 11. Henceforth cited as *A*.

23. "I cannot deny that I deem Anselm's Proof of the Existence of God *in the context of his theological Scheme* a model piece of good, penetrating and neat theology, which at every step I have found instructive and edifying" (*A*, 9; emphasis added).

24. As a good student of Ricoeur, he rightly complains that negative theology and the theology that confines the sacred "to the domain of abyssal

abjection . . . share a common aversion to any mediating role for narrative imagination" (*GMB*, 7). Kearney also critiques the negative theology of Marion (31–33).

25. Taking biblical texts seriously is not the same as appealing to them as the norm for one's thinking about God. That is why Kearney remains a phenomenologist rather than a theologian. But there is no reason why theologians, who read the same texts in a different posture, should not both learn from and challenge his readings.

26. See Nick Wolterstorff, *Divine Discourse: Philosophical Reflections on the Claim That God Speaks* (New York: Cambridge University Press, 1995), especially chapters 1–7. Wolterstorff places emphasis on promises and commands as the most typical divine speech acts.

27. Herbert Marcuse, *One-Dimensional Man* (Boston: Beacon Press, 1964).

28. Note the mutual exclusion of the either/or expressed in this "rather than."

29. Switching the priority of actuality and possibility does not remove our discourse from the abstract, dare one say "Scholastic," category of being, for actuality and possibility are modal modifiers of being. We are talking about actual and possible *being*.

30. In speaking of God as *posse* rather than *esse*, Kearney claims to be making "a liberal borrowing from Nicholas of Cusa" (*GMB*, 2). My reading of Cusa suggests that he provides no support for Kearney's "may be." In most of his writings, he seems quite traditional in giving priority to actuality over possibility. When, after his Easter discovery of 1464, he speaks, in *On the Summit of Contemplation*, of God as *Posse* and even *Posse Ipsum*, this strikes me less as a departure from that classical view than as a reformulation. Like others trying to formulate the uniqueness of the divine existence, he speaks of it as the actuality that, unlike any other actuality, is the ultimate ground of all possibility. See *Selected Spiritual Writings*, translated by H. Lawrence Bond (New York: Paulist Press, 1997).

31. "I will make of you a great nation, and I will bless you, and make your name great, so that you will be a blessing . . . and in you all the families of the earth shall be blessed" (Genesis 12: 2–3; cf. Genesis 15).

32. 2 Samuel 7.

33. "I will put my law within them, and I will write it on their hearts, and I will be their God, and they shall be my people" (Jeremiah 31:33, in the context of Jeremiah 31:31–34).

34. The quarrel between Catholics and Protestants about the role of Peter's successors in this does not concern the unconditional character of the promise itself.

35. Nicholas Wolterstorff, "God Everlasting," in *God and the Good: Essays in Honor of Henry Stob*, edited by Clifton J. Orlebeke and Lewis B. Smedes (Grand Rapids, Mich.: Eerdmans, 1975), reprinted in and cited from *Con-*

temporary Philosophy of Religion, edited by Stephen M. Cahn and David Schatz (New York: Oxford University Press, 1982), 77. Henceforth cited as *GE*.

36. *The Consolation of Philosophy*, translated by Richard Green (Indianapolis: Bobbs-Merrill, 1962), 115.

37. Jerusalem Bible, King James Version, and NRSV, respectively. NRSV gives as alternative translations both "I am what I am" and "I will be what I will be."

38. For my own hermeneutical-phenomenological defense of Buber's future-tense reading, see *God, Guilt, and Death* (Bloomington: Indiana University Press, 1984), 238 and 295 n. 82.

39. *Confessions*, VII, 9, 20–21. Subsequent references in text are by book and chapter numbers.

40. On the importance of God as voice in Augustine, see my "Divine Excess: The God Who Comes After," in *The Religious*, edited by John D. Caputo (Oxford: Blackwell, 2002), 258–276.

41. Verse 11 by his count, since, unlike modern translations, he counts the traditional title as verse 1.

42. In both passages, "Lord" signifies the Tetragrammaton, YHWH, as given in Exodus 3:15.

43. *Expositions of the Psalms*, vol. I, translated by Maria Boulding, O.S.B. (Hyde Park, N.Y.: New City Press, 2000), 147.

44. Wolterstorff recognizes that the matter is not cut and dried. He writes, "It might seem obvious that God, as described by the biblical writers, is a being who changes, and who accordingly is fundamentally noneternal." Then, after repeating this "seem obvious" or "seems evident" at least half a dozen times more, he writes, "However, I think it is not at all so obvious as on first glance it might appear that the biblical writers do in fact describe God as changing" (*GE*, 88–89).

Kearney's Wager
Patrick Burke

1. John P. Manoussakis, "From Exodus to Eschaton: On the God Who May Be," *Modern Theology* 18, no. 1 (January 2002): 95–107 (see also the revised version under the title "Prosopon and Icon," in this volume).

Is the Possible Doing Justice to God?
Dominique Janicaud

1. Martin Heidegger, *Identity and Diffrence*, translated by Joan Stambaugh (New York: Harper Torchbook, 1974), 71.

2. "Was mit den formalen Bedingungen der Erfahrung übereinkommt ist möglich" (Kant, *Kritik der Reinen Vernunft*, A 218, B 265).

3. Malebranche, *Entretiens sur la Métaphysique* (Paris: Vrin, 1948), 87: "Mais tous les êtres et créés et possibles, avec toute leur multiplicité, ne peuvent remplir la vaste étendue de l'être."

4. As it seems to be the case in *The God Who May Be*: "Since onto-theology defines God as the absolute priority of actuality over possibility, it may be now timely to reverse that priority" (*GMB*, 99–100).

5. See Jacques Derrida, "Comme si c'Était Possible, 'Within Such Limits,' . . . ," *Revue Internationale de Philosophie* 3, no. 205 (1998): 497–529.

6. "L'impossible ne s'évanouit pas comme ce qui se contredit. Il est impossible au sens où l'on dit: cette vie est impossible; cette vie est impossible alors qu'elle est. L'être réalise l'impossible" (Emmanuel Levinas, *Sur Maurice Blanchot* [Montpellier: Fata Morgana, 1975], 67).

7. For instance, "pure being in the manner of onto-theology" (*GMB*, 4).

8. "What kind of divinity comes after metaphysics?" (*GMB*, 2).

9. I would like to express a very special thanks to Charles Cabral, who most graciously helped me with the redaction of this essay.

The God Who May Be and the God Who Was
Craig Nichols

1. See Friedrich Nietzsche, *The Gay Science*, translated by Walter Kaufmann (New York: Vintage Books, 1974), §125. Cf. Friedrich Nietzsche, "Thus Spoke Zarathustra," in *The Portable Nietzsche*, edited by Walter Kaufmann (New York: Viking Press, 1968), §3.

2. My interpretation of the postmodern "nothing" as the "con-text" of being centers on Heidegger's *Auseinandersetzung* with German idealism. The nothing of which Heidegger speaks is not an empty *thing*. It is, rather, that which we experience as most concrete in our daily lives. It is the revelation of ourselves in the context of our world, the emergence of selfhood and otherness, and the emergence of the possibility of coherence (fittingness, jointure) between the two spheres. It is shared history, understood as the destiny into which we are thrown. At bottom, it is the metanarratival *contextualization* of the meaning of human existence. I introduce the common Heideggerian hyphen here—hence, "con-textualization"—in order to highlight the unity of duality, or identity in difference, of the two equiprimordial concepts Heidegger implies with his conception of the nothing. The "with" (*con*) that accompanies the linguistic house of being in which we dwell, that is, the hermeneutical "living text" of historical human existence, is precisely the nothing that sets the boundaries and opens the horizon of possibility and meaning of human existence. But this nothing does not merely frame the text of being from the outside; rather, it permeates it, revealing the inner coherence of its structure. Hence, the meaning of the Latinate "con-text" (or in German, "*Kon-text*") is poignantly revealed in the imbedded structure of the alternate German word for context: *Zusammen-hang*, the inner "tendency" (*Hang*) of being to "hang together" (*Zusammen*) as a coherent whole (i.e., for Heidegger, in the *Fug* of *physis*). The fundamental possibilities of meaning that lay open for Western humanity at the inception of Greek metaphysical thinking reached their conceptual, or idealistic, closure and

ultimate expression in Hegel's absolute system (i.e., Plato's *idea*, or *eidos*, of universality having become actual and absolute). Pressing toward a transcendence of the system of Western metaphysics, on a quest for the unthought ground of the system qua the nothing that makes it possible, Heidegger came to realize, in the *Kehre*, that the nothing into which *Dasein* projects itself as transcendence does not merely provide the context of *Dasein*'s existence, or even *Dasein* multiplied into a historical aggregate (through its communal destiny as *Mitsein*); rather, the nothing that gapes open before *Dasein*, the rift into which it is thrown, is more profoundly the contextual nothing of *systematicity in general*, which has become fully expressed in concrete particularity through Hegel's absolute system. In the *Kehre*, the nothing comes to the fore as the very context (or "con-text") of being for Heidegger, eclipsing the former priority he had given to the question concerning the meaning of being and the ontological difference—or, rather, placing these issues in a new light, a new *con-text*.

3. Richard Kearney, *The God Who May Be* (Bloomington: Indiana University Press, 2001), 13, 17.

4. Ibid., 47.

5. Ibid.

6. Ibid., 48.

7. Ibid.

8. Ibid., 48–49.

9. Ibid., 1.

10. See Richard Kearney, *Strangers, Gods, and Monsters* (New York: Routledge, 2003).

11. Ibid., 17. Note the parallel metaphor used by Nietzsche to describe his *Übermensch*: "Zarathustra . . . spoke thus: 'Man is a rope, tied between beast and overman—a rope over an abyss. A dangerous across, a dangerous on-the-way, a dangerous looking-back, a dangerous shuddering and stopping. . . . What is great in man is that he is a bridge and not an end: what can be loved in man is that he is an *overture* and a *going under.*'" Friedrich Nietzsche, "Thus Spoke Zarathustra," in *The Portable Nietzsche*, edited by Walter Kaufmann (New York: Viking Press, 1968), §4.

12. Kearney, *Strangers, Gods, and Monsters*, 18.

13. Kearney, *The God Who May Be*, 1.

14. Ibid., 34.

15. For instance, while hailing the positive value of Derrida's "deconstructive critique of inherited onto-theological notions of both potentiality and presence" for "a new eschatological understanding of God as *posse*," Kearney proffers the following critique (which can be applied, in the end, to Levinas as well): "Derrida points to such possible paths but he does not choose to walk them. In the heel of the hunt, he prefers ghosts to gods. He prefers, as is his wont and right, to leave matters open. He reserves judgment. . . . This is where we part company" (ibid., 98–99).

16. Ibid., 37.

17. See Martin Heidegger, *Phänomenologie des Religiösen Lebens* (1921), vol. 60 of *Gesamtausgabe* (Frankfurt am Main: Vittorio Klostermann Verlag, 1995).

18. See especially Martin Heidegger, *Introduction to Metaphysics*, translated by Gregory Fried and Richard Polt (New Haven, Conn.: Yale University Press, 2000), 159–72.

19. I am here drawing rather freely from Paul Ricoeur's discussion of the four primary myths of evil which have served as the narratival foundation of subsequent Western speculation concerning the problem of good and evil (i.e., the "ritual" vision, the "tragic" vision, the "Adamic" myth, and the "Orphic" myth). See Paul Ricoeur, *The Symbolism of Evil*, translated by Emerson Buchanan (Boston: Beacon Press, 1967).

20. F. M. Cornford offers a very helpful interpretation, originally published in 1912, of the early shift in meaning of foundational Greek religious-philosophical concepts (highlighting especially the *moira-dike* dichotomy) in his now classic, albeit somewhat controversial, work *From Religion to Philosophy* (Princeton, N.J.: Princeton University Press, 1991).

21. Gadamer presents a parallel heightening of the Greek concept of *logos* through the Christian idea of incarnation; see Hans-Georg Gadamer, *Truth and Method*, 2nd ed., translated by Joel Weinsheimer and Donald G. Marshall (New York: Crossroad, 1989), 418ff.

22. For a revealing account of the manner in which Hegel's speculative pneumatology completes the lacking component in dogmatic Christian theology that Von Harnack identified (i.e., through a retrieval of Luther's dialectics of Spirit), see Alan M. Olson, *Hegel and the Spirit: Philosophy as Pneumatology* (Princeton, N.J.: Princeton University Press, 1992).

23. Martin Heidegger, *Hegel's Concept of Experience* (New York: Harper and Row, 1970), 31.

24. When Heidegger took up, in 1950, another close reading of the *Phenomenology of Spirit* (having done so in several earlier lecture courses), this time focusing on the Introduction, he again highlighted the significance of the concept of absolution for Hegel, but this time he demonstrated far more clearly the religious nuances of this conception, for both himself and for Hegel, in relation to the revelatory possibilities inherent in the Greco-Christian (or ontotheological, or "eschatologico-theogonical") concept of *parousia* (presence). He further developed the ontotheological critique made in the winter semester of 1930–31, stating now: "At the beginning and throughout the first section, it seems that Hegel is trying to meet the current critical demands, that knowledge must be examined. Actually, his concern is to point out the Absolute in its Advent with us." This advent of being requires a particular sort of receptivity that will stand finally as a core difference between Hegel and Heidegger; Heidegger comments: "The first step which knowledge of the Absolute must take is to accept and receive the Absolute

in its absoluteness, that is, in being-with-us. This being-present-to-us, this *parousia*, this Advent, is part and parcel of the Absolute in and for itself" (ibid.).

25. Ibid., 39.

26. *Parousia*, the presence of being for Heidegger, is set in opposition to Hegel's view of being as the objectivity of an immediately representing subjectivity that has not yet found itself. Unlike his earlier critique, his later thought recasts the conception of *parousia* in the context of his own retrieval of primordial *physis* as the con-text of Hegel's system (i.e., as the jointure of being). Thus, opposing Hegel's absolute willfulness of *parousia*, Heidegger locates the hidden meaning of *parousia* in the revelation of truth as *a-letheia*, the self-revealing arrival in unconcealment characteristic of primal *physis*: "But this arriving presence that occurs in the representation of consciousness as skepsis is a mode of being present which, like the Greek *ousia*, arrives from a concealed area where nature is as yet unthought" (ibid., 69).

27. Theodore Kisiel provides a detailed exposition of Heidegger's development of this point in the early religion courses of 1920–21. Especially pertinent is the analysis of Heidegger's interpretation of First and Second Thessalonians; see Theodore Kisiel, *The Genesis of Heidegger's "Being and Time"* (Berkeley: University of California Press, 1993), 179–91. Kisiel poignantly comments: "Against the eschatology of the late Judaism of Paul's time, which put the primacy on a future event which is to be awaited, the temporality of Christian facticity emphasizes the moment of decision between past and future in which the Christian constantly stands, in the present, 'before the God of old' (*emprosthen*, with connotations of both time and place), from which the future receives its sense. Temporality thus first arises from this context of actualization before God" (ibid., 189).

28. Heidegger explores the *ab-grund*, or "abyss," of presence in a most revealing way, *as the possibility of systematicity*, in his 1936 lecture course on Schelling's 1809 *Freiheitsschrift*. See Martin Heidegger, *Schelling's Treatise on the Essence of Human Freedom*, translated by Joan Stambaugh (Athens: Ohio University Press, 1985).

29. This Idea pushes itself forward via its own will to presence and absolves the violence of its imposition historically by reconciling all being back to itself, hence saving its other from the isolation of its separated selfhood — that is, absolving itself. Hegel's will to power of the absolute, therefore, highlights the necessity of the forward drive of the absolute's self-absolution, but subsumes within this grand, benevolent *moira* the intuitional pull that equiprimordially constitutes the movement. This can be seen in Hegel's subsumption of the *Phenomenology of Spirit*, the original means of entrance into the system, to the position of a mere moment (or set of moments) within the grand whole that it first made possible. (See G. W. F. Hegel, *Encyclopedia of the Philosophical Sciences*, vol. 3, translated by William Wallace and A. V. Miller [Oxford: Clarendon Press, 1971], §§413–39.) This is, furthermore,

probably the reason why Heidegger was so preoccupied with Hegel's *Phenomenology* rather than with the *Encyclopedia* (cf. Heidegger's discussion of this relation in §1 of his 1930 lecture course on Hegel's *Phenomenology:* Martin Heidegger, *Hegel's Phenomenology of Spirit*, translated by Parvis Emad and Kenneth Maly [Bloomington: Indiana University Press, 1988)]).

30. This means that he cannot simply pull the positivity of the *Phenomenology* out of its context and absolutize it vis-à-vis the system (as Schelling in effect did), that is, simply insisting that there is no resolution of the conflict and leaving it at that [incidentally, a situation in which Levinas likewise finds himself]). Rather, the doctrinally inscribed inner tension of ontotheology becomes in Heidegger's post-Hegelian adventism a waiting for the meaning of presence in the midst of the abyss of meaning (the con-textual nothing) left unclarified by Hegel's taking for granted of the hidden pull toward presence required by the system.

Christianity and Possibility
Jeffrey Bloechl

1. Jean-Luc Marion, *God Without Being*, translated by Thomas A. Carlson (Chicago: University of Chicago Press, 1991), xix.

2. We should not forget that, in his Zurich seminar of 1951, Heidegger states that were he to have written a theology, the word "being" would not have appeared in it. The philosophy that he did write meditates profoundly on being and thus remains silent about a God who would remain beyond being. M. Heidegger, *Gesamtausgabe*, vol. XV (Frankfurt: Klostermann, 1986), 436–37.

3. Emmanuel Levinas, *Totality and Infinity* (Pittsburgh: Duquesne University Press, 1969), 104. For his part, Kearney writes that we "co-accomplish creation" (*GMB*, 108).

4. Bernard of Clairvaux, *Steps to Humility* (London: St. Austin Press, 2001), 33–39.

5. Etty Hillesum, *An Interrupted Life: The Diaries of Etty Hillesum, 1941–1943*, translated by A. Pomerans (New York: Pantheon, 1983), 151.

6. Ibid., 194.

7. Cf. ibid., 180 and 71.

8. Etty Hillesum, *Letters from Westerbork*, translated by A. Pomerans (New York: Pantheon, 1986), 116.

9. Hillesum, *An Interrupted Life*, 173.

10. Ibid., 52.

11. Ibid., 128; see also 125.

12. Friedrich Nietzsche, *Will to Power*, translated by R. J. Hollingdale and Walter Kaufmann (New York: Vintage, 1987), 124.

Quis ergo Amo cum Deum Meum Amo?
Brian Treanor

1. Emmanuel Levinas, *Totality and Infinity: An Essay on Exteriority*, translated by Alphonso Lingis (Pittsburgh: Duquesne University Press, 1969),

49. The radically other is an event that always surpasses or overflows my idea of the other, an *ideatum* that always surpasses my *idea*. For Levinas, the event of the other reveals itself in a manner that *kath' auto* escapes our understanding or comprehension of it. To be other is to be incomprehensible, infinite. Nevertheless, deconstruction will critique Levinas for not being rigorous enough in his account of alterity.

2. See, for example, the various contributors to *Questioning God*, edited by John D. Caputo, Mark Dooley, and Michael J. Scanlon (Bloomington: Indiana University Press, 2001); and John D. Caputo, *On Religion* (New York: Routledge, 2001), 1–2.

3. This is not to conflate the work of Derrida and Caputo. However, in terms of the argument made in this paper, contrasting Kearney's position and deconstruction, their positions are taken as more or less the same. In terms of the proximity of Derrida and Caputo, see Caputo, *The Prayers and Tears of Jacques Derrida: Religion Without Religion* (Bloomington: Indiana University Press, 1997).

4. On "religion without religion," see Jacques Derrida, "Sauf le Nom," in *On the Name*, edited by Thomas Dutoit, translated by David Wood, John P. Leavey Jr. and Ian McLeod (Stanford, Calif.: Stanford University Press, 1993), 71; *The Gift of Death*, translated by David Wills (Chicago: University of Chicago Press, 1995), 49; and "Circumfession," in Geoffrey Bennington and Jacques Derrida, *Jacques Derrida*, translated by Geoffrey Bennington (Chicago: University of Chicago Press, 1993), 151ff.

5. Graham Ward, "Questioning God," in *Questioning God*, 274–90 (especially 285). Henceforth cited as *QG*. In all fairness, Caputo is well aware of this difference between Augustine and Derrida. Deconstruction embraces Augustine's question at the apex of its perplexity, prior to Augustine's "answer." "The difference between Augustine and Derrida is that while both decide-in-the-midst-of-undecidability, Derrida has made explicit the determinability and undecidability that inhabit the faith and hope that sustain him, whereas Augustine comes to rest in the historically determinate decision he has made in the midst of this undecidability." John D. Caputo, "What Do I Love When I Love My God? Deconstruction and Radical Orthodoxy," in *Questioning God*, 312. Henceforth cited as *DRO*.

6. "'This place is unique. It is the One without name. It gives rise to (*donne lieu*), perhaps, but without the least generosity, neither divine nor human. Not even the dispersion of cinders is promised there, not given death.' What did you expect to find in the desert?" Caputo, *The Prayers and Tears*, 159, citing Jacques Derrida, "Foi et Savoir: Les Deux Sources de la 'Religion' aux Limites de la Simple Raison," in *La Religion*, edited by Jacques Derrida and Gianni Vattimo (Paris: Seuil, 1996), 86.

7. See my "Divine Others and Human Others: An Inquiry into the Influence of Søren Kierkegaard on Emmanuel Levinas," in *Proceedings of the American Catholic Philosophical Association* 75 (2001).

8. Kearney notes that certain early Christian writers used *persona* and *eikon* synonymously (*GMB*, 19).

9. John Caputo, "Richard Kearney's Enthusiasm: A Philosophical Exploration of *The God Who May Be*," *Modern Theology* 18, no. 1 (January 2002): 92. Henceforth cited as *RKE*.

10. See, for example, the collection from the first Villanova Conference on Religion and Postmodernism: *God, the Gift and Postmodernism*, edited by John D. Caputo and Michael J. Scanlon (Bloomington: Indiana University Press, 1999).

11. "*Quissity*" would be the English cognate of Jean-Francois Courtine's translation of Heidegger's *Werheit* as *quissité*. See Jean Greisch, "'*Idipsum*': Divine Selfhood and the Postmodern Subject," in *Questioning God*, 237.

12. Nevertheless, while thinking God as *posse* keeps one from presuming apodictic knowledge regarding the unfolding of the divine plan, it is not clear that it ensures the ecumenical attitude that Kearney himself advocates with respect to already unfolded parts of that plan. He could address in greater detail how the "eschatological May-be," *which unfolds "as a should-be* (Sollen-sein)," remains above sectarian religious conflict *hic et nunc* (*GMB*, 100; emphasis added).

13. Simon Critchley, *Very Little . . . Almost Nothing: Death, Possibility, Literature* (London: Routledge, 1997), 80. Cited in Kearney, *The God Who May Be*, 77.

14. For example, "undecidability is a structural ingredient of faith" and "deconstruction is a certain faith. Indeed, what is not?" (*PT*, 63, 149). Or again, "Derrida thinks that, precisely because of his notion of undecidability, everything begins and ends in faith" (*DRO*, 296).

15. I wish to acknowledge the benefits derived from discussing these issues with the students of my postmodernism class at Loyola Marymount University and to acknowledge especially the contributions of Jesse Mills on this topic.

16. Augustine, *Confessions*, Book X, Chapter 6. Kearney recently noted that while Derrida "quite rightly passes for an atheist," he (Kearney) quite rightly passes for a theist.

Divinity and Alterity
Felix Ó Murchadha
This article is a reworked version of my contribution to a panel discussion of Richard Kearney's book *Strangers, Gods, and Monsters* (London: Routledge, 2003). This accounts for its conversational tone in places.

1. R. Otto, *The Idea of the Holy* (New York: Oxford University Press, 1958), 25–30.

2. Cf. E. Husserl, *Ideas Pertaining to a Pure Phenomenology and to a Phenomenological Philosophy*, vol. 1 (The Hague: Kluwer, 1983), §58.

3. Heidegger, "The Essence of Grounds," in *Pathmarks* (Cambridge: Cambridge University Press, 1998), 70, n. 45.

4. Cf. J. Manoussakis, "The Fourth Reduction," in this volume.

5. Ibid.

6. R. Kearney, *Strangers, Gods, and Monsters* (London: Routledge, 2003), 5 (henceforth *SGM*).

7. Levinas, *Otherwise Than Being* (Dordrecht: Kluwer, 1991), 76.

8. Otto's work was influential on Heidegger, especially his *Die Götter Griechenlands* (Frankfurt am Main: Klostermann, 1987).

9. R. Kearney, *Poétique du Possible* (Paris: Beauchesne, 1984), 241–50.

On the God of the Possible
Stanislas Breton

1. All citations refer to this work.

2. This is an idea originally posed by Whitehead, who discusses it in his *The Making of Religion*, but from an entirely different perspective.

3. Jean Wahl has coined these two terms in order to indicate the two directions that the language of transcendence could take.

4. For Kearney's treatment of Eckhart's thought, one should take into consideration the lengthy notes 13 and 65 (120–21 and 129–30).

5. "Cum intellectus resolvat ad esse, oportet et hoc transire . . . nam et ipsum deum sub hoc nomine, immo sub omni nomine, debet transire anima," cited by Vladimir Lossky in *Théologie et Connaissance de Dieu chez Maître Eckhart* (Paris: Vrin, 1960), 195.

6. This is the definition of the human soul as given by Thomas Aquinas in his commentary on Aristotle's *De Anima* (book 3, 429b, lect. 7, para. 681 in the Pirotta edition, Turin, 1936).

7. From *Le Paradoxe du Comédien*.

8. The Neoplatonists distinguish between two types of nothingness, the one based on deficiency, the other on excess. Similarly, Greek grammar distinguishes between two adverbs of negation: *ouk* and *me*. The first indicates absence or privation; the second suggests the act of thought or will. Cf. B. Cassin, *Parménide, sur la Nature et sur l'Étant* (Paris: Le Seuil, 1998), 202–203.

Questions to and from a Tradition in Disarray
Joseph S. O'Leary

1. Plotinus met opposition to the notion of the One as self-caused, and he expresses his own qualms about this concept, which seems to defy logic and imperil divine simplicity, much as Descartes was to do later (see M. Narbonne, "Plotkin, Descartes, et la motion de *causa sui*," *Archives de Philosophie* 56:177–95). The defense of this usage in *Enneads* VI, 8, 20 is reminiscent of Descartes's acrobatics on the same theme. Marion, in reply to Narbonne, unconvincingly equiparates Plotinus's doubts about the *causa sui* with the medieval rejection of it (Marion, *Questions Cartésiennes*, vol. 2 [Paris: Vriu, 1966]). This topic has now been magisterially illuminated by Vincent Car-

raud, *Causa sive Ratio: La Raison de la Cause de Suárez à Leibniz* (Paris: Presses Universitaires de France, 2002). Strangely, Marion finds a secret sympathy with the *causa sui* in Suárez, whose metaphysics is so pervaded by discussions of causality and who treats God as part of metaphysics rather than its external principle. Marion quotes J. Whittaker as claiming that self-constitution is only a "philosophical relic" in Proclus. In that case, the influence of Proclean self-constitution on Eriugena and Hegel is a startling demonstration of the power of relics. That Proclus rejects Plotinus's application of *causa sui* to the One is no argument against the similarity between Plotinus and Descartes (*pace* Marion). Plotinus's language is perhaps more figurative than that of Descartes, and its upshot is a defense of the freedom of the One rather than an effort to subject it to causal law. Nonetheless, despite Marion's attempts to attenuate this, the *causa sui* is applied to the One even more clearly than in Descartes in the sense of efficient causality (under erasure). In freeing the One from chance, Plotinus invokes the authority of reason: "that which is in accordance with rational principle (*logos*) is not by chance." Yet the One is above reason as its root: "it is like the principle and fundament of a mighty tree living according to rational principle which remains itself by itself but gives to the tree existence according to the rational principle it receives" (*Enneads* VI, 8, 15 [31–32, 34–37]). Marion argues that Descartes' use of the *causa sui* subjects God to a universal principle of causality, anticipating the Leibnizian imperium of the principle of sufficient reason, and providing the target of Heidegger's comment that the *causa sui* is the inevitable name of God in onto-theo-logy. Since only with Descartes is God subordinated to metaphysical reason, he claims, medieval thought does not fit under the rubric of onto-theo-logy or metaphysics. This would entail a severe curtailment of Heidegger's questions. If instead we think of Plotinus's discussion of the One as *causa sui* as belonging to what Heidegger, in *Der Satz vom Grund*, calls the "incubation period" of the principle of sufficient reason, then we can pursue the overcoming of metaphysics on a broader front in the ancient texts.

More concerned than Plotinus with absolute self-grounding, and writing without the shield of the *hoion*, Marius Victorinus says of God the Father: "sibi causa est ut hoc ipsum sit quod exsistit" (*Adversus Arium* IV, 6, 38). Perhaps this merely means that the only reason God exists is that God exists. Werner Beierwaltes claims that Victorinus's "highly differentiated trinitarian theory of the Trinity is the immediate—or also mediated (through Porphyry)—effect of Plotinus's idea of the self-causation of the absolute"; he sees this as "an outstanding testimony that without philosophy there cannot be a self-conscious theology reflecting on its conceptual possibilities, and that philosophy can unfold productively in Christian theology without anxiety about Hellenization" (Beierwaltes, *Das wahre Selbst* [Frankfurt: Klostermann], 151–52). But if the urge to found things in a *causa sui* marks both the most ambitious reach and the most crippling limitation of metaphysics in its attempt to think being in a radical fashion, as Heidegger maintains, it can hardly be recommended to theology in its search to think the God of revelation.

Rejection of the *causa sui* is a ritual apotropaic gesture among medieval philosophers, as if they were haunted by the traumatic memory of Gnosticism and its self-generating pluriform divinity. Even Eriugena confines the *causa sui* idea to what comes after the first principle. If *deus se ipsum fecit* (*Periphyseon* III, 674A), it is in the sense that God generates or expresses himself in willing creation; "God, by manifesting Himself, is created in a marvelous and ineffable manner in the creature" (678C). Even Eckhart declares that *nihil est causa sui ipsius* (*LW* II, 470), following Aquinas (*Summa Theologiae* I, q. 2, a. 3) and Augustine (*De Trinitate* I, 1). Nonetheless, Plotinus's daring and problematic idea lingers in the background of the medieval discourse on necessary being and aseity in Jewish, Islamic, and Christian scholasticism. This is perhaps more the case in Islamic and Jewish theology. Avicenna states: "Its existence, which is necessary, is due to itself"; for Gersonides, God "has his existence from himself."

Mystic Maybes
Kevin Hart

1. Augustine Birrill, *Res Judicatae* (New York: Scribner's, 1893), 184.

2. Matthew Arnold, *Literature and Dogma*, in *Dissent and Dogma*, edited by R. H. Super, *The Complete Prose Works of Matthew Arnold*, vol. 6 (Ann Arbor: University of Michigan Press, 1968), 151. Henceforth cited as *LD*.

3. William of St. Thierry, *The Mirror of Faith* (Kalamazoo, Mich.: Cistercian Publications, 1979), 28.

4. John of Salisbury, *Metalogicon*, edited by C. C. J. Webb (Oxford: Clarendon Press, 1929), III.

5. The point is discussed by Peter J. Casarella in his "Nicholas of Cusa and the Power of the Possible," *American Catholic Philosophical Quarterly* (Winter 1990), §1. I am indebted to Casarella's discussion.

6. Wolfhart Pannenberg, *Basic Questions in Theology*, vol. II, translated by George H. Kehm (Philadelphia: Fortress Press, 1971), 161. Henceforth cited as *BQ*.

7. Wolfhart Pannenberg, *Theology and the Kingdom of God*, edited by Richard John Neuhaus (Philadelphia: Westminster Press, 1969), 62.

8. Paul Ricoeur, "Toward a Hermeneutic of Revelation," in *Essays on Biblical Interpretation*, edited by Lewis S. Mudge (Philadelphia: Fortress Press, 1980), 94. Henceforth cited as *THR*.

9. Wolfhart Pannenberg, *Systematic Theology*, translated by Geoffrey W. Bromiley, 3 vols. (Grand Rapids, Mich.: William B. Eerdmans, 1991–98), 1:360.

10. See my essay "The Kingdom and the Trinity," in *Religious Experience and the End of Metaphysics*, edited by Jeffrey Bloechl (Bloomington: Indiana University Press, 2003).

11. See Wolfhart Pannenberg, *Metaphysics and the Idea of God*, translated by Philip Clayton (Grand Rapids, Mich.: William B. Eerdmans, 1990), 6.

12. Eberhard Jüngel, *God as the Mystery of the World: On the Foundation of the Theology of the Crucified One in the Dispute Between Theism and Atheism*, translated by Darrell L. Guder (Grand Rapids, Mich.: William B. Eerdmans, 1983), viii. Henceforth cited as *GMW*.

13. Eberhard Jüngel, *Theological Essays*, edited and translated by J. B. Webster (Edinburgh: T. and T. Clark, 1989), 116. Henceforth cited as *TE*.

14. Ricoeur published *La Métaphore Vivre* in 1973; Jüngel"s "Metaphorische Wahrheit. Erwägungen zur Theologischen Relevanz der Metapher als Beitrag zur Hermeneutik Einer Narrativen Theologie" appeared the following year in a joint publication by Jüngel and Ricoeur, *Metapher. Zur Hermeneutik religiöser Sprache* (Munich: Kaiser,1974).

The Maker Mind and Its Shade
Jean Greisch

1. In my book, I analyze the development of philosophy of religion as an academic discipline during the last two centuries while focusing on five paradigms of reason: "speculative" reason (Schleiermacher, Hegel, Schelling, Rosenzweig); "critical" reason in the Kantian and neo-Kantian sense (Kant, Cohen, Tillich, Troeltsch, Duméry) but also in the sense of Feuerbach, Nietzsche, and Bloch; "phenomenological" reason (Husserl, Otto, Scheler, Heiler, Wach, van der Leeuw, Eliade) up to the last generation of French phenomenology (Chrétien, Lacoste, Marion, Henry, including the critical questions of Janicaud); and "analytical" reason (Wittgenstein, James, up to "Wittgensteinian fideism"). In that book, I endeavor to work out a fifth "hermeneutical" paradigm of philosophy of religion through a discussion of Heidegger, Gadamer, and Ricoeur. Many of the questions I am struggling with while finishing this book are similar to those raised by Kearney in his *God Who May Be*, which the subtitle presents as a *Hermeneutics of Religion*.

2. Didier Franck, *Nietzsche et l'Ombre de Dieu* (Paris: Presses Universitaires de France, 1998). On this topic, see my essay "L'Assombrissement de l'Être et les Ombres de Dieu," *Transversalités, Revue de l'Institut Catholique de Paris* 83 (July–September 2002): 85–103.

3. Regarding negative theology, I have tried to discuss the positions of Marion and Derrida in my essay "Du 'Non-Autre' au 'Tout-Autre': Le Spectre de la Théologie Négative," in *Théologie Négative*, edited by M. Olivetti (Milan: Cedam, 2003), 147–70.

4. Jean-François Mattéi, *Heidegger et Hölderlin: Le Quadriparti* (Paris: Presses Universitaires de France, 2002).

5. Paris: Gallimard, 1992.

Divine Metaxology
James Olthuis

1. See Pierre Hadot, *Philosophy as a Way of Life: Spiritual Exercises from Socrates to Foucault* (Oxford: Blackwell, 1995).

2. Emmanuel Levinas, *Totality and Infinity*, translated by A. Lingus (Pittsurgh: Duquesne University Press, 1969), 304. "Ethics is the spiritual optics" (78).

3. Emmanuel Levinas, *Otherwise Than Being*, translated by A. Lingus (The Hague: Martinus Nijhoff, 1981), 162.

4. Kearney places his Ricouerian "*dia-logos* of oneself-as-another" between the modernist "*logos* of the One and the [postmodern] anti-*logos* of the Other" (*SGM*, 18). Although with Kearney, I am concerned that an anti-logos of the Other jeopardizes actual connection between different people, I wonder if a *dialogos* of oneself-as-another sufficiently honors the alterity of the other. Perhaps we would do well to conceptualize the *logos* as a *meta-logos*, that is, a with-*logos* in which people in their empirical dissymmetry are able to negotiate connections of mutuality. See my "Ethical Asymmetry or the Symmetry of Mutuality?" in *Knowing Other-Wise*, edited by James Olthuis (New York: Fordham University Press, 1997), 131–58.

5. And perhaps that is all Kearney desires. After all, he makes a point of insisting that he is not making a universal claim so much as risking a wager that may help us on our way (*SGM*, 19).

6. See Rodolphe Gasché's astute remarks with reference to Derrida's "perhaps": "The 'perhaps' articulates rigorously the wavering ontological status of the gift's event." *Inventions of Difference* (Cambridge, Mass.: Harvard University Press, 1994), 194, 228.

7. I have no problem when *perichoresis* is used as a confessional term describing the mystery of God's mutual indwelling with us. My problem arises when the term is employed theologically, as it is used today, for example, by Jürgen Moltmann, first to detail the mystery of the inner life of God, after which this intradivine communion is set up as the model for communion among humans. See Catherine Lacugna's discussion in *God for Us* (San Franciso: Harper San Francisco, 1973), 270–78.

8. See John P. Manoussakis, "From Exodus to Eschaton," *Modern Theology* 18, no. 1 (January 2002): 107, n. 17. Let me add at this point that I have the utmost respect for Zizioulas's efforts in *Being as Communion* (New York: St Vladimir's Seminary Press, 1985) to develop an ontology of communion centered in God as love. But here, too, I am concerned about dangers of ontotheological speculation, as, for example, when Zizioulas comments: "[t]his love . . . is not something 'common' to the three persons, that is, like the common nature of God. . . . When we say that 'God is love,' we refer to the Father, that is, to that person which 'hypostasizes' God, which makes God to be three persons" (46).

9. In Scripture, talk of God doing the "impossible" is doxological, not philosophical, rooted in the incomparable character of God. See Walter Brueggemann, "'Impossibility' and Epistemology in the Faith Tradition of Abraham and Sarah," in *The Psalms and the Life of Faith* (Minneapolis: Fortress Press, 2001).

10. Jacques Derrida, edited by Thomas Dutoit, *On the Name*, translated by David Wood, John P. Leavey Jr., and Ian McLeod (Stanford, Calif.: Stanford University Press, 1995), 25, 26.

11. Jacques Derrida, *Given Time*, translated by Peggy Kamuf (Chicago: University of Chicago Press, 1992), 103.

12. Jacques Derrida, *Limited Inc.*, edited by Gerald Graff, translated by Samuel Weber and Jeffrey Mehlman (Evanston, Ill.: Northwestern University Press, 1988), 148.

13. Jacques Derrida, *The Gift of Death*, translated by David Wills (Chicago: University of Chicago Pres, 1995), 6.

Theopoetics of the Possible
B. Keith Putt

1. Charles Winquist, *Epiphanies of Darkness: Deconstruction in Theology* (Philadelphia: Fortress Press, 1986), 49.

2. Ray Hart, *Unfinished Man and the Imagination: Toward an Ontology and a Rhetoric of Revelation* (New York: Seabury Press, 1979), 28. Henceforth cited as *UM*.

3. Jacques Derrida, *Points . . . Interviews, 1974–1994*, edited by Elisabeth Weber (Stanford, Calif.: Stanford University Press, 1995), 130. Kearney writes that "historical memory [read: tradition] needs *both* empathic belonging *and* critical distance" (*SGM*, 183).

4. Kearney claims that *persona* always exceeds any attempt to categorize it or to speak about it. It transcends both perception and imagination; however, its very "beyondness" impels language and imagination to "grasp it — especially in the guise of metaphor and narrative" (*GMB*, 10).

5. Derrida's interpretation of aporia inculcates many of the issues that Kearney addresses in his imaginative theological method. According to Derrida, aporia references "the difficult or impracticable, here the impossible, [*sic*] passage, the refused, denied, or prohibited passage, indeed the nonpassage, which can in fact be something else, the event of a coming or of a future advent" (*Aporias*, translated by Thomas Dutoit [Stanford, Calif.: Stanford University Press, 1993], 8). As will be apparent later in this essay, "event," "advent," and the future as a "coming" figure significantly in Kearney's theology of a God Who May Be.

6. Gordon D. Kaufman, *An Essay on Theological Method* (Missoula, Mont.: Scholars Press, 1979), 13, 27. Henceforth cited as *ETM*.

7. Thomas Hobbes, *Leviathan*, edited by Michael Oakshott (New York: Macmillan, 1962), 23.

8. Kearney points out that Husserl actually refers to the open *telos* of existence as "God" and the power that motivates imagination to project that *telos* as "grace." Consequently, even in this "secular" phenomenological theory, there is a theological character to the imagination (32–33).

9. Of course, Heidegger reverses the traditional Aristotelian order: "It is evident that energy, or activity, is prior to potentiality" (*Metaphysics* IX, 8).

10. Kearney constantly emphasizes the existential importance of the narrative imagination for how humans interact with reality. He claims, in good Socratic fashion, that "the unnarrated life is not worth living" (*OS*, 14).

11. Garrett Green, *Imagining God: Theology and the Religious Imagination* (San Francisco: Harper and Row, 1989), 85. Henceforth cited as *IG*.

12. Garrett Green, *Theology, Hermeneutics, and Imagination: The Crisis of Interpretation at the End of Modernity* (Cambridge: Cambridge University Press, 2000), 205.

13. Paul Ricoeur, *Figuring the Sacred: Religion, Narrative, and Imagination*, edited by Mark I. Wallace, translated by David Pellauer (Minneapolis: Fortress Press, 1995), 230. Henceforth cited as *FS*.

14. Paul Ricoeur, *The Philosophy of Paul Ricoeur: An Anthology of His Work*, edited by Charles E. Regan and David Stewart (Boston: Beacon Press, 1978), 238.

15. Paul Ricoeur, *From Text to Action: Essays in Hermeneutics*, translated by Kathleen Blamey and John B. Thompson (Evanston, Ill.: Northwestern University Press, 1991), 2:171. Henceforth cited as *TA*.

16. Paul Ricoeur, *Essays on Biblical Interpretation*, edited by Lewis S. Mudge (Philadelphia: Fortress Press, 1980), 117.

17. Parmenides prescribes a corporeal monism to being that excludes any potentiality or mutability, since both rely upon some notion of non-being. Non-being cannot be, for Parmenides, precisely because it cannot be thought, since to think the "not" is in essence not to think. Consequently, he disallows any reality to movement, temporality, history, or change (see Parmenides, fragments 3 and 4, in Kathleen Freeman, *Ancilla to the Pre-Socratic Philosophers* [Cambridge, Mass.: Harvard University Press, 1962], 42). Since being has been equated to God in the ontotheological tradition, God cannot be temporal, mutable, or kinetic, but must be understood as an "epiphany of the eternal present (see Jürgen Moltmann, *Theology of Hope* [New York: Harper and Row, 1975], 84). Henceforth cited as *TH*.

18. Westminster Confession, 2:1; emphasis added.

19. The Exodic naming "signals an inextricable communication between God and humans, a commitment to a shared history of 'becoming' . . . God may henceforth be recognized as someone who 'becomes with' us, someone dependent on us as we are on Him. God's relation with mortals is, in other words, less one of conceptuality than of covenant" (*GMB*, 161).

20. The phrase "Divine Perhaps" comes not from Kearney but from the Old Testament theologian Terence Fretheim, who interprets God's relation-

ship with Israel as one of spontaneity and reciprocal response. Scripture indicates in several passages (Ezekiel 12:1–3, Jeremiah 26:2–3, and Isaiah 47:12) that God leaves God's future actions open and uncertain, awaiting Israel's response to the divine Word. Who God will be and what God will do, then, depend upon the decisions made by God's people. "Perhaps" they will respond; "perhaps" they will repent; "perhaps" they will obey. Although God knows what God will do in reaction to the various particular responses that might come from Israel, God does not know which of those reactions will actualize. Fretheim contends that "Israel's response[s] . . . contribute in a genuine way to the shaping not only of its own future, but to the future of God." See *The Suffering of God* (Philadelphia: Fortress Press, 1984), 45–47.

21. *WI*, 75–78. See also *GMB*, 37, 103–105; and *GWMB*, 170.

22. Jürgen Moltmann, *The Future of Creation*, translated by Margaret Kohl (Philadelphia: Fortress Press, 1979), 55.

23. See ibid., 29; Jürgen Moltmann, *The Experiment Hope*, translated by M. Douglas Meeks (Philadelphia: Fortress Press, 1975), 52–53; Jürgen Moltmann, *The Way of Jesus Christ*, translated by Margaret Kohl (New York: HarperCollins, 1985), 317.

24. Jacques Derrida, "As if It Were Possible, 'Within Such Limits' . . ." in *Negotiations: Interventions and Interviews, 1971–2001*, edited and translated by Elizabeth Rottenberg (Stanford, Calif.: Stanford University Press, 2002), 367. Henceforth cited as *AIP*.

25. John D. Caputo, *Deconstruction in a Nutshell: A Conversation with Jacques Derrida* (New York: Fordham University Press, 1997), 117–118. Derrida treats the issues of event, advent, and the invention of the other (*l'invention de l'autre*) extensively in "Psyche: Inventions of the Other," in *Reading de Man Reading*, edited by Lindsay Waters and Wlad Godzich (Minneapolis: University of Minnesota Press), 25–65, and in "As if It Were Possible," 343–370. Expecting the impossible, as in remaining open to the unprogrammable ad-vent of the God Who May Be, makes one the "greatest," according to Kierkegaard: "One became great by expecting the possible, another by expecting the eternal; but he who expected the impossible became the greatest of all (*Fear and Trembling*, edited and translated by Howard V. Hong and Edna H. Hong [Princeton, N.J.: Princeton University Press, 1983], 16).

26. Kearney also seems to utilize a language that corresponds to Derrida's idea of *l'invention*, at least with his notion that one must remain open in order to receive the incoming of the other. When writing of the desire for God, Kearney quotes from Gide's *Nourritures Terrestres:* "Let your desire be less expectation than a readiness to receive" (*GWMB*, 79).

27. It lies beyond the scope of this essay to engage Kearney's critique of Derrida and Caputo in depth. Suffice it to say, however, that his criticisms have merit at certain points, especially in regard to the two deconstruction-

ists' predisposition to avoid giving specific content to their quasi-transcendental structures. At other points, though, his criticisms derive from a misreading of their texts, for example, his persistence in confusing undecidability and indecision. Undecidability becomes, for Kearney, the summary of all he finds wrong with deconstruction and radical hermeneutics, because he misinterprets undecidability as prohibiting any decision, as leaving individuals forever riding the pendulum between two alternatives. Take, for instance, his analysis of Caputo's polarity between a meaningful belief in God and an acceptance of the anonymity and abyssal nature of *khora*. When Caputo inquires rhetorically into whether one has to choose between God and *khora*, Kearney answers for Caputo with "No." But that is not how Caputo would answer. In several of his texts, Caputo makes it clear that undecidability is *not* synonymous with indecision. On the contrary, undecidability is the quasi-transcendental ground for making decisions. Were it not for undecidability, there would be no decision to be made. If a matter were programmed, calculated, and formalized according to some objective algorithm of choice, then no decision would be possible or necessary. Decision arises only when there is uncertainty, when there is genuine possibility between two or more alternatives; and under those circumstances, undecidability demands that choices be made. In his best Left Bank rabbinical French, Caputo would contend that within the context of undecidability, "Il faut choisir," it is necessary to choose. See Caputo, *Deconstruction in a Nutshell*, 137; *The Prayers and Tears of Jacques Derrida: Religion Without Religion* (Bloomington: Indiana University Press, 1997), 338 (henceforth cited as *PT*); "Richard Kearney's Enthusiasm: A Philosophical Exploration on *The God Who May Be*," *Modern Theology* 18 (January 2002): 93.

28. "It is because our desire is human that we have to see to believe, that we need signposts and signals on our night journey, sentinels to guard and guide us on our undecidable way toward the absolute other" (*DG*, 126).

29. Kearney proposes to engage alterity in order "to say something about the unsayable, to imagine images of the unimaginable, to tell tales of the untellable, respecting all the while the border limits that defer all Final Answers" (*SGM*, 10).

30. The idea of response naturally carries with it the idea of responsibility—the ability to respond to the summons of the Other. Mark Dooley addresses the issues of imaginative variations and responsibility within the context of Kierkegaard's thought and concludes, "To be truly responsible, for Kierkegaard, is to affirm the possibility *of imagining otherwise*, of calling into question what has been traditionally celebrated as truth, reason, ethics, and community with a view to making each of these structures own up to its contingent configuration." *The Politics of Exodus: Søren Kierkegaard's Ethics of Responsibility* (New York: Fordham University Press, 2001), 107; emphasis added.

31. S. D. Goitein proposes an interesting morphological correlation between God as love and the Exodic naming of Yahweh. By comparing the

Hebrew Tetragrammaton *YHWH* with certain Arabic roots, he suggests that the term references passionate emotion, somewhat akin to the passion of jealousy. He concludes that *ẹhyehāsherẹhyeh* may be translated as "I shall passionately love whom I love" ("*YHWH* the Passionate: The Monotheistic Meaning and Origin of the Name *YHWH*," *Vetus Testamentum* 6 [January 1956]: 2). Were one to couch Goitein's naming of God in a more Kearneyesque nomenclature, one might translate the Exodic naming as "I Am the God Who May Be as Loving Potency."

32. Kearney references Zephaniah 3:17, where the prophet writes of God's dancing for Israel with shouts of joy (*SGM*, 207).

33. For an excellent, if brief, Trinitarian reading of Kearney's theology of God as *Posse*, see John P. Manoussakis, "From Exodus to Eschaton: On the God Who May Be," *Modern Theology* 18 (January 2002): 99–100.

34. Søren Kierkegaard, *Repetition*, edited and translated by Howard V. Hong and Edna H. Hong (Princeton, N.J.: Princeton University Press, 1983), 131, 148, 186. Henceforth cited as *R*.

35. John D. Caputo, *Radical Hermeneutics: Repetition, Deconstruction, and the Hermeneutic Project* (Bloomington: Indiana University Press, 1987), 20. Henceforth cited as *RH*.

36. As Mark Dooley puts it, repetition "keeps the individual moored to time, to the implacable stream of motion and change." See Dooley, *The Politics of Exodus*, 98.

37. John D. Caputo, "In Search of a Sacred Anarchy: An Experiment in Danish Deconstruction," in *Calvin O. Schrag and the Task of Philosophy After Postmodernity*, edited by Martin Beck Matuštík and William L. McBride (Evanston, Ill.: Northwestern University Press, 2002), 238; emphasis added.

38. John D. Caputo, "Instants, Secrets, and Singularities: Dealing Death in Kierkegaard and Derrida," in *Kierkegaard in Post/Modernity*, edited by Martin J. Matuštík and Merold Westphal (Bloomington: Indiana University Press, 1995), 234. Caputo's correlation of repetition and faith repeats Kierkegaard's claim that "repetition begins in faith" (*Concept of Anxiety*, edited and translated by Reidar Thomte [Princeton, N.J.: Princeton University Press, 1980], 18).

39. Jacques Derrida, *On Cosmopolitanism and Forgiveness*, translated by Mark Dooley and Michael Hughes (London: Routledge, 2001), 27.

40. For Caputo's perspectives on forgiveness, consult *Against Ethics: Contributions to a Poetics of Obligation with Constant Reference to Deconstruction* (Bloomington: Indiana University Press, 1993), 106–112; *Prayers and Tears*, 226–229; and "Reason, History, and a Little Madness," in *Questioning Ethics: Contemporary Debates in Philosophy*, edited by Richard Kearney and Mark Dooley (London: Routledge, 1999), 84–104.

41. Kearney understands that "desire responds to the double demand of *eschaton* and eros. God's desire for us — our desire for God" (*GMB*, 79).

Is God Diminished If We Abscond?
Mark Patrick Hederman

1. Buber continues, "Levinas, in opposition to me, praises solicitude as the access to the otherness of the other. The truth of experience seems to me to be that he who has this access apart from solicitude will also find it in the solicitude practised by him—but he who does not have it without this, he may clothe the naked and feed the hungry all day and it will remain difficult for him to say a true Thou. If all were well clothed and well nourished, then the real ethical problem would become wholly visible for the first time." This was one of the last things written by Martin Buber before he died in 1965. "Replies to My Critics," in *The Philosophy of Martin Buber*, edited by P. A. Schilpp and M. Friedman (LaSalle, Ill.: Open Court, 1967), 723.

2. Martin Heidegger, *Poetry, Language, and Thought* (New York: Harper and Row, 1971), 125. Henceforth cited as *PLT*.

3. " 'Our customary consciousness lives on the tip of a pyramid whose base within us (and in a certain way beneath us) widens out so fully that the farther we find ourselves able to descend into it, the more generally we appear to be merged into those things that, independent of time and space, are given in our earthly, in the widest sense worldly, existence' [Rilke, letter, quoted by Heidegger]. True, this presence, too, like that of the customary consciousness of calculating production, is a presence of immanence. But the interior of uncustomary consciousness remains the inner space in which everything is for us beyond the arithmetic of calculation and, free of such boundaries, can overflow into the unbounded whole of the Open" (*PLT*, 128). This is "the innermost region of the interior" (129).

Prosopon and Icon
John Panteleimon Manoussakis

An earlier version of this essay was published in a book symposium on R. Kearney's *God Who May Be*, as "From Exodus to Eschaton: On the God Who May Be," *Modern Theology* 18, no. 1 (January 2002): 95–107). In *The God Who May Be* (Bloomington: Indiana University Press, 2001), Richard Kearney cites that first version of this essay by the draft title "I-M-Possible: Contrapunctus et Augmentationem." I decided that it should appear in this volume, in a much revised and extended form, because parts of this text (especially the analysis of a phenomenology of the *prosopon*) were referenced and discussed by a number of other contributors in this volume (e.g., Keith Putt, James Olthuis, Brian Treanor, and David Tracy).

1. Martin Heidegger, *Identity and Difference* (New York: Harper and Row, 1969), 72.

2. My responsibility for the Other, as Levinas argues, or, better yet, the face-to-face (and thus *prosopic*) relationship with the Other, is such an exceptional case where freedom, an immemorial freedom, "predates" even my

very existence: "Responsibility for the Other, for the naked face of the first individual to come along. A responsibility that goes *beyond* what I may or may not have done to the Other or whatever acts I may or may not have committed, as if I were devoted to the other man *before* being devoted to myself. Or more exactly, as if I had to answer for the other's death *even before being*. A guiltless responsibility, whereby I am none the less open to an accusation of which no alibi, spatial or temporal, could clear me. It is as if the other established a relationship or a relationship were established whose whole intensity consists in not presupposing the idea of community. A responsibility stemming from a time *before* my freedom — *before* my (*moi*) beginning, *before* any present. A fraternity existing in extreme separation. *Before*, but in what past? Not in the time preceding the present, in which I might have contracted any commitments. Responsibility for my neighbour dates from *before* my freedom in an immemorial past, an unrepresentable past that was never present and is more ancient than consciousness of. . . . A responsibility for my neighbour, for the other man, for the stranger or sojourner, to which nothing in the rigorously ontological order binds me — nothing in the order of the thing, of the something, of number or causality. It is the responsibility of hostage which can be carried to the point of being substituted for the other person and demands an infinite subjection of subjectivity. Unless this anarchic responsibility, which summons me from nowhere into a present time, is perhaps the measure of the manner or the system of an immemorial freedom that is *even older than being*, or decisions, or deeds" ("Ethics as First Philosophy," in *The Levinas Reader*, edited by Sean Hand [Oxford: Blackwell, 1989], 83–84; emphasis added).

3. Such a provocative claim was first formulated in the thought of the Greek Church Fathers, and it was again unearthed and brought to its full rigor in the pivotal work of John of Pergamos (Zizioulas).

4. It is worthwhile to rethink, at this point, the phronetic character of ecclesial practice. We have not been baptized in the name of the Being and the Essence and the Substance, nor do we pray to the Divinity or Godhead. Instead, the Church baptizes us in the name of three *persons* (the Father, the Son, and the Holy Spirit), and we call God "our Father" when we pray. "Father" and "Son" are terms that par excellence denote a personal and a relational association. A father can not possibly be what he is without a son, and the son is never a son without a father. Both John of Pergamos and Karl Rahner have called attention to the fact that in modern handbooks of dogmatics, the chapters are so arranged that "on the One God" precedes "On the Trinity," an arrangement that expresses the misunderstanding that the principle of God's existence lies on His single substance rather than on His Trinitarian-personal way of existence. *Being as Communion* (New York: St. Vladimir's Seminary Press, 1985), 40, 58.

5. I am greatly indebted here and for the analysis that follows to a series of articles by the Metropolitan of Pergamos, John Zizioulas, most notably

his "Human Capacity and Human Incapacity," *Scottish Journal of Theology* 28 (1975); "Communion and Otherness," *St. Vladimir's Theological Quarterly* 38, no. 4 (1994); and "On Being a Person: Towards an Ontology of Person-hood," in *Persons, Divine and Human,* edited by Christoph Schwöbel and Colin Gunston (Edinburgh: T. and T. Clark, 1991).

6. Maximus the Confessor (c. 662) would agree with this interpretation. In a comment on Dionysius's *Ecclesiastica Hierarchia,* he writes that "shadow refers to the Old Testament, icon to the New and Truth to the future condition" (*PG* 4, 137D); following this tripartite hermeneutic principle, the event of Christ's transfiguration is the *icon* that was foreshadowed in Exodus and will become fully true eschatologically in the Kingdom.

7. For a complete historical as well as theological account of the importance of this synthesis, one should consult Metropolitan of Pergamos John Zizioulas's excellent treatment in *Being as Communion* (New York: St. Vladimir's Seminary Press, 1985). For the relevance of this synthesis for the theology of the icons, see Christoph Cardinal Schönborn's *God's Human Face: The Christ-Icon* (San Francisco: Ignatius Press, 1994). Cardinal Schönborn rightly observes that "the distinction between *ousia* and *hypostasis*" and the synthesis (or identification) of the latter with that of the *prosopon* (supported by Gregory of Nyssa) were completely "unknown to the pre–Christian philosophers" and "a stroke of genius on the part of the Cappadocians" (31). Gregory of Nyssa in his *Letter on the Distinction of Essence and Hypostasis* (usually attributed to Basil the Great as his 38th Letter) explicitly connects the two terms: "Ὥστε ἡ τοῦ Υἱοῦ ὑπόστασις οἱονεὶ μορφὴ καί πρόσωπον γίνεται τῆς τοῦ Πατρὸς ἐπιγνώσεως" (8, 26).

8. One should remain attentive to the various nuances that the terms *ekstasis* and *hypostasis* carry, especially after their use (almost as hallmarks of their respective philosophical systems) by Heidegger and Levinas. Kearney's work on the *possible* seeks to reconcile this phenomenal contradiction into an eschatological understanding of the person.

9. "In this sense we might best describe ourselves as actors (figurants) in a play authored by *personne.* . . . To interpret a role is, therefore, to respond to the script of the *persona* who speaks through the other, to figure and play out this role as a one-for-the-other, as one through (*trans*) the other" (*GMB,* 17). These lines could serve as pretext to whomever wishes to misread Kearney's intentions. Basil the Great in a letter (no. 214) makes clear the crucial distinction between *prosopon* (face) and *prosopeion* (mask); the latter degenerates the plurality and the otherness of the person into the monism and the sameness of the mask. On the danger of mistaking the *prosopon* as a mask, see also Cardinal Schönborn's remarks in reference to Gregory of Nyssa's *Letter on the Distinction of Essence and Hypostasis*: "In order to employ the term *prosopon* to the full extent of its meaning, that is, in the sense of 'proper face' and 'personal countenance,' we must make sure that any restricted use only as 'mask' or 'role' is avoided, and that this *prosopon*

is indeed supported by its proper existence, by a subsistence, in short: by a hypostasis, so that this countenance (*prosopon*) is the expression of person" (*God's Human Face*, 33).

10. It is telling, I believe, that in Sartre's own version of Hades (*No Exit*), it is precisely this face-to-face relationship with the Other that makes the Other be hell. Sartre reverses the entire model down to the slightest detail; where for the Greeks the underworld is defined as the absence of seeing (Hades), the Sartrean hell is the place of constant and compulsory vision (the lights never turn off, one cannot sleep, one has no eyelids, etc.).

11. S. Kierkegaard, *The Concept of Anxiety*, edited and translated by Reidar Thomte (Princeton, N.J.: Princeton University Press, 1980), 123, 124.

12. Ibid., 128–29.

13. Of course, the ecclesial understanding of the Eucharist plays with both meanings of communion. The Eucharist is the actual communion one receives, but also the means of communion, first, among the participants themselves and, through this relationship, with the one participated (Christ). There are other, far-reaching, and essential considerations about the Eucharist that need to be taken into account; first of all, its eschatological character is of paramount importance. As an event that unfolds in a time beyond time (in the temporality of *kairos* and not of *chronos*), in the Christic chiasmus of the horizontal axis of history with the vertical, consecrating descent of the Holy Spirit, the Eucharist bridges the divisions and cancels out the fragmentations effected by the categories of space and time. Theologically understood, the catholicity of the Eucharist (and therefore of the Church) means that every time the broken bread and the common cup are shared by the faithful, the event of the Church, in her geographical and historical entirety, is occasioned. Simply put, around the Eucharistic table are present all of those who believed, believe, and will believe in Christ's death and resurrection, from the time of His incarnation to the time of His second coming, regardless of their physical (race, gender, age) or social (class, educational, moral) differences. These differences are not simply obliterated for the sake of a homogeneous uniformity; they are, rather, "lifted up" in the "negation" (κατάργησις, *Aufhebung*) effected by the assumption of the fullness of human nature in the "collective person" (κοινόν πρόσωπον) of Christ (as Cyril notes; see *PG* 73, 161c). They were introduced by the fall of the old man, Adam, and they were overcome by the resurrection of the new man, the second Adam, "so that God may be all in all" (1 Corinthians 15:28). Last, one should pay attention to the praying practice of the Church: all the prayers are phrased and expressed from a communal "we" (e.g., "*Our Father . . .*"). How little sense would it make for one in the Church to say "*my* Father . . ."!

14. One problem, however, remains unresolved: What happens (to me) if, or when, the Other refuses, or simply is unable, to see in me his or her Other? What happens when for the Other I am not another Other, but only

a third? What happens when the reciprocity of the prosopic relationship is never returned? Isn't it, then, the case that my rejection by the Other breaks down the symmetry of love? Doesn't the Other's unavailability turn my chance to live Paradise into the experience of everyday hell? How, then, do we account for the fact that the very same "structure" of being a *prosopon* can be either my salvation or my condemnation, depending on such fragile and arbitrary factors as chance, infatuation, preference, and so on?

15. In the translation by H. Lawrence Bond of *Nicholas of Cusa, Selected Spiritual Writings* (New York: Paulist Press, 1997), 241.

16. See my study "The Phenomenon of God: From Husserl to Marion," in *American Catholic Philosophical Quarterly* 78, no. 1 (2004): 53–68.

17. Hans Urs von Balthasar, *The Glory of the Lord: A Theological Aesthetics*, vol. 1, *Seeing the Form*, edited by Joseph Fessio and John Riches, translated by Erasmo Leiva-Merikakis (San Francisco: Ignatius Press, 1998), 301–2.

18. Translated by H. Lawrence Bond, ibid., 243.

19. Jorge Luis Borges, *Selected Poems* (bilingual edition), edited by A. Coleman (New York: Viking, 1999), 81 (the translation has been slightly modified).

20. De Visione Dei was written in 1453. As Nicholas wrote his text — which is nothing else than a mystical meditation on the art of icons — great changes in the artistic universe were happening around him. Some thirty years earlier (c. 1425), Masaccio had painted one of his Madonnas (*Madonna con Bambino e Sant' Anna*, Uffizi, Florence), a work that moves between two worlds — the Middle Ages and the Renaissance — and thus marks the passage from the one to the other. Masaccio employed here the groundbreaking technique of chiaroscuro, developed earlier by Giotto. Lighting and shadowing, used appropriately, can convey the false impression of depth on the two-dimensional surface of the canvas. Thus, perspective was at last achieved. In Masaccio's *Madonna con Bambino* we still see an icon (the austere and somehow "stiff" style of Byzantine technique), perhaps for the very last time. At the same time, something entirely new is to be seen here, a painting (the naturalness and aliveness of a Renaissance work). After Masaccio, Western art used perspective ad nauseam for more than five centuries. By which time, with the illusions of perspective long exhausted, the arrogance (or naïveté) of the artist who struggles to represent nature as faithfully as possible was finally satisfied; in fact, it was more than satisfied, it is satiated, for one detects a certain feeling of grossness in the need to move to the other extreme, that of iconoclasm, as it has been so vividly represented by abstractionist art. With this historical background in mind, it becomes interesting, I think, to read Cusanus's text as a praise of icons, these fading works of art that seem to lack any sense of perspective and, next to the masterpieces of the Renaissance, are made to look (as at least some modern art historians have read them) like little more than a series of primitive caricatures. But 1453 was a year not only of artistic changes. It is

the year that Constantinople fell, and with it the more than a millennium-old Byzantine Empire that gave rise to and nourished the spirituality of the icons. Writing *De Visione Dei* was Cusanus's way to bid a solemn farewell to a civilization that he profoundly admired and to a city that he himself had come to know, albeit in its twilight.

21. The term was coined by the Russian theologian and philosopher Pavel Florensky. See "Against Linear Perspective," in *Utopias: Russian Modernist Texts 1905–1940*, edited by Catriona Kelly (New York: Penguin Books, 2002), 70–75.

22. Aristotle, *Categories*, VII (6a37). Nicephorus's texts reads as follows "And I think it is not inappropriate to add this as well to the argument: that the icon expresses a relationship with the original and is the effect of a cause. For this reason it is necessary that the icon belongs and is classified among those things that express relation. The things that express relation are called what they are on the grounds of their relationship to something different [from themselves] and their reciprocal relationship with each other, for example, a 'father' is the father of a son and a 'son' is called so insofar as he is the son of a father, in a similar way a 'friend' is someone's friend. In the same way, too, an original always implies its icon and an icon is that of its original. One could not say that something is an icon without the relationship with this someone [whom the icon represents]. What is different is introduced and regarded together with the other." From *Antirrheticus I*, PG 100, 277 D.

23. Let me note here that the key term *perichoresis* was first used in this context (by Gregory of Nyssa in his *Epistle 101*, PG 37, 181C) and only later applied (by Pseudo-Cyril, in his *De Trinitate*, PG 77, 1144B) to the relationship of the Persons in the Trinity.

24. In Maximus's *Epistula XV* ("On the Common and the Particular, i.e., on the Essence and the Hypostasis"), PG 91, 556 A–C).

25. By Procopios of Gaza (c. 538) in his *Commentary on Genesis* (PG 87, 361A).

26. Traditionally attributed to Justin the Philosopher and Martyr, but recent scholarship places it under the name of Theodoretos of Cyrene (c. 458). *Exposition Rectae Confessionis*, PG 6, 1212A.

27. Humanity as the Other of God, on which God is dependent, makes sense *only* if understood in terms of the *Economical* Trinity—that is, the Trinity in its (historic) relation to humanity and to creation in general, especially through the Incarnation and Ascension of the second Person. In the *Immanent* or *Ontological* Trinity (i.e., the relationship of the three Persons with each other), the Other of God is always God as the Other (Person). The human Other and the divine Other constitute two distinct moments of otherness viewed under the two different angles of speaking about the Trinity, the Economical and the Ontological, respectively. I am thankful here to the Metropolitan of Pergamos, John Zizioulas, who, in a private conversation,

brought this potentially self-contradicting point to my attention and suggested the maintaining of the distinction between Economical and Ontological Trinity as its solution. I also thank him for reading my text so carefully.

28. Kazantzakis would say that Christ's option to say "no" constitutes His last and, perhaps, the most important of all temptations that He has to fight and overcome.

Richard Kearney's Enthusiasm
John D. Caputo

1. *Being and Time*, translated by John Macquarrie and Edward Robinson (New York: Harper and Row, 1962), §7c, 63.

2. Jacques Derrida, "*Comme si c'Était Possible,* 'Within Such Limits' . . . ," *Revue Internationale de Philosophie* no. 3 (1998): 497–529. Henceforth cited as *CSP*.

3. See my *On Religion* (London and New York: Routledge, 2001), 11.

4. A longer version of the following remarks is to be found in my response to Richard Kearney in *A Passion for the Impossible: John D. Caputo in Focus*, edited by Mark Dooley (Albany: State University of New York Press, 2003).

5. Jacques Derrida, *On the Name*, edited by Thomas Dutoit (Stanford, Calif.: Stanford University Press, 1995), 95. For a commentary, see John D. Caputo, *Deconstruction in a Nutshell* (New York: Fordham University Press, 1997), 96–105.

6. Emmanuel Levinas, *Of God Who Comes to Mind*, translated by Bettina Bergo (Stanford, Calif.: Stanford University Press, 1998), 69.

7. See my *Radical Hermeneutics* (Bloomington: Indiana University Press, 1987) and *More Radical Hermeneutics* (Bloomington: Indiana University Press, 2000).

8. Emmanuel Levinas, *Autrement qu' Être ou au-delà de l'Essence* (The Hague: Nijhoff, 1974), 212; *Otherwise Than Being or Beyond Essence*, translated by Alphonso Lingis (The Hague: Nijhoff, 1981), 167.

In Place of a Response
Richard Kearney

1. "On the Gift: A Discussion Between Jacques Derrida and Jean-Luc Marion, Moderated by Richard Kearney," in *God, the Gift, and Postmodernism*, edited by John D. Caputo and Michael J. Scanlon (Bloomington: Indiana University Press, 1999), 54–78, 61.

2. Geoffrey Bennington and Jacques Derrida, *Jacques Derrida*, translated by Geoffrey Bennington (Chicago: University of Chicago Press, 1993) 154.

3. Jean-Luc Marion, *God Without Being*, translated by Thomas A. Carlson (Chicago: University of Chicago Press, 1991).

4. Jean-Luc Marion, "Le Phénomène Saturé," in *Phénoménologie et Théologie*, edited by Jean-François Courtine (Paris: Criterion, 1992), 79–128;

"The Saturated Phenomenon," translated by Thomas A. Carlson, *Philosophy Today* 40 (1996): 103–24. See also Dominique Janicaud et al., *Phenomenology and the "Theological Turn"* (New York: Fordham University Press, 2000).

5. Martin Heidegger, *Introduction to Metaphysics*, translated by Gregory Fried and Richard Polt (New Haven, Conn.: Yale University Press, 2000).

6. Richard Kearney, *The God Who May Be: A Hermeneutics of Religion* (Bloomington: Indiana University Press, 2001).

7. See Catherine Keller's *The Face of the Deep: A Theology of Becoming* (London: Routledge, 2002).

8. Emmanuel Levinas, "Ethics of the Infinite," in Richard Kearney, *States of Mind: Dialogues with Contemporary Thinkers* (New York: New York University Press, 1995), 177–99.

9. Exodus 3:14.

10. Etty Hillesum, *An Interrupted Life* (New York: Owl Books, 1991). Cited in *The God Who May Be.*

11. Matthew 9:19–23; Luke 8:43–48.

12. John 2:1–11.

13. Matthew 10:27, 19:26; Luke 18:27.

14. Richard Kearney, *Poétique du Possible: Phénoménologie Herméneutique de la Figuration* (Paris: Beauchesne, 1984).

15. "Desire of God" (with discussion), in *God, the Gift, and Postmodernism*, edited by John D. Caputo and Michael J. Scanlon (Bloomington: Indiana University Press, 1999), 112–145, 135.

16. Ibid., 140, note 43.

17. Ibid., 139, note 43.

18. Richard Kearney, introduction to *Strangers, Gods, and Monsters* (New York: Routledge, 2002).

19. Peter Sutcliffe is the serial killer known as the "Yorkshire Ripper." He claimed that his killing spree was a divine mission.

20. Nietzsche asks in section 55 of the *Will to Power* (edited by Walter Kaufmann, translated by Walter Kaufmann and R. J. Hollingdale [New York: Vintage Books, 1968]): "Does it make sense to conceive a god 'beyond good and evil'?"

21. Richard Kearney asks Derrida the following question in his interview with him in Richard Kearney, *Debates in Continental Philosophy: Conversations with Contemporary Thinkers* (New York: Fordham University Press, 2004): "But did not Judaism and Christianity represent a heterogeneity, an 'otherness' before they were assimilated into Greek culture?" To which Derrida replied: "Of course. And one can argue that these original, heterogeneous elements of Judaism and Christianity were never completely eradicated by Western metaphysics. They perdure throughout the centuries, threatening and unsettling the assured 'identities' of Western philosophy. . . ."

22. Jacques Derrida's *Schibboleth—pour Paul Celan* (Paris: Galilée, 1986) and "Circumfession: Fifty-nine Periods and Periphrases" form the text *Jac-*

ques Derrida, cowritten ("Derridabase") and translated by Geoffrey Bennington (Chicago: University of Chicago Press, 1993).

23. Derrida's essay "Donner la Mort" appears in *L'Éthique du Don: Jacques Derrida et la Pensée du Don*, edited by Jean-Michel Rabaté and Michael Wetzel (Paris: Métailié-Transition, 1992). The English version of the essay is titled *The Gift of Death*, translated by David Wills (Chicago: University of Chicago Press, 1995).

Contributors

Jeffrey Bloechl, Associate Professor of Philosophy and Edward Bennett Williams Fellow at the College of the Holy Cross, has published widely in contemporary Continental philosophy and philosophy of religion. His major works include, as author, *Liturgy of the Neighbor: Emmanuel Levinas and the Religion of Responsibility* (2000), and as editor, *Religious Experience and the End of Metaphysics* (2003). He is Series Editor of *Levinas Studies: An Annual Review* (2005 onward), and is currently at work on a book-length study of the structure of call and response in phenomenology and theology.

Stanislas Breton (d. 2005), philosopher and theologian, was the author of numerous books in French, including *Philosopher sur la Côte Sauvage* (2000), *Vers l'Originel* (2000), *Causalité et Projet* (2000), *L'Avenir du Christianisme* (1997), and *L'Autre et l'Ailleurs* (1995).

Patrick Burke is Professor of Philosophy at Seattle University. An expert in the philosophy of Maurice Merleau-Ponty, he also concentrates his research on phenomenology, ethics, and aesthetics, with a current emphasis on Renaissance philosophy of art.

John D. Caputo is the Thomas J. Watson Professor of Religion and Humanities at Syracuse University and the David R. Cook Professor Emeritus of Philosophy at Villanova University. His many books on religion and postmodernism include *Radical Hermeneutics* (1987), *The Prayers and Tears of Jacques Derrida* (1987), and *On Religion* (2001).

Jacques Derrida (d. 2004) was Director of Studies at the École des Hautes Études en Sciences Sociales in Paris and visiting professor at the University of California, Irvine. His numerous publications include *On Grammatology, The Post Card, Spurs: Nietzsche's Styles, Dissemination,* and *Margins of Philosophy.*

William Desmond is Professor of Philosophy and Director of the International Program of Philosophy in the Higher Institute of Philosophy, Katholieke Universiteit Leuven (Louvain), Belgium; and David R. Cook Visiting Chair in Philosophy, Villanova University. His recent books include *Beyond Hegel and Dialectic* (1992), *Being and Between* (1995), *Ethics and the Between* (2001), and *Is There a Sabbath for Thought* (2005).

Jean Greisch is Professor of Philosophy at the Institut Catholique de Paris. He is the author of *L'Âge Herméneutique de la Raison* (1985), *L'Arbre de Vie et l'Arbre du Savoir: Les Racines Phénoménologiques de l'Herméneutique Heideggérienne* (2000), and a trilogy under the title *Le Buisson Ardent et les Lumières de la Raison. L'invention de la Philosophie de la Religion* (2002).

Kevin Hart is Professor of English at the University of Notre Dame. A noted poet, he has published books of poems that include *Flame Tree: Selected Poems* (2001), *New and Selected Poems* (1995), *Penial* (1991), *Your Shadow* (1984), *The Lines of the Hand* (1981), and *The Departure* (1978). Hart is also the author of *A. D. Hope* (1992) and *The Trespass of the Sign: Deconstruction, Theology, and Philosophy* (1989).

Mark Patrick Hederman is a monk and former headmaster at Glenstal Abbey in Ireland. A frequent lecturer in the United States, Hederman is the author of *The Haunted Inkwell: Art and Our Future* (2002) and *Kissing the Dark: Connecting with the Unconcious* (1999). He has also edited, with Richard Kearney, *The Crane Bag Book of Irish Studies (1977–1981)* (1982).

Dominique Janicaud (d. 2002) was Professor of Philosophy at the Université de Nice. He was the author of numerous books on Heidegger (*Heidegger: From Metaphysics to Thought*, 1995; and *Heidegger en*

France, 2002) as well as on phenomenology (*Phenomenology and the "Theological Turn,"* 2000).

Richard Kearney holds the Charles B. Seelig Chair in Philosophy at Boston College and is a visiting professor at University College Dublin. His recent publications include *On Stories* (2001), *The God Who May Be* (2001), and *Strangers, Gods, and Monsters* (2002).

Catherine Keller is Professor of Constructive Theology in the Theological and Graduate Schools of Drew University. Her many publications include *Face of the Deep: A Theology of Becoming* (2003) and *Apocalypse Now and Then: A Feminist Guide to the End of the World* (1996).

John Panteleimon Manoussakis teaches philosophy at Boston College and the American College of Greece. He has been educated in philosophy, classical literatures, and religion. He has published articles on the philosophy and phenomenology of religion and has presented his work at a number of conferences in Europe and the United States. He is the coeditor of *Traversing the Imaginary: Encounters with Richard Kearney* (with Peter Gratton, 2003) and *Heidegger and the Greeks* (with Drew Hyland, 2006), and the author of *Theos Philosophoumenos* (2004; in Greek).

Jean-Luc Marion is Professor of Philosophy at the University of Paris IV (Sorbonne) and the John Nuveen Professor at the University of Chicago Divinity School, Department of Philosophy, and the Committee on Social Thought. He is the author of *Sur l'Ontologie Grise de Descartes* (1975), *Sur la Théologie Blanche de Descartes* (1998), *God Without Being* (1991), *The Idol and the Distance* (2001), *Being Given* (2002), and *In Excess* (2002).

Sallie McFague is the former Carpenter Professor of Theology Emerita at Vanderbilt University and presently Distinquished Theologian in Residence at the Vancouver School of Theology. She is the author of *Metaphorical Theology* (1982), *Models of God* (1987), *The Body of God* (1993), and *Life Abundant: Rethinking Theology and Economy for a Planet in Peril* (2000).

Craig Nichols received his Ph.D. in philosophy from Boston University. Among his interests are the philosophies of Kant and Heidegger and the philosophy of religion. His publications include

"Primordial Freedom: The Authentic Truth of *Dasein* in Heidegger's *Being and Time*," in *Thinking Fundamentals*, vol. 9, edited by David Shikiar (2000).

Joseph S. O'Leary, born in Cork in 1949, has a doctorate in theology from Maynooth College. He has worked on Patristic theology (Origen, Gregory of Nyssa, and Augustine). His books *Questioning Back: The Overcoming of Metaphysics in Christian Tradition* (1985) and *Religious Pluralism and Christian Truth* (1996) are essays in fundamental theology in dialogue with Heidegger, Derrida, and Buddhist philosophy. He has lived in Japan since 1983 and teaches at Sophia University.

James H. Olthuis is Professor of Philosophical Theology and Ethics at the Institute for Christian Studies in Toronto. A practicing psychotherapist, Olthuis is the editor of *Knowing Other-wise: Philosophy at the Threshold of Spirituality* (1997) and author of *I Pledge You My Truth* (1975), *Keeping Our Troth: Staying in Love Through the Five Stages of Marriage* (1986), and *The Beautiful Risk* (2001).

Felix Ó Murchadha, D.Phil. (Wuppertal), is currently a lecturer in philosophy at the National University of Ireland, Galway. He was educated at University College Galway and University College Dublin, Ireland; McMaster University, Canada; and Bergische Universität Wuppertal (Germany). His publications include a monograph on Heidegger titled *Zeit des Handelns und Möglichkeit der Verwandlung* (1999) and numerous articles and book chapters focusing on hermeneutics, phenomenology, time, and the philosophy of religion.

B. Keith Putt (Ph.D. Rice University) is Professor of Philosophy at Samford University. Among his numerous publications are " 'Too Deep for Words': The Conspiracy of a Divine 'Soliloquy' " (in *The Phenomenology of Prayer*, ed. Bruce Ellis Benson and Norman Wirzba [2005]); "Faith, Hope, and Love: Radical Hermeneutics as a Pauline Philosophy of Religion," (in *A Passion for the Impossible*, ed. Mark Dooley [2003]); and "Prayers of Confession and Tears of Contrition: A Radically 'Baptist' Hermeneutic of Repentance" (in *Religion With/Out Religion*, ed. James Olthuis [2002]).

David Tracy is the Andrew Thomas Greeley and Grace McNichols Greeley Distinguished Service Professor of Catholic Studies and

Professor of Theology and of the Philosophy of Religion in the Divinity School and the Committee on Social Thought at the University of Chicago. His publications include *The Analogical Imagination: Christian Theology and the Culture of Pluralism* (1981), *Plurality and Ambiguity: Hermeneutics, Religions, and Hope* (1987), and *On Naming the Present: Reflections on God, Hermeneutics, and Church* (1994).

Brian Treanor received his M.A. in philosophy from California State University, Long Beach, and his Ph.D. in philosophy from Boston College. He has presented papers and published in the areas of ethics, philosophy of religion, aesthetics, and literature. He is currently an Assistant Professor at Loyola Marymount University, where he is finishing a manuscript addressing various accounts of alterity in Continental philosophy.

Merold Westphal is Distinguished Professor of Philosophy at Fordham University and author of numerous articles and books on the philosophy of religion from Kant and Hegel to today. His recent publications include *Suspicion and Faith: The Religious Uses of Modern Atheism* (1998), *Overcoming Onto-theology: Toward a Postmodern Christian Faith* (2001), and *Transcendence and Self-transcendence* (2004).

Index

onto-eschatology. *See* eschatology.
Origen, 358

Pannenberg, Wolfhart, 212–15, 218, 358
Pascal, Blaise, 71, 79–80, 95, 97, 104, 168, 353
Plato, 9, 13, 19, 27, 57, 59, 64, 91–92, 119, 141, 160, 170, 178, 189, 200, 205, 213, 224–25, 262, 314, 325, 330–32, 341, 356, 395, 405
prosopon, 6–7, 11, 14, 21–23, 26, 28–29, 31–32, 79, 81, 95, 107, 111, 131, 135, 143, 145, 147–49, 153, 230, 258, 278, 283–89, 346–49, 353, 391–92, 421, 423

radical orthodoxy, 140, 186, 409
Rahner, Karl, 216, 227, 422

reciprocity, 28, 198, 253, 256, 267, 284, 368, 425
Ricoeur, Paul, 6–7, 11, 49, 110, 115, 120, 153, 157, 188–89, 211–12, 214, 218, 223–26, 232, 246, 248–49, 253, 266, 268, 271, 310–11, 318–19, 326, 340–46, 349, 351–52, 381

Schleiermacher, Friedrich, 133, 186, 238, 348, 379, 414

Tillich, Paul, 347, 363

Wittgenstein, Ludwig, 338, 414

Zizioulas, John (Metropolitan of Pergamos), 235, 415, 422, 426

Perspectives in
Continental Philosophy Series
John D. Caputo, series editor

14. Mark C. Taylor, *Journeys to Selfhood: Hegel and Kierkegaard*. Second edition

15. Dominique Janicaud, Jean-François Courtine, Jean-Louis Chrétien, Michel Henry, Jean-Luc Marion, and Paul Ricœur, *Phenomenology and the "Theological Turn": The French Debate*

16. Karl Jaspers, *The Question of German Guilt*. Translated by E. B. Ashton. Introduction by Joseph W. Koterski, S.J.

17. Jean-Luc Marion, *The Idol and Distance: Five Studies*. Translated with an introduction by Thomas A. Carlson

18. Jeffrey Dudiak, *The Intrigue of Ethics: A Reading of the Idea of Discourse in the Thought of Emmanuel Levinas*

19. Robyn Horner, *Rethinking God as Gift: Marion, Derrida, and the Limits of Phenomenology*

20. Mark Dooley, *The Politics of Exodus: Søren Kierkegaard's Ethics of Responsibility*

21. Merold Westphal, *Toward a Postmodern Christian Faith: Overcoming Onto-Theology*

22. Edith Wyschogrod, Jean-Joseph Goux, and Eric Boynton, eds., *The Enigma of Gift and Sacrifice*

23. Stanislas Breton, *The Word and the Cross*. Translated with an introduction by Jacquelyn Porter

24. Jean-Luc Marion, *Prolegomena to Charity*. Translated by Stephen E. Lewis

25. Peter H. Spader, *Scheler's Ethical Personalism: Its Logic, Development, and Promise*

26. Jean-Louis Chrétien, *The Unforgettable and the Unhoped For*. Translated by Jeffrey Bloechl

27. Don Cupitt, *Is Nothing Sacred? The Non-Realist Philosophy of Religion: Selected Essays*

28. Jean-Luc Marion, *In Excess: Studies of Saturated Phenomena*. Translated by Robyn Horner and Vincent Berraud

29. Phillip Goodchild, ed., *Rethinking Philosophy of Religion: Approaches from Continental Philosophy*

30. William J. Richardson, S.J., *Heidegger: Through Phenomenology to Thought*

31. Jeffrey Andrew Barash, *Martin Heidegger and the Problem of Historical Meaning*

32. Jean-Louis Chrétien, *Hand to Hand: Listening to the Work of Art*. Translated by Stephen E. Lewis

33. Jean-Louis Chrétien, *The Call and the Response*. Translated with an introduction by Anne Davenport

34. D. C. Schindler, *Hans Urs von Balthasar and the Dramatic Structure of Truth: A Philosophical Investigation*

35. Julian Wolfreys, ed., *Thinking Difference: Critics in Conversation*